SAFE INVESTING
and other money matters

By the Editors of MONEY Magazine

Oxmoor House®

Money
SAFE INVESTING
and other money matters

Illustrations By Patrick McDonnell

Library of Congress Catalog Number:
Hardcover 91-067883
Softcover 91-067881

Hardcover ISBN: 0-8487-1075-4
Softcover ISBN: 0-8487-1106-8

Manufactured in the United States of America
First Printing 1992

Published by arrangement with Oxmoor House, Inc.
Book Division of Southern Progress Corporation
P. O. Box 2463, Birmingham, AL 35201

Safe Investing and other money matters
Senior Editor: Clark Scott
Editorial Assistant: L. Amanda Owens
Designer: Nancy Johnson
Fact Checker: Frances C. Marshman
Copyreader: Kay Vance

Art Director: James Boone
Director of Manufacturing: Jerry Higdon
Production Manager: Rick Litton
Associate Production Manager: Theresa L. Beste
Production Assistant: Pam Beasley Bullock

To order *Money* magazine, write to: *Money*, P. O. Box 54429, Boulder, CO 80322-4429

Money Staff
Managing Editor: Frank Lalli
Assistant Managing Editors: Frank B. Merrick, Caroline Donnelly, Tyler Mathisen
Senior Editors: Joseph S. Coyle, Richard Eisenberg, Eric Gelman, Diane Harris, Joanna L. Krotz, Kevin S. McKean, Eric Schurenberg, Michael Sivy
Associate Editors: Denise M. Topolnicki, Walter L. Updegrave
Senior Writer: Jerry Edgerton
Staff Writers: Gary Belsky, Derek T. Dingle, Kerry Hannon, Beth Kobliner, Lani Luciano, John Manners, Marsha Meyer, Suzanne Seixas, Ruth Simon, John Sims, Marguerite T. Smith, Teresa Tritch, Penelope Wang, Clint Willis
Chief of Reporters: Katharine B. Drake
Deputy Chief: Sian Ballen
Senior Reporters: Debra Wishik Englander, Carla A. Fried, Jersey Gilbert, Jordan E. Goodman, Prashanta Misra, Holly Wheelwright
Reporters: Lesley Alderman, Elizabeth Fenner, Mary Granfield, Roberta Kirwan, Miriam A. Leuchter, Deborah Lohse, Elizabeth M. MacDonald, Baie Netzer, D. Jacqueline Smith, Daphne D. Mosher (mail)
Art Director: Sandra DiPasqua
Associate Art Director: Traci Churchill
Design Department: Joseph E. Baron, Helene Elek (designers), Maria Taffera (assistant designer)
Picture Editor: Deborah Pierce
Deputy Picture Editor: Miriam Hsia
Assistant Picture Editor: Leslie Yoo
Editorial Manager: Jacqueline T. Zanca
Copy Deputies: Patricia A. Feimster, Mark Hudson Giles
Editorial Systems Manager: Andrew Schwartz
Copy Desk: Sukey Rosenbaum (senior coordinator), Kathleen Beakley, Henry S. Hample, P. Nigel Killikelly, Jeanne L. McGough, Bill O'Connor, Sarah Plant, Suzanne Justin Riggio, Judith Ryan, Eve Sennett, Margaret J. Stefanowicz
Editorial Production Manager: Karen Harper Diaz
Editorial Production: Sally Boggan, Gary S. Costello
Contributing Editors: Steve Gelman, Cheryl Russell
Contributing Writers: Anthony Cook, Junius Ellis, Marlys J. Harris, Andrea Rock, Robert Wool

Editor's Note

Congratulations! By picking up this book you have already demonstrated considerable investment savvy. To the uninitiated, "safe investing" can seem to be an oxymoron, like "jumbo shrimp." People think that, by its nature, investing is a risky undertaking. But they are wrong.

In fact, the bigger risk is run by those who cautiously stash all their funds away in bank accounts and other low-paying savings vehicles. They risk the near certainty that their money will lose ground to inflation. Meanwhile, prudent investors in stocks, bonds, and mutual funds can prosper—and still sleep soundly at night.

Safe Investing—the sixth in a series of annuals from the Editors of *Money* and Oxmoor House—is designed to make you even savvier. It's our aim to put you in the ranks of those prudent, prosperous, well-rested investors. This book contains the most useful and important information on investing that has appeared in *Money* magazine's pages in the past 12 months—including a round-up of the best investments for 1992. Our emphasis is on mutual funds, clearly the best way for individuals to get into stocks and bonds. With funds, the small investor can enjoy the kind of diversification and professional management otherwise available only to institutions.

But the scope of this book is much greater than you might think. We offer help with all aspects of your finances—budgeting, spending, borrowing, savings, insurance, taxes, your home, just to name a few. We even provide 15 pages of advice on starting your own business; it begins on page 59.

And in our final chapters, we present three of the exclusive rankings that are a hallmark of *Money* magazine. Beginning on page 153, *Money*'s first-ever Car Cost Ratings give the total ownership costs, including depreciation, insurance, and maintenance, for more than 500 '92 models. On page 165, we rank the 100 colleges providing the best education for the tuition dollar, followed by an alphabetical guide to over 1,000 schools. And, lastly, starting on page 189, are our Mutual Fund Rankings, including the top performers in 13 fund categories and an alphabetical guide to over 1,000 funds.

We are proud of the breadth and depth of expertise packed into this single volume. We think it will make *Safe Investing* an indispensable tool for managing your money in the coming year.

Caroline Donnelly
Assistant Managing Editor, *Money*

Contents

Get up early, work late—and strike oil.
– John D. Rockefeller, Jr. explaining the secret of his success.

INVESTMENTS

Safe Ways to Make Money Now

"Almost anybody can lose his shirt on Wall Street," millionaire Joseph Kennedy once remarked, "if he's got enough capital to start with and the proper inside information." *Almost* anybody, nothing. Everybody who was along for the 1987 crash and the capricious stock market swings since then knows exactly for whom that shirt-swiping bell tolls.

The problem is, with inflation eating up your capital on any investment returning less than about 6%, you have to do something with your money or lose it just by the passage of time. What you want are *safe* investments. In this chapter, we eschew insider tips and, instead, focus on investment strategies of the keep-your-shirt and add-to-your-wardrobe variety, specifically, ways to build a diversified portfolio for steady, long-term growth.

Exactly how you should deploy your investment money depends on how and when you ultimately plan to use it. That's why your first step should be to clearly define your goals and priorities. The shorter the time until you'll need your money, the more you should put in cash investments and short-term bonds that keep your principal safe. For goals that are more than five years off, you should invest heavily in stocks, which, over 10 or 20 years, almost always outperform every other type of investment. This chapter explains how you can take advantage of the best investment opportunities available now. For portfolio strategies geared to specific goals, see the chapters on college saving (beginning on page 75) and retirement investing (beginning on page 135).

The safest way for small investors to buy into the stock market is through mutual funds. They provide professional management and broad diversification. But it would be foolish to think you can sink your money into funds and then forget about them. The stories in this chapter explain how to invest safely in mutual funds (page 15), choose between the different types (page 17), and keep up with your fund's performance (page 27). A complete guide to over 1,000 funds, including rankings of the top 5-year performers, begins on page 189.

Today's Best Investments

In the recovery ahead, small investors can earn 10% to 15% on stocks and 7% or more on income investments.

Just about everything you could buy went up in 1991, but in the year ahead investors will need to be extremely selective. So even though the approaching elections are a plus overall for small investors, you still need a rundown of the best ways to get the highest returns on your investments—without subjecting yourself to unreasonable risks.

This story spotlights the most promising moves you can make with mutual funds, stocks, income investments, and cash, as well as some assets that may deserve a modest place in your portfolio—foreign stocks, real estate, and gold. Equally important, it will help you steer clear of a variety of investments that could ruin your chances for a prosperous year. Once you've read this overview, you can turn to the stories that follow for smart long-term investment strategies for the decade ahead.

Right now, investors should favor the shares of stocks that can deliver consistent earnings growth. But even if income is not important to you, your diversified holdings should also include stocks that pay above-average dividends; they will likely do well as money-fund investors search for higher yields. If income is important, look for conservative issues; don't reach for the highest payouts on long-term bonds or income stocks with low credit ratings. Instead, aim for yields of as much as 7.5% in less risky short- and intermediate-term bonds or top-quality utility stocks. We recommend the following portfolio strategy:

• Spread your money among stocks, bonds, and cash investments. Small investors should balance stock and equity-fund holdings with less risky investments such as bonds, certificates of deposit, and money-market funds.

• Keep 25% to 35% of your money in stocks. You should never entirely eliminate equities from your portfolio: In the long run, they outpace most other investments by at least two percentage points a year. Given the favorable outlook for 1992 as a whole, you should divide your money between small-company mutual funds, which are likely to be the best performers, and conservative equity funds or blue-chip stocks that would hold up better in a market decline. Then if share prices dive early in the year, you can raise your equity holdings to as much as 50%.

• Put 25% of your portfolio in bonds or other income investments. We recommend that you stick with conservative choices—intermediate-term bonds with maturities of seven to 10 years—or top-quality utility stocks.

Our interest-rate forecast is defensive. Most economists think that inflation will stay low, around 3.5%. We think the Bush Administration, however, will speed up the economy so much in the election year that consumer prices could rise faster than most investors expect—at a 4% to 5% annual rate, at least for a few months. An inflation scare could easily cause long-term rates to spike up to 8.5% or higher. Bonds with maturities of less than 10 years will minimize your risk of principal losses, and utilities will protect you against any longer-term increase in inflation; whereas bond interest payments are fixed, utilities can raise their dividend payouts over time.

• Maintain a large cash reserve. Even though yields on money funds and CDs are at 14-year lows, you should keep as much as 40% of your portfolio in secure short-term investments. Don't take risks to get the highest available yield. Your chief objective should be safety so that you have money to buy stocks or bonds if their prices fall to bargain levels.

• And if you are a sophisticated investor, consider diversifying beyond the basics. Investments such as foreign stocks, real estate, and gold can help boost your return while trimming the overall risk of your portfolio. You don't need a pollster to tell you that's the strategy for winning investment returns.

Here's a quick rundown of our experts' top picks, as well as the investments you should avoid. Stock prices and interest rates quoted in this story reflect their November 1991 values. While our predictions are based on an investment's three- to five-year potential, you should consider its current price before you buy. If an investment you like seems pricey, hold off. You may be able to pick it up cheap if the market skids temporarily later.

Stock Funds: *Small-stock portfolios will lead the pack.*

Buy funds that invest in the shares of small companies. Such stocks gained 37.5% through the middle of November 1991—but despite that run-up they have climbed only 49% since 1983, versus 133% for the S&P 500. Thus, you can anticipate big profits in funds such as T. Rowe Price Small Cap Value (minimum investment of $2,500; 800-638-5660), which generally holds shares of the tiniest firms—those with market capitalizations of $100 million or less. Such stocks may be underpriced because they are neglected by analysts.

Columbia Special ($2,000 minimum investment; 800-547-1707) holds an eclectic mix of small and medium-size stocks, with about 50% of the fund's portfolio in fast-growing companies such as biotech firm Genzyme; the rest is in less popular stocks, a group that recently included capital-goods manufacturers.

Buy the funds that hold fast-growing or undervalued blue-chip stocks. Such funds could deliver double-digit total returns this year and are less volatile than small-company portfolios. Janus Fund (minimum investment of $1,000; 800-525-8983) holds the shares of stable growers, such as drug manufacturer Merck and discount retailer Wal-Mart, that can boost their earnings by 15% or more annually. The fund also likes foreign stocks that may offer even faster growth—such as Teléfonos de Mexico, the Mexican telephone company that analysts expect to show 30% annual profit growth through mid-decade.

T. Rowe Price Capital Appreciation ($2,500 minimum; 800-638-5660) buys companies with overlooked growth potential; recent holdings included battered giants IBM and Polaroid.

Avoid sector funds that have outpaced the stock market by wide margins. Funds that invest exclusively in one of the market's hottest corners—such as biotechnology or financial services— gained 50% or more in 1991. Among them: Financial Strategic Financial Services, up 67%, which holds shares of banks, insurance companies, and brokerages. Although the fund has proved adept at finding the best values in its sector, the fund is likely to give back gains in any market sell-off.

Stocks: *Look for steady growth and financial strength.*

Buy stocks of large, established growth companies that can deliver earnings gains even in tough times. Some of the safest stocks could also be among the market's biggest winners this year as investors who are worried about the anemic economy look for secure havens. Pharmaceutical companies, such as Merck (NYSE, $145), are likely candidates for gains. The world's leading producer of prescription drugs, Merck is headed for its sixth straight year of double-digit growth in earnings, sales, and dividends. Its recently introduced blockbuster drugs—which include Mevacor and Zocor to treat high cholesterol—will help boost earnings by as much as 20% annually over the next three to five years.

A string of successful acquisitions has profoundly transformed Philip Morris (NYSE, $67.75) from a tobacco company to broadbased consumer-goods business. In fact, the company now derives more than half of its $60 billion in annual revenues from brand-name foods such as Oscar Mayer, Bird's Eye, and Jell-O. Profits are likely to grow by as much as 22% a year through the mid-1990s.

Buy the shares of small to medium-size companies whose leadership positions in niche markets ensure steady profit growth. As a result of the stock market's strong gains in 1991, some of these stocks are pricey now, but you should consider buying them if they drop to more attractive levels in a stock market decline. For example, you could select a target price of $84 for $835 million U.S. Surgical (NYSE, $94), which controls more than 80% of the market for surgical clips and internal staples. Analysts say that with no meaningful competition and continuing demand for its products the company can boost its earnings by 65% this year and by 30% to 35% annually after that.

More conservative investors may want to consider Automatic Data Processing (NYSE, $37.25), the nation's largest payroll processor, if its price drops to $32. ADP has racked up 41 straight years of double-digit profit growth, and analysts say the company could boost its earnings by at least 15% annually through 1996.

Avoid the stocks of companies in industries that are in long-term decline. Contrarian investors may be tempted to buy General Motors (NYSE, $30.50), Ford (NYSE, $24.25),

and Chrysler (NYSE, $11.50). But the risks are too great, and the payoff too uncertain. The Big Three U.S. automakers posted a combined loss of $1.7 billion in the third quarter of 1991 on their way to the biggest annual deficits in their histories. And it's not just the recession: All three have been losing market share to Japanese competitors for five years. With no relief in sight—their total share of the U.S. market is now 64%, versus 66% a year ago—earnings growth at these firms will be poor at least through 1995.

Income Investments: *Favor reliable dividends and rising payouts.*

Buy Treasury notes with intermediate maturities or funds that hold them. These issues mature in four to 10 years, recently yielded as much as 7.4%—only about half a percentage point less than 30-year Treasury bonds—and are roughly 35% less volatile than long-term issues. The best buys now are 10-year Treasury notes (7.4% yield). Investors willing to pay for the convenience of a mutual fund that holds intermediate-term Treasuries should choose one with expenses below 0.8% a year such as Benham Treasury Note Trust (minimum of $1,000; 800-472-3389) or recently launched Vanguard Intermediate-Term Treasury (minimum of $3,000; 800-662-7447).

Buy high-quality intermediate-term municipals or funds that hold them. Municipal issues rated AA or AAA by agencies such as Standard & Poor's recently offered tax-exempt yields of about 5.3%—equivalent to a taxable payout of 7.4% or more for investors in the 28% federal tax bracket or above. Consider general-obligation issues backed by the states that have the strongest finances, such as AAA State of Maryland General Obligation 6.7s of 1996, which recently traded at $1,020 to yield 5.2%, and AA+ State of Georgia General Obligation 6.75s of 1997, recently traded at $1,068 to yield 5.3%.

As an alternative, consider an intermediate-term muni-bond fund that has at least 75% of its portfolio in munis rated A or better. Such funds yield about 5.6%, equivalent to a taxable yield of 7.8% or better for top-bracket investors. Two of the best: Vanguard Municipal Intermediate Term ($3,000 minimum; 800-662-7447) and Dreyfus Intermediate Municipal Bond ($2,500 minimum; 800-645-6561).

Buy pre-refunded municipal bonds. These issues, backed by Treasuries held in escrow accounts, carry no credit risk and recently paid tax-exempt yields of around 5.3%. Two solid picks: Piedmont Municipal Power Agency South Carolina 9.7s, recently yielding 5.3%, selling for $1,198 per bond and pre-refunded to mature at $1,030 in 1996; and Austin Texas Utility Revenue 10.25s, 5.2% yield, trading at $1,177 per bond, pre-refunded to mature at $1,020 in 1995.

Buy shares of electric utilities that have solid finances and rising dividends, or a utility mutual fund. Some electric utility stocks with strong financial backing recently paid yields up to 7.8%. And unlike bonds, which pay a fixed rate of interest, these utilities are likely to raise their dividends by as much as 5% annually over the next five years. That should boost their share prices at similar rates, providing investors with annual total return of 9% or better. Top utilities to buy now include: Central & Southwest (NYSE, $50.25), which recently was yielding 5.8% and is likely to deliver annual dividend growth of 5.5% over the next five years for a total return of over 11%; and Kentucky Utilities (NYSE, $25.50), which had a 5.9% yield and projected dividend growth of 3.5% for a total return of about 9.5%.

As an alternative, you can buy shares in a mutual fund that holds utilities. Two sound choices are Fidelity Utilities Income Fund ($2,500 minimum investment; 800-544-8888) and Stratton Monthly Dividend Shares (minimum investment of $2,000; 800-634-5726).

Avoid the high-yielding shares of financially troubled utilities. Payouts of 8% or higher often signal that a utility's shares are depressed because the company lacks financial strength. Centerior Energy (NYSE, $18.75), yielding 8.5%, must pay out 94% of its current earnings

to maintain its dividend, and also operates in slow-growth markets such as Cleveland.

Cash: *Shop for above-average yields—but put safety first.*

Buy government money-market funds that hold only direct obligations of the U.S. government. Their portfolios are free of default risk, and some recently yielded as high as 5.8%. Better yet, in most states the income from these funds is exempt from state and local taxes, which can add half a percentage point or more to your after-tax return. Two high-earning choices in this category are: United Services Government Securities Savings Fund ($1,000 minimum; 800-873-8637) and Dreyfus 100% U.S. Treasury Money Market Fund, LP ($2,500 minimum; 800-645-6561).

Buy high-grade short-term taxable bond funds. These funds hold diversified portfolios of U.S. government or corporate securities that mature in one to five years and are only slightly more volatile than money funds. The safest choices among corporate funds, which can yield up to 8.4%, are those that invest primarily in issues rated AA or better. Two examples: Neuberger & Berman Limited Maturity Bond (minimum of $5,000; 800-877-9700) and Scudder Short-term Bond (minimum of $1,000; 800-225-2470).

Government funds carry no credit risk at all. Interest from those that hold only direct U.S. government obligations is usually exempt from state and local taxes; they recently yielded as much as 6%. Here's your best choice now: Vanguard Fixed-Income U.S. Treasury—Short-term ($3,000 minimum; 800-662-7447).

Buy adjustable-rate mortgage funds that carry no sales charge. These funds are about as stable as short-term bond funds, and they offer yields of up to 7.4%. The funds invest in adjustable-rate mortgages, whose interest rates are reset semiannually or annually; such adjustments sharply reduce the funds' price sensitivity to changes in interest rates.

Until recently, investors had to shell out sales charges of as much as 4% for ARM funds. But since September 1991, two fund families have launched the first no-load entries in the category: Benham Adjustable Rate Government Securities Fund ($1,000 minimum; 800-472-3389) and T. Rowe Price Adjustable Rate U.S. Government ($2,500 minimum; 800-638-5660).

Avoid single-state tax-exempt money funds. Because they invest in the municipal securities of a single state, these funds yield as much as 4.5%, and for that state's residents, the income is typically exempt from state as well as federal income tax. But that advantage isn't worth the extra risk of holding a portfolio that lacks diversification across state lines. Analysts say it's possible that a tax-free money fund could suffer principal losses of as much 5%—and single-state funds are the likeliest candidates.

Foreign Investments: *Don't miss out on growth abroad.*

Buy diversified funds that invest in overseas stocks; they can help you ride out any setback in the U.S. market. T. Rowe Price International Stock Fund ($2,500 minimum; 800-638-5660) has posted annual returns of 18% over the past 10 years, versus 14.7% gains for the average international fund. More than half the $1.4 billion fund's holdings are in Western Europe. Portfolio manager Martin Wade has plowed another 16% of the fund's assets into booming Pacific Rim countries—such as South Korea, Malaysia, Singapore, and Thailand.

Real Estate: *Stick with cash-rich investment companies.*

Buy shares in financially strong real estate investment trusts (REITs) that own undervalued properties. These companies, whose shares are traded on exchanges like any other stock, pool investor cash to buy properties or make mortgage loans. As the real estate market begins to improve in some areas of the country, well-managed REITs that are able to acquire quality properties for bargain prices can offer yields of 6% or higher and the potential for solid capital gains of 5% or more over the next year. Richmond's United Dominion Realty Trust (NYSE, $18.50; 6.9% yield) is poised to capitalize on the depressed real estate market in the Southeast: The $295 million REIT has assembled $52.5 million in bank lines of credit, which it can use to buy new properties. Since May 1991, United Dominion—which owns more than 10,000 apartments and 1.7 million square feet of retail space—has bought 1,160 apartment units in North Carolina and Virginia. Such acquisitions could help fuel 12% earnings growth in 1992.

Gold: *Buy the mines, not the metal.*

Buy shares of leading gold-mining companies with a strong competitive edge. Gold recently fetched a paltry $364 per ounce, a far cry from its peak of $850 in 1980. Although few analysts expect a rebound soon, some mining firms have glittering prospects. Those that earn above-average profits and are increasing their production can post strong earnings gains even when the metal's price remains stagnant. Among them: $619 million Newmont Mining (NYSE, $38.25). The firm's strict cost controls and superior mining technology enable it to spend far less than competitors to pull gold from the ground—$200 an ounce, versus an industry average of $250. Newmont's earnings are likely to grow by 15% or more this year as the company boosts its annual production of gold by an estimated 6.6% to 1.6 million ounces.

Buy shares in leading precious metals mutual funds. Such funds allow you to reduce your risk by investing in a wide range of mining companies operating in different countries. Vanguard Gold and Precious Metals Portfolio ($3,000 minimum investment; 800-662-7447) has earned annual returns of 7.5% over the past five years, compared with 3.3% for the fund's average competitor. David Hutchins, the manager of the fund, spreads his mining-share portfolio among the stock markets of North America, South Africa, and Australia.

Avoid gold bullion and coins. Not only is the price of the actual metal likely to stay flat in 1992, it can cost plenty to buy and hold the stuff. Banks and brokers charge markups and fees that can range as high as 10% if you invest less than $5,000 in bullion or coins such as the Canadian Maple Leaf or the American Eagle; you may also incur annual storage costs of 0.5% to 1.5%. The typical markups on collectible coins purchased through dealers are even worse—up to a gold-digging 30% or more.

Risk-Reducing Fund Strategies

You can't give up on the stock market if you want superior long-term results. But you can play it safe using these tried-and-true principles.

If you're a mutual fund investor, the ups and downs in fund performances in recent years may have made you uneasy about the safety of stock funds as an investment. Don't give up on them yet. Over the long run, inflation will cripple your capital worse than an occasional sour market ever could. To stay ahead of rising prices, you need stocks, period. And while it may seem strange to say so given the rollercoaster results of the market since 1987, stock funds still offer real opportunities. Your goal as a mutual-fund investor in the 1990s, as always, must be to accommodate equity investing's risks while still giving yourself a shot at stock funds' superior long-term returns. The task begins with smart fund selection, and *Money*'s Mutual Fund Rankings (beginning on page 189) will help you there. But investment technique is likely to be equally important, particularly to your peace of mind. Here, then, is a close look at five proven risk-reducing strategies for making money in mutual funds today:

Seek out low-cost funds. In the roaring 1980s, gains-hungry investors paid no more attention to fund expenses than drag racers do to gas mileage. Who cared about costs as long as stock funds were piling up average annual gains of 15.5% and bond funds were churning out 11.1% a year?

In the present decade, when analysts expect yearly returns to be three to five points lower, fees and expenses will loom larger, steepening losses and slowing subsequent recoveries.

For instance, a no-load fund with a 9.75% gross return and a low 0.75% annual expense ratio would build $10,000 into $23,670 over the next 10 years. A 4% load fund with a stiff 1.5% charge would knock that down to $21,210.

As a rule, avoid domestic stock funds with annual expenses that total more than 1.5% of assets. In evaluating international funds, in which the costs of doing business overseas jack up fees, cut out any fund charging more than 2% a year. With bond funds, insist on expenses below 1%.

Dollar-cost average. Investing a fixed amount of money at regular intervals—say, $100 to $500 a month—wrings much of the risk out of stock funds with little effort.

For one thing, it prevents you from committing your whole stash at a market peak. And if your mutual fund's share value does drop, your next installment payment automatically picks up more of the lower-priced shares. That cuts your average cost per share and boosts your eventual gain.

Build a well-balanced, diversified portfolio. Most investors are at least familiar with the don't-put-all-your-eggs-in-one-basket logic of diversification. But many really don't understand how powerful a risk-reducing tactic it is. Martin Sass of M.D. Sass Investors Services in New York City calculates that in a truly disastrous year, in which long-term Treasury yields rise by three percentage points and the stock market falls by 20%, a moderately conservative portfolio split evenly between stocks and intermediate-term bonds would drop only 9.4%. A superskittish mix featuring 25% in equities would lose just 5.6%. Better yet, sensible diversification costs you relatively little in performance. For example, over the past 30 years, a portfolio split evenly between stocks and five-year Treasury notes provided 87% of the gain of Standard & Poor's index of 500 stocks while fluctuating in value only 60% as much.

Emphasize intermediate-term bond funds. Typically, the longer the maturity of the bonds in a fund's portfolio, the higher the fund's yield—but also the steeper its losses when interest rates rise. The trade-off is rarely even. When you extend your portfolio's maturity much past five years, you get a little more yield and a lot more risk. For instance, if interest rates rose by two percentage points—as they did in 1987—the price of the most recently issued 30-year Treasury bonds would fall by 19% while the comparable five-year issue would drop only 8%.

Interest-rate leverage cuts both ways, of course; as rates fell about one percentage point in the last four months of 1990, long-term bonds garnered capital gains of about 9%, compared with 4% for five-year bonds. But if you're willing to take the risk to capture bigger gains, don't buy longer-term bonds. Add to your position in stocks.

Split your stock fund allotment among managers with different styles. Over any investment period of 10 years or more, funds with differing investment philosophies will take turns outperforming—and being outperformed by—those with other philosophies (see "Choosing among Different Fund Styles" at right). For example, the money-management firm Trinity Investment Management in Cambridge, Massachusetts, examined the returns of traditional growth-stock mutual funds, small-company growth funds, funds taking a value approach (investing in stocks trading below the value of their assets or earnings), and those that combined growth and income.

In 18 of the past 21 years, the average return of at least one of those four groups exceeded that of the S&P 500. And the annual average difference between the best- and worst-performing styles was a whopping 14.4 percentage points. Foretelling exactly how and when investing fashions will change, however, is like trying to predict when long, Elvis-like sideburns will come back in style. Analysts say that you should instead divide your money among funds with different styles. That way you won't be left behind when one sector of the market moves up sharply. For example, coming out of a bear market, you could put 40% of your stock-holdings into value funds. Reason: Value investing typically pays off best at the end of a bear market and in the early part of a new bull.

Three solid, no-load value entries you might want to consider are Gabelli Asset (800-422-3554); Lindner Fund (314-727-5305); and Selected American Shares (800-553-5533).

Another 20% to 30% of your stock allotment could go into no-load small-company funds like Pennsylvania Mutual (800-221-4268), managed by Charles Royce. Royce seeks to control his downside in the mercurial small-company sector by focusing on shares trading below their inherent worth.

Other worthy small-stock funds include Nicholas II (414-272-6133) and GIT Equity Special Growth (800-336-3063).

Though the small-company funds have gained only 50% on average from their peak in mid-1983, compared with 123% for value funds and 94% for growth, many analysts believe the group may regain its spark once the economy shows signs of picking up. If so, the surge could be spectacular: From 1975 through 1982, the little guys returned 600%—nearly double the gain of any other equity group.

Reserve another 20% to 30% of your stockholdings for growth funds. The category's 32% average return from the beginning of 1987 to the end of 1990's third quarter topped both the value funds' 25% and small-company funds' 13%. Solid no-load candidates include SteinRoe Special (800-338-2550); Janus Venture (800-525-3713); and no-load Counsellors Capital Appreciation (800-888-6878).

Your smallest allocation, about 10% to 20%, should go into solid-performing, modest-expense international funds such as Vanguard Trustees' Commingled International (800-662-7447) and T. Rowe Price International Stock (800-638-5660).

The internationals' 17.9% annually compounded gain from 1985 through 1990 has made them by far the top-performing fund category. But with foreign economies weakening and the battered U.S. dollar, analysts expect that overseas funds will sooner or later be knocked out of first place.

Why not bypass internationals entirely? Because markets often confound even the most confident expectations. By diversifying among different types of funds, you acknowledge the unpredictability of markets and lessen the damage if you're wrong. In an uncertain market, diversification is king. Whatever happens, if you spread your money among assets and among investment styles, you should be able to sleep at night.

Choosing among Different Fund Styles

Why can't your fund beat the S&P? The key is knowing how investment style powers funds—and then acting on it.

If money talks, then a small but growing minority of mutual-fund shareholders are saying they've had it with fund managers. At the Vanguard group, for example, one of the hottest-selling funds has been the Index Trust-500 Portfolio, which attracted some $140 million—half again as much as any other stock fund in the group. What's significant about that is the $2.6 billion fund has no human stock pickers in charge. Using computer trading models, it simply attempts to match the returns of Standard & Poor's index of 500 stocks. And as its shareholders have no doubt noticed, both the fund and the S&P have beaten the typical all-too-human manager eight years running.

For investors, equity funds' persistent inability to beat the S&P is only one of many frustrations. Among the complaints:

Inconsistency. Of the top 25 equity funds in the five years to January 1, 1986, none reappeared among the top 25 over the five years to January 1, 1991—and six actually slipped into the bottom half of the 1,241 stock funds tracked by Lipper Analytical Services.

Broken promises. After years of claiming that they would surely prove their mettle in a down market, managers got their chance in 1990—and blew it. The S&P, which fell 3.1%, not only held up better than the average stock fund (off 5.3%) but also lost less than defensive categories such as growth and income (down 4.2%) and equity income (off 5.8%).

Less performance at more cost. Even as performance relative to the S&P worsened since 1982, annual expenses levied by the average mutual fund have risen by 22%, from 98¢ for each $100 of assets to $1.20.

Such disappointments raise fundamental questions for investors: Can you really put much faith in a manager's long-term performance? Have the top managers of the past lost their touch? And, most basic of all, perhaps: Is there any point in investing in anything but an index fund? The answers to those questions, according to the money managers and mutual-fund analysts interviewed for this story, are yes, not necessarily, and yes. Says San Francisco investment adviser Kurt Brouwer: "Mutual funds as a group have underperformed partly because the kinds of stocks that many of them invest in—small and mid-size firms—have been out of style. When they come back into style, the funds should again outgain the S&P."

Understanding the role of investing style in fund performance will help you increase your returns, starting now. Helping you gain that understanding—and use it to your advantage—is what this story is about.

Winners in Five Investing Styles

These funds were among the best in their investment style, measured by risk-adjusted returns. But no style wins all the time. The two value entries, for example, lagged the S&P over five years but beat the index over 10 years, a period that includes their strong showing in the early 1980s.

FUND NAME	% gain to 4/1/91 One year	% gain to 4/1/91 Five years	% gain to 4/1/91 10 years	Years since 1981 fund outperformed the S&P	Five-year expense projection	Minimum initial investment	Telephone
GROWTH							
AIM Weingarten	27.6%	117.2%	401.2%	7	$120	$1,000	800-347-1919
Twentieth Century Select	16.3	75.6	352.0	8	55	None	800-345-2021
GROWTH AND INCOME							
Founders Blue Chip	17.6	74.1	276.3	5	55	1,000	800-525-2440
Investment Company of America	15.2	84.2	365.7	7	86	250	800-421-0180
VALUE							
Lindner Fund	3.8	73.5	357.1	6	41	2,000	314-727-5305
Selected American Shares	27.9	85.6	369.4	5	60	1,000	800-553-5533
SMALL COMPANY							
Janus Venture	24.3	121.5	N.A.	4[1]	64	1,000	800-525-3713
Pennsylvania Mutual	7.3	57.5	305.0	4	54	2,000	800-221-4268
INTERNATIONAL							
Scudder International	1.5	89.5	317.7	5	74	1,000	800-225-2470
T. Rowe Price International Stock	0.7	102.6	338.8	6	61	2,500	800-638-5660
S&P 500-STOCK INDEX	**14.4**	**86.3**	**316.4**	—	—	—	—
GENERAL EQUITY FUNDS AVERAGE	**12.3**	**58.7**	**239.1**	—	—	—	—

[1] Since the fund's inception in 1985 **Source:** Lipper Analytical Services

Style, in a mutual fund context, refers to a fund's investment approach. Most mutual-fund managers realize that they can never hope to own the best-performing equities all the time. So they try to get an angle on the market in the long run by subscribing to a particular stock-picking philosophy, or style, and sticking with it. Some pros, like Harry Hutzler and Jonathan Schoolar of AIM Weingarten, load their portfolios with classic growth stocks whose earnings are expanding 16% or more annually. Others, like Eric Ryback and Robert Lange of Lindner Fund, favor bargain-basement "value" shares whose prices are low compared with the per-share value of the company's earnings or assets. Still others, like James Craig of Janus Venture, go for promising small or mid-size companies, while managers like Erik Borgen of Founders Blue Chip favor established corporations that pay steady, generous dividends. (For performance data and phone numbers for these and other leading funds in five different investment categories—growth, growth and income, value, small company, and international—see the table at left.)

What you need to keep in mind is that no style stays on top forever. As the economy and the stock market move through the business cycle, different approaches slide in and out of favor. And while a skillful portfolio manager can make a fund clearly stand out from its peers, no fund is entirely exempt from the following five rules of the style game:

A fund's investing style accounts in large measure for the difference between its performance and that of the averages. As every fund investor has observed, funds tend to rise when the broad stock market jumps and to fall when it slips, regardless of the investment approach. But style is crucial in determining whether a fund soars or slumps farther than the average fund or the S&P. In a study comparing the performance of major investment styles over the past 22 years, Cambridge, Massachusetts money manager Trinity Investment Management found that the average difference between the best- and worst-performing domestic styles each year was a whopping 14 percentage points. Had you managed to switch into the

average fund in the best-performing group at the start of each year, you would have clocked an annualized return of 16.7%. That's 7.6 percentage points a year better than the S&P and two points better than the No. 1 publicly available fund over the period, Twentieth Century Select. By contrast, if you had the ill fortune to choose the worst-performing style each year, you would have gained a meager 4% annually.

No style wins all the time. Value funds, with an 11.1% annualized total return, had the best average performance in the Trinity study, but they still lagged other mutual-fund styles for long stretches of time. Since 1988, for example, value funds have risen an ordinary 9.2% a year, even as growth funds gained 11.3% and growth and income funds climbed 12.7%. Small-company funds, by contrast, turned in the worst average performance over the past 22 years, with an 8.6% annualized return; but they, too, had their day. In 1977, for example, small-company funds led their nearest competitors, growth funds, by an eye-popping 14.5 points.

The cycles of over- or underperformance usually last two years or more. If you miss the first few months of a strong performance by one category, don't assume it is too late to get aboard. That's because when a certain style starts to outgain the S&P, it generally stays ahead for at least two years. Similarly, when it lags, it tends to fall behind for a couple of years. Small-company funds seem to go through particularly long cycles: Their most recent run of superior performance lasted from 1975 to mid-1983, while their most recent down cycle dragged on from 1983 until January 1991.

Different styles tend to dominate at different points in the economic and market cycles. Value, for example, often shines in the early stages of a bull market, while growth grabs the lead when the economy heats up. One reason is that investors tend to stay nervous even after stocks begin to rise. Skittish investors favor bargain-priced value shares because they feel such stocks won't tumble further. Indeed, when the first pullback hits a new bull market, value often does hold up better than growth. For example, the average value fund gained 2.3% in the bearish third quarter of 1983, while the average growth entry dropped 3.3%. "Later in the cycle, when people become confident that the recovery is established, growth takes over," says money manager Kenneth Fisher.

Other investment styles also march to their own drummers. Growth and income funds tend to do best when a rally is accompanied by sharply falling interest rates, which makes their high-dividend stocks that much more attractive to investors. As a result, growth and income funds gained 26.8% in 1982 (versus 21.6% for the S&P), when interest rates fell from 14.2% to 10.5%. International funds fare best when foreign markets are strong and the dollar is falling, since that increases the dollar value of their foreign currency trading profits. Hence, internationals gained a sizzling 31.6% a year between 1985 and 1987 as the dollar dropped more than 35% versus the yen and the Deutsche mark.

To some extent, small-company funds ride along with the market and the economy. But they also appear to move in a cycle of their own, driven at least partly by the tastes of institutional investors. Normally, such investors prefer secure, well-researched, big-company stocks. As long as those stocks perform, as they did for most of the past nine years, the institutions stick with them. But when small companies become compelling bargains compared with larger stocks, the big money edges into high-growth small companies. Since such companies have relatively few shares outstanding, even a minor shift by institutions toward small stocks can send their prices into orbit.

The same cycles help determine whether the average fund beats the S&P 500. While many investors regard the S&P as a neutral benchmark, the index is actually heavily slanted toward big, established stocks with billions of dollars of shares outstanding. (That's why the fairest way to judge individual funds is in comparison with others of the same type or against indexes that track their market sector, such as the Russell 2000 for small-company

stocks or the Morgan Stanley EAFE index for international stock funds.) In the 1980s, the big S&P companies benefited from corporate cost cutting, which gave a one-time boost to earnings, and from the growth of index investing and program trading, which increased demand for S&P stocks simply because they were in the index. Most of all, takeovers, real and rumored, lifted the S&P. "Takeovers concentrated on big stocks," notes A. Michael Lipper, president of Lipper Analytical Services, "and that helped drive up the S&P." Most of these conditions no longer exist, however, and momentum seems to be shifting to the kind of small and medium-size equities that fund stock pickers have long favored. The last time little stocks took charge—between 1975 and 1982—the average equity fund beat the S&P by 5.6 percentage points a year. Unfortunately, patterns in the stock market never repeat themselves precisely. So in putting the foregoing information to use, tread carefully. Mutual fund analysts recommend observing three prudent rules:

• Diversify your equity holdings among different styles of funds. By now you probably can recite in Urdu the virtues of diversifying among stocks, bonds, and cash to reduce your overall risk. The rationale for diversifying among different stock-picking approaches is the same: Spreading your risk keeps your investment portfolio from capsizing if one investment style runs aground.

Once you have a foothold in every investment style, your most crucial step is to decide which fund categories get the greatest weight. Currently, many market analysts point to value and small-company growth funds as the most promising candidates. Both have been laggards in recent years, both typically fare well in the early stages of economic recovery, and both began to make encouraging moves even before the stock market surged in January and February 1991, coinciding with the allies' Persian Gulf victory.

Judging from past performance, value funds should be among the top performers for at least 12 months after the recession ends. In fact, two years after the beginning of the bull markets in 1975 and 1982, the average value fund had built a 15 percentage-point lead over the average growth fund. Part of the advantage comes from value funds' concentration in hard-hit cyclical companies, which often rise the most in a recovery. And the underpriced stocks that value funds own tend to have higher dividend yields than the S&P. Over time, that can give the funds a leg up on the index.

Ken Gregory, editor of the mutual fund advisory newsletter *L/G No-Load Fund Analyst,* feels that the case for small-company funds is equally persuasive. "Our strongest call is that small-cap stocks will do well over the next two to three years and maybe longer," says Gregory. But considering the headlong advance that small-company funds made in 1991, be price-conscious when getting into the sector.

• Pick individual funds that stand out in comparison with their peers. Getting your style allocations right is only part of the battle. Even if you overweight the right categories, you can still fall flat if you pick a laggard fund within its sector. Ideally, you want funds, such as the 10 in the table on page 18, that have consistently outrun the competition in their class, while taking no more than average risks.

• Reconsider your allocations at least once a year. Although you should look forward two years or more in making your allocations, it still pays to rebalance your portfolio annually and to review your allocations when the market undergoes a meaningful change. For example, if small-company stocks eventually reach price/earnings multiples more than 60% to 75% higher than the S&P, it will be time to cut back on your small-stock funds. After all, if the history of investment styles proves nothing else, it's that no winning streak lasts forever.

Why Good Brokers Sell Bad Products

The reason, of course, is money—for them, not you.

Don't be surprised if you start hearing more from your broker about the mutual funds his firm manages. Be warned, though: Apart from a handful of stalwarts, the private-label funds managed by the major national brokerages—Dean Witter, Merrill Lynch, Paine Webber, Prudential, and Shearson—have been mediocre, or worse. Yet, that has not prevented the five prestigious firms from making money on them. In all, they pull in roughly $2.6 billion a year in commissions, management fees, and other revenues from their house brands, according to Lipper Analytical Securities. And in these days of slimmer stock-trading commissions and reduced underwriting revenues, they want more. Several big brokerage firms, for example, are stepping up their mutual fund marketing efforts. Merrill Lynch, for one, recently spent a large portion of its ad budget—which, in 1990, totaled more than $24 million—on the company's first major campaign for its in-house funds. The sales push began with 30-second TV spots on the major networks; Merrill also ran fund ads in nearly a dozen magazines (including *Money*) and hundreds of local newspapers. The firm also revamped all of its fund brochures and sales materials.

Among some of the other firms' sales tactics:

Higher commissions for selling the house brand. In April 1991, Prudential—which pays its brokers up front on both its front- and back-end load funds—boosted its salesmen's take on its private-label funds from 40% to 45% of the total sales commission, while it held the brokers' share on funds from outside load groups, such as Colonial and Kemper, constant at 30% to 40%. (On an in-house fund, the brokerage firm keeps the rest of the commission, which typically runs from 4% to 8.5% of the amount invested; on an independent fund, the outside sponsor also gets a small cut.) Result: On a typical $10,000 transaction, a Prudential broker pockets as much as $75 more for putting you in the house special. Paine Webber brokers collect as much as 11 percentage points more for selling their company's own funds, while

Big Doesn't Necessarily Mean Better with Brokerage Funds

Although the five leading brokerage houses are big fish in the mutual-fund pond—managing 25% of the industry's $1.2 trillion in assets—they don't always make a splash on the performance charts. Following is a look at each family, starting with the largest:

Merrill Lynch. With more than $100 billion in its 44 mutual funds, Merrill Lynch is second only to Fidelity Investments ($131 billion) in assets managed. The firm has one of the steadier records among the house brands we studied. Of its 22 nationally available funds with five-year records to April 1991, half had better than average returns within their categories and only three ended up in the bottom quarter for the period. "Our philosophy is to aim more for consistency than for outstanding performance in any given period," says Arthur Zeikel, president of Merrill Lynch Asset Management. Four Merrill funds ranked in their sectors' top quarter. They are Capital A (up 73.4%), Corporate—High Income A (up 44.5%), Corporate—Intermediate Term (up 45.6%), and Municipal—Insured A (up 43.8%). But Merrill's standing slipped somewhat over the past three years as only 40% of its funds posted above-average gains.

Shearson. Boosting performance has been a major goal for Jerome Miller, who took over Shearson's $50 billion group in 1989. In 1990, he dumped or reassigned the managers of nine of his 36 funds. With good reason. Twelve of the 34 Shearson funds with three-year records placed in the bottom quarter of their categories. And three funds came in dead last over the five years to April 1991: Investors Special Equity (down 3.3%), Global Opportunity (up 19.3%), and Intermediate Government (up 37%). On the plus side, Telecommunications—Income (up 98.2%), Aggressive Growth (up 102.8%), and Appreciation (up 83.8%) all finished in the top quarter for the five years.

Dean Witter. Mediocrity has been the watchword for Dean Witter's 42 funds. Over the five years to April 1991, not one stock or bond fund in the $47 billion group ranked in the top quarter of any category. High Yield was the worst of the battered junk-bond funds, down 20% since 1986.

That major embarrassment aside, most of Dean Witter's other funds have been about average. Five of eight funds posted above-average five-year returns in their categories. But the three-year figures aren't as pleasing: Just under half beat the averages during that time.

Prudential. "We recognize we've had some weak spots," admits Michael Downey, head of Prudential's $36 billion, 53-fund group. That's putting it lightly. Of 25 Prudential funds with three-year records, eight clustered in the bottom fourth in their categories. The biggest clinker: GNMA B (up 39.7%), the worst five-year performer of 23 GNMA funds. Downey also has a few winners. Over the past five years, Utility Fund B (up 74.7%) took first in its group and Government Intermediate (up 42.1%) made the top quarter.

Paine Webber. With $20 billion in 31 funds, Paine Webber has outrun some bigger competitors. More than 55% of its funds scored above-average three- and five-year gains, the highest percentage of the five wire-house families. Two rank in the top fourth of their categories for five years: Classic Growth (up 75.8%) and U.S. Government Income (up 47.5%).

The firm's biggest shortcoming has been its fixed-income funds: Three were in the bottom quarter of their categories over five years. Fund chief Joyce Fensterstock blames the poor showing on Paine Webber's erstwhile focus on yield. "That put some of our funds' track records in the middle or bottom third," she says. She hopes for better results from the group's new fixed-income managers and from their new emphasis on total return.

Dean Witter pays as much as five points more. Only Merrill and Shearson still use the same commission system for both in-house and outside funds.

Locking out the competition. In 1991, Dean Witter forbade outside fund groups from making sales presentations in Dean Witter's offices. The goal: to boost sales of the firm's own funds from 60% to 75% of its total fund sales. Investors might justifiably wonder why the brokerage executives are flogging their own funds so vigorously when the firms get roughly the same commission for selling independent funds. The answer, simply put, is annual fees. Chief among them is the investment management fee, typically 0.4% to 1% of fund assets a year, or as much as $10 million on a $1 billion fund. The marketing or distribution charges known as 12b-1 fees, common on brokerage funds, bring in as much as 1% of fund assets a year; the brokerage generally keeps 90%. Some firms also pick up a few million dollars a year per fund for processing fundholder accounts. And the more assets that brokers can funnel into the brokerage-house funds, the fatter the fees grow since they are charged to a bigger pool of assets. It all adds up. Dean Witter's $10.2 billion U.S. Government Securities, for example, pulled in $135.8 million for the firm in 1990. Shareholders didn't make out nearly so well, however: The fund ranked a lowly 20th out of 23 GNMA funds over the five-year period ending in December 1990, with a total return of only 45%.

Unlike sales loads, moreover, annual fees pour in whether investors are buying or not. It's not only the level of income that's attractive, but also that the fees are there year after year. Prudential's fund operation earned $88 million in 1990, for instance, while the firm as a whole lost $250 million.

No one could begrudge the firms their profits if they provided real performance. But not even the brokerages themselves are satisfied with their funds' results. (For a head-to-head comparison of the house-brand funds' performance, see the box at left.) Shearson, for example, changed the managers of nine of its 36 funds in 1990. Prudential removed six of 25,

while Paine Webber replaced all three of its bond-fund managers. Dean Witter reportedly hopes to start almost from scratch by acquiring an existing fund group. It could then merge such turkeys as U.S. Government Securities and Option Income into funds with better records.

Not all house specials are wimps. Standouts include Merrill Lynch Capital A (up 79.1% for the five years to May 1991, compared with 66.1% for the average growth and income fund), Prudential-Bache Utility (up 77.9% versus 60.4% for the typical utility fund), and Shearson Aggressive Growth (up 86.7% versus 55.9% for its average competitor). But if your broker calls with one of the firm's "hot" funds, don't bite until you've received satisfactory answers to the following questions:

What is the fund's record? Most brokerage firms made their big plunge into the fund business late and then scrambled to catch up with more established competitors. Shearson, for instance, has 36 funds today but ran only one before the mid-1980s, while Paine Webber's 31-fund stable has no fund older than Classic Atlas, founded in 1983. The result: Investors suffered as the big wire houses struggled to come up with investment strategies that worked. To avoid such start-up troubles, stick with funds that have outperformed the average in their category for at least three years.

What can go wrong? Too often brokerage firms come up with a product their brokers can easily sell rather than one suited to their customers' risk tolerance. In the 1980s, for example, many brokers hawked funds with high yields, without paying enough attention to whether the funds could deliver that yield without undue risk to the fundholders' principal. "There has been a greater proportion of what we'd call product disappointments sold by the big brokerages," says Avi Nachmany, an analyst with Strategic Insight, the mutual-fund research and consulting arm of Jesup Josephthal & Company. Needless to say, a brokerage's "product disappointment"—be it a junk-bond fund that collapses in a recession or a Ginnie Mae fund wracked by mortgage prepayments—can be a customer's worst nightmare.

How do the fees compare with those of similar funds? Many brokerage funds carry excessive operating costs. Take Shearson Multiple Opportunities, for example. The $164 million fund is freighted with annual expenses of 3%. That's high for a fund that has whipped the S&P 500 just once in its four-year history. One rule of thumb: Shy away from front-end-load funds in which annual fees exceed the following levels: 1.3% of assets on a domestic stock fund, 1% of assets on a taxable bond fund, and 0.7% on a tax-exempt fund. If the fund carries a back-end load, don't pay more than 0.2 percentage points above those cutoffs.

What happens if your broker switches firms? If you like your broker, you'll probably want to stay with him if he moves from, say, Dean Witter to Merrill Lynch. If you own a fund managed by an independent company, transferring the shares to your broker's new firm will involve some annoying paperwork. But transferring a house-brand fund is so much trouble that few investors try it. One alternative is to leave the old account open—though you'll have to continue paying an account fee if the fund is in an IRA or, at Merrill Lynch or Paine Webber, if the account is inactive. Another choice is to sell the old fund and buy a new one. But, first, research the terms of both sales: You could pay twice if you dump a fund with a back-end load and buy one with an up-front charge.

What should you do if you already own a house fund? Stay put if the fund's performance record is solid and you're comfortable with its risk level. If not, you should consider switching to one of the brokerage house's stronger performers. (You won't have to pay a sales charge, except in some cases when the new fund has a higher load than the one you're leaving.) You could also redeem your fund shares, but you'll have to pay if the fund carries a back-end load and you've owned it for less than five or six years.

Little-Known Money-Makers

These pint-size funds offer agility, solid gains, and sometimes even the chance to chat with the pro who's managing your money.

Of the approximately 1,100 publicly sold stock funds, there are a good 400 or so that few investors ever hear of, no matter how strong their performances. The reason: They're too small to get much press. Funds with less than $25 million in assets don't show up in *Money*'s annual rankings or even in newspaper listings, unless they have more than 1,000 shareholders. Advertising isn't likely to bring them attention either, since few have the budget for it.

Small funds rarely make headlines, but some do earn shareholders a good bit of money.

That's certainly true of the eight plucky funds discussed here. All were under $25 million in assets in late 1990 (some have since grown), and all are run by managers who have topped the 35.7% gain of the average equity fund over the three years to January 1991. These funds typically succeed for the same reasons as any well-run fund: savvy stock picking and, in some cases, well-timed defensive moves into cash. But they also enjoy an important advantage because of their size—agility. An elephant such as $13 billion Fidelity Magellan, for example, leaves footprints that can easily drive a stock's price up when the fund is buying or push it down as it sells. A $25 million fund, by contrast, can flit in and out of stocks with barely a ripple. That allows little funds to react quickly—and profitably—to changes in the economic outlook. Smallness also means that little funds can acquire shares of thinly capitalized small companies in sufficient quantity to have an impact on their portfolios.

Small funds do have one major drawback: steep annual expenses. The average fund with less than $25 million spends $1.85 of every $100 of assets a year on investment advisory fees, legal costs, and other expenses, according to the mutual-fund data firm Lipper Analytical Services. In a fund with more than $500 million, economies of scale cut costs to a yearly average of just 79¢ per $100 invested.

Therefore, in addition to limiting our list to managers with above-average three-year gains (and, if applicable, five-year returns), we eliminated from our search any selection with a front- or back-end sales charge or an annual expense level that tops 2%. Our eight up-and-comers are presented here in alphabetical order:

Fontaine Capital Appreciation. The son of a Rhode Island bread deliveryman, Richard Fontaine won shareholder gratitude as manager of a T. Rowe Price fund—also called Capital Appreciation—that skirted the worst of the 1987 crash and returned an index-whipping 39.5% between 1986 and 1988. A student of the so-called value school of investing, Fontaine buys securities that others shun at what he hopes are bargain prices. Fontaine, who owns 10% of the $7 million fund's shares, cuts risk by loading up on cash when he thinks the market is set to fall. That helped the fund return 6% in 1990 despite the market's 3% loss. Holding down fund costs has called for more painful solutions. Fontaine has gone without a management fee since the fund's September 1989 inception and paid $40,000 in fund bills out of his own pocket. "I wouldn't pay a money manager more than 1.5% of assets," he explains, "and I don't think anyone else should."

Monetta Fund. This $6 million small-company growth fund is tiny, but manager Robert Bacarella traces its origins to something smaller still: an investment club he started in 1975 with four friends. To keep a lid on the risks of investing in small-company stocks, Bacarella is quick to sell any holding that climbs 30% or drops 10% from the fund's purchase price. "We're one of the few firms to use market sentiment to tell us what something is worth," he says. That still leaves the fund subject to stomach-churning ups and downs. Monetta slid 8% in one four-week period in 1990, for example, when several technology holdings posted weak earnings. "When buying small technology companies," he says dryly, "you have to be very careful about believing what management says."

Northeast Investors Growth. When it comes to stock picking, portfolio manager William Oates prefers not to take risks. His $27 million, 32-stock Northeast Investors Growth fund is nearly fully invested in top-quality blue chips like Johnson & Johnson and Kellogg. The result: a 52% gain over the three years to January 1991, 19 percentage points more than the average equity fund. "Before I make a purchase," he says, "I ask myself, 'Is this an investment I would like to own? Is it something I can live with for a while?' " If it is, he buys—and usually holds for three to five years. Oates, who owns 5% of Northeast's shares himself, asks his fellow investors to call or write him with comments or questions. On average, eight do each week.

Robertson Stephens Emerging Growth. With a three-year total return of 80.5%, this $25 million small-company growth fund is the top performer in our group. About 85% of the 50-stock portfolio is in computer, medical, and service companies. That reflects the expertise of both manager Bob Czepiel, a former Wall Street technology stock analyst, and Robertson Stephens, the San Francisco investment house that sponsors the fund. But Czepiel also credits his success to a kind of judicious impatience. "A stock either goes up, or it goes out of our portfolio," he says. "And if it goes up too quickly, we get rid of it, too." Most stocks are held for less than six months, making for a steep annual turnover rate of 272%.

Twentieth Century Giftrust. The $30 million Giftrust is the smallest fund in the $9 billion Twentieth Century group. But president James Stowers still expects the eight-year-old fund to be the family's top long-term performer. "Because of its size, the fund can invest in smaller companies than our other funds," he says. Indeed, the 43-stock growth fund has a solid five-year total return of 93%, versus the 86% gain scored by the S&P 500-stock index. The fund has an unusual feature, however: You can buy it only as a gift. Shares are then held in an irrevocable trust that the beneficiary cannot tap for a preset period of at least 10 years. That limits Giftrust to investors who want to help fund a child's education, say, or leave money to charity. Stowers and four money managers keep Giftrust fully invested in companies whose earnings and revenues are accelerating. As a matter of fund policy, Stowers won't discuss specific investments. Giftrust is one of the riskiest choices because of its damn-the-torpedoes strategy. In 1990, for example, it fell by 17% (after gaining 50% in 1989). "When the market goes down, we temporarily look sick," admits Stowers, "but when it bounces off the bottom, we go like gangbusters."

U.S. Income. J. David Edwards sees managing money as a form of art. "I build mosaics and patterns of investment strategy," says Edwards, who has managed money for banks and pension funds for half his life. Certainly, the recent returns on his eight-year-old U.S. Income look lovely to shareholders. Up 49.4% over the three years to January 1991, the $7.5 million income-oriented stock fund outgained the average equity fund by an impressive 14 percentage points.

One of 12 San Antonio-based United Services funds, 30-stock U.S. Income is one of the most conservative picks. "We're a lot less volatile than a growth fund," Edwards says, "but in 1989 we gained 38%, outperforming the S&P by six points." In 1990, he had less to boast about: A losing bet on natural gas and telephone stocks produced an 8.7% decline. U.S. Income's prospectus allows Edwards to buy bonds as well as REITs and other high-yielding stocks, but he prefers utilities. Depending on his economic outlook, he tinkers with the mix in his portfolio.

Wasatch Growth. Before becoming the lead portfolio manager of $5.5 million Wasatch Growth fund in 1986, Samuel Stewart, Jr. spent three years teaching finance at Columbia University in New York City. But academe left

Up-and-Comers for the 1990s

These eight unheralded stock funds, ranked here by their three-year returns, enjoy a combination of savvy management and nimble size that could make them strong performers in the 1990s—and wise buys now, before the economy kicks into gear again. Net assets are as of December 31, 1990.

FUND NAME	Net assets (millions)	% gain (or loss) to January 1, 1991 One year	Three years	Annual expenses (per $100)	Minimum initial investment	Telephone (800)
Robertson Stephens Emerging Growth	$25.0	9.5	80.5	$1.88	$5,000	766-3863
Monetta Fund	6.0	11.4	57.9	1.50	100	666-3882
Northeast Investors Growth	27.0	1.4	52.1	1.77	1,000	225-6704
U.S. Income	7.5	(8.7)	49.4	2.00	1,000	873-8637
Wasatch Growth	5.5	10.4	42.1	1.50	5,000	551-1700
Wayne Hummer Growth Fund Trust	26.0	5.1	39.5	1.50	1,000	621-4477
Twentieth Century Giftrust	30.0	(17.0)	38.5	1.00	250	345-2021
Fontaine Capital Appreciation	7.0	6.1	10.5[1]	1.50	2,500	247-1550
AVERAGE EQUITY FUND	645.0	(5.3)	35.7	0.79	—	—

[1] Since inception (September 28, 1989) **Source:** Lipper Analytical Services

Stewart unsatisfied. "At the university, it was all theory and no practice," says Stewart. Practice proved almost perfect in 1990: The Salt Lake City fund gained an impressive 10.4%. Stewart and his three co-managers look to invest in roughly 40 fast-growing small companies. But such shares can be risky. "We used to put 5% of our portfolio in every company we owned," says Stewart. "Then we found out some of these companies are hard to get out of in a hurry." Now Wasatch invests no more than 1% of fund assets in any holding unless all four managers approve a larger stake.

Wayne Hummer Growth. The $26 million Wayne Hummer Growth Fund Trust outperformed the average stock fund by four percentage points over the three years to January 1991. But don't look for razzle-dazzle in its 33-stock portfolio. Says Alan Bird, a money manager for Chicago brokerage firm Wayne Hummer for the past nine years: "Our strategy is so apple pie and motherhood it's almost nauseating." That's one way of putting it. Certainly, the portfolio assembled by Bird and co-manager Thomas Rowland is moderate on risk and strong on Midwestern flavor. "Most of these companies I've followed for 20 years or more," says Bird, who was a security analyst for Northwestern University for 16 years. Bird and Rowland look for companies with upstanding financial credentials. They want a return on equity of at least 15% that can be maintained over time, increasing earnings and dividends, low debt, and a solid market position. Says Bird, who holds on to his choices for a superlong average of about five years: "The ideal stock is one you'd never want to sell."

Keeping a Watchful Eye on Your Mutual Fund's Performance

Regular checkups can make all the difference in your payoff.

One of the chief benefits of investing in a mutual fund is that you are hiring a professional to manage your money. But there is no guarantee that the fund won't sink because of bad investment decisions or a weak stock market. Thus, a wise investor examines his fund's annual and quarterly reports, analyzes its statement of account, which most funds send to shareholders at least quarterly, and periodically looks up the value of the fund's shares in a newspaper's financial pages. Then, if the fund starts to founder, you can cut your losses by moving your assets elsewhere.

A three-month checkup is probably all you need if your money is in a diversified long-term growth or growth and income fund and you don't plan to touch the balance for several years. That way you will find out about serious management problems before it is too late to do anything about them, but you won't be tempted to make mistaken changes in strategy because of short-term dips in the stock and bond markets. If you have invested in maximum-capital-gains or sector funds, however, and hope to sell your shares for a short-term profit, you probably should turn to the financial pages for your fund's performance at least once a week or even every day. Then you will be able to respond quickly to sudden changes in the fund's fortunes.

Most investors, but especially those in highly volatile stock funds, will also want to pay close

How Are Your Mutual Funds Doing?

Performance figures such as those in the fund rankings starting on page 189 are useful for comparing mutual funds, but they do not tell how well your fund has done for you, since you probably opened your account on a different date from the ones on our list and added to it from time to time.

This worksheet will help you estimate your rate of return over the past two years or less. To fill in the blanks, get out your most recent fund statement and the one for the beginning of the period you are examining. (For simplicity, the sample statement below combines two years.)

	Your fund	Example
1. The number of months for which performance is being measured (not more than two years).		19
2. The value of your investment at the start of the period. The figure in the example came from multiplying total shares owned on January 4, 1990 (101.141) by the share price ($53.46).		$5,407
3. The value of your shares now. In the example, we multiplied shares owned on July 5, 1991 by the share price on that date.		$8,837
4. Dividend income and capital-gains distributions paid to you in cash (not reinvested) during the period.		$111
5. Net redemptions or investments during the period not including reinvested distributions. In the example, we subtracted the $500 redemption on January 15, 1991 from the $2,000 investment on June 1, 1990.		$1,500
6. Computation of your gain or loss: Step A: Add line 2 to half the total on line 5.		$6,157
Step B: Add lines 3 and 4, then subtract half the line 5 sum.		$8,198
Step C: Divide the step B result by the step A figure.		1.33
Step D: Subtract the numeral 1 from the result of step C, then multiply by 100.		33%
7. For your annualized return, divide 12 by the number on line 1. Multiply the result by the step D percentage, then by 100.		20.8%

SAMPLE MUTUAL FUND INC. 1000 MAIN ST. NEW YORK, NY 10020

PAGE 1 OF 1
1990-91 STATEMENT

SAM SAMUELS
SANDY SAMUELS
3 OAK ROAD
MAYFIELD, MO 63010

ACCOUNT NO. 98765432101

		YOUR DISTRIBUTION OPTION IS	
		INCOME REINVEST	CAPITAL GAINS IN CASH

STATEMENT DATE	TRANSACTION DATE	TRANSACTION DETAIL DESCRIPTION	DOLLAR AMOUNT OF TRANSACTION	SHARE PRICE	SHARES THIS TRANSACTION	TOTAL SHARES OWNED
		BEGINNING BALANCE				82.435
1/4/90	1/4/90	INVESTMENT	1,000.00	53.46	18.706	101.141
4/18	4/6	INCOME REINVEST AT .250	25.29	52.25	.484	101.625
4/18	4/6	SHORT-TERM CAPITAL GAIN AT .450	45.52	—	—	101.625
6/1	6/1	INVESTMENT	2,000.00	55.37	36.121	137.746
7/17	7/4	INCOME REINVEST AT .250	34.44	57.04	.604	138.350
10/23	10/10	INCOME REINVEST AT .250	34.59	61.89	.559	138.909
1/15/91	1/15/91	REDEMPTION	500.00	66.10	-7.564	131.345
1/26	1/17	INCOME REINVEST AT .200	26.27	66.13	.397	132.742
1/26	1/3	SHORT-TERM CAPITAL GAIN AT .500	65.87	—	—	132.742
4/26	4/3	INCOME REINVEST AT .300	39.82	65.88	.604	133.346
7/18	7/5	INCOME REINVEST AT .250	33.34	66.02	.505	133.851

attention to such economic bellwethers as the Dow Jones stock averages, yields on U.S. Treasury bills, quarterly trends in the gross national product, and changes in the Commerce Department's monthly index of leading economic indicators. Such information is published in the business sections of most daily newspapers. If the stock market starts to sink, interest rates suddenly lurch upward, or the economy turns sour, you can quickly adjust your portfolio to take advantage of these developments or avoid sizable losses that could result from them.

In tracking your fund, you can use one or more of the following three performance measurements:

Net asset value. A fund's NAV is the value of the fund's outstanding shares at the close of the trading day. Since daily gains and losses in NAV are often published in newspapers, such figures are the most accessible indicator of a fund's performance.

Yield. This figure tells you how much dividend income your investment is generating yearly as a percentage of the fund's latest net asset value. You can usually find your fund's current yield in its quarterly or annual report, by calling the fund's customer relations department, or by referring to an independent source such as *Money*'s Mutual Fund Rankings beginning on page 189. A caveat: If you are comparing your fund's yield with that of another portfolio, you should make sure that both use the same method of calculating yields.

Total return. This is the most comprehensive and, to most investors, the most useful measure of how a fund is doing. Total return is the sum of all dividend and capital-gains distributions the fund has made in a given period and any increase or decrease in the portfolio's net asset value.

Although some funds publish their total returns in ads and brochures, many do not. Therefore, you may have to calculate your fund's total return from the information in its quarterly statement. To get an approximation of your fund's total return for any period up to one year without going through detailed computations, you can use this shortcut: Take the fund's NAV at the end of a particular time period, add any dividend or capital gains the fund distributed to you during the period, divide by the NAV at the beginning of the period, subtract the number 1, then multiply by 100. Thus, if your fund had a net asset value of $12 at the end of the year, paid $1 in dividends and $1 in capital gains, and had an NAV of $11.50 at the beginning of the year, your approximate total return for the 12-month period would be 21.7%. The worksheet at left will help you do this calculation for periods as long as two years.

Money's Mutual Fund Rankings provide the one-year total return for 1020 funds and three-, five-, and 10-year compounded total-return figures for funds that have longer-term records.

When comparing the performance of your fund with that of others, you should keep in mind that, in contrast to *Money*'s Mutual Fund Ranking calculations, the initial sales charge is usually not taken into account when figuring total return. Since a sales load reduces the amount of money you have working for you in a fund, a load fund must achieve a higher rate of return than a no-load to earn you the identical amount of money. For example, a fund that charges an 8.5% load would have to earn 15.4% a year over a three-year period for its total return to equal that of a no-load fund that earns just 12% yearly.

Your fund's total return gives you only half the performance picture. To know whether that return was adequate, you need to compare it with those of funds with similar investment objectives. Of course, even if your fund stacks up well against similar funds, there is still a chance that the type of fund you are in is performing worse than the market in general. To find out, compare your fund's total return with a market gauge such as Standard & Poor's 500-stock index. If your fund consistently underperforms that stock market average by more than a few percentage points, you should start looking for a portfolio with a better record.

Investing Myths That Could Hurt You

All too often, the conventional wisdom isn't very smart.

Investing has always been fertile ground for dubious generalizations. Let a stock-market bore corner you at a party, and you will inevitably get an earful of maxims and truisms. Some of these are of the fatuous "buy low, sell high" variety. But other conventional wisdom can actually be hazardous to your wealth.

The problem is, most investing myths contain a grain of truth. But following any rule of thumb uncritically could be costly, since it may fail without warning. Here's the scoop on 10 widely held misconceptions:

Myth 1: Blue chips are stocks you own for life. Buying the shares of financially strong companies that offer better-than-average growth prospects and holding them for 10 years or longer is a sensible strategy. But no one should put stocks in a drawer and forget about them. Some of the so-called Nifty Fifty—shares of giant blue-chip companies popular with institutional investors in the early 1970s—never recovered from the 1972-74 bear market when this group lost half its value on average. Xerox, for example, which traded as high as $171 a share (adjusted for subsequent splits) in 1972, dropped 70% over the next two years. Then, because competing Japanese copier makers were capturing Xerox's market, the stock never managed to make a major comeback.

Myth 2: Small investors who try to time the market usually wind up losing. This is true if by "timing" you mean moving all of your money in and out of stocks to try to catch short-term market swings. But it pays to manage your

holdings actively, taking into account share-price levels and the general outlook for stocks. If the Dow Jones industrial average is trading at an average P/E ratio of 15 or higher and has a dividend yield of less than 3% after a bull market lasting three years or longer, you would be foolish not to sell some of the stocks in which you have large profits and build up your cash reserves. By contrast, when stocks drop more than 20% from their highs—as many did in 1991—you should be looking for chances to add to your holdings.

Myth 3: An undervalued stock will be bid up to its true worth within a year or two. Many investors rely on a contrarian strategy: They buy out-of-favor shares that trade at below-average price/earnings ratios or that appear cheap relative to the worth of a company's assets. Then they wait for other investors to recognize the stocks' true worth and bid up their prices. So far, so good. That's the basis of sound value investing. Many individuals, however, underestimate how long they might have to wait. From the beginning of 1987 through September 1990, for instance, the 20% of stocks in the S&P 500 index with the lowest P/E ratios produced no price gains at all, even though the average price of stocks in the S&P 500 rose 43% during that period.

Myth 4: Investors who buy stock in odd lots get killed on commissions. You usually do have to spend a little extra to buy an odd lot—that is, typically less than 100 shares. For most issues, you will pay an additional eighth of a point

(12½¢) a share to compensate brokers for the inconvenience of trading a small amount of stock. Beyond that, brokers generally do not charge higher commissions for such trades, except in one case: A small odd lot of a stock priced below $20 may run up against the minimum commission of $35 to $50 at many brokerages. Even so, if you are buying shares that you plan to hold for three to five years, the overall effect of a slightly higher price will be tiny—lowering your annual return by perhaps a tenth of a percentage point.

Myth 5: You need at least $25,000 to buy individual stocks. You can greatly decrease the risk of owning stocks by dividing your money among industries that react to disparate economic conditions. Many individuals think that this requires a portfolio of $25,000 to $100,000 invested in two or three dozen stocks. In fact, though, you can put together a reasonably well-diversified portfolio for as little as $10,000 and get 75% of the benefit you would have by diversifying among a full 500 stocks. People who have portfolios smaller than $100,000 should concentrate on five well-diversified stocks and add to those positions as they get more money.

Myth 6: Foreign stocks are too tricky for most small investors. The shares of some 700 foreign companies trade in the U.S. in the form of American Depositary Receipts (ADRs), and 57 of the largest are listed on the New York Stock Exchange. Six others are listed on the American Stock Exchange, and 86 more leading foreign issues are traded over the counter in the computerized NASDAQ system. Small investors can buy and sell these shares as easily as U.S. issues. Moreover, information about those companies is readily available; many are followed by analysts at large U.S. brokerages.

Myth 7: U.S. government bonds are the safest investment you can make. It is out of the question that the U.S. government or its agencies, such as the Government National Mortgage Association (Ginnie Mae), could ever default on debt obligations. But investors are mistaken to think that default is the biggest risk

that bondholders face. Two other dangers are far greater: that rising interest rates could cause the prices of long-term bonds to fall and that inflation could erode the purchasing power of the bonds' principal. The size of a bond's price decline when rates rise depends on the issue's term to maturity. With a two-percentage-point rise in rates, a three-year Treasury bond will drop 5%, a 10-year bond 12%, and a 30-year issue 18%. In addition, a steady 4% to 5% annual rate of inflation would erode the purchasing power of a 20-year bond's principal by as much as 65% by the time the bond matures. In fact, studies show that Treasury bond total returns have outpaced inflation in only 37 of the past 64 years.

Myth 8: Zero-coupon bonds provide a predictable return. If you choose a bond that matures when you need a specific amount of money—to pay college tuition or set yourself up in retirement, for example—then a zero's return is indeed predictable. But if you buy a long-term zero and then decide to sell well before maturity for some reason, you may be in for a shock. The prices of such issues are about 60% more volatile than those of ordinary bonds that pay cash interest. If, for instance, you put $20,000 into a 20-year zero-coupon Treasury at the rate of 8.5% and rates later jumped to 10.5%, the price of your zero-coupon bond would fall by about 25%. You would, therefore, lose $5,000 if you suddenly needed money and had to sell.

Myth 9: Mutual funds are the best way for small investors to buy bonds. If you want to invest in convertible issues or in municipals, it makes sense to go through a mutual fund. Analyzing individual bonds is difficult for you to handle alone, and you would need $25,000 to $50,000 for adequate diversification. But if you want to invest in Treasuries, where there is no risk of default, diversification and bond selection are inconsequential. By investing in bonds through a mutual fund, you would, therefore, end up paying annual management and operating expenses—averaging 0.79% of assets for Treasury funds—with little benefit. On a $10,000 investment, that would cost you $79 a year.

Myth 10: Gold is the best hedge against inflation. It has been, historically, but only when inflation was 9% or more and seemed likely to get worse, as it did in 1979-80. That's why gold peaked at $825 an ounce in January 1980. Since then, gold has fallen 55% even though inflation has boosted consumer prices by a total of 72% by ticking along at an average rate of 5% a year. Since most economists believe that annual inflation will average 5% or less during the 1990s, gold is unlikely to keep pace with those steady increases in consumer prices. In short, gold now looks like a mediocre investment at best.

Socially Responsible Investing

You can pick among the many stocks and mutual funds that take ethical stances—and still come out ahead.

By the tens of thousands, Americans are refusing to compromise their social and political principles in the quest for investment profits. As a result, so-called socially responsible investing is today's fastest-growing money-management style. The pros who invest in companies that, for example, seek to improve the environment or workers' welfare and shun firms in the tobacco or nuclear-power industries manage more than $625 billion. (For a list of 50 top socially responsible investments, see the table on pages 34-35.) Moreover, converts to the clean-and-green trend are discovering that, contrary to what they have heard from Wall Street types in the past, they can invest for the common good and still beat the average common stocks. Consider the evidence:

• Of the five ethical mutual funds in existence since 1986, four beat the average returns for their respective fund categories for the five years through 1990 by four to 13 percentage points. The clear winner: Pax World, which topped the average balanced fund 71.1% to 57.4% and was the only fund to get an A rating for risk-adjusted return in *Money*'s rankings.

• In 1990, when four out of five equity funds in *Money*'s rankings posted losses, Pax World was up 10.5%. Two of the other six socially conscious stock funds made money as well: Dreyfus Third Century was up 3.6%, and Calvert Social Investment Managed Growth registered a 1.8% increase.

• The Domini Social Index, a benchmark of 400 ethical stocks that was created in April 1990, gained 19% for the 12 months to April 30, 1991, compared with 18% for the S&P 500.

It's little wonder the word is spreading that you don't have to sacrifice your principal to your principles—and that more small investors are welcoming the news. Never willing to pass up a profit-making opportunity, Wall Street is going green, too. Today, there are 17 socially conscious mutual funds and other ethical investment products—among them the top-performing Eco-Logical unit investment trust—up from only six in 1985. In addition, at least eight large brokerage firms, including Shearson Lehman, Prudential Securities, and Smith Barney, now offer research or money-management services that are especially geared to socially responsible investors.

Such ethical investing also has spread far beyond the hard core of environmental and political activists. Prodded by demands from the public that they green their portfolios, pension funds now provide more than $500 billion, or 80%, of the money invested according to some sort of socially conscious criteria. For example, last year, TIAA-CREF, the teachers' retirement fund with assets of $90 billion, was pressuring companies it owned to stop doing business in South Africa, as was the New York City pension system, with $45 billion in assets.

Despite the growing evidence that socially conscious investing can be profitable, most professionals are still not convinced it will work over the long term—say, 20 years or more. These pros dismiss the ethical funds' one, or even five, years of solid performance as largely a fluke and question the wisdom of restricting your investment universe.

Adherents of socially conscious investing counter by noting that most practitioners use such broad criteria in picking stocks that some 70% of the 1,000 largest U.S. companies qualify. "Since typical small investors own at most 25 stocks," says Bruce Lehmann, an associate professor of economics and finance at Columbia University's business school, "limiting the universe to a modest extent won't have much impact on returns."

Most mainstream clean-and-green investors start by steering clear of alcohol and gambling stocks, as well as corporations that do business in South Africa, make armaments, produce nuclear power, or pollute. Next, the investors subject the remaining stocks to standard financial tests to rule out poor performers and spot promising buys. Finally, they screen the survivors to identify the ones that meet more detailed social criteria.

The thinking behind this approach is that doing good pays off. Companies that ignore the environment, say, risk becoming targets of liability suits. Those that follow insensitive personnel policies may have growing difficulty retaining first-rate workers. And firms that consciously contribute to the community can build good will with customers and increase sales.

Keep in mind, however, that some clean-and-green-minded investors follow strict, limiting rules. For example, some invest solely in companies with at least two women among their directors—a test passed by just 74 of the firms in the S&P 500. And others who favor stringent bans on animal testing avoid all drug companies and nearly all consumer-products companies. Such inflexibility makes diversification nearly impossible and, thereby, increases your investment risk.

There is yet another complication: Even adherents who follow liberal criteria often disagree on a company's ethical rating. Consider the debate over Amoco, a $28.5 billion natural gas producer and an industry leader in alternative energy research. The company's white hat turned black in 1978 after its tanker Amoco Cadiz spilled 68 million gallons of oil off Brittany. When Calvert fund managers asked investors whether Amoco was still an acceptable stock, it was overwhelmingly rejected. Nonetheless, many other money managers who consider socially conscious criteria continue to hold Amoco shares.

As with most investing, the clean-and-green approach requires careful analysis of a firm's finances as well as its record on social and environmental issues, using data collected from government agencies, private watchdog groups, and the company itself. Because such research is too difficult for most individuals, small investors are probably best off sticking with solid, socially conscious mutual funds such as the nine listed in the accompanying table. Check a fund's prospectus, however, to be sure that the manager's goals match your own. Dreyfus Third Century, for example, buys certain defense stocks, whereas Pax World will not hold any.

If you want to invest in individual stocks, you will probably need guidance from a money manager or newsletter that is in harmony with your social criteria. (For a directory of such experts, send $35 to the Social Investment Forum, 430 First Avenue North, Suite 290, Minneapolis, MN 55401.)

Still, if the Green Spirit moves you, fear not. As long as you don't overdo a good thing, you can invest according to your canons of social responsibility and pick winning stocks and mutual funds.

The 50 Best Clean-and-Green Investments

To put together this list of ethical investments, *Money* asked Franklin Research & Development, which publishes *Investing for a Better World* (617-423-6655), to identify the 50 most promising stocks, mutual funds, and cash investments that meet widely accepted social-investing criteria.

Franklin first excluded all companies connected with alcohol, animal testing, gambling, nuclear power, South Africa, tobacco, and weapons manufacturing. After that, Franklin ranked the shares of 1,000 companies in three categories of social responsibility. With 1 as the highest rating and 5 as the lowest, the firms that qualified scored 2.5 or better in each category. Thirty stocks with solid investing fundamentals are listed in the table, starting with those that had the best overall ratings. Companies with an environmental rating of 1 were outstanding in pollution control, hazardous-waste reduction, and energy conservation. Firms that earned a 1 rating for employee relations excelled in at least three of the

STOCKS	Environmental rating	Employee practices rating	Corporate citizenship rating	May 1991 price	P/E	Earnings growth rate	Yield
BLUE CHIPS							
Dayton Hudson	2	1	1	$75.00	12.9	16.5%	1.9%
Digital Equipment	1	1	2	66.25	15.6	5.0	N.A.
Stride Rite	2	1	1	46.25	18.9	21.5	1.0
Xerox	2	1	1	56.75	10.9	11.5	5.3
Amoco	2	2	1	54.75	15.0	8.0	4.0
Cabot Corporation	2	2	2	32.25	11.9	19.5	3.2
Minnesota Mining	1.5	2	2.5	87.75	14.5	10.0	3.6
Stanley Works	2	2	2	34.75	14.5	11.0	3.5
McDonald's	2	2.5	2	33.25	12.1	15.0	1.0
Northwest Corporation	2.5	2	2	28.00	10.0	10.5	3.3
GROWTH							
Apple Computer	1	1	1	$50.25	10.6	15.0%	1.0%
Ben & Jerry's	1	1	1	19.25	16.7	15.0	N.A.
H.B. Fuller	1	1	1	45.75	17.6	14.5	1.4
Sunrise Medical	1.5	1	2	27.75	20.0	19.0	N.A.
Nucor	1	2	2	82.75	23.6	17.0	0.6
Thermo Electron	1	2	2	36.75	18.8	19.0	N.A.
TJ International	1	2	2	21.00	35.0	9.5	2.0
Donnelly	2.5	1	2	46.50	15.5	12.5	2.2
Unum	2.5	1	2	66.25	12.2	18.5	1.6
Wellman	1.5	2	2	20.75	9.9	20.0	0.6
UTILITIES							
Sierra Pacific	1	2	2	$22.25	10.9	2.5%	8.3%
Brooklyn Union	1.5	2.5	1.5	28.75	11.3	3.5	6.6
Atlanta S&L	2	2	2	33.50	14.6	5.0	6.1
Energen	2	2	2	16.75	9.9	8.0	5.6
Idaho Power	2.5	2	2	26.25	13.1	6.5	7.1
Southern New England	2.5	2	2	33.00	12.5	5.0	5.3
Southwest Bell	2.5	2	2	53.00	13.8	8.5	5.4
Ameritech	2.5	2.5	2	63.25	13.0	5.5	5.4
People's Energy	2.5	2.5	2	24.50	11.4	3.5	7.0
Pacific Enterprises	2.5	2.5	2.5	33.25	11.7	5.5	10.5

Price/earnings ratios reflect estimated earnings for 1991. Annual earnings growth rates are projections for the next five years. Current rates may change. **N.A.** Not available. **Sources:** Franklin Research & Development, IBC/Donoghue's, Institutional Brokers Estimate System, Lipper Analytical

following areas: promotion of women and minorities, action on child care and AIDS, fringe benefits, commitment to on-the-job safety, and fair bargaining with unions.

Franklin based corporate citizenship ratings on community involvement and charitable giving, such as funding low-income housing, scholarships, and job-training programs. Again, the 1-rated companies were among the best in three areas.

Survivors were then measured against investment criteria, excluding blue chips selling far above the average market P/E of 17, and required at least a B+ financial rating from *Value Line Investment Survey.*

Among smaller growth stocks, *Money* looked for trend-setters in socially conscious activities, such as plastics recycling. Because small stocks are volatile, only aggressive investors should consider them.

The 10 utilities on the list offer total returns of 10% a year or higher, based on the May 1991 yield and projected earnings growth rates for the next five years. They also have *Value Line* safety ratings of B+ or better.

For mutual-fund investors, the choices are limited since only about a dozen funds follow ethical investing principles; nine are currently open and tracked by Franklin. They are listed in order of their total return for 1990.

Among cash investments, those offered by banks that lend locally for socially conscious projects are included. These banks are all federally insured through the Federal Deposit Insurance Corporation (FDIC) and accept out-of-state deposits. The money-market funds on the list hold only the securities of corporations that meet broad social screening tests.

MUTUAL FUNDS	Total return for 1990	Total return for 1988-90	Minimum initial investment	Maximum initial sales charge	Telephone
Pax World	22.4%	58.8%	$250	None	800-767-1729
Progressive Environmental	22.4	N.A.	1,000	4.50%	800-826-8154
Calvert-Ariel Appreciation	21.6	N.A.	2,000	4.75	800-368-2748
Dreyfus Third Century	21.5	58.6	2,500	None	800-645-6561
Parnassus	17.3	20.7	2,000	3.50	800-999-3505
Calvert SIF-Bond	14.5	31.8	1,000	4.75	800-368-2748
Calvert SIF-Growth	12.3	31.3	1,000	4.75	800-368-2748
New Alternatives	11.7	38.6	2,650	5.66	516-466-0808
Calvert SIF-Equity	10.1	38.5	1,000	4.75	800-368-2748

CASH INVESTMENTS	May 1991 rate	Effective annual yield	Minimum initial investment	Bank safety rating	Telephone
Vermont National Bank 2½-year CD	6.77%	7.00%	$500	**	800-544-7108
South Shore Bank 2½-year CD	6.38	6.58	200	**	800-669-7725
Vermont National Bank one-year CD	6.53	6.75	500	**	800-544-7108
Elk Horn Bank one-year CD	6.15	6.29	1,000	***	501-246-5811
South Shore Bank one-year CD	5.88	6.05	200	**	800-669-7725
Vermont National Bank six-month CD	6.39	6.60	500	**	800-544-7108
Elk Horn Bank six-month CD	6.00	6.09	1,000	***	501-246-5811
Community Capital Bank six-month CD	5.49	5.64	1,000	**	800-827-6699
South Shore Bank MMDA	5.88	6.04	2,500	**	800-669-7725
Calvert SIF-Money Market	5.71	5.87	1,000	N.A.	800-368-2748
Working Assets Money Fund	5.48	5.63	1,000	N.A.	800-533-3863

Services, Value Line. Veribanc bank safety ratings are based on fourth-quarter 1990 data—*** for the highest financial standing, ** for high, * for low, and no stars for the lowest or where no data are available. Detailed reports available from Veribanc ($45 each; P.O. Box 461, Wakefield, MA 01880).

**Banks will lend you money if you can
prove you don't need it.** — Mark Twain

PERSONAL FINANCE

Understanding Banks, Budgets, Credit & Insurance

One of the trends that marks the baby boom generation's coming of middle age is an increase in personal savings and a reduction of debt. But according to *Money*'s most recent Americans and Their Money poll, fully 27% of those surveyed say they had not saved or invested a single dollar over the previous 12 months. And a substantial 37% say that installment debt payments eat up a hefty 10% or more of their incomes.

If you fall into one or both of these groups, it's time to take steps to turn your financial life around. Even if you're already headed in the right direction, this chapter can help you organize your finances better to achieve the goals that are important to you.

The first step in any money-management plan is to monitor your income and outgo regularly to control expenses and ensure that part of your funds go into savings and investments. The worksheets on pages 40-43 provide an easy way to figure your net worth and set up a personal budget. You should also set aside a cash cushion for emergencies, usually an amount equal to at least three months living expenses. Given the shaky condition of many banks and savings and loans today, finding a safe place for your ready cash requires some forethought, but it sure beats the alternative (see story on page 38).

The banking industry isn't the only one experiencing widespread problems; insurance companies are also failing at an alarming rate these days. You can protect many of your assets with the right insurance (for tips on auto insurance, see page 49), but it's equally important to find the right insurer (page 47). Getting a grip on installment debt is trickier. Not everyone has the willpower or even the means to meet every expense with cash. But no one has to be a patsy for credit card companies anymore. By shopping around, you can easily cut as much as 8% off what most companies' charge in interest and dispense with annual fees altogether (page 44). It's safe to say that it's an unsafe world out there. But you don't have to be a genius or even lucky to protect what you have or to achieve some degree of financial security. Sometimes it's as simple as managing your money wisely.

Keep Your Savings Safe

Your emergency fund won't give you much peace of mind if it's not secure.

The rising tide of bank failures has pushed the Federal Deposit Insurance Corporation (FDIC) Bank Insurance Fund to the brink of insolvency. Over the past five years, 896 insured banks have gone belly up—compared with 840 failures in the previous 50 years. And the worst may be yet to come. A 1990 report by three leading bank economists prepared for a congressional subcommittee warns that a severe recession could trigger a wave of bank failures costing up to $63 billion—seven times what is in the fund now.

Aside from the risks at banks and savings institutions, there are other, less obvious dangers. Money-market mutual funds, which are committed—but not legally obligated—to hold their share prices constant at $1, have been rattled by defaults on commercial paper, the investment most funds buy for their portfolios. Parent companies have eaten the losses so far, but they probably won't forever. Any loss on a money fund would most likely be small, probably just a cent per share, but the potential for worse exists.

In the worst cases, you could face total loss—although that would be extremely rare. More likely, losses would be small—5% or less. But even a small loss is unnerving if you are unprepared for it. And since a few situations can be truly disastrous, you should always invest with full knowledge. Here is a detailed rundown of the rules you need to follow:

Bank accounts and CDs. Always insist on federal insurance. Scattered across the country are hundreds of banks, S&Ls, credit unions, and investment companies that are either uninsured or covered by state or private insurance that may be inadequate. Remember, also, that not every investment at a federally insured bank is automatically covered. Banks regularly sell uninsured investments ranging from mutual funds to deferred annuities. They may also sell uninsured investments that appear to be CDs.

Another danger: nonbanks offering savings certificates, essentially uninsured CDs. In 1990, for example, IDS Certificate Company, which is owned by American Express, sold an estimated $1.6 billion worth of its certificates, which were yielding 7.4% to 7.9%. Surprisingly, the company had an easy time selling them. But despite the company's marketing brochure, which promises lofty returns "without any risk of losing your original investment," these certificates are backed only by the financial reserves of IDS Certificate Company.

Despite the FDIC's woes, federally insured money-market deposit accounts (MMDAs) and CDs are still ultimately guaranteed by the U.S. government. But even with such insured investments, savers can be denied access to their money or lose interest if an institution goes under.

When a bank is failing, federal regulators first try to shift accounts to a healthy institution. While that is usually done without disruption, the new bank will probably offer you a lower rate on MMDAs and CDs that have not yet matured. And if you don't take up their offer within two weeks, the bank could switch your money into an even lower-yielding passbook savings account or a checking account that pays no interest.

The scenario gets nastier if regulators can't arrange to transfer accounts and have to liquidate a failed bank to pay depositors. Over the past three years, that has happened in less than 5% of the cases where federal regulators have had to intervene. In liquidations, outstanding checks are usually returned and you may lose access to your cash for a month or more, forfeiting interest on your deposit during that time.

Even if you are dealing with an FDIC-insured account, you can still get tangled in the safety net. If you are one of the 98.5% of bank account holders who have less than $100,000 on deposit with any single federally insured bank or thrift, you have no problem. But if you have accounts that total $100,000 or more (including both principal and interest), you will have to worry about the FDIC's often Byzantine regulations.

Sometimes in the past, the FDIC has decided to guarantee all deposits. But, generally, a federally insured bank or thrift is protected up to $100,000 per depositor in each of four categories: individual accounts, joint accounts, Individual Retirement Accounts, and Keogh accounts. But the rules governing insurance coverage are complex; for example, a joint or trust account that is not set up correctly might not be covered separately. The bottom line: Smart savers with more than $100,000 should spread their money among several banks.

Money-market funds. Don't assume money funds are as secure as insured bank accounts. Recent defaults on commercial paper have led the Securities and Exchange Commission to re-examine the risk in these funds and propose new regulations to enhance their safety. Money funds are safe overall, but they're not insured. It is possible to lose money.

So far, that hasn't happened because fund management companies have stepped in to make good their funds' losses. But there's no guarantee they will continue to do so in the future. Any losses, though, would probably be tiny. In March 1990, for example, T. Rowe Price's Prime Reserve fund held $42 million of Mortgage Realty Trust commercial paper, which defaulted. Even if T. Rowe Price had not reimbursed the fund, a $42 million hit would have cost investors only a penny per $1 share.

If the prospect of even such a minimal loss bothers you, there are ways to protect yourself. For the highest possible level of safety, buy funds that invest only in U.S. Treasury bills. But be aware that some Treasury funds invest in repurchase agreements, or "repos"—securities offered by a bank or brokerage that are backed by Treasuries. Though losses in repos are rare, they can occur if the bank or brokerage goes bankrupt and creditors try to claim the Treasury collateral.

Similarly, there are U.S. government funds that invest in the securities of government agencies, such as the Federal National Mortgage Association (Fannie Mae) or the Farm Credit system. The chance of default on these securities is barely above zero. But when government funds and Treasury-only funds have similar yields, ultraconservative investors are better off with Treasuries. An added bonus: The Treasury-only funds pay interest that is exempt from state taxes, boosting their yields in high-tax states such as California and New York. Interest from U.S. agency paper is not exempt from taxes in many states.

Potential losses can be greater on tax-free funds, which invest in the short-term debt of states and municipalities. With their tax-exempt status, these funds have surged in popularity, almost doubling in number and size in recent years. But even though these funds invest in securities backed by state and local governments, it is a huge mistake to equate them with U.S. government funds. No state has the ability to print money to pay off its debts as the federal government can.

Tax-exempt funds that invest in the securities of many states offer enough diversity to keep the potential losses in a default relatively small. There's a greater risk, though, in funds that restrict themselves to debt issued in one state. This is especially true with states such as Massachusetts and New York that have budget problems. While no one is suggesting single-state funds are on the brink of default, security-minded investors may want to avoid them.

Figuring Your Net Worth

Calculating your net worth—what you own minus what you owe—is the first step toward taking control of your financial life. From there, you can set your goals—a vacation, a house, a comfortable retirement, an ample estate for your children—and devise strategies to reach them. Anyone with a calculator can complete this worksheet in two to three hours. If you are married or living with someone, you should involve your partner. You already have most of the information to fill in the blanks, or you can get it free from your broker, banker, and others. Your insurance agent can supply the current cash value of your life insurance if it's not in the policy. Your banker will calculate the interest on your savings. You can look up most stock prices and some bond prices in newspapers and get any others from a broker. To find out what your house or condo is worth, consult a real estate

ASSETS

CASH:

Cash on hand	$ _____	Clothing, furs	_____
Checking accounts	_____	Jewelry	_____
Savings accounts	_____	Other possessions	_____
Money-market funds	_____		
Life insurance cash value	_____	**REAL ESTATE:**	
Money owed you	_____	Homes	$ _____
		Other properties	_____

MARKETABLE SECURITIES:

Stocks	$ _____	**PENSION:**	
Bonds	_____	Vested portion of company plan	$ _____
Government securities	_____	Vested benefits	_____
Mutual funds	_____	IRA	_____
Other investments	_____	Keogh	_____

PERSONAL PROPERTY:

		LONG-TERM ASSETS:	
Automobiles	$ _____	Equity in business	$ _____
Household furnishings	_____	Life insurance	_____
Art, antiques, other collectibles	_____	Annuities	_____
		TOTAL:	$ _____

broker or note the asking prices of similar homes for sale in your neighborhood. Remember to subtract all selling costs, such as the real estate broker's 6% commission and the 2% your stockbroker charges, and allow for any taxes you'll owe on the proceeds.

When computing your net worth, don't overlook pension plans and other employee benefits such as profit sharing and thrift programs and unexercised stock options. Your company can tell you what the vested portions of your pension and other benefits are worth now.

You can get an estimate for your car by asking a car dealer to look at the blue book, published by the National Automobile Dealers Association.

To make sure you're moving toward your financial goals, you should redo your personal balance sheet at least once a year.

LIABILITIES

CURRENT BILLS:

Rent $ _____

Utilities _____

Charge accounts _____

Credit cards _____

Insurance premiums _____

Alimony _____

Child support _____

Other bills _____

TAXES:

Federal $ _____

State _____

Local _____

Taxes on investments _____

Other _____

MORTGAGES:

Homes $ _____

Other properties _____

DEBTS TO INDIVIDUALS: $ _____

LOANS:

Auto $ _____

Education _____

Home improvement _____

Life insurance _____

Other _____

TOTAL: $ _____

What you own minus what you owe equals your net worth: $ _____

Setting Up a Personal Budget

On the face of it, budgeting is a simple process of keeping expenses in line with income. By devoting a few hours each month over the next three months to considering your income and your outgo, you can reduce overspending, free up money for savings and investments, and build a cash reserve for any sudden urge to splurge.

In the first month, you keep track of how much money comes in and, more important, how much goes out. The second month, you look at your cash flow with an eye toward realigning your spending to match your financial goals and expectations. By the third month, you'll check to see that your revised spending patterns are workable, and fine-tune any trouble spots.

The accompanying cash-flow worksheet will help you begin. You'll need to gather your records from the past year. They are likely to include such items as pay stubs, canceled checks, credit-card statements, other bills, sales receipts, tax returns, bankbooks, and dividend statements. You should continue to collect your canceled checks and other statements through the year to measure how well you meet your budgeting objectives and to calculate any taxes you might owe.

To figure out your monthly income, add up your salary, dividends, interest, child support, and any other money you receive during the year and divide by 12. You do the same thing with your expenses: Look at your outgo for an entire year and then spread each item over 12 months even though there will be some you don't pay monthly. The purpose is to smooth out your expenses so that you never have to invade your savings for unexpected bills. If you are self-employed, for example, or if some of your earnings are not withheld, you'll need to budget your taxes. You can consult a tax table or ask your accountant to determine your bracket and estimate the bill.

Some outlays, notably mortgage or rent, are fixed every month and easy to determine. But it's hard to assign a dollar amount to less frequent and more variable expenses. Set aside about 1% of the selling price of your house or condo for maintenance. Figure on 3% of the replacement cost to keep the car going and the dishwasher washing. But if this is the year you plan to put a new roof on the house or get the engine overhauled on the aging VW, your outlays are likely to be greater.

After tallying your expenses and income, you may still find that your budget doesn't balance. It's not so much sloppy bookkeeping as that a sizable portion of most people's earnings disappear into that never-never land known as miscellaneous. If

INCOME		EXPENSES	
Salary and bonuses	$ _____	Mortgage payments	$ _____
Dividends	_____	Food	_____
Interest	_____	Utilities	_____
Proceeds from the sale of securities	_____	Transportation	_____
Alimony	_____	Property taxes	_____
Child support	_____	Education	_____
Other income (rents, royalties, fees, etc.)	_____	Health care (doctors, dentists, drugs)	_____
TOTAL MONTHLY INCOME:	$ _____	Clothing (purchases, cleaning, laundry)	_____

you want to get a handle on where your money is really going, try to keep a journal and jot down expenses as you go along.

Once you have figured out where your money is going, then devote the second month of your program to trimming any excesses in the budget so you can build up your savings and investments. It should take only an hour or two to study your plan, decide where you are overspending, and how to redistribute your resources.

Some broad guidelines are useful in putting together a budget: Allocate 65% of your take-home pay for fixed expenses including rent, mortgage payments, utilities, and food. You should allow another 20% for such variable outlays as household repair, recreation, or clothing. Put aside 10% for insurance premiums and property taxes, and the last 5% for savings. If yours is a two-paycheck family, you should put away another 5% of *each* salary. And, if your take-home pay exceeds $1,200 a month apiece, fixed expenses will probably be less than 65%, so each of you should be able to save as much as 10%.

You're in good shape if 10% or less of your after-tax income is going to pay credit-card and other charge-account bills. If those expenses creep beyond 15% of your income, you're losing the battle of the budget. At 20%, you'd better leave those cards at home.

During the third month, you should evaluate your cash-flow statement and adjust it so you can live on it. If you've underestimated your entertainment expenses or neglected to add the cost of a babysitter to your evenings out, now is the time to amend the budget. Successful budgeting depends on being neither too rigid nor too loose. If you are passionate about movies and want to see three or four films a week, then adjust your spending in some other area.

The reason that you have a budget is to generate extra cash at the end of each month for savings and investments. Your first goal is to build a "strategic reserve" for any financial emergencies. In the past, you were expected to stockpile enough cash to cover six months' expenses, but inflation has made that kind of cache impractical for many people. Figure on stashing at least three months of after-tax income away in a money-market fund, Treasury bills, short-term bank certificates, or other liquid savings against the day you lose your job—however unlikely that is—or some other crisis. Once this security blanket is tucked around you, you can begin using your savings allocation for longer-term investments.

Personal care (hairdresser, gym classes, etc.)	_____	Investments	_____
Child care	_____	Savings	_____
Household help	_____	Personal allowance	_____
Entertainment and travel	_____	Other	_____
Gifts and donations	_____		
Loan or installment debt repayment	_____		
Insurance premiums	_____	**TOTAL MONTHLY EXPENSES:**	$ _____

Cutting the Cost of Your Credit Cards

Competition alone won't turn Plasticland into a buyer's market. But you can beat annual fees and high rates by using the right strategies.

There's an unintended message in all those perfervid ads and letters streaming your way lately, urging you to sign up for the credit card of your dreams. Rejoice! For the first time in their lavishly profitable history, the major card issuers may need you more than you need them. At last, the major banks that dominate the world of plastic are feeling the winds of competition blowing against their near-20% interest rates and $20 annual fees. The intruders include AT&T's Universal Visa and MasterCard, Sears' no-fee Discover, and soon-to-be launched no-fee Prime Option Visa, American Express' medium-rate (16.75%) Optima, and Japan Credit Bureau's American Express-like JCB charge card. All are pushing into a saturated market at a time when many banks, hobbled by soured real estate loans, are counting on their lucrative credit-card line of business more than ever.

So plastic will finally be getting cheaper, right? The answer is yes, if you make it happen yourself. Cardholders will increasingly refuse to pay annual fees. But they haven't yet shown the same sensitivity to high interest rates, which is how credit-card costs really mount.

Moreover, even as competition heats up, significant savings are threatened by a countervailing trend: consolidation. Large banks are devouring smaller, usually less expensive issuers—the 10 largest bank-card issuers now hold 53% of all plastic debt, up from 47% in 1988. As a result, the supply of low-rate, low-fee cards dwindles, while bargain issuers who do survive must bump up rates and fees to cover the costs of duking it out for customers

with the big banks. Clearly, then, you can't just sit by idly and wait for rates and fees to vanish. Instead, here are six strategies you can use right now that could shave as much as 8.8 percentage points off your credit-card interest and eliminate annual fees altogether:

Shop for the lowest interest rate you can find. Customers lured by deals on annual fees are missing the crucial point for the two-thirds of cardholders who maintain a credit-card balance: You'll nearly always save more by choosing a low-rate card, even one with an annual fee, over a high-rate card with no fee. (Most holders actually opt for the worst combination—high rates and high fees.) On a $1,200 average balance, your annual interest cost on a major bank card charging 19.8% comes to $237.60. (Chances are you'll pay an $18 to $20 annual fee, too.) By comparison, the yearly interest for the same balance on a Visa or MasterCard charging 13.9% would be just $166.80. Even when you add in an annual fee of $25, you come out ahead with the lower rate.

You can obtain lists of nationally available lower-rate Visa and MasterCards by writing to Bankcard Holders of America (560 Herndon Parkway, Suite 120, Herndon, VA 22070; $1.50) or Ram Research's Cardtrak (Box 1700, Frederick, MD 21702; $5). Lists of no-annual-fee cards are also available. Look for undesirable trade-offs before you leap, however. One of the lowest-rate bank cards in the country, Arkansas Federal Savings, generally applies strict credit standards and then holds its new cardholders to a $1,000 to $2,000 credit limit.

You might also shop among your current connections. Many credit unions offer cards with fixed rates averaging around 15.2%, and some of the 2,600 alumni, fraternal, and professional groups like the American Association of Retired Persons and the National Education Association issue cards that beat the behemoths by four points or more.

Don't pay annual fees. The one-third of cardholders who do pay off their balances each month needn't be concerned about interest rates, since they don't pay interest. So to maximize savings, choose a no-fee card with a grace period. (The bank still makes money through so-called interchange fees—charges that merchants pay to the issuer when they accept your plastic, generally 2% of your total purchase amounts.)

Competition has added a profitable twist for those who regularly use a card, make timely payments, and carry a balance. If you are among this number, call your card issuer when the annual fee bill arrives and ask to have the charge waived. Although most major issuers deny that they do so, industry insiders tell another story. Says one consultant, who asked not to be identified: "Most issuers are waiving fees when customers call to cancel, in order to save the account." His advice: "It's definitely worth trying." Some banks have adopted a compromise approach: The $20 annual fee for a nationally available Visa or MasterCard is automatically waived for the first two calendar years. After that, there's no fee if you pay at least $25 in annual interest. If you use your card frequently but pay up every month, you might try to get the annual fee deep-sixed by arguing that your card usage generates significant interchange fees. While you may not be considered an ideal customer, you may still be a cash cow worth milking if you charge more than $3,500 a year. If the bank won't waive your fee, resist the urge to cancel a card you use until you have a replacement in hand.

Time purchases and payments carefully. Under most credit-card agreements, an interest-free grace period—typically 25 days between the billing date and the due date—applies only if you pay your balance in full; if you don't, most issuers will assess interest on new-purchase amounts almost immediately.

If you pay in full each month, you can get the most from the grace period by making big credit purchases just after your statement closing date and paying your bill on time, of course, but at the last minute. By so doing, you'll get interest-free use of the credit-card loan for some 50 days, a float that on, say, $3,000 in a money-market fund yielding 6.5% would let you earn an additional $27.

If you maintain a credit balance, adopt the reverse tactic: Buy big-ticket items toward the end of the billing cycle and, more importantly, pay as much of the bill as possible each month as soon as you get your bill. This slows the interest-rate meter and lowers your cost.

Some issuers offer a low interest rate but no grace period. That's a good deal if you keep a balance running each month. If you never carry a balance or do so only occasionally, go for a low-rate card with a grace period.

Monitor who owns your card. If your account is sold to another issuer (a fate that has befallen nearly one in 10 cardholders since 1989 as banks sell assets to raise cash), chances are your terms will change, too—for the worse. Buyers tend to be the major issuers, specializing in above-average rates and fees. Your best defense is to shop for a new card as soon as you're notified of the sale. That way, you'll be sure that you won't be blindsided by a sudden fee or rate increase or, worse yet, cancellation if the new owner takes an unfavorable view of your credit record.

Carry no more than three cards. Keep one no-annual-fee card with a grace period for purchases you plan to pay off in full each month, and a low-interest-rate card for purchases you want to finance, ideally also without an annual fee. Keep a third low-rate card for business use only. If you're a sole proprietor, you're allowed to take a tax deduction for the interest you pay on financed business expenses; a business-use-only card will help you keep tax records in order and substantiate the expenditures if you're ever audited. For salaried employees, an

American Express corporate card—if your employer provides one—fills the third-card niche. Otherwise, stick with two.

Even if your superfluous cards are fee-free and you're never tempted to charge a cent, banks and other lenders may count the total credit available to you as if you'd already spent it, thus sometimes disqualifying you for other borrowing, such as a car loan or even a mortgage. So notify your banks in writing that you want your unused cards canceled. Follow up with a note to the credit bureaus regarding your action; your credit-card issuer can tell you which bureaus to inform.

Resist the come-ons. If you're paying upwards of $18 for a standard card or $35 for a gold card because you like the enhancements, ask yourself if you will ever use them. Indeed, some of the most popular perks, such as buyer protection and rental-car insurance, apply only after your own homeowners, renters, or auto insurance pays off. If you truly believe you'll use an enhancement someday, find out just how it would kick in should you make a claim. American Express and Visa have quietly restricted their buyer-protection coverage to $1,000 per-claim—previously there had been no per-claim limit—and excluded from protection anything stolen from a car.

Also bear in mind that many issuers now offer enhancements on lower-cost standard cards and even on some thrifty cards. And if you're creditworthy, you can get your credit limit raised as high on a standard card as on a gold. How? Just ask.

Keep Their Eyes Off Your Credit Data

"Congratulations! You're pre-approved. Return the enclosed application..."

Sound familiar? Those envelopes crowding your mailbox, offering MasterCards, Visas, automobile loans, and home-equity lines of credit—all yours for the asking—are not just phony come-ons. You *have* been pre-approved, but you may be outraged to learn *how.*

Chances are, your name came from a credit bureau that was paid by a marketer to comb its records for target customers like you. This increasingly common procedure, known as prescreening, is a departure from credit bureaus' primary function of providing prospective lenders, insurers, and employers with your borrowing history when *you* apply to them. Why the new line of business? It's lucrative, of course. Credit bureaus charge marketers as much as $100 for every 1,000 screened names of people who, say, pay bills on time or maintain balances on their revolving charge accounts.

Credit bureau officials argue that they merely cull lists, like other data-base marketers, and then give out only names and addresses. "We're creating consumer opportunity and protecting privacy at the same time," says Marty Abrams, consumer affairs director for TRW, one of the nation's biggest credit bureaus.

But consumer advocates say that besides tempting some people to overextend themselves, prescreened offers are often more expensive than services that don't have to cover the cost of screening. Some also call prescreening an invasion of privacy. "The credit bureau system is not voluntary," says Evan Hendricks, editor of the 10-year-old biweekly *Privacy Times.* "If you participate in the economy at any level, the bureaus have a file on you, and their data are more sensitive than what most direct marketers use."

Congress is considering legislature that would require credit bureaus to notify you when they plan to release your name to marketers and give you the chance to stop them. But here's what you can do now to opt out of prescreening: Write to any of the big national bureaus—Equifax, Trans Union, or TRW (TRW Marketing Services, 600 City Parkway West, Orange, CA 92668; Attention: Mail Preference Services). Say: "Please see that my name, which may appear in your files as (give all forms of your name that the bureaus may have), and address are not given out for marketing purposes." The bureau will pass on your demand to its competitors.

Don't Gamble with Your Life Insurance

As insurance companies collapse at a record rate, we tell you how to learn if yours is financially unstable and what to do if it is.

Rather than peace of mind and family security, life insurance too often conjures up another image these days—high-stakes gambling. Just lay your premium on the table, watch your insurer roll the dice, and pray that the company doesn't crap out. In 1990, 30 life and health insurers with total assets of $1 billion went bust, compared with a mere five with total assets of $41 million in 1981. The life insurers most at risk are those with huge holdings of junk bonds and troubled commercial real estate. And when an insurer fails, hundreds of thousands of people can suddenly be left with policies or annuities that won't live up to their promises.

What should jittery policyholders and annuitants do? The surprising answer for most people, according to life insurance experts: Stay put. The industry is a lot sounder than you may think. Experts estimate that 95% of insurers are in no danger of collapse.

And even if your company is in jeopardy, switching to another may be unwise. Dropping an annuity or a cash-value life policy—one with a built-in savings fund—can be prohibitively expensive, unless you have owned it for at least seven years. In addition, almost every state has a backup system, called a guaranty fund, which essentially is a promise by insurers licensed to do business in the state that, if one of them fails, the others will put up the money to reimburse its customers. (The exceptions are Louisiana, New Jersey, and Washington, D.C., which have no such funds.)

Most states limit the amounts that policyholders and annuitants can get back, though.

Generally, guaranty fund cash-value reimbursements are capped at $100,000 per insured life or annuity and at $300,000 in combined death benefits and cash value if the customer has died. (Your state insurance department can tell you about the terms of your guaranty fund.) Worse yet, the guaranty funds have never been tested by insurance failures as costly as recent insolvencies, so no one knows how well the funds will respond.

If you are looking for a new policy or annuity, or want the peace of mind of knowing that your present insurer is sound, give the company the following step-by-step checkup. Your insurance agent and your state insurance department can assist you. (You will find the names of the 11 sturdiest U.S. life insurers in the table on page 48.) The safest insurers meet these criteria:

High ratings for financial stability. The ratings, awarded by private analytical firms, are based on a company's claims-paying performance, the quality of its investments, and its ability to withstand economic downturns. The five major ratings services are: A.M. Best of Oldwick, New Jersey (which rates 1,379 companies on a scale of A+ down to NA-7); Duff & Phelps of Chicago (61 companies, AAA to CCC); Moody's of New York City (72 companies, Aaa to C); Standard & Poor's of New York City (450 companies, AAA to C); and Weiss Research of West Palm Beach, Florida (1,740 companies, A+ to F). For maximum security, deal only with insurers that have one of the three highest grades from at least two of the ratings agencies and are not rated below the fourth grade by another. Remember, however, that the ratings aren't foolproof. For one thing, since insurers must pay $17,000 to $25,000 a year to be rated by Moody's, S&P, and Duff & Phelps, many companies decline to be graded. For another, the agencies' assessments of the same company often differ.

Few junk bonds and problem real estate loans. Analysts disagree about how much is too much when it comes to these investments, which along with foreclosed real estate are known as high-risk assets. But be cautious if such assets are more than twice a company's total capital.

You can get helpful data on assets and capital from Weiss or A.M. Best. Weiss (800-289-9222) sells a one-page *Personal Safety Brief* about a

specific insurer for $25 and a more detailed 18-page *Personal Safety Report* for $45. Best (908-439-2200) offers its own in-depth analysis, *Best's Advanced Company Report,* for $15.

Reasonable interest rates on annuities. Most insurers recently paid roughly the same rate on their annuities, but a few lure customers with higher rates. High rates can sometimes mean high risk, signaling that a company may be headed for trouble.

Fifty years or more of experience in the life insurance and annuity business. Such a company will have withstood several boom-and-bust insurance cycles, so you can count on its weathering tough times in the future.

After you've learned whether your insurer meets the safety criteria, you must decide whether it will pay to transfer your business to a safer company. Unfortunately, switching can be time consuming—the paperwork can take several weeks and finding a new insurer even longer—and expensive, if you have to pay surrender fees on your old policy or annuity. So before committing yourself to changing companies, talk over your plans with at least two insurance agents and let them review each other's advice. That way, you can compare one agent's recommendations with the other's and avoid missteps based on sales pitches or unrealistic policy projections.

Don't cash in your current policy until you get a new one. Before selling you a policy, your new insurer will most certainly insist that you obtain a medical exam. If your health has deteriorated since you purchased your original policy, the new insurer might turn you down.

The cost of switching will depend on the type of policy you have now and how long you've owned it. Moving from one company's term policy to another's term or cash-value coverage is simple and cheap. Your only cost will be the new premium.

But determining the costs of exchanging annuities—or of swapping one cash-value policy for another—is extremely tricky. Your calculations must include how much you've already paid in, the account value of the

America's Safest Life Insurers

These 11 insurance companies, ranked by assets, are the only ones selling policies to the general public that get the highest ratings for financial soundness from A.M. Best, Standard & Poor's, and Moody's. For the names of agents in your area, call the insurers' home offices (some companies do not sell in every state). None of the companies hold significant amounts of junk bonds or troubled real estate, and each has been selling life insurance for at least 50 years.

Insurer	Assets (in billions)	Telephone
Prudential	$133.5	201-802-6722
Metropolitan	103.5	800-638-5433
New York Life	39.9	212-576-7000
Connecticut General	37.4	203-726-6000
John Hancock	33.7	800-922-5050
Northwestern Mutual	31.4	414-271-1444
Principal Mutual	27.5	800-247-9988
Massachusetts Mutual	27.2	413-788-8411
Nationwide	12.3	614-249-7111
State Farm Life	12.1	309-766-2311
Guardian Life	6.2	212-598-8000

annuity or the cash value of the policy, and the insurer's surrender charges. In most cases, you will almost certainly lose money by switching annuities if you have owned yours for less than seven years. That's because companies routinely assess surrender penalties on contracts cashed in—as much as 7% of the annuity's value in the first year and one percentage point less each year thereafter. And you'll owe a 10% tax penalty on withdrawals made before you reach age 59½.

Insurance experts say you'll often take a loss if you swap a life insurance policy you've held for less than 10 years. For example, assume a non-smoking man, aged 45, bought a $100,000 whole life policy in 1986 for an annual premium of $1,900. If he surrendered the insurance policy 5 years later, he would probably get back about $6,090 in cash value, or $3,400 less than all of the premiums that he had paid. In fact, David Woods, an insurance agent in Springfield, Massachusetts, calculates that the man would likely have to wait until 1996 or so before the whole life policy's projected cash value of $19,815 would exceed his $19,100 in total premiums. If his cash value had been more than the cost of all his premiums, the man would also owe income taxes on the difference, unless he switched to another insurer's policy with what is called a 1035 exchange. Named for a section of the tax code, it lets you move your cash value, or an annuity's account balance, directly from one company to another without getting your hands on the money. You can obtain a 1035 exchange form from your agent.

If you have built up cash value in a life insurance policy and want instant access to the earnings, there is a penalty-free way to get your money. You can borrow from the insurance company an amount that is equal to your cash value and then put the money in some safer investment elsewhere. You will owe no surrender charges. Your cost will be the difference between the interest you pay on the loan and that of your new investment. Some insurers will also cut the rate earned on your cash value by roughly two percentage points. You never have to pay back the loan, though any outstanding balance will be subtracted from your death benefit or from your cash value if you let the policy lapse. But at least you'll have tilted the odds in your favor in the event that your insurer comes up a loser.

How to Save $1,000 on Auto Insurance

Get rid of unnecessary coverage, low deductibles, and other premium wasters. Above all, get on the phone and shop till you drop.

Auto insurance premiums increased at an annual rate of 8% over the past decade, from an average payment of $290 a year in 1981 to $650 in 1991. How can you fight back? By shopping for the cheapest insurer, making intelligent coverage choices, and driving safely. Such steps could cut your auto insurance bill by $200 to $600, or possibly as much as $1,000.

By far the most effective way to slash your costs is to compare quotes from at least five companies whenever you enter the market for a new policy. Whatever kind of driver you are and wherever you live, differences among competing insurers—such as whether they sell directly to consumers or through agents—all but guarantee you will find coverage in a wide range of prices. *Money*'s survey of large insurers found that premiums for identical policies in the same city could differ by as much as $1,000 a year.

Whatever you do, don't simply accept some independent insurance agent's assurance that he or she can find you the best price. In fact, the most expensive policies tend to be the very policies that independents sell. The reason: Companies that market through independent agents must pay higher commissions than do those that employ their own sales force, such as State Farm and Nationwide, or those that sell policies directly to customers, such as Amica Mutual. There are exceptions, however, so it often pays to get prices from several companies and then to challenge an independent agent to beat them.

Before you start comparing premiums, figure out how much protection you need. A standard package includes six basic coverages: bodily-injury liability, property-damage liability, collision, comprehensive, uninsured-motorist coverage, and medical (or, if you live in a state with no-fault insurance laws, personal-injury protection). Your goal is to eliminate the coverage you don't need and to take no more than necessary of the rest.

You definitely should *not* skimp on the two liability coverages: bodily injury, which pays medical bills for anyone you may injure, and property damage, which covers any car or other property that you might damage in an accident. Most states require you to buy a minimum amount of each. Bodily-injury minimums range from $20,000 to $50,000 for each victim, up to $40,000 to $100,000 an accident; property damage ranges between $5,000 and $25,000.

These minimums almost certainly fall short of your needs. Most advisers recommend getting bodily-injury coverage of at least $100,000 a person up to $300,000 an accident. If your net worth exceeds $300,000, get at least $200,000 a person and $500,000 an accident, especially in a lawsuit-happy state like New York, where auto accidents wind up in court three times as often as they do in the country as a whole. If the value of your assets exceeds the maximum limits of your insurer's bodily-injury

protection, you might consider bolstering your coverage with an umbrella liability policy, usually available as an add-on to your homeowners policy. This insures you against judgments in excess of your auto and homeowners protection. To get it, you generally have to insure both your home and car with the same company, and you may have to carry liability well above the minimum. Geico, for example, requires umbrella policyholders to have bodily-injury coverage of $300,000 a person. You should also get at least $50,000 in property-damage coverage. In an unlucky moment, you could easily cause far more damage than would be covered under the typical state minimum package of $5,000 to $25,000.

How much does all of this cost? A married couple in their mid-thirties living in Dallas and driving a 1988 Audi 90 and a 1991 Ford Taurus might pay $793 a year to insure the two cars with Nationwide. Liability coverages of $100,000 an injured person up to $300,000 an accident, plus $50,000 in property damage, would consume around $356 of that sum, of which $237 would go for bodily-injury coverage and $118 would pay for property-damage protection. For another $120, the couple could add a $1 million umbrella policy.

Another essential part of any basic package is uninsured-motorist coverage ($20,000 to $40,000 is required in many states). If you were to have an accident involving an uninsured driver, this coverage would pay for injuries to your passengers, your own "pain and suffering," and other expenses that health plans do not pick up. Coverage runs about $40 a year for $100,000. Pay it.

When it comes to other parts of the typical insurance policy, however, you should look for chances to shave costs. Start with collision and comprehensive coverages, which together might absorb more than 40% of your total premiums. Collision pays for accident damage to your car, while comprehensive covers most other risks to the car, ranging from theft to natural disasters. Unlike the coverages discussed so far, both are subject to deductibles of anywhere from $50 to $1,000. (The deductible is the amount you pay out of your own pocket before the insurance kicks in.) Choosing high deductibles can lower your premiums considerably. Typically, for every $100 your deductible rises, the cost of your collision coverage drops by 7% to 15%. Your comprehensive coverage might drop 15% to 30%.

Because collision and comprehensive are so costly, it rarely makes sense to carry them on cars more than five years old. As a rule, drop collision if the most you can expect to receive as a settlement would equal just a few years' premiums. Some advisers recommend holding on to comprehensive, however. Their reasoning: If someone steals your car, you might recover at least enough to meet the down payment on a replacement.

There is also room to save on medical coverage, an optional feature usually offered outside no-fault states. This pays physicians' fees, hospital bills, and sometimes funeral expenses for the driver or passengers. Your life and health insurance probably render this coverage unnecessary. Possible savings: as much as $100 a year.

If you live in one of the 15 states with no-fault insurance—which generally requires your insurer to pick up your damages even if someone else caused the accident—you may have to buy personal-injury protection, or PIP. This covers your medical bills as well as some portion of wages lost if you are disabled in an accident. If your health plan agrees to be the primary payer for accident-related medical bills, you could cut your PIP costs by as much as 40%.

Though your agent is likely to offer you a range of other minor coverages, you can probably dispense with them. If you own two cars, for example, you needn't spend $15 or so a year for rental-reimbursement coverage, which pays $15 to $25 a day for as long as 30 days toward a rental car when your car is being repaired after an accident. Likewise, if you belong to a motor club like AAA, you can get along fine without towing insurance. That's another $15 or so in savings. Apart from cutting unnecessary coverages, your best chance

for putting a lid on premiums is to be a low-risk driver. Staying out of accidents and traffic court, for example, could save you roughly 40% in premiums. Many insurers will permit two or three violations (including speeding tickets) or one accident within a three-year period before bumping you from the elite of their "preferred" customers—those who get the lowest rate—to the ranks of their "standard" or, worse, "nonstandard" risks.

If you do have a spotted driving record, your insurance company may refer you to one of its subsidiaries for higher-risk drivers, and you'll pay more. If you have a serious violation like a drunken-driving conviction, however, you may not find an insurer willing to write you a policy at any price. In that case, an agent can direct you to a state insurance pool, where everyone is granted the coverage they request—though often at premiums four times as high as a preferred rate.

If you are buying a new car, you can also cut costs by favoring models with histories of few insurance claims. Claims records are compiled for hundreds of models by the Insurance Institute for Highway Safety in Alexandria, Virginia. (IIHS data are used to grade more than 500 different 1992 models for insurance costs in the *Money*'s Car Cost Ratings that begin on page 153.)

When you start phoning insurers, ask not only about current premiums but also about possible future costs: How much will premiums rise if you get a speeding ticket or two? What if you get into an accident?

Finally, don't wait for your agent or some other salesperson to volunteer information about discounts for which you may qualify—ask. Most companies give a 10% to 15% break for insuring both your house and your cars with them. Also, driver's education can trim premiums for new drivers and seniors by 5% to 10% at Geico and USAA, while Allstate gives breaks of between 5% and 15% for car safety features such as air bags and anti-lock brakes. Some companies even give nonsmokers discounts of up to 25%.

***The trouble with the rat race is that even
if you win you're still a rat.*** – Lily Tomlin

CAREERS

Taking Charge of Your Life

The Organization Man, that consummate all-for-the-company and the-company-for-all employee who flourished in the 1950s, died sometime in the 1980s, leaving those who're still struggling to make a living in the decades ahead less secure, but more protective of their own career interests. In the post-war boom, the Organization Man could count on his company for regular promotions and raises, safe in the knowledge that his job would be there as long as he pulled his weight. Things are different now. When bad times hit companies in the 1990s, layoffs and belt-tightening often result. One consequence is that employees no longer see their companies and their careers as synonymous. Another consequence is the emergence of thousands of small, privately owned businesses each year and a constantly shifting job force.

Career counselors say that the skills most in demand today are computer expertise, technical writing, managerial prowess, and foreign languages. In this era of skimpy raises and corporate downsizing, the professional who can piggyback one or more of these talents onto his or her current area of expertise will enjoy both the greatest job security and the best salary. You may also boost your career prospects if you're willing to relocate to a place with a fast-growing job market. (For a list of cities and occupations most in demand, see the story on page 54).

Most of this chapter is devoted to helping the aspiring business owner realize his or her dream of self-determination. We take you through the process of business ownership, from recognizing the best opportunities of the 1990s (page 59) to finding the right location for your business (page 68), raising the cash you'll need (page 65), and deciding whether to buy an existing enterprise or start from scratch (page 70).

It's important how you manage your career, whether you're working for someone else or yourself. Unless you're independently wealthy, your biggest income-producing investment won't be stocks or bonds or even real estate, but your job.

Where to Find the Best Jobs

Two California cities, Los Angeles and Anaheim, top the list of the best white-collar job markets for the 1990s.

Americans have been pulling up stakes and pursuing prosperity since the days of the Conestoga wagon. An estimated 1.3 million heads of household moved annually during the 1980s, nearly half of them doing so primarily either to take a new job or to look for one. This characteristically American wanderlust has its roots in our national faith in a person's ability to improve his circumstances—and in the power of the U.S. economy to reward those who try. One key is the economy's deep diversity, which permits regional job markets to thrive even when the country as a whole is

slipping into recession. As the economy sputters into the 1990s, a number of these regional pockets of opportunity will continue to flourish. For workers thwarted by recession-worn local job markets, such oases could make the difference between career progress and stagnation. That's where this story can help. In the table on pages 56-57, we've named 48 metropolitan areas that are expected to be the hottest job markets through 1996. Though many of these locales were hit hard by the recession, they figure to recover to account for 59% of the professional and managerial jobs created

Where Women Execs Win Out

White-collar women are in demand in these cities, where the percentage of working women in professional and managerial jobs handily exceeds the U.S. average of 26%. Most of these areas are dominated by service industries, which have traditionally promoted women.

Metropolitan area	% of working women in white-collar jobs	% of all jobs held by women
Washington, D.C.	37.4%	34%
San Francisco	36.1	45
Boston	35.6	47
San Jose	33.9	44
New York City	32.6	45
Nassau County, New York	32.4	42

Source: Bureau of Labor Statistics

Where There's Always Work

To find a job that's here today and still here tomorrow, look for a city dominated by a university or government offices. All of these metro areas—each of which ranked in the bottom 10% for unemployment every year from 1983 to 1989—are either college towns or capital cities.

Metropolitan area	% average unemployment 1983-89	% unemployment October 1990
Iowa City, Iowa	2.5%	1.7%
Raleigh, North Carolina	3.2	2.6
Burlington, Vermont	3.2	3.1
Lincoln, Nebraska	3.3	1.6
Columbia, Missouri	3.4	N.A.
Washington, D.C.	3.6	3.4

Source: Bureau of Labor Statistics **Notes:** N.A. Not available

by 1996, according to the Washington, D.C. research firm Woods & Poole Economics.

Of course, there is more to relocating than simply picking one of the hot job markets off our list and calling the movers. You have to weigh a whole matrix of issues: How will a move affect your spouse's career? Will it disrupt your kids' education? Will you have to take a loss on your house? (For a checklist of questions you will need to consider before deciding to relocate, see the box on page 58.) Still, investigating an area's economic prospects before you move is your best defense against what could be a nightmarish miscalculation. The last thing that you want is to relocate for a new job and wind up laid off in a strange city.

Our projections suggest that professional and managerial job growth will outpace population increases in areas such as California and Miami, which serve as gateways to global markets, and those like Texas and much of the Midwest, where previous local recessions have already shaken out weak employers. Major research centers or seats of government are also pipelines for jobs. That explains the strong outlook for Raleigh-Durham, Boston, and Washington, D.C. Not surprisingly, the greatest number of jobs will be added in cities with large, highly diverse economic bases. Los Angeles heads the list; it is projected to create some 113,000 new top-level, white-collar jobs by 1996. Bear in mind, however, that many of the cities with strong five-year outlooks—particularly those dependent on the recession-whipped financial and retailing industries—are currently struggling with unemployment rates above the national average of 6.1%. Those job markets may take as much as a year or more to hit their stride.

An area's overall economic health, of course, is of less concern to you than the extent of opportunity available in your particular line of work. No city, however prosperous, is a haven for every occupation. Washington, D.C., for example, is expected to be the third hottest metropolitan area through 1996, creating some

Where College Grads Thrive

Because of the recession, the class of 1991 will average 10% fewer job offers than grads the previous year. But they will have an edge in the areas below. For the sake of comparison, only 24% of jobs nationwide require degrees.

Metropolitan area	% of jobs requiring a college degree	Total 1991 employment (millions)
Washington, D.C.	39%	2.8
San Jose	38	1.1
San Francisco	38	1.3
Boston	36	1.6
Oakland	33	1.2
Bergen County, New Jersey	32	0.9
Seattle	32	1.2
Essex County, New Jersey	32	1.2
Denver	32	1.1
St. Louis	31	1.4

Sources: Bureau of Labor Statistics, Woods & Poole Economics Inc.

Where the Money Is

If you're ambitious, set your sights on working within commuting distance of these high-rent markets. Even in the least tony here, Anchorage, the typical household pulls down 92% more than the U.S. average of $36,500.

Metropolitan area	Average household income	% above U.S. average
Stamford, Connecticut	$91,480	151%
Nassau County, New York	89,082	144
Bergen County, New Jersey	80,236	120
San Jose	80,072	119
Middlesex County, New Jersey	79,671	118
Anaheim, California	78,387	115
Lake County, Illinois	75,581	107
Essex County, New Jersey	70,551	93
Washington, D.C.	70,296	93
Anchorage	70,175	92

Source: Woods & Poole Economics Inc.

Top Job Markets across the Country

These 48 metropolitan areas led by Los Angeles will provide the largest number of white-collar jobs between now and 1996, according to Washington, D.C. economics firm Woods & Poole. The occupations listed as being in most demand are those expected to grow faster than the national average through 1996.

Metropolitan area	Estimated new professional/ managerial jobs by 1996	Ratio of job growth to population growth	Occupation in most demand	Occupation in least demand	Average household income	Relative cost of living (U.S. average equals 100)
1. Los Angeles	113,000	1.09	Photographers Architects Respiratory therapists	High school teachers Special education teachers Speech therapists	$62,905	124
2. Anaheim, CA	108,000	1.10	Marketing managers Real estate managers Management analysts	Journalists Vocational counselors Elementary school teachers	78,387	128
3. Washington, D.C.	81,000	1.21	Management analysts Personnel specialists Personnel managers	Industrial engineers Mechanical engineers Respiratory therapists	70,296	130
4. Dallas/Fort Worth	78,000	0.96/ 1.05	Underwriters Electrical engineers Real estate managers	Social workers Special education teachers High school teachers	59,012/ 48,190	105/94
5. Atlanta	77,000	0.99	Management analysts Kindergarten teachers Underwriters	Special education teachers Mechanical engineers Industrial engineers	55,529	101
6. San Francisco/Oakland	67,000	0.84/ 0.95	Management analysts Biologists Commercial artists	Special education teachers Industrial engineers Vocational counselors	69,124/ 64,666	128/124
7. Chicago	54,000	2.85	Chemists Physicians Mechanical engineers	Real estate managers Special education teachers Kindergarten teachers	61,186	124
8. Nassau County, NY	48,000	1.27	Lawyers Psychologists Commercial artists	Real estate managers Kindergarten teachers Management analysts	89,082	156
9. Phoenix	46,000	1.10	Electrical engineers Architects Computer systems analysts	Chemists Business agents Management analysts	51,967	102
10. Tampa/St. Petersburg	44,000	1.17	Respiratory therapists Underwriters Real estate managers	Chemists Accountants Biologists	45,502	103
11. Houston	44,000	0.89	Civil engineers Architects Chemists	Business agents Special education teachers Journalists	49,980	99
12. Philadelphia	41,000	2.61	Underwriters Chemists Speech therapists	Business agents Civil engineers Mechanical engineers	57,447	128
13. San Jose	40,000	2.04	Personnel specialists Physical therapists Kindergarten teachers	Underwriters Respiratory therapists Lawyers	80,072	124
14. Riverside, CA	39,000	0.91	Civil engineers Psychologists Electrical engineers	Photographers Journalists Speech therapists	48,698	112
15. Orlando	38,000	1.01	Underwriters Respiratory therapists Photographers	Biologists Chemists Civil engineers	51,510	104
16. San Diego	38,000	1.21	Real estate managers Management analysts Computer systems analysts	Underwriters Chemists High school teachers	52,389	132
17. Boston	37,000	1.81	Technical writers Physical therapists Biologists	Real estate managers Special education teachers Personnel specialists	67,090	130
18. Fort Lauderdale	36,000	1.13	Physical therapists Designers Pharmacists	Mechanical engineers Vocational counselors Social workers	59,705	114
19. Minneapolis/St. Paul	33,000	1.20	Technical writers Computer systems analysts Industrial engineers	Education administrators Management analysts Medical administrators	58,226	99
20. Middlesex County, NJ	33,000	1.19	Accountants Personnel specialists Engineers	Therapists Physical scientists Life scientists	79,671	128
21. West Palm Beach, FL	33,000	1.18	Architects Management analysts Managers	Chemists Kindergarten teachers High school teachers	57,529	114
22. Denver	28,000	0.91	Technical writers Physical therapists Vocational counselors	Underwriters Respiratory therapists Systems researchers	53,569	101

Sources: Woods & Poole Economics Inc., Bureau of Labor Statistics, American Chamber of Commerce Researchers Association. **N.A.** Not available

Metropolitan area	Estimated new professional/ managerial jobs by 1996	Ratio of job growth to population growth	Occupation in most demand	Occupation in least demand	Average household income	Relative cost of living (U.S. average equals 100)
23. Sacramento	26,000	1.14	Real estate managers Personnel specialists Special education teachers	Mechanical engineers Industrial engineers Electrical engineers	$51,726	109
24. Baltimore	25,000	1.35	Underwriters Management analysts Personnel specialists	Mechanical engineers Respiratory therapists Industrial engineers	57,035	112
25. Miami	24,000	1.87	Lawyers Special education teachers Education administrators	Industrial engineers Mechanical engineers Computer systems analysts	51,311	112
26. Seattle	23,000	1.23	Real estate managers Underwriters Management analysts	Chemists High school teachers Pharmacists	58,095	112
27. Detroit	23,000	0.80	Mechanical engineers Industrial engineers Marketing managers	Biologists Journalists Civil engineers	58,014	118
28. Raleigh/Durham, NC	23,000	1.08	Medical administrators Business agents Physical therapists	Respiratory therapists Elementary school teachers Lawyers	50,441	102
29. Charlotte, NC	22,000	1.12	Architects Electrical engineers Industrial engineers	Biologists Psychologists Respiratory therapists	48,669	101
30. Columbus, OH	21,000	1.23	Technical writers Special education teachers Kindergarten teachers	Physical therapists Commercial artists Elementary school teachers	49,015	104
31. New York City	20,000	0.98	Journalists Commercial artists Designers	Respiratory therapists Special education teachers Elementary school teachers	58,540	130
32. Oxnard/Ventura, CA	19,000	0.93	Business agents Marketing managers Personnel specialists	Pharmacists Lawyers Biologists	64,117	126
33. Essex County, NJ	18,000	1.71	Chemists Underwriters Systems researchers	Respiratory therapists Speech therapists Special education teachers	70,551	128
34. Austin	18,000	0.99	Special education teachers Vocational counselors Accountants	Physicians Respiratory therapists Financial managers	47,598	97
35. Pittsburgh	17,000	0.80	Chemists Registered nurses Speech therapists	Real estate managers Management analysts Business agents	50,627	104
36. Nashville	17,000	1.09	Business agents Photographers Underwriters	Mechanical engineers Chemists High school teachers	48,780	99
37. Las Vegas	17,000	1.01	Pharmacists Civil engineers Commercial artists	Management analysts Education administrators Speech therapists	49,341	109
38. Bergen County, NJ	16,000	1.67	Accountants Personnel specialists Engineers	Teachers Physical scientists N.A.	80,236	128
39. San Antonio	16,000	1.20	Real estate managers Photographers Physicians	Registered nurses Social workers Speech therapists	46,110	97
40. Greensboro, NC	16,000	1.22	Personnel managers Marketing managers Managers	Biologists Real estate managers Civil engineers	48,770	103
41. St. Louis	15,000	1.79	Chemists Computer systems analysts Speech therapists	Business agents Vocational counselors Real estate managers	55,838	99
42. Salt Lake City	15,000	1.16	Special education teachers Kindergarten teachers Elementary school teachers	Underwriters Business agents Management analysts	48,787	92
43. Monmouth County, NJ	14,000	1.34	Accountants Personnel specialists Computer specialists	Life scientists Physical scientists Architects	64,900	128
44. Hartford	14,000	1.20	Systems researchers Computer systems analysts Technical writers	Real estate managers Education administrators Management analysts	66,217	129
45. New Orleans	13,000	1.15	Civil engineers Physicians Lawyers	Vocational counselors Social workers Special education teachers	43,462	96
46. Indianapolis	13,000	1.23	Underwriters Respiratory therapists Speech therapists	Architects Civil engineers Social workers	51,277	99
47. Richmond	13,000	1.03	Systems researchers Personnel specialists Underwriters	Respiratory therapists Mechanical engineers Industrial engineers	55,131	110
48. Cincinnati	13,000	1.69	Marketing managers Speech therapists Registered nurses	Vocational counselors Electrical engineers Journalists	52,098	103

81,000 new white-collar jobs overall—but if you are an industrial engineer, you'd probably find work more easily in No. 19, Minneapolis.

If you don't already long to live in one region or another, you might start your search for a promising area by calling your professional organization or the trade publications in your field and asking which cities have the best opportunities. (If you're not sure where to find these sources, check *The Encyclopedia of Associations* or *SRDS Business Publication Rates and Data*, which are available at most libraries.) Some groups, including the American Institute of Architects and the American Institute of Chemical Engineers, maintain nationwide data bases to match job-hunting members with

employers. Many others at least publish journals with help-wanted ads.

Once you've zeroed in on a few likely places, call the local chambers of commerce and ask which local firms in your field are expanding. However, you should bear in mind that local boosters have a tendency to overemphasize the positive aspects of their area businesses. Therefore, you may want to double-check what you hear from them with the director of labor market information at the state's labor department. Ask for the occupational projections, which estimate the demand for jobs in areas across the state.

Working couples obviously face a particularly touchy problem in choosing where to live. In eight out of 10 couples, it is the husband who has been transferred or been recruited and the wife who has to look for work in the new city, experts say. That often means that a wife finds herself moving to an area where there is less demand for her skills than for her husband's. (For the cities in which a larger-than-average proportion of working women hold upscale jobs, see the table on page 54.)

Women who find themselves in such straits can expand their job-hunting contacts by joining the National Association for Female Executives (127 West 24th Street, New York, NY 10114), a networking group. For $29 a year, membership provides access to 500 local chapters covering virtually every metropolitan area. While two careers may complicate the decision of where to move, working couples benefit from financial flexibility.

Once you and your spouse find a city with mutually acceptable job prospects, you still need to decide if you could maintain your standard of living there. Unfortunately, many of the most promising job markets have steep costs of living. It costs 56% more to live in No. 8 Nassau County, New York, for example, than in the average metropolitan area.

Housing expenses account for the bulk of these differences. Indeed, the Employee Relocation Council reports that 82% of the employees who refused corporate transfers in 1990 did so because of high housing costs in their proposed destinations. For that reason, it may pay to concentrate some of your efforts in

Are You a Candidate for a Move?

Would moving improve your career prospects? If demand for your profession is stagnant nationally—as it is for purchasing managers and aeronautical engineers, for example—moving is likely to change nothing but the scenery. You may be better off training in a new line of work. Things may not be as bad as you think where you are. It generally takes four to eight months to find a white-collar job. If you haven't been looking that long, don't give up on your home market.

How quickly would your family adapt to a new location? Teenagers tend to be hardest hit by separation from their peers. Younger kids can more easily take a move in stride. Ideally, your spouse should be able to find a job with undiminished prestige in your new location. Bear in mind that only about 10% to 15% of companies help relocating spouses find work, as a matter of policy. But you may be able to negotiate such assistance with your new employer.

How smoothly could you transfer from your present housing market? If you're considering a more expensive area, will the equity in your current home cover a typical 20% down payment, or will you have to draw down other assets? With homes lingering on the market these days for three to six months, you might consider leaving one spouse behind until the house sells. The alternatives are renting or leaving the house vacant, both of which could ultimately drive down the price your home fetches.

the relatively inexpensive housing markets among our top 48 metro areas—such as St. Louis, New Orleans, Salt Lake City, or many of the cities in Texas.

However pessimistic you may be about the career prospects in your current location, stay put until you or your spouse has a firm job offer elsewhere. Outplacement advisers point out that slumps currently affecting many regions will not last forever. It generally takes four to eight months for an executive to find a job even in the most promising regions; therefore, your own area might begin to recover before you could expect to get established somewhere else. On the other hand, if your local job market has been sluggish for years, a move to a more prosperous city may make sense even before you've nailed down a job— especially if you are young and largely free of financial responsibilities.

The Hottest Opportunities of the 1990s

Profits will soar for firms in fields like health care and training. The key to success lies in developing a distinctive niche.

Recession or recovery, boom or bust, the one thing constant about the American economy is that it's constantly changing. Yet, despite economic upheaval—and, in many cases, because of it—now could be the perfect time to start, or expand, your business. The reason is that each new economic earthquake buries old markets as it thrusts up new ones. And it is small, agile firms—like the one you might start or currently run—that can reach emerging ground first. During the boom days of the 1980s, small businesses had to worry about large companies squashing them if they tried to enter new turf. Now they can stake claims in markets that they never had access to before. In 1990, for example, companies with 100 or fewer workers grew between two and three times faster in their number of employees than did larger firms, according to the American Express small-business index. Many of those companies grew by practicing "nichecraft"—the art of finding a small but profitable market. Then, too, it never hurts to be in a hot business at the right time. Though the U.S. economy is forecast to grow only about 2.3% a year this decade, versus 2.7% in the 1980s, there will still be plenty of room for small firms to prosper in such burgeoning fields as health care, education, and environmental services.

Here, in descending order of total market size, are six sectors that promise the greatest growth this decade:

Retailing. Nichecraft will be especially vital for the roughly 25% of new businesses each year that seek a slice of the $1.8 trillion annual retail trade. The reason is simple: While the traditional mass marketers like Sears are taking a beating (the $32 billion giant was unseated as the nation's No. 1 retailer in 1990 by the $32.6 billion discount chain Wal-Mart and $32.1 billion K Mart), more specialized firms like The Gap, which sells stylish leisure clothing at affordable prices, have zoomed ahead. And experts predict that the trend toward value and specialization will only gather steam.

The trick, of course, will be to pick the right niche. For example, with real estate prices either down or sluggish across much of the country, the $101-billion-a-year home improvement market is expected to grow 10% annually for the next few years as Americans fix up their homes instead of moving. That should mean plenty of business for specialty stores that stock, say, every variety of bathroom fixture or every imaginable kind of tile. The same kind of fine-bore marketing strategy could be applied to any of the other retailing areas that are expected to grow 10% a year or more during the decade; they include consumer electronics, home hobby goods, and apparel. Entrée into specialty retailing can also be gained through franchise outfits. One example is the Decorating Den, a Bethesda, Maryland firm (800-428-1366) with more than 1,100 outlets that trains you to sell custom draperies and home furnishings. Start-up costs can run about $15,000, but a successful franchisee can gross between $50,000 and $100,000 a year (for tips on shopping for a franchise, see page 72).

Health care. The prognosis is good for small firms in this market, which analysts expect to grow 150% to $1.5 trillion annually by the year 2000. True, many of the opportunities will be reserved for specialists like doctors and nurses. But not all.

Consider the fact that the baby-boom generation—those born between 1946 and 1964—is now cruising into its middle years, when most people spend more on their health. By 2001, the number of 45- to 54-year-olds will have grown nearly 50% to 38.7 million, and they will command a stunning 25% of the nation's spending power. Experts say those facts virtually guarantee rising demand for health-related products and services: stores that sell health foods and vitamins, for example; weight-control programs; and sports gear and fitness centers designed for middle-aged athletes.

The boomers' parents are aging, too. The ranks of Americans 65 and over will swell 10% to 35 million by 2000, and the 85-and-up group will grow 37% to 4.6 million. That should mean a healthy market for products and services that help the elderly to maintain independence. Your company might provide transportation, deliver food and prescriptions, run errands, or perform clerical tasks like completing health

insurance forms. Established firms can jump in, too. If construction is your trade, for example, you might make a specialty of modifying homes to accommodate wheelchairs or walkers.

Meanwhile, there will be a growing volume of work for the many small companies—like Hex "FF" of Los Angeles—that serve doctors' offices, labs, and hospitals. This four-person firm, founded in 1981, grossed $300,000 last year installing software to help private labs track their records and billing.

Environmental work. With annual revenues in the environmental services field expected to blossom from $120 billion in 1991 to $265 billion by the turn of the century, nurturing the environment will keep many small firms green. Already, environmentally related businesses account for three of the eight fastest-growing categories of Yellow Pages listings in the country. And, as in the health-care field, an advanced degree is helpful but not critical.

Anyone who collects plastic, glass, or aluminum refuse efficiently, for example, can grab part of the $16.9 billion recycling industry. *The Environmental Business Journal*, a newsletter in San Diego that tracks the industry, says the recycling market will advance at a brisk 14% a year now that 30 states have passed comprehensive recycling laws. Nine states—California, Indiana, Iowa, Maine, Massachusetts, Michigan, New Mexico, New York, and Washington—plan to reclaim 50% of their trash by 2005.

Small firms should dominate two of the fastest-growing environmental industries: testing, a $2.2-billion-a-year business expanding at 20% annually; and engineering, a $10 billion segment growing 17% a year that designs the solutions to environmental problems. But they will also claim a share of the much larger $80 billion market for environmental treatment and purification, in part thanks to the performance of companies that are run by nonscientists.

Privatization. You used to have to work in the public sector to be a public servant, but no more. Today, entrepreneurs are saving money for the taxpayer—and making it for themselves—by providing services like transportation, maintenance, refuse collection, and even jail management for states and counties. By 1996, federal, state, and local governments are expected to spend an estimated $100 billion a year on such privatized services. You'll see more small businesses benefiting from this as financially strapped cities and states explore cheaper ways to maintain services.

For your business, the opportunities could be as specialized as computerizing medical records at the city hospital or as broad-based as landscaping the municipal parks and grounds. But don't get scared off by the Herculean sound of these labors; most public business comes in bite-size chunks. The state of Florida, for example, recently spent $3.5 million to hire 12 small firms to run 21 drug treatment facilities for the prison system. And a survey of 1,000 city and local officials showed that nearly three-quarters think privatization generally is a good idea, and one-quarter have already turned to private firms to take over government services. A classic example is tiny Ecorse, Michigan (pop. 12,430), which saves an estimated $1.5 million a year hiring private companies to do the work once done by the city attorney, clerks, and janitors.

Training and education. With approximately one in 10 Americans unable to read so much as a restaurant menu, it's no surprise that big companies have to look far and wide for able-minded employees. A survey by the consulting firm Towers Perrin and the Hudson Institute concluded that 40% of large and medium-size corporations reject 10 or more job applicants for every one they hire. And a third of them spend $2,000 a head training new workers. Those facts help explain why the $30-billion-a-year employee training industry is likely to grow at a rate of 3% a year for the next decade. They also spell opportunity for the many small firms that specialize in finding and training new hires.

The biggest winners will be people who tailor programs to a specific industry. There is also money to be made in helping the schools head off illiteracy in the first place. The average U.S. school district will educate nearly 20% more fifth-graders in 2000 than it did in 1988, since American mothers are having more

babies these days (4.1 million in 1990) than at any time since the baby boom. To prepare for that onslaught, school districts are investing heavily in educational materials and technology—much of it from smaller companies. Forecasters expect the educational materials market to grow 38% to $1.1 billion by 1995, and that for technology—like in-school computers and software—to leap 79% to $2.7 billion.

While you obviously need special training and experience to create materials like educational software, you don't have to have any such expertise to sell them or to supply the computer gear that they run on. Moreover, schools will need local providers for many conventional goods and services—everything from bus service to chalk to napkins for the cafeteria. To succeed, though, your company will have to meet the needs and regulations of individual school systems. So do your homework. Seek the counsel of administrators, school board members, purchasing agents, teachers, and even parents. Find out the system's requirements and standards. And ask about any new or special purchasing programs.

Business consulting. The corporate belt tightening that raised unemployment among U.S. managers and professionals to nearly 800,000 in 1990 has at least one positive side effect: As large companies dump whole divisions, like marketing, public relations, or advertising, they need to replace those functions somehow. That gives small firms an opportunity to move in. *Consultants News,* a trade newsletter, estimates that corporations spent more than $13 billion on such consultants in 1990. Demand could grow 15% a year.

The market for data processing, including programming and general computer services, should increase 12.5% annually to $474 billion by the year 2000. And data-base marketing—the collection and sale of information on everything from what brand of cornflakes people buy to where they go for vacation—will skyrocket 30% a year to $32 billion through 1996. And as with educational services, your company does not need to devise the software that manipulates this data. You can participate in the growth in many other ways—sales, market research, and advertising. There is even room, as was true for other areas of opportunity, for the inspired low-tech approach. Consider the case of John Cotugno, formerly president of a Florida company that manufactured and sold dental implants. About two years ago, Cotugno began to notice that it was getting easier to make reservations for lunch in Boca Raton restaurants. Putting two and two together, he realized that corporate cost cutting was putting a crimp in expense-account meals. "More white-collar professionals were chained to their desks for lunch—so I thought they might need a food service that would cater to them." So Cotugno and a partner paid $100,000, plus a slice of revenues, for the rights to franchise a company called Wee-Bag-It that delivers custom-made brown-bag lunches. With three stores and six franchises, it is already pulling in some $630,000 a year—a classic case of following gut instincts to profit.

A Blueprint for Starting a Business

It takes more than a sharp idea to make a great company. Here's how to get your firm up and running.

Planning. Discipline. Caution. They are the last things you want to hear about when you're caught up in the excitement of turning a business idea into fact. But without a carefully drawn blueprint, your chances of success are almost nil. Indeed, at least half of start-up failures can be traced to faulty planning up front. Here are eight steps to help get your business off the ground:

Make sure that you're cut out to be an entrepreneur. If your main aspiration is to get rich, forget it. Successful entrepreneurs usually have their eyes on something bigger—like a passionate desire for independence or a belief in a business idea. Next, ask yourself this tough question: Does my family have enough cash to survive without my income for 18 months? That's how long it takes the average successful start-up to turn a profit, and most entrepreneurs plow 30% to 100% of profits back into the firm for at least three years.

Sharpen your business idea. Your next mission is to zero in on the product or service you will sell. A would-be retailer, for example, might begin with an idea for a store that sells all manner of kitchenware. But in an era when "nichecraft"—tailoring your product or service to a narrowly defined market segment—is expected to separate the winners from the losers, and maybe especially so in retailing, you might ultimately conclude that your outlet will be most profitable if it specializes in high-priced restaurant-quality cookware.

To hone your business concept, bounce your idea off as many knowledgeable people as will listen. Talk to trusted work associates, potential customers or suppliers, and even local business school professors. Don't spill the idea to potential competitors, of course. To protect yourself, you can ask people to sign a one-paragraph confidentiality agreement; for sample agreements, consult business law texts at your local public library.

Gauge the demand for your product or service. All embryonic outfits need a solid marketing plan. That means figuring out who your customers will be, why they will want your product or service, how you will deliver it, and what you will charge. The key to an airtight plan is richly detailed research, and you have a choice as to how to get it. You can hire a professional firm, or you can do it yourself. If you hire a pro—your local chamber of commerce may make referrals—expect to pay $2,000 or more, depending on the complexity of the research. If you gather market facts yourself, which is fine for most businesses except those developing highly specialized products like computers, your most powerful tools will be the telephone and the automobile, as you call on potential customers and suppliers to discuss how your product or service can beat the competition's. Don't neglect the local library, either, where publications like the *U.S. Industrial Outlook*, put out by the Commerce Department, give an industry-by-industry forecast of future economic activity.

For a crash course in a particular market, seek out a big trade show. There you'll find customers, suppliers, and competitors under one roof. One of the trickiest parts of your marketing plan will be setting the price. Start by projecting your expenses, breaking them into such categories as sales, manufacturing, distribution, and administration, and then dividing each category into subcategories covering, say, labor and materials. Then calculate how much you'll need to charge to break even and compare it with the competition's price. If your break-even is much lower than the other guy's price, check your estimates to make sure you haven't overlooked something. If it's equal to or higher than his price, you'll need to show that your product or service is superior in some way.

Write a detailed business plan. You are now ready to draft a 20- to 50-page plan that describes your company in great detail. It's the same as drawing a blueprint for a house before you start nailing down the boards: If you don't want to take the trouble, you're not ready to own a business; go back to working for someone else. (See the box below for specifics on creating a plan.)

How to Write a Business Plan

Face this unavoidable fact of entrepreneurial life: You have to write a business plan. Raising money is almost impossible without one. And even if it weren't, you need to put your ideas on paper as a guide for yourself. The hallmarks of winning plans:

Follow standard format. Begin with an executive summary. That's the two- or three-page introduction outlining what your company will do, how it will be financed and organized, and who will be its customers and suppliers. Though brief, the summary is crucial. A banker or venture capitalist probably sees upwards of 1,000 such plans a year, so a compelling introduction may be your only real chance to grab his or her attention.

After the summary come three critical seven- to 10-page sections: a market overview that describes in detail who will buy the product or service, why, and at what price; a financial discussion that explains how money will be raised and spent, and how long the company will take to make a profit; and biographies of the owners and managers, showing their experience and expertise.

Spell out the finances in detail. Include a projected income statement showing all anticipated sources of revenue and expenses, as well as a balance sheet that lists projected assets and liabilities. Also include a five-year forecast of cash flow—basically a view of whether you'll have enough cash coming in to meet expenses. Pay special attention to making accurate spending forecasts for such easy-to-underestimate outlays as those for marketing and professional services like legal and accounting fees.

Create customized versions for different readers. Keep the essential facts of your plan the same, of course, but tailor the narrative to answer specific readers' questions. If you are seeking a bank loan, for example, write a version that concentrates on your expected cash flow, since that's what will prove to the banker whether you can make the payments on your loan.

Raise cash. This is often the most critical and frustrating step. Besides traditional sources like family members, friends, banks, and venture-capital firms, be sure to try so-called angels—private investors who put money into promising start-ups. (For more on funding sources, see "How to Raise the Cash You Need" at right.)

Line up tax and legal counsel. Start your search for a pro by getting references from a few local businesspeople whom you respect. You need someone who understands and works with entrepreneurs. Also ask for referrals from local business groups such as the chamber of commerce.

One of the first things your lawyer should do is advise you on how to structure your company. Nine times out of 10, it's a good idea to incorporate, because it keeps the firm's assets and liabilities separate from yours, so creditors can't go after your home or property. The procedure for incorporating varies from state to state but generally takes two to four weeks and costs from $350 to $700, including attorney's fees.

If you do incorporate, you'll have to choose whether your firm will be what the Internal Revenue Service calls an "S" or a "C" corporation. For most start-ups, the S route makes sense. That way, all the company's income flows directly to its owners and is taxed at the individual rate rather than at the often higher corporate level. Plus, the income is taxed only once. In a C corporation, income gets taxed when it's earned by the firm, then again when the corporation pays you dividends. If you have a partner, your attorney should also draw up what is sometimes referred to as a "prenuptial" agreement—a contract specifying how you will divide business assets in case you break up or one of you dies. You might also use the agreement to stipulate how certain corporate decisions will be made. Figure on spending $750 to $2,500 for this vital document.

Your attorney's other major task will be to protect valuable original ideas or products.

Common sense dictates how much protection you need: If you're opening a standard dry cleaning company, you can probably skip it. But if you've got a catchy name or a particularly eye-grabbing logo, you should register it with the federal government's Patent and Trademark Office (cost: $1,000 to $3,000, including attorney's fees). If you've invented a new product or technology, you may need to file for a patent—a one- to three-year process that costs around $840 if you try to do it yourself, and upwards of $3,000 if, more sensibly, you hire a patent attorney.

Become a sales machine. Like it or not, once you launch your venture, selling will take up 80% to 95% of your time. "When I was starting out, I just got on the phone and sold, sold, sold," recalls John Arensmeyer. He made about 400 cold calls to marketing directors in the first four months alone, he says. But the effort paid off. His Sausalito, California company, which produces direct-mail promotions using computer disks, grossed in the "low to mid six figures" in 1990.

Move fast and hang loose. Finally, as a small-business owner, never forget that speed, creativity, and adaptability are your biggest competitive advantages. If something isn't working, junk it. If new market niches present themselves, seize them—fast. And keep your sense of humor always. Just ask Nancy Trent, founder of Trent & Company, a New York City-based public relations firm. When Trent landed her first big contract—a $120,000 deal in 1987—she worried that it would fall through if the client knew she was working from her apartment. So before the client's first visit, Trent moved her furniture out to the stairwell, installed temporary office trappings, and persuaded six friends to pose as employees. "The client later told me that he saw through the ruse," Trent laughs, "but thought that anyone who'd pull a stunt like that would work hard for him." The client was right: Trent's revenues have grown an average of 100% a year.

How to Raise the Cash You Need

Despite the credit crunch, you can still find money—if you know where to look.

Every start-up needs capital and, as a company founder, you'll need to become a skilled fund raiser—a job that is growing tougher and tougher. Pummeled by the recession and a rising tide of bad loans, nearly a third of banks surveyed by the Federal Reserve in January 1991 had tightened standards for small-business lending since October 1990. And U.S. venture-capital firms, which invested $2.9 billion in new companies in 1987, plowed in only half that sum in 1990.

Nevertheless, you can get the money you need. The problem is not a lack of funding sources but a lack of knowledge of how to find them. Here's a look at your 10 best cash sources, starting with the easiest to tap:

Your own resources. Dip into your own pockets first—and not just because it's convenient. The sooner you take outside money, the more ownership in your company you'll have to surrender. Draw on your bank and savings accounts first, then stocks, bonds, or mutual funds. (Try to hold back three months' living expenses for emergencies, however.)

Next, take advantage of the equity in your home. You can take out a second mortgage, but a more flexible approach might be to open a home-equity line of credit that you can draw on only as needed. In either case, the bank will lend you as much as 80% of your home's appraised value, and the interest on as much as $100,000 of the loan will be tax deductible.

As a last resort, consider dipping into your tax-deferred retirement accounts. But note: If you're younger than 59½, you'll pay a 10% penalty plus regular income tax on money from an Individual Retirement Account, and 10% plus tax on lump-sum distributions from a 401(k).

Friends and family. Turn to relatives, friends, and business associates next. Often, they aren't as worried about quick returns as other outside investors would be.

Outright gifts are one way to get such money. But, more often, you'll either have to borrow it or sell relatives a stake in the firm. If you borrow, keep the arrangement strictly business: Pick up a standard promissory note form at a stationery store, fill it out, and have your attorney review it at a fee of $150 or so. (You could also pay the lawyer $400 to $800 to draw up a more elaborate document from scratch.) And don't set the interest rate more than a point or so below prime. Otherwise, the Internal Revenue Service may consider the loan a gift and require the donor to pay gift tax. If you surrender equity, get your lawyer to write up the terms (cost: $500 to $1,000) to head off disputes later.

If Uncle Bob and Aunt Margie still hesitate to bet their nest egg on your bright idea, ask if they'd guarantee a loan instead.

Angels. The term "angel" refers to any informal private investor—often a businessperson like you who wants to put excess cash to work. According to a landmark 1988 study by Knoxville economist Robert Gaston, some 720,000 angels invest $32.7 billion of equity in small businesses each year, making them these firms'

Angling for an Angel

William Wetzel, Jr. of the University of New Hampshire, an expert on the business-funding benefactors called angels, talked with *Money* about tapping this key cash source:

What will an angel want to know about me? Mainly that you and the other managers of your company have integrity and competence, which you could demonstrate by providing six personal and professional references, for example. But angels are also motivated by nonfinancial considerations, like wanting to create jobs or develop socially useful technology. So be sure to mention any such benefits that your enterprise may entail.

What should I know about an angel? Get a résumé and two or three references, especially the names of other entrepreneurs he or she has financed. Then call them to see whether they were satisfied. Ask how much technical or management guidance the angel provided and whether it proved helpful or just meddlesome.

How much money should I ask for? As much as you need. Angels usually invest $25,000 to $50,000 each, but you can get more by dealing with five or six angels at once, since they sometimes prefer to invest as a group.

How should the investment be structured? It's best to give up straight equity—a percentage of ownership of your business, represented by common stock—rather than, say, a loan that can be converted into stock. The simpler the deal, the easier it will be to raise money from other investors later. And nail down the investor's exit options early. If he expects to cash out by selling securities back to you, be sure the terms are laid out in the agreement and tied to the firm's performance.

Can I swing the deal alone or should I get help? You will need a lawyer familiar with state and federal securities law. Your attorney should also be experienced in negotiating venture financing so he can help you get the best deal. Legal fees can run $10,000 to $20,000 for an uncomplicated $500,000 angel transaction—but if your lawyer saves you even 5% or 10% of your company's equity, that cost will be worth it.

largest source of equity capital. Still, finding an angel can be tough. Enlist the help of lawyers, accountants, bankers, and local business-people. You should concentrate your search within 50 miles of home, because angels usually like to keep an eye on their investments. The Association of Venture Clubs (c/o Jim Jensen, 265 East First South Street, Suite 300, Salt Lake City, UT 84111) keeps a list of about 100 venture clubs nationwide that bring together angels and entrepreneurs, and computerized services like the Venture Capital Network (617-253-7163) do the same thing. For advice on how to deal with an angel once you've found one, see the box at left.

Your suppliers and customers. Trade credit from suppliers, a type of loan often overlooked by small-business people, pumped a whopping $195 billion into small outfits in 1988, the most recent year for which reliable data are available. Established firms can get it most easily, of course, but start-ups sometimes qualify, too. You can also raise cash by demanding early payment from customers.

Banks. The founders of small start-ups have always had trouble getting commercial bank loans, and today it's tougher than ever. Very few banks are interested in making $50,000 loans that take as much paperwork as $500,000 loans at only a tenth of the profit. (See "Bargaining with a Banker" at right.)

The SBA. If you're turned down for a bank loan, don't give up: Ask whether that same bank would make the loan if it were guaranteed by the Small Business Administration (SBA). The federal agency's guaranteed loan program—which helped 16,730 small businesses borrow $3.8 billion in fiscal 1990—can back as much as 85% of loans of up to $750,000 (the average is $230,000) from both bank and regulated nonbank lenders, such as the Money Store. The SBA caps rates at $2\frac{1}{4}$ to $2\frac{3}{4}$ points over prime, plus a fee equal to 2% of the loan. About a quarter of such loans go to start-ups.

Seek your loan, if possible, at an institution that the agency has designated as a Preferred or Certified lender (call your local SBA office to find one), since that will speed the paperwork. If you don't have an accountant or lawyer to help you, ask the bank to recommend a loan packager who can complete the complex paperwork (cost: about $1,000).

The SBA also makes direct loans to certain types of small businesses, such as those headed by Vietnam veterans or the disabled. And if you need funds for research and development, the SBA-administered Small Business Innovation Research program (800-U-ASK-SBA) made R&D grants totaling $432 million in fiscal 1990 to small businesses.

Your city or state. As traditional sources of capital have grown stingier, state and local governments have become more generous. Start your search for such funds with the mayor's or county executive's office, which can direct you to the official or department in charge of economic development. Set up a meeting to discuss financing, stressing how your business will benefit the area.

The state economic development agency in your state capital should be your next stop. Or consult the biannual *States and Small Business* guide (Government Printing Office; 202-783-3238), which lists major state aid programs.

Venture-capital firms. The ideal candidate for venture capital—equity funds placed by an investment firm that backs unproven young businesses—is a one- or two-year-old company that has the potential to quintuple in value within three to five years. Venture firms typically invest a minimum of $500,000 to $1 million. If your business qualifies, consult your library's *Pratt's Guide to Venture Capital Sources* for firm names. Then seek a lawyer or an accountant who can give you a personal introduction to nearby ones. But be prepared for frustrations. You may have to shop around.

Corporate partners. In lieu of venture capital, some small firms are forming partnerships with larger companies; experts estimate that 40% to 60% of Fortune 500 companies are involved in such deals. The advantage to you, of course, is access to capital. Your partner, in turn, gets into

Bargaining with a Banker

William J. Rossman, who is president and CEO of Mid-State Bank & Trust in Altoona, Pennsylvania and first vice president of Robert Morris Associates, a trade association for bank lenders, gave *Money* the following tips on the best way to go after a bank loan:

How should I prepare myself when I first meet with my banker? Bring your business plan and three of your latest tax returns. Be ready to say how you intend to use the loan, and what your company's balance sheet will look like during the next three years. You might also consult Robert Morris Associates' *Annual Statement Studies* at your public library beforehand, so that you can compare your company's key financial ratios to the norm for your industry. If they are at variance, the banker will want to know why.

What should I look out for in the loan document? Try to strip out any terms that you may not be able to live up to. For example, the bank might try to stick you with a debt-to-worth ratio—a measure of how much debt you have for each dollar of equity—that your profits simply can't sustain.

What if I'm turned down? Be persistent. Ask why the bank rejected your application. Ask to have it re-evaluated—after making any changes the bank suggests. And try other banks, too, of course.

How can I make my case more effectively so I'll have a better chance of getting a loan? Come in with a confident, positive attitude and present your business in an honest manner, pointing out its hazards as well as its promise. Bankers want to know whether you have a realistic attitude and have planned for the inevitable setbacks.

Can I bargain for a better loan rate? Yes. Go to more than one bank, and play each off the other in negotiating. Some banks require a business to open a deposit account before they'll lend. Ask about special deals: If you have an account, you might be able to negotiate the loan rate down by one-half to 1½ percentage points. But always choose the bank that best meets your needs, such as one that won't change loan officers on you every few months; that might not be the one that offers the lowest rate.

an attractive market instantly and ultimately shares in your profits. As your business grows, a good partner may also bring a distribution network, licensing fees, or joint product development opportunities that stop competitors from leapfrogging you. One more tip: Look first for a partner among your big customers or suppliers.

The stock market. You probably have a better chance of being struck by lightning than of taking your start-up public, especially if you need less than $5 million. The market for small initial public offerings, or IPOs, has been comatose since the stock market crash of 1987 (only 65 small companies went public in 1990, raising a feeble $495.7 million, as against 292 issues worth $3.6 billion in 1986). Even if you qualify, fees and expenses will chomp 15% to 20% out of the capital you raise. Nevertheless, it's an option worth considering. For companies with proprietary products or unique services in a "hot" industry, an IPO just might find a market.

Finding the Right Location

Hunting for a locale used to be as scientific as using a divining rod to find water. Now, smart owners check out the demographics.

Finding the right location for a small business these days demands as much science as art. Whether you're launching a new company, moving an existing one, or merely opening a branch office, you'll need to draw on everything from market research to consumer psychology to find the optimal site. Such information was once too expensive for smaller firms to afford. Today, though, you can get much of it free from the chamber of commerce and other public or civic groups, or at prices as low as $100 from private demographic research firms like Urban Decision Systems of Los Angeles or National Planning Data in Ithaca, New York.

To be sure, data gathering is no substitute for common sense, and you will have plenty of legwork to do on your own. When used properly, however, demographic research can function like a safety net—not necessarily guiding you to the perfect location, but at least steering you away from a choice so poor that it could spell disaster.

If you are like most businesspeople—including 80% of those who launch start-ups—you'll stay right in the town where you now live. Choosing a location, then, will be an exercise of microresearch that takes place in your own backyard. Your first step is to learn all you can about your best customers—either who they are or, for first-time owners, who they will be. Don't mistake them for your steadiest customers. The regular who stops by a convenience store every day for a doughnut and a cup of coffee may not spend half as much as the harried father who rushes in once a week to buy two $11 boxes of Pampers. Your aim should be to figure out the basic demographics and habits of your clientele so you can seek locations where they are plentiful.

If you already run a business, two of their most important characteristics—their spending habits and addresses—may already be in your back invoices. Or you can gather this information directly by asking customers to fill out a short questionnaire. If you're launching a new company, you'll have to substitute guesswork for some of this research. But you can at least visit firms like the one you plan to open and eyeball the clientele.

Once you know who your best customers are (or will be), start looking for neighborhoods where lots of them live. You will probably want to locate your business in or near such a spot. Here's where a little demographic research can help. Start your quest at the chamber of commerce, city planning commission, economic development agency, or local office of the U.S. Census Bureau. These groups often have valuable demographic data—average family income, length of residence, age of house, and so forth—for each of your city's census tracts (one tract contains roughly 4,000 people). Such data, available free or at a nominal cost of $10 or so, may give you clues on picking the choicest location. A hardware store, for instance, might benefit from moving to a neighborhood where relatively well-to-do young families are moving into older homes, on the presumption that many of them will want to do major renovations.

If you are willing to spend a little extra money, you can turn to private demographic and life-style database firms for some of this information. The seven biggest ones are: CACI (800-292-2224); Claritas (703-683-8300); Donnelley Marketing Information Services (800-866-2255); Equifax (800-866-6510); National Demographics & Lifestyles (800-525-3533); National Planning Data (607-273-8208); and Urban Decision Systems (800-633-9568). For $100 or so, most will furnish basic demographic data on some or all of your metro area. For another $150, they'll prepare a custom report that shows which neighborhoods would be most promising for your business. If you are opening an Italian restaurant, for instance, Equifax can tell you how often people in each census tract dine in ethnic eateries—and how much they spend.

Several of the firms help you home in on desirable customers by subdividing residents according to their buying habits and preferences. Claritas, for example, has assigned every zip code in the nation to one of some 40 colorfully named life-style groups.

If, say, you were looking to start a beverage store that specialized in imported beer, you might search out zip codes like 95132 (San Jose)—part of Claritas' "Young Suburbia" group. Residents there show a strong preference for foreign over domestic brews. But Claritas might steer you away from zips like 22190 (Waterford, Virginia, part of "God's Country"), where the average age and income are similar to those of 95132 but where people prefer the good old American stuff. Claritas will charge you $500 or so to produce a customized report along these lines.

Be warned, though, that you cannot rely solely on research reports in your hunt. Demographic information is sometimes out of date. Moreover, much information at the block-by-block level comes from computer estimates, not hard numbers. So you must always double-check the data yourself. You must also keep in mind how large the trade area will be for your firm. That's the region around your shop from which you draw 60% to 80% of your customers.

The trade area for most small businesses is about three to five miles in radius. But it can be much larger or smaller; for a radio-dispatched computer repair company, for instance, it could be 20 or 30 miles wide. The trade area is important because it tells you how near you need to be to your best customers. Ideally, you should seek a location that includes the maximum number of choice neighborhoods within your trade area's radius.

Once you have several locations in mind for your business, begin winnowing them down. Visit city hall or the planning office to see whether zoning regulations would keep you out (retailers and restaurateurs: Pay particular attention to regulations governing signs). Also find out if planned roads or developments could affect your choice.

Next, rule out spots that your competitors already control. The simplest way is to check their addresses in the Yellow Pages or your industry's business directory. Data-base firms can help in this phase of your research, too. If you are opening a fried chicken outlet in Boston, for instance, you could order a map of existing fast-food restaurants in the metro area from Equifax for $350. But make sure the information is up to date. Equifax updates its restaurant data base from phone books and business directories every year, which is adequate. But if the data are more than, say, two years old, then you might as well forget about them.

You should now have narrowed your search to one or two neighborhoods. If so, start looking at individual properties. Scan through commercial real estate listings in the classified section of your newspaper or seek out a commercial real estate broker. If your business caters to the retail trade, where location is critical to sales, you should look at five sites or so before renting. If you're a wholesaler looking for warehouse space, you might be able to get away with inspecting three or fewer. In either case, sit down at the end of your visits and rank the properties according to basic real estate criteria like the ones listed below:

Cost versus value. Which site offers the best market for the price? In a mall, for example, you can count on anchor stores to draw shoppers, but you pay for it. A nearby strip shopping center may attract sufficient customers at 10% to 30% less in rent. And if you are starting a business consulting firm, you may be able to get by with not-so-posh digs if clients rarely visit your office.

Access and traffic patterns. Are there major streets nearby? Can customers—or your employees—drive in and out easily? Is the traffic flow sufficient? Don't rely on data from the mall developer or broker. Instead, gather your own data and do on-site research.

Physical characteristics. Is the building attractive and well maintained? Does it have ample parking? Will your retail outlet be visible from the street? If you are in need of warehouse space, is it sufficient? If a problem should crop up—such as a burst pipe or an electrical short—how quickly will the management make the necessary repairs?

Leasing terms. With many regions in a real estate slump these days—rental rates for commercial office space have dropped about 12% on average over the past two years—you are likely to find plenty of bargains. Concessions of as much as 30% are common on existing office space in some cities. Of course, market research and demographics alone cannot make the decision for you. Give your instincts plenty of play. But if your intuition is balanced by the right kind of information, you're less likely to go wrong. Then you can enjoy choosing many more sites in the future as your business grows.

Buying a Business Readymade

Solid small companies are trading at bargain prices these days. To snag one with real potential, follow these rules of buying and selling.

Attention, small-business shoppers: Your timing is perfect. While big companies tagged with "For Sale" signs wither on the vine, small operations are being snapped up like bottles of vintage champagne. True, aggregate sales figures are notoriously difficult to compile in the highly localized field of small-business

transactions. But the newsletter *Mergerstat Review* estimates that fully 30% more businesses in the $5-million-and-under range were sold in 1990 than in 1989, while prices dropped 11% because of the soft economy.

The principal advantage of buying an existing business, rather than starting one from scratch, is that you face less risk when you take over a firm that is already up and—you hope—prospering. But just because the risk is lower and the market is hot, don't expect buying a small business to be a snap. Acquiring the right company makes even the ordeal of closing on a house look easy.

As in a home purchase, your basic strategy is to survey the market, make a choice, and then negotiate hard. But you'll also have to research the company's history and earnings potential and then, before you settle on the price, exhaustively analyze the company's worth. The entire purchasing process can take as much as two years and cost from $30,000 to more than $100,000, largely in legal and accounting fees.

The first question to answer, of course, is what type of business you want. Most experts advise that you stick with an industry you already know. If you're hankering for something new, you may find that your skills can be applied in an industry only distantly related to your current one. The manager of an auto manufacturing plant might find that his skills suit him to run most any kind of assembly line, from one that makes aircraft parts to one that makes golf carts. (If you yearn to range even farther afield, you might buy a franchise; see the box on page 72.)

One systematic way to search for related businesses is through the *Standard Industrial Classification Manual,* which is available at most libraries. This 705-page tome, compiled by the federal Office of Management and Budget, divides all U.S. industries into nine major categories and thousands of subcategories. Fields related to construction, for example, include everything from land clearing to sprinkler-system installation.

Once you pinpoint an industry, look for specific companies. First, though, decide whether you want to manage the business yourself or hire pros to do it. If you prefer the hands-on approach, go after any business you can afford. If you want others to take charge, you need a business with enough gross revenues (generally $5 million or more a year) to cover the cost of their salaries.

To identify specific companies, work the grapevine of local accountants, attorneys, and bankers, as well as suppliers to the industry that interests you. Accountants can be especially useful, since they're often the first to know when a client wants to sell. You could also consult lists of buyers and sellers, like the quarterly *World M&A Network* ($335 a year; 202-628-6900) and *Admax* (single issue $25, $45 for three months, $150 a year; 800-327-9630).

Besides searching on your own, you might enlist the help of a business broker or two. Like real estate brokers, they usually work for the seller (who generally pays a 10% commission for small businesses), so you must sometimes take their observations with a grain of salt. But knowledgeable brokers can provide the names of four or five businesses for sale of the type you're seeking, plus information on each firm's history, finances, management, and worth. To find a broker, seek leads from friends, business acquaintances, and your accountant. You could also call professional groups like the International Business Brokers Association (508-369-2490) in Concord, Massachusetts. Look for brokers who have experience in your area of interest. And use only those who have closed five to 10 deals in the past two years to be sure they're experienced.

After you've chosen a company to bid on, your real work begins. The first step is to have the owners sign a letter of intent—you'll sign it, too—in which they promise not to sell the business to anyone else while you research its value. This document, which should be drawn up by your attorney (average cost: $1,500), will indicate a tentative sale price. But that price will be subject to change based on what you, your attorney, and your accountant discover when you tackle the next two formidable tasks: due diligence and valuation.

Due diligence, which ordinarily takes 60 to 90 days and costs $20,000 to $60,000 in legal, accounting, and research fees, is basically an intensive homework assignment in which you and your advisers examine the health of the company. Start by asking for key documents—five years of financial statements, tax returns, and budgets—plus lists of accounts payable and receivable, inventory, and equipment. Then ask for copies of agreements with major customers and suppliers, checking to see whether the company has done its work on schedule and paid its bills on time. Have your lawyer investigate any lawsuits against the company that could hurt your bottom line. Check the status of the firm's facilities to see, for example, if an important lease is about to expire. And talk to major customers to see if they're satisfied with the company's service. If the owners won't provide this kind of information, that's a strong warning sign about the company.

At the same time, you must decide what the company is really worth. Don't try to do it alone; get a certified appraiser familiar with the industry to do it under your close supervision (to find a suitable pro, call the American Society of Appraisers at 800-ASA-VALU). The reason is that there are at least a dozen common methods of valuation and, because each

Franchises: Shortcut to Success

Buying a franchise combines the excitement of starting a business with the safety net of the franchisor's system, which can dictate everything from storefront design to sales reporting. Plus, studies show that fewer than 5% of franchise outlets fail every year, compared with nearly 8% of start-ups. Nevertheless, franchising can be risky. Here's how to proceed:

Don't go into a business you know. Contrary to the advice when buying a business, in franchising it is actually harder to succeed in a field you already know—since your ingrained habits keep you from adhering to the franchisor's formula. For a list of the roughly 2,400 franchises available worldwide (about 90% are U.S.-based), call 800-543-1038 to order the International Franchise Association's *Franchise Opportunities Guide* ($15 plus $5 shipping).

Review all documents thoroughly. Write or call the franchisor for a copy of its 50- to 100-page Uniform Franchise Offering Circular (UFOC), which is required by federal law to disclose 22 categories of information ranging from corporate financial results to the franchise agreement. Then have your attorney review it thoroughly (legal fees: $500 to $1,500). Watch out for:

• Renewal policy. A typical franchise contract lasts 10 to 15 years. Check that you won't have to pay a second franchise fee—which can range from $1,500 to $50,000—when you renew. Also, if fewer than 90% of franchisees are renewing, it could mean many are unhappy with the company.

• Exclusivity. Verify that another franchisee can't open up shop near enough to cut into your business.

• Trademark registration. Make sure the company name and logo are trademarked. If they're not, or if the trademarks are being contested in court, you could wind up erecting new signs and changing order forms—and everything else—at your expense.

Do some independent digging. The UFOC tells you the length and content of the franchisor's training program, for example, but not whether it's any good. Yet, 50% of franchisees in one recent survey said their training was either barely adequate or poor. So call or visit seven to 10 franchisees (the UFOC lists them) to learn the real story. Also ask questions like: How much did it really cost to get started? How much did you make the first year? And, most important, would you buy the franchise again?

Scrutinize start-up costs. Most will be stated in the UFOC, including the franchise fee, the monthly royalty (generally 4% to 10% of sales), and an advertising fee (1% to 3%). But you'll also need money for working capital, inventory, construction, and equipment. The total tab for opening a McDonald's, for example, could easily go as high as $600,000.

Now look for financing. It's easier to raise money for a franchise than for an independent business, since the failure rate is lower. Gulf American (800-228-9868), for example, a small-business lending company in Panama City, Florida, gives franchise loans averaging $325,000 with no points and an adjustable interest rate for terms of seven to 25 years. A few franchisors will even advance you part of the cash themselves. You'll find a list of them in the IFA's spring/summer guide.

approach yields a slightly different view of the company's worth, you should use at least two or three of them. For example, the so-called fair-market-value-of-assets approach essentially answers the question: How much are this company's plant, machinery, and other properties really worth? That's important to know if you're buying a company that has tangible assets—a machine shop, say, that owns the building and the land it stands on—but less critical with a service business like a small insurance company that has only its office equipment for tangible property. A method called discounted future earnings, on the other hand, could be useful for valuing any company; it answers the question: How much will I earn on my investment?

Be aware also that in closely held companies, the profit-and-loss statement and balance sheet don't always tell the full story. An owner-manager may have been paying himself a $200,000 salary, for example, when you could hire someone to run things for less than half that. For more information, consult *Valuing Small Businesses and Professional Practices* by Shannon Pratt (Business One Irwin). If your due diligence has been thorough, your assessor could complete his valuation in just a few weeks at a cost of $10,000 or so. If he or she needs to gather more data, though, this part of the acquisition process could run 60 to 90 days and cost as much as $50,000.

After you've investigated the firm and assessed its value, you'll make one more key decision: whether to buy its stock outright or only its assets. You may want to avoid a stock purchase, for example, if you're going after a construction firm or a chemicals company that could be facing outstanding damage lawsuits from injured workers or customers. When you buy stock, you inherit the company's prior legal liabilities, whereas when you purchase its assets, you do not. Thus, if the company was a gasoline distributorship that happened to be fighting a couple of lawsuits for fuel spills, you could acquire its trucks and customer lists without being held liable for earlier pollution (you'd still be liable if one of your trucks dumped fuel the next day, however).

Only after you've taken all these safeguards can you safely hammer out a final contract of sale and seek financing. Banks and venture capitalists are unlikely to lend more than about 50% of the company's asset value (for tips on how to raise money from them, see "How to Raise the Cash You Need" on page 65). So ask the current owner to lend you some of the money. Realistic sellers know they're going to have to take back a promissory note for some of their sale price. A business owner may finance as much as two-thirds of the deal, with the money paid back in monthly installments at interest rates equal to or slightly below prime.

Finally, buying a business is so complex that you should always proceed slowly and methodically. Your most valuable asset—even more than cash, loans, or astute advisers—will be patience.

I was thrown out of college for cheating on the metaphysics exam; I looked into the soul of the boy next to me. — Woody Allen

COLLEGE

The Low-Cost Approach to Higher Education

Given the cost of college today, your child's education can easily become the biggest expenditure of your lifetime. The annual charges for tuition, fees, room, and board reached $5,248 at public colleges and universities in the 1990-91 academic year and $13,318 at private institutions. And that's just the average. A year at Harvard will set you back $22,080.

To make matters worse, reasonably priced financial help for middle-income parents is disappearing. Just 10 years ago, any student could get a low-cost federal loan. Today, such loans are available only to students deemed needy under a government-approved formula that, in some cases, rules out families earning as little as $35,000. As a result, middle-class parents must fall back on their own resources.

In this chapter, *Money* tells you how to invest to build your college fund (see the story on page 76), get the best deal on financial aid (page 80), and borrow wisely to close the gap (page 85). But, most important, you'll learn that, contrary to what you may think, you don't have to pay top dollar for a high-quality education. *Money*'s analysis found that America's top college value today is Rice University, which charges $12,600 for tuition, room, and board—a little over half the cost of Harvard with no drop-off in the education delivered. And Rice is not the only superb value. Beginning on page 165, you'll find out about the 100 public and private schools that offer the best education for the money. Then, starting on page 167, we compare tuition and fees, the cost of room and board, the average amount of financial aid, and other vital information on 1,011 four-year colleges and universities.

You can almost always find comparable value at a lower price. If your child is interested in a program at a school with a tuition of $16,000 a year, why not look at one of the same quality that costs only $12,000? The information in this chapter and *Money*'s College Value Rankings can help you get your money's worth.

Smart Investing and Savings Moves You Can Make Now for College

Whether your child is into rattles or rap music, there are ways you can be sure of meeting the challenge of college costs.

If you think paying for college is getting tougher, you're right: During the 10 years through 1989, American families' median income grew by only 2.3% after inflation, while the annual charges for tuition, fees, room, and board jumped an average of 30.7% at public colleges and universities and 50.5% at private institutions during the same period. With relatively moderate increases in 1990 of 2.4% and 4.8%, respectively, the average bill was: public, $5,248; private, $13,318. You can't control those costs, but you can find ways to pile up money for them whether your child is a toddler or a teenager.

Since your best strategy will depend on how much time you have before your first tuition bill, this story has been divided into three sections that describe investments that are most suitable for families with kids 10 or more years away from college, five years away, and only one year away.

The general rules on the pages that follow can help you avoid the most common mistakes made by parents of college-bound children:

For long-term growth, you must own stocks.
You may be tempted to lock in safe yields with such standbys as certificates of deposit and Treasury bills. But their yields probably won't keep pace with college costs, which are expected to rise about 7% a year for the next decade, while inflation averages 5%. According to data from Ibbotson Associates, a Chicago

investment research firm, T-bills have lagged inflation by 0.2 percentage points a year during the past half-century. Only a well-diversified portfolio that includes stocks as well as bonds and cash can deliver the growth you need without the risk of severe losses. Although stocks fluctuate in value more widely than other assets, they generally post much larger gains over long periods.

Using Ibbotson data, Ken Gregory, editor of the newsletter *L/G No-Load Fund Analyst* in San Francisco, found that stocks have delivered average annual returns of 10.3% over the 56 separate 10-year periods since 1926, beating out the 4.6% return of medium-term Treasury bonds and the 3.5% posted by short-term Treasury bills.

Yet, you don't want to put all of your money in stocks even when your child is still in diapers. Based on past performance, an all-stock portfolio could drop as much as 43% in a single year. And stocks occasionally deliver subpar performance over periods of as long as a decade.

Don't count on financial aid. If you meet the income limits described in the worksheet, "Estimate Your Share of the Tab" on pages 82-83, you may end up getting substantial help from the government and the school your child attends. But if college is more than a couple of years off, you have no reliable way of estimating how much. The rules may change, as may your own finances.

There are other reasons to save as much as you can. Raymond Loewe, president of College Money, a Marlton, New Jersey firm that helps parents plan for college bills, estimates that a typical family with an annual income of $66,000, a net worth of $266,000 (including home equity), and one child entering college this fall would be asked to pay as much as $17,800 of each year's college costs.

Don't rely on your home equity as a substitute for college savings. Many homeowners reaped windfall profits during the real estate boom of the 1970s and early 1980s. But most analysts expect housing prices to outpace inflation by no more than one percentage point over the next decade.

Don't look for the perfect college investment. There are no special high-yielding, ultrasafe investments just right for parents of college-bound kids. Banks, brokers, and other financial institutions often label ordinary products—ranging from zero-coupon bonds to variable-rate CDs—as ideal college investments. But no single investment can be guaranteed to grow as fast as college costs.

Start saving now. If you set aside even small amounts each month, you can end up with surprisingly large sums, given enough time.

Think twice before investing in your son's or daughter's name. Under current law, the first $500 of a child's investment income is not taxed and the next $500 is taxed at the child's rate; but anything above $1,000 is taxed at the parent's rate until the child is 14, eliminating most of the tax benefits. And if you expect to qualify for financial aid, you're far better off

A Guide to the Leading Loans

The table below describes the most widely available education loans. (State- and school-sponsored loans as well as other attractive borrowing options are described in the accompanying story.) Any credit-worthy family facing college education bills is eligible; there are no maximum income limits. The loans are made through banks, savings and loans, and other lenders. For more information, call the sponsor's 800 number. Except where noted, rates are variable and have no caps.

Name	Sponsor	Maximum amount	Rate equals...	Maximum term	Up-front fees	Repayment deferral
PLUS	U.S. Department of Education 800-562-6872	$4,000 a year per child	One-year T-bill rate plus 3.25 percentage points adjusted annually; 12% cap. Recent rate: 9.3%	10 years	3%	Principal and interest only, depending on lender
PLATO	University Support Services Inc. 800-767-5626	$25,000 a year per child	Greater of 30- or 90-day commercial paper rate plus 4.85 percentage points, adjusted monthly. Recent rate: 10.75%	15 years	4% plus $55	Principal
TERI	The Education Resources Institute 800-255-8374	$20,000 a year per child	Prime rate plus 1.5 to 2 percentage points, adjusted monthly. Recent rate: 10% to 10.5%	20 years	5%	Principal
EXCEL and SHARE	Nellie Mae Inc. 800-634-9308	$20,000 a year per child	Prime rate plus 2 percentage points, adjusted monthly. Recent rate: 10.5%. Also available: fixed rate, prime plus three to four points. Recent rate: 11.95%	20 years	5%	Principal
Knight Extended Re-payment Plan	Knight Tuition Payment Plans 800-225-6783	Full cost of education	91-day T-bill rate plus 4.5 percentage points, adjusted quarterly; 18% cap. Recent rate: 9.5%	10 years	$55	None
ABLE	Knight Tuition Payment Plans 800-225-6783	Full cost of education	Prime rate plus 2.5 percentage points, adjusted quarterly; 18% cap. Recent rate: 11.5%	15 years	$55	None
ExtraCredit	The College Board 800-874-9390	Full cost of education	91-day T-bill rate plus 4.5 percentage points, adjusted quarterly; 18% cap. Recent rate: 9.5%	15 years	$45	None

keeping your college savings in your name. Reason: Children are expected to contribute up to 35% of their savings to college costs, parents only 5.6% at most.

Now you're ready to begin investing. The three model portfolios that follow were devised by Roger Gibson, a highly regarded Pittsburgh investment adviser and author of *Asset Allocation: Balancing Financial Risk* (Business One Irwin). His guiding principle is that you want to invest more conservatively as you get closer to needing the money. Gibson recommends the first of the three portfolios for savings that you will not have to draw on for at least 10 years. The second is suitable for savings that you will start spending in about five years; the third is for savings that your family must begin to spend within a year or so. If you have more than one child headed for college, you can divide your savings into separate portfolios and invest the money according to the children's different ages.

Investors with savings of less than $10,000 should stick with mutual funds that hold diversified portfolios of stocks, bonds, or other assets.

If you are starting out with no savings at all, you will have to build up and diversify your portfolio in stages. Later, you may be dealing with sizable sums; when rearranging your portfolio, shift your money gradually from one investment to another to reduce the risk of selling stocks or bonds at an unfavorable moment. For example, if you are transferring $10,000 from stocks to cash, shift $2,500 every six months over two years.

Ten or More Years to Go

Stocks: 65%; bonds: 20%; cash: 15%. Expected annual return: 10%.

Based on historical performance data, a portfolio like the one above can be expected to earn a compound annual return of 10% over 10 years or longer and to decline by more than 6% in only one out of every six years. For added safety and growth potential, you should split your equity holdings among different types of stocks or mutual funds. Start by investing about a third of the money earmarked for equities in blue-chip stocks, which are shares of leading companies with strong finances, steady earnings, and dividend growth.

Hugh Johnson, chief investment officer of First Albany, a brokerage firm in Albany, New York, recommends companies that have sales of $5 billion or more with low to moderate debt, average earnings growth of 8% or better over the past five years, and dividend yields of at least 3%.

Put another third of your equity investments in large-company growth stocks, which are shares of companies with well-established products in fast-growing markets. Such companies should see better earnings growth than most firms.

Investment advisers urge even cautious investors to put 15% of their equity stake in mutual funds that hold small-company growth stocks, which include shares of companies with annual revenues of less than $500 million. Such stocks gained 27% during the first six months of 1991, nearly double the 14% gain of the S&P 500. Despite that surge, many analysts maintained that small stocks were cheap compared with large-company stocks, which rose far faster for most of the past decade.

For added diversification, invest another 15% of your equity holdings in mutual funds that purchase overseas stocks.

When buying bonds, you can eliminate the danger of default by going with Treasury securities, since the federal government backs their principal and interest payments. The price of Treasuries will vary as interest rates fluctuate, but if you hold them to maturity, you will always get back your principal in full. Your best choices are the intermediate-term Treasury notes, which mature in three to 10 years. Over the past 15 years, such issues have delivered total annual returns of 10%, topping the 9.6% returns for long-term government bonds, and they were 40% less volatile—their prices moved in a narrower range.

Investors should also consider the tax-free yields of high-quality municipal bonds; for people in the 28% federal tax bracket or above (taxable income of more than $35,800 a year for couples, $21,450 for singles), a yield of 6.5%, for example, is equivalent to a taxable payout of 9% or better. For safety, most analysts recommend buying five or more different tax-exempt issues, which requires a stake of at least $25,000. Or you can buy shares in a mutual fund, making sure that at least 90% of its portfolio consists of bonds rated A or better. Be aware, however, that some advisers do not recommend bond funds for money you will need at a specific time, since fund shares may be trading for less than you originally paid when you need to redeem them.

For the cash portion of your portfolio, consider short-term bond funds, which offer better yields than savings accounts or money-market funds, with little added risk.

Five Years to Go

Stocks: 45%; bonds: 20%; cash: 35%. Expected annual return: 9%.

Around the time that your child enters junior high school, you should begin to shift your savings into safer investments. The above portfolio will cut your expected annual return to about 9%, but, on the positive side, your losses will usually be limited to 2% or so in any single year.

To reduce your risk further, replace the international and small-company stockholdings recommended in the previous section with more conservative total-return stocks, which pay above-average dividend yields. Among such stocks, First Albany's Hugh Johnson favors companies with five-year profit growth of 12% or better, dividend yields of at least 3.5%, and P/E ratios no higher than their average P/E over the past decade.

Your taxable fixed-income holdings should remain in Treasuries. But when you buy more of them, stick to issues that will mature around the time that your child will enter college. That way you can avoid selling bonds before maturity, when they may be worth less than face value.

Firm up your cash position by moving half your stash into a government money fund. Such funds invest in Treasury bills and short-term securities issued by government agencies, so they are virtually free of default risk. Moreover, the interest they pay is usually exempt from state and local taxes, which boosts the effective yield by roughly half a percentage point.

How Much Must You Save?

Use this worksheet to figure out how much you must set aside each year for future college costs. The calculation assumes the following: your child will enter college at age 18, at which point you will stop saving; your investments will earn 8% a year after taxes as long as the money lasts; and you will make your contributions at the end of each year.

1. Current annual college costs (use $5,248 average for public school and $13,318 for private; or use the cost of a specific school) _____

2. Future costs of first year of college (line 1 times factor from column A in the table below) _____

3. Future total cost of four years of college (line 2 times 3.91) _____

4. Amount you need to invest at the end of each year (line 3 times factor from column B below) _____

AGE OF CHILD	A	B
Newborn	3.38	0.0267
1	3.16	0.0296
2	2.95	0.0330
3	2.76	0.0368
4	2.58	0.0413
5	2.41	0.0465
6	2.25	0.0527
7	2.10	0.0601
8	1.97	0.0690
9	1.84	0.0801
10	1.72	0.0940
11	1.61	0.1121
12	1.50	0.1363
13	1.40	0.1705
14	1.31	0.2219
15	1.23	0.3080
16	1.14	0.4808
17	1.07	1.0000

Source: Moss Adams, Seattle

One Year to Go

Stocks: 30%; bonds: 15%; cash: 55%. Expected annual return: 8%.

When your child is within a year or two of college, you should further prune your stockholdings, although you will still want the growth that stocks can provide during the four or five years that your son or daughter is in school. You can expect an average annual return of about 8% on the portfolio above, with little likelihood of significant losses. The stocks you continue to hold should be total-return issues (or mutual funds invested in them). For bonds, stay with short-term Treasury notes maturing at the time you must pay college bills, and keep your cash in government money funds.

That simple strategy is not advisable, however, if you think your family will qualify for financial aid. In that case, you should sell all the stocks and bonds on which you have capital gains by the end of the calendar year in which your child becomes a high school junior. Reason: Under financial aid rules, you will be expected to contribute to college costs as much as 47% of any capital gains realized during the year before you apply for assistance, but only 5.6% of your assets.

If your savings fall short of the amount you need, don't be disheartened. For one thing, you can probably cover a lot of the remaining costs out of your current income. But you should probably continue to make contributions to IRAs, Keoghs, 401(k) plans, and similar accounts that you can fund with pretax earnings, even if that means you must borrow money to pay college costs. That's because the tax savings and other benefits, such as company matching contributions to 401(k) plans, usually outweigh the cost of loans.

The table on page 77 lists the leading federal, nonprofit, and commercial programs that offer low-cost loans to parents of college students whether or not they qualify for financial aid. Often, such loans allow parents to put off some or all of their loan payments until the child graduates from college.

Parents who bought homes in the 1970s or early 1980s may have substantial equity to borrow against. Interest on a home-equity loan of as much as $100,000 is tax deductible. For a borrower in the 28% federal income tax bracket, that reduces the net cost of a home-equity loan from a 10.2% rate, for example, to about 7.3%.

When you combine all of the tools at your disposal, you may find that paying for college is easier than you thought.

How to Win the Financial Aid Game

Learning the unspoken rules can improve your chances of getting the money you need.

Competing fiercely for fewer kids, colleges are increasingly using beefed-up financial aid packages to attract outstanding prospects. The competitive spirit may soon take hold even among the 30 or so elite schools like Harvard, Yale, and Princeton that routinely reject far more applicants than they admit. In 1991, the eight Ivy League colleges avoided federal antitrust charges by agreeing not to exchange information about their financial aid practices or to coordinate their awards. The colleges had argued that it was in the best interest of the students to receive identical aid packages from the schools. That way, students who got into two or more of the Ivies could choose among them on factors other than cost. But critics, including the Justice Department, contended that the system deprived students of the benefits of open-price competition. Although the Ivies say they still plan to grant aid strictly on the basis of financial need, at least the possibility now exists that they will vie for the best scholars with financial incentives.

This new competitive atmosphere may boost your son's or daughter's chances of finding one or more colleges willing to offer all the aid you need, preferably with a package that's heavy on grants and scholarships and light on loans. This story will tell you how to apply for aid and will take you inside the decision-making process so that you can be sure to get every penny you deserve.

Will any colleges reject your child just because he or she asks for financial help? That's the first question on many parents' minds and, indeed, some prestigious schools, including Brown and Smith, publicly acknowledge that they reject some otherwise qualified candidates because they cannot afford to give them sufficient financial help. But don't let that keep you from applying for aid. For one thing, if you need substantial help to pay college bills, who else is going to give it to you? And, in general, a request for money doesn't hurt students who comfortably meet the college's academic standards. "Non-need blind admissions policies affect marginal students who need lots of aid," says Kalman Chany, president of Campus Consultants, a New York City firm that advises parents applying for financial aid.

Ideally, you could find out whether your family qualified for aid—and for how much—before your child even applied to a college. That way, you could shop around knowing how much each school would cost. But you won't get that kind of information from college financial aid officers. "We don't want to give parents an answer up front, then have to backpedal and create bad feelings after we get their financial aid application," says Michael

Brown, director of financial aid at Union College in Schenectady, New York.

That doesn't mean your child must shop in the dark, however. Schools calculate financial aid by first figuring out how much you can afford to pay—what financial aid officers call your "expected family contribution." The

Filling Out Those Fussy Forms

You enter the financial aid sweepstakes by completing one or more of the applications described below. All of them, available from high school guidance offices, ask for detailed information about your income, savings, and investments. You mail your applications to the company listed on the form, which calculates the amount of money you will be expected to contribute toward your child's college expenses; the result is sent to the schools you designate. Although colleges' deadlines vary, try to apply for aid as soon as possible after the new year—some schools run out of cash for latecomers.

• The Financial Aid Form (FAF) is the one that you usually fill out for colleges that require the Scholastic Aptitude Test (SAT). You must pay $9.75 to have the College Board process your application and send the results to one college; each additional school costs you $6.75.

• The Family Financial Statement (FFS) usually goes to colleges that require the American College Test (ACT). Cost for processing by the American College Testing Program: $5.50 for the first report, $4 for each additional copy.

• Two companies entered the business last year: United Student Aid Funds and CSX Commercial Services. Their forms, SingleFile and the Application for Federal and State Student Aid (AFSSA), are processed at no cost to you. If you want to use one of the newcomers, check first with the financial aid officers at the schools to which your child is applying.

• Some state college systems and private schools also ask you to fill out their own aid forms. And if your child applies for early admission, you may have to complete a preliminary aid application as well as the standard one.

Estimate Your Share of the Tab

This worksheet can help you estimate how much you will be expected to contribute toward your son's or daughter's college costs. The table, based on the complicated formulas that are used to determine eligibility for financial aid, makes the following assumptions: there are two parents, only one of whom is working; the oldest parent is 45; only one child is going to college; state and local taxes equal 8% of family income; and the parents do not itemize deductions on their tax return. Various other factors, including high medical bills or ownership of a business, may sharply raise or lower the actual amount of aid to which you are entitled.

Complete steps 1 and 2 to determine your income and assets. Use those figures to find the parents' expected contribution in the table, and enter that figure in step 3. Then complete steps 4 and 5 to calculate the student's expected share and the total family contribution. If that amount is greater than the school's total annual cost, you will not qualify for aid. If it is less, you probably will be offered a financial aid package to make up the difference.

ASSETS	Number of children	Parents' pretax income					
		$30,000	$40,000	$50,000	$60,000	$70,000	$80,000
$40,000	1	$2,500	$5,000	$7,900	$10,900	$13,900	$16,900
	2	1,900	4,000	6,800	9,800	12,800	15,800
	3	1,400	3,100	5,800	8,800	11,800	14,800
	4	800	2,400	4,700	7,700	10,700	13,700
$60,000	1	3,300	6,100	9,000	12,000	15,000	18,000
	2	2,500	4,900	8,000	10,900	13,900	16,900
	3	1,900	4,000	7,000	9,900	12,900	16,000
	4	1,300	3,000	5,800	8,800	11,800	14,800
$80,000	1	4,100	7,300	10,200	13,100	16,100	19,100
	2	3,200	6,100	9,100	12,000	15,100	18,100
	3	2,500	5,000	8,100	11,100	14,100	17,100
	4	1,800	3,800	7,000	9,900	12,900	15,900
$100,000	1	5,100	8,400	11,300	14,200	17,300	20,300
	2	4,100	7,200	10,200	13,200	16,200	19,200
	3	3,200	6,100	9,200	12,200	15,200	18,200
	4	2,400	4,800	8,100	11,100	14,100	17,100
$120,000	1	6,300	9,500	12,400	15,400	18,400	21,400
	2	5,100	8,300	11,300	14,300	17,300	20,300
	3	4,100	7,200	10,400	13,300	16,300	19,300
	4	3,100	6,000	9,200	12,200	15,200	18,200
$140,000	1	7,400	10,600	13,500	16,500	19,500	22,500
	2	6,200	9,500	12,500	15,400	18,400	21,500
	3	5,100	8,300	11,500	14,400	17,500	20,500
	4	4,000	7,100	10,300	13,300	16,300	19,300

Source: Peterson's College Database © 1991 Peterson's Guides Inc.

1. PARENTS' INCOME:

Enter your adjusted gross income as reported on your IRS Form 1040, line 31. _____

Enter the sum of all nontaxable income (for example, child support and tax-exempt bond interest). _____

Add back deductions taken for contributions to IRAs and Keogh accounts for the year. Enter the total here. _____

2. PARENTS' ASSETS:

Enter the equity in your home (its value minus any unpaid balance on your mortgage or home-equity loan). _____

Enter the value of investments such as stocks, bonds, mutual funds, or real estate (other than your home). _____

Enter the sum of all cash, bank, and money-market accounts. _____

Enter the total here. _____

3. PARENTS' CONTRIBUTION:

Use your answers from sections 1 and 2 to find the parents' expected contribution in the table. Enter that number here. _____

4. STUDENT'S CONTRIBUTION:

Enter $700 or 70% of the student's taxable and nontaxable income, whichever is greater. _____

Enter 35% of his or her assets, including bank accounts and investments. _____

Enter the total here. _____

5. TOTAL FAMILY CONTRIBUTION:

Enter the sum of sections 3 and 4. _____

institution then makes up some or all of the difference with a package of loans and grants. You can estimate your expected contribution by filling out the simplified worksheet at left. (The official figure will be calculated when you apply for aid.) For a more precise estimate, you can complete the questionnaires in *Don't Miss Out: The Ambitious Student's Guide to Financial Aid* (Octameron, Box 2748, Alexandria, VA 22301); *The College Cost Book 1992* (College Board); or *Applying for Financial Aid*, a brochure available in high school guidance offices or from ACT Financial Aid Services, Educational Services Division-11, P.O. Box 168, Iowa City, IA 52243.

Once you've estimated your share, you can come up with the other key number in the aid game: your actual need. You arrive at that figure by subtracting your family contribution from the total annual cost of the college in question. Thus, if your expected family contribution is $5,000 and the annual cost is $15,000, your need is $10,000. At a school with a total tab of $5,000 or less, your need would be zero.

But the arithmetic doesn't end there. As part of your investigation, you must ask financial aid officers about the schools' own policies. Colleges must use a federal formula in doling out government funds, but they can make up their own rules when divvying up their own dough. And only about a quarter of all four-year colleges even say they will meet 100% of your need; you can find out how much of the gap a school will bridge by consulting *Money*'s College Value Rankings that begin on page 165 or *Peterson's 1991 College Money Handbook* (Peterson's Guides).

The same reference book can tell you whether a school's typical aid package is weighted toward loans and work/study jobs or more desirable grants. Most selective private colleges split aid about 75% to 25% in favor of grants, but some have a much lower ratio. For instance, Notre Dame's ratio is 54 to 46 in favor of grants. Most students at the university must take on substantial loans and a job of up to 12 hours a week (paying a maximum of $1,800 for the academic year) before they are even considered for a grant, says Joseph Russo, the university's financial aid director.

But those ratios are only averages. Sought-after students can get more attractive packages from most schools through what financial aid officers call "preferential packaging." The term, which you won't find in any college's promotional viewbook, refers to the practice of offering aid packages sweetened with lots of grants and scholarships to students rated most desirable by the admissions office. Recipients can be brains, jocks, minorities, or even "geos"—financial aid jargon for kids who hail from states that aren't well represented on campus. To qualify as an academic all-star, your child will have to land in the top 25% of students that the college has admitted, based on high school class rank, grade point average, and college entrance exam scores. You can gauge your progeny's chances of achieving this favored status at specific schools by checking profiles of entering freshmen in *Lovejoy's College Guide* (Monarch).

Viewbooks also don't tell you how a scholarship from your local Moose Lodge or PTA will affect an aid package, so you'll have to ask financial aid officers. Most colleges deduct the value of outside scholarships from their own grants. There are exceptions, however, such as UCLA, which uses such scholarships to reduce a student's loan burden instead.

If you get a lowball aid offer from a school that your child wants to attend, you can try haggling with the financial aid officers. Some will make adjustments only if you can document a change in your financial situation, such as the loss of your job or divorce. With others, you may be able to make the case that your child is something special and deserves more help, says Donald Moore, director of financial aid at the State University of New York at Oneonta and author of *Financial Aid Officers: What They Do To You and For You* (Octameron). "But if parents cannot prove that their child is particularly bright, athletic, or, say, a gifted tuba player, they won't have a leg to stand on."

A financial aid officer willing to bargain is more likely to give you a better mix of grants versus loans than to reduce the amount you are expected to pay. "Schools generally limit financial aid officers to budging 10% at most on your need figure," says Judith B. Margolin, author of *Financing a College Education* (Plenum). There are times when you may be able to play one school's offer against another's, but only if the colleges consider themselves to be academic equals. "If someone shows us a scholarship from another competitive school, we'll take a hard look at it and may match it if we consider the student very desirable," says Walter Cathie, associate vice president for financial resources at Carnegie Mellon University in Pittsburgh.

Two heartening developments work in favor of parents who want to bargain over aid. First, competition among colleges for top students has led to a boom in dollars for scholars—merit awards that have no connection to financial need. Such bonuses accounted for 23%, or $452.7 million, of all scholarships and grants at private colleges during the 1987-88 academic year, up from 15%, or $138.7 million, in 1970-71, according to the National Association of Independent Colleges and Universities. Most elite institutions, such as Stanford, Yale, and the University of Pennsylvania, still shun

Searching for Scholarships

College financing experts routinely advise students not to bother seeking out the usually small scholarships offered by the local Lions Club and other organizations, because college financial aid officers subtract the value of such awards from their own grants. Happily, the conventional wisdom isn't always right; some schools will use any money your child wins to reduce his or her loan burden, leaving grants intact. For leads on scholarships for which your child may be eligible, consult these guides, which can be purchased and are available in public libraries and high school guidance offices:

• *The A's and B's of Academic Scholarships* (Octameron, Box 2748, Alexandria, VA 22301)

• *Financing a College Education* (Plenum)

• *Peterson's 1992 College Money Handbook* (Peterson's Guides)

• *The College Blue Book: Scholarships, Fellowships, Grants and Loans* (Macmillan)

non-need scholarships. But merit awards have increased most dramatically at prestigious liberal arts colleges. Each year, for example, Johns Hopkins offers 20 Beneficial-Hodson awards for as much as 60% of tuition to students who rank in the top 5% of their high school classes, boast grade point averages of at least 3.8, and score 1,400 or better on the SAT. And Emory University gives free rides to a dozen accomplished students it designates as Woodruff Scholars.

Second, there's good news if your child wants to attend a state university: State grants based on merit alone increased by 82% to $70 million between 1983-84 and 1989-90. Politicians know that attracting top talent is one way to burnish their state system's reputation.

Once you have the best possible deal in hand, ask the school's financial aid officer what you can expect when you reapply for financial aid in future years—and how high your kid's grades will have to be to avoid losing grants and scholarships. "In the vast majority of cases, you'll get a similar package if your financial situation hasn't changed much and your kid remains in good academic standing," says Margolin.

Even with all the conditions in your favor, most college experts recommend that your child apply to one or two financial safety schools—ones you could afford without any help at all. That way, you will have some protection even if you end up a loser in the financial aid game.

How to Get Top Dollar

The company that processes your aid application determines how much your family will have to pay toward college costs by applying the government-mandated formula known as the congressional methodology. After some allowances—for example, a family of four with one child in college is allotted a measly $15,940 for living expenses—the formula works like this:

Parents are deemed able to contribute up to 5.6% of their assets and 47% of their after-tax income each year. Students must kick in 70% of their after-tax income, with a minimum of $700 a year for freshmen and $900 for sophomores, juniors, and seniors (even if they don't work), plus 35% of their savings.

You can improve your chances of winning more financial aid by making these moves:

• Don't save money in your child's name, as students are expected to contribute a far greater percentage of their assets than are parents.

• Cash in any investments by December 31 of your child's junior year in high school. The capital gains you incur during the year before you apply for aid count as income, and you'll be asked to contribute far more of your income than of your assets.

• Have your child pay for his new stereo or computer with his own money, because the aid formula takes more of his savings than yours.

• Stash retirement savings in a 401(k), IRA, or Keogh, which are not counted as assets under the aid formula. But be warned: Some private colleges count them as assets on their own financial aid forms.

• Borrow against your house for major purchases. Under the aid formula, credit-card debt and other consumer loans aren't subtracted from your net worth; mortgage debt is. Thus, taking out a home-equity loan rather than borrowing some other way will actually increase your eligibility for aid.

I feel very honored to pay taxes in America. The thing is, I could probably feel just as honored for about half the price. — Arthur Godfrey

TAXES

How to Beat the IRS at Its Own Game

Once upon a time, how much you paid to the Feds defined your tax situation. Today, your federal tax bill is only the beginning. Taxes at all levels—federal, state, and local—have embarked on a protracted trip north. And you'll be along for the chilling ride unless you learn to recognize the true total costs of your taxes and marshal appropriate defenses.

First of all, you'll need to get a grip on just how the federal tax hikes that are part of 1990's deficit-reduction law will affect you. The devil will be in the details of deduction tightening, which is now Congress' preferred method of raising extra revenues even as it avoids the politically riskier approach of hiking official tax rates. In this chapter, we distill the new wisdom of dealing with the IRS into 11 tax-cutting strategies that you can act on now (see page 88). We also offer advice on relatively painless ways to prepare your own tax return (page 94).

One thing you can do to help yourself is to not hurt yourself. Each year, millions of taxpayers who prepare their own returns make costly errors, often resulting in audits and penalties, or, at the very least, overpayment of their taxes. Obviously, a little mistake-avoidance can go a long way (see page 96).

Another thing you can do is concentrate more than ever on reining in your local property taxes—the fastest growing of all major taxes in recent years. To beat that bite, there are four simple steps to challenging a property assessment and winning a reduction in your local real estate tax bill (see page 92).

Unfortunately, despite the optimism that greeted tax reform in 1986 and efforts by politicians in recent years to call taxes anything else—"revenue enhancements," for example—the reality is that taxes by any name are going up and will continue to do so in the years ahead. More than ever, to be a winner, you'll have to become an expert at playing the game.

11 Ways to Beat the Feds

The new, unkinder tax law calls for basic shifts in strategy.

What will it cost me?" That's the question millions of taxpayers have been asking ever since October 1990, when Congress hiked taxes as part of its five-year, $500 billion deficit-reduction package. If you don't like the bottom line, be prepared to get serious about long-term tax planning. Gone are the happy days when a March write-off hunt was all you needed before filling out your 1040. Now you have to adhere to three broad guidelines:

Don't waste time chasing after increasingly trivial itemized deductions. Not only have long-cherished write-offs disappeared (among the lost: deductions for interest on personal debts), but also the value of most remaining deductions have been reduced for taxpayers with incomes of six figures or more. These write-offs—including ones for home mortgage interest, state, and local taxes, and miscellaneous expenses—have been cut by an amount equal to 3% of every dollar by which your adjusted gross income (AGI) exceeds $100,000. For example, a taxpayer with an AGI of $150,000 will see deductions worth $10,000 trimmed to $8,500. What's more, personal and dependent exemptions, worth $2,150 per person in 1991, are phased out for couples with an AGI above $150,000 and singles who earn more than $100,000. (The phaseout ends at $272,500 for couples and $222,500 for singles.)

As a result of the cuts in deductions and exemptions, single taxpayers who earn six figures will pay a marginal tax rate of nearly 32.5%; a couple with two children and an AGI in the phaseout range of $150,000 to $272,500 will face almost 34%, versus 28% in 1990.

Make long-term commitments to tax-deferred accounts. Your best defense against the new taxes is time. There are really no quick tax breaks anymore. To minimize your taxes now takes planning that stretches over years. Financial advisers urge clients to contribute as much as they can to tax-deferred accounts, such as company 401(k) retirement plans and deductible Individual Retirement Accounts (IRAs), to invest in high-quality, tax-exempt municipal bonds or bond funds, and to make maximum use of tax-cutting trusts in their estate plans.

Count on taxes rising again well before 1996. You probably guessed that long ago. The 1996 date is when the current budget projections expire. By then, we will know just how overly optimistic Congress' economic assumptions may turn out to be.

Despite all that, sound tax planning is still possible. The following 11 crucial steps will help you do it, whatever your income or tax bracket. They fall into three categories—income, investments, and estates.

Your Income

No matter what Congress does to taxes in the future, you can cut your bill by trimming the most important number on your return—your AGI. That way, more of your income will end up in your pocket rather than the tax collector's. Thus, our list begins with four AGI-shrinking strategies and then moves on to other tax-cutting devices. (AGI is your total income minus a few tax-favored items, such as deductible IRA contributions and alimony that you pay. Taxable income, the amount on which your tax rate is based, is your AGI minus all of your deductions and exemptions.)

Put every penny you can in tax-deferred retirement savings plans. The simplest way is to make maximum contributions to a 401(k) plan at work. Nearly a quarter of all American workers are offered 401(k)s (most large corporations have them), yet only 56% of eligible employees make use of them. In 1990, the law authorized your employer to let you stoke a 401(k) with up to $7,979 pretax, although most employers impose lower limits. Earnings grow tax deferred until withdrawn after age 59½. In addition, companies typically chip in 50¢ for every dollar you contribute up to 6% of your salary.

Open a flexible spending account (FSA) at work. Next to tax-deferred retirement plans, FSAs are your best shelter, enabling you to pay medical and dependent-care expenses with before-tax dollars. Moreover, FSA money escapes federal, state, and local income taxes plus Social Security payroll taxes. In 1990, nearly 40% of large corporations offered these accounts, but only an estimated 20% or so of eligible workers signed up for them, chiefly because of misunderstandings about how the FSAs operate.

With an FSA, the law allows you to earmark as much as $5,000 for care of your children and other dependents. Another amount, set by employers and usually about $4,000, is for unreimbursed medical expenses. (With both types of FSAs, however, your employer may set lower limits.) A $5,000 FSA is worth $1,550 in federal tax savings alone if you're in the 31% bracket; $1,400 in the 28% bracket, which applies to couples with projected income of $35,800 to $86,500 and singles earning $21,450 to $51,900. The only catch: You must spend the money in the year you commit it to an FSA; if you don't, you lose it. Sounds scary, although in fact contributions are rarely forfeited.

Many two-earner couples can realize even greater savings if their FSAs are funded by the lower-earning spouse. Say a husband and wife

figure they'll cover $6,000 in expenses from their FSAs. Let's assume that the husband earns $65,000, the wife $35,000, and they are in the 31% federal tax bracket. If the wife opens the FSAs, the federal tax savings will come to $2,319. If the husband funds the accounts, those tax savings drop to just $1,947. Reason for the $372 difference: The 6.2% Old Age and Survivors Disability Insurance portion of the Social Security tax was levied only on wages up to $53,400 in 1991. Thus, all of the wife's contributions to the FSAs escaped that tax; none would have if the husband had made them, since they would have come off the top of his income.

Moonlight. The tax breaks made possible by burning the freelance oil can significantly offset the tax you'll owe on the extra earnings. You can shelter as much as 20% of your self-employment income after deductible expenses annually in a Keogh retirement plan or in a combination of a Keogh and a simplified employee pension (SEP). You can open either account even if you are covered by a pension at your regular job as long as your combined contributions don't exceed $30,000 a year. Here's how the plans work: You can fund a so-called money-purchase Keogh with up to 20% of your taxable business income, but once you decide on a percentage, you must stick with it every year. For greater flexibility, experts suggest you fully fund an SEP—you're allowed to salt away and deduct up to 13.04% of your net business income—and then put the remaining 7% of your profit into a money-purchase Keogh. The SEP lets you change the percentage you contribute—or even not make one at all—in future years, while the Keogh contribution ensures that you will dutifully tuck something away each year.

Give income-producing assets to your children. Every kid under age 14 that earns up to $500 a year should have an investment or savings account in his or her name. Reason: Annual earnings of up to $500 are tax-free because of the child's standard deduction. By giving a child assets producing that much income, you reduce your AGI and cut your tax bill—by

$140, assuming you're in the 28% bracket. The next $500 will be taxed at your child's rate—presumably 15%—for a tax bill of $75 on $1,000 of unearned income. The tax due if the assets were in your name: $280. Any earnings above $1,000 will be taxed at your rate until the child turns 14.

Accounts for children under 18 should be opened at banks, brokerages, or mutual funds under the Uniform Transfers to Minors Act (UTMA) or, in some states, the Uniform Gifts to Minors Act (UGMA).

Consider tapping your retirement stash. With tax rates just about guaranteed to go up, now may be an opportune time to withdraw money from your tax-deferred retirement plans. If you're under age 59½, you can avoid the 10% early-withdrawal penalty by arranging to take the money in equal annual installments according to IRS life-expectancy tables. You must continue the withdrawals for five years or until age 59½, whichever comes later.

Many financial advisers urge retirees to start withdrawing money from their tax-deferred accounts after age 59½ but well before they reach 70½, the age at which the law requires you to start taking money out. If you let your account grow untouched until then, your mandatory payout could swell your AGI, pushing you into a higher tax bracket and even boosting your income to the point that your Social Security benefit becomes taxable. The formula: If your AGI plus your tax-exempt income and half your Social Security benefit exceed $32,000 for couples or $25,000 for singles, as much as half of your Social Security benefit is taxable. Too many retirees wait until they're 70 to start taking their money out and, then, at age 71, 72, 75, and so on, they find themselves paying more tax than at any time since they retired.

Worse yet, by the time you reach age 70½, Congress may have hiked the federally taxable portion of your Social Security benefit above the 50% mark.

Watch out for the alternative minimum tax (AMT). This arcane levy is imposed on filers whose tax breaks reduce their bill below an amount that's considered their fair share. Only 130,000 taxpayers paid the AMT in 1989, but the AMT rate rose to 24% in 1991 from 21% and an estimated 317,000 had to wrestle with it.

Figuring out whether you are AMT-bound demands help from an accountant or other skilled tax pro. So if you suspect you might have a problem, ask him to project your current year's tax and your AMT liability, preferably at the time that you do this year's return. If you seem to be running afoul of the AMT, your adviser can suggest several ways to reduce or even eliminate the bite.

Pay off your consumer debts. You can no longer deduct any of the interest you pay on credit-card balances, car loans, and other consumer borrowing. If you can't liquidate such debt, try to convert the nondeductible interest payments into deductible ones like those on a home-equity loan. For sole proprietors, experts suggest this strategy: Use cash earmarked for a business expense to pay off your plastic. Then charge the business purchase on your credit card if you can't get lower-cost credit elsewhere. Since interest on business loans is fully deductible, your 19% credit-card interest will drop to 13.7% after taking the write-off, assuming you're in the 28% bracket. To establish a paper trail, reserve that credit card solely for business use.

Your Investments

You'll be disappointed if you're among the 65% of *Money* subscribers who said in our Gallup poll that they favored a capital-gains tax break. Rather than offer a new approach, the 1990 law revives an old distinction between long- and short-term gains. If you're in the 31% bracket and sell appreciated assets that you've owned for less than a year, your gain is taxed at 31%. If you've held the asset for more than a year, however, the official rate drops to 28%. Bear in mind, though, that if you have a six-figure AGI, your capital-gains rate rises as you lose deductions and exemptions, just as do your regular income tax rates. (If you're in the

15% or 28% bracket, your gains are taxed at 15% or 28%.)

For all the niggling complexity, the capital-gains rate shouldn't make a hoot of difference in deciding when to sell an investment. If you're confident that your appreciated asset won't drop in value, go ahead and hold onto it until a year is up and enjoy the tax break. But if you keep it just to save a little on taxes, you're making a bad choice.

Consider buying municipal bonds or bond funds. The higher your total income tax burden, the better tax-exempt munis look. Munis offer interest free of federal and, usually, state and local taxes if you live in the state where the bonds were issued. If you're a New York City investor in the 31% federal bracket—which works out to a combined effective tax rate of nearly 40%—you would have to find a taxable investment paying 11.7% to make as much money after tax as you could on a 7% muni bond or bond fund.

Investigate tax-deferred annuities for retirement savings. Annuities may make sense if you meet these conditions: you are in the 28% or 31% federal tax bracket, have at least $10,000 to invest, plan to retire in 10 or more years, and have maxed out on other tax-favored retirement savings plans, such as a 401(k) or IRA. Sponsored by insurance companies, annuities are sold by brokers, financial planners, and insurance agents. You get to sock away money that grows tax deferred until withdrawn. If you make a withdrawal before age 59½, however, you'll pay a 10% penalty plus income taxes on the earnings.

You should subject annuities to rigorous comparison shopping. Among the basics: Beware of sales charges greater than 3.5% to 6% and surrender charges that don't decline over time. Buy only an annuity offered by an insurer rated A or A+ for financial soundness by A.M. Best, the insurance rating firm, or AAA by Standard & Poor's. Also avoid insurance companies that keep more than 15% to 25% of their portfolios in junk bonds and commercial real estate; the Best's and S&P reports cover this subject.

Your Estate

Current law lets you give tax-free gifts of $10,000 a year to each of as many recipients as you wish ($20,000 if you give jointly with your spouse). You can also pass an estate of $600,000 to your heirs tax-free. You should consider using the two remaining strategies before a revenue-hungry Congress decides to take them away.

Turn gift-giving into a habit. Bestowing money and property on others within the $10,000 annual limits while you're alive removes the assets from your estate, thus reducing its value and lowering eventual estate tax. To identify assets that will yield the best tax breaks when given away, consult an estate-planning attorney. Some general guidelines:

If your primary goal is to reduce your current income taxes, then you should give income-producing property, such as high-yielding stocks, to a child aged 14 or older. That way, the child will pay the tax at his or her rate, which is usually just 15%.

To escape gift and estate tax, give property with a low present value and a high potential for appreciation, such as growth stocks. Obviously, it's much easier, given the annual limits, to remove an asset from your estate when it's worth $10,000 than when it's worth $40,000 or $50,000.

Consider setting up charitable trusts. These trusts let you reduce your taxable estate by donating assets to a charity. At the same time, you can get an income tax deduction for the value of the charity's interest in the gift. Charitable trusts, once viewed as for the rich only, are increasingly available to middle-income earners. If you have $50,000 or more to give, for example, consider establishing a charitable remainder annuity trust. This device lets you remove assets from your taxable estate by bequeathing them to a charity. You also get to take a deduction for your gift and continue to collect income from the assets until you die. That may be the next best thing to taking it with you. But consult an attorney to be sure a trust is suitable for your situation.

Taming Your Local Taxes

Like thousands of others, you may be overpaying your property tax.

If you suspect that property taxes are taking a bigger bite out of your income, you're not paranoid—you're perceptive. In 1989, the last year for which statistics are available, property taxes consumed $3.51 out of every $100 that Americans earned. That may not sound like a lot of money, but it represents a nettlesome 8% jump from $3.26 per $100 of personal income in 1982.

It is no wonder, then, that most of the 1,029 taxpayers in a 1990 survey by the Advisory Commission on Intergovernmental Relations, a government research group in Washington, D.C., objected to property taxes more than any other levy. The deep-seated, anti-local-tax sentiment led to taxpayer revolts that year in Colorado, Illinois, Kansas, New Jersey, Oregon, the Washington, D.C. suburbs, as well as New York's Long Island and Ulster County.

Whether or not you take part in such a large-scale citizen action is beside the point anyway. But you may have cause to mount your own personal tax protest by staging an effective appeal of your local levies. This story will help. By following the four steps outlined below, you can determine whether your property taxes are too high and, if they are, fight for a reduction. If your case is solid, you have a four-in-five chance of winning. The smart steps to take:

First, find out whether you qualify for any special tax breaks. Many states reduce property taxes for veterans, low-income homeowners over age 65, and the disabled.

Next, check the accuracy of your home's assessed value. Your property tax bill is calculated by multiplying your locality's tax rate by your home's assessed value, which is determined by the local tax assessor. If the assessment is too high, you must determine why and propose an alternative. To do this, ask the assessor for copies of your property record card, which lists characteristics such as lot size and the number of rooms, and, if possible, the worksheet on which he or she calculated your bill. If you find errors in these documents—like the wrong number of bathrooms—you can usually win a tax reduction with one visit to the assessor's office.

Don't be discouraged if your home is overvalued for more subtle reasons. Consider the case of retired gym teacher Carol Tesmer of Palatine, Illinois, who successfully fought a 61% increase in her 1990 tax assessment. It would have upped the tax bill on her modest two-bedroom house from $1,212 to $1,956. "I stood there and cried when I got the assessment," recalls Tesmer. "But after I got that out of my system, I decided I wouldn't let them tax me out of my home." Sure that the assessor had overvalued her house, Tesmer marched to his office armed with photographs showing the flood damage that rainwater runoff from a neighbor's property frequently causes to her one-acre yard. The assessor cut her assessment increase to 31% on the spot, which resulted in a first-year tax savings of $372.

You should also check the assessor's estimate of your home's market value, especially since prices have plunged as much as 30% in some areas since 1988. This step is simple in the 19 states where property is assessed at 100% of its fair market value. You merely check your property record card for your home's assessment, which is the same as its market value. Chiefly to make taxes more politically palatable, the other states practice fractional assessment, meaning that your house is assessed at some percentage, called the assessment ratio, of its market value. Such partial assessment can trick you into thinking that you're getting a tax break when you're not. For example, if your town uses an assessment ratio of 40% and your house is worth $100,000, it should be assessed at $40,000. But suppose it's erroneously assessed at $50,000. If you don't know that your town uses fractional assessment, you may not realize that your property is overvalued.

If your locality has not revalued properties within the past two years, the assessor may determine your assessment using a so-called sales ratio that expresses a relationship between house values set by the assessor and the prices that homes have actually fetched in the past two years. A sales ratio of 90%, for example, means that home values have declined by 10%. Ask the assessor for the sales figures he used and your home's property record card so you can check the math. For example, if your house is worth $225,000 and your town uses a sales ratio of 90% and an assessment ratio of 40%, multiply $225,000 by 90% to get $202,500. Then multiply that figure by 40% to arrive at your home's correct assessed value of $81,000.

The math may check out, but you may still disagree with the assessor's estimate of your home's market value. To make your case, ask the assessor or a local real estate agent for recent sale prices of three to five houses in your town that are comparable to your property in size and location. Then compare the assessor's property record cards for those houses with that for your own. Finally, drive by each of the houses to verify that their exteriors and neighborhoods are comparable to your own home's. It's also a good idea to photograph those houses, as well as yours, so you can substantiate your claims.

Present your arguments by precisely following your locality's appeals procedure. You usually start with an oral plea before the local assessor.

If he or she won't budge, you must state your case on an appeals form and request a hearing before the local, county, or regional board of equalization. Ask the assessor for the board's schedule; many meet for only one to two months after assessment notices are mailed. Try to attend a board meeting in advance of your hearing to get a feel for the process. When it's your turn, bring photocopies of any documents and photos that support your oral arguments. The board will generally hand down its decision within a couple of weeks of your hearing. If you lose, you can take your case to the state property tax board and, if necessary—and the taxes in question justify it—to the state supreme court.

Consider hiring professional help. If you fear you're not persuasive enough to sway the assessor or higher authorities, get a pro to do your bidding. You can engage a tax attorney to plead your case, but his $500 to $1,500 fee may dwarf your tax savings. A growing army of more than 2,000 property tax consultants is also eager to assist, for a fee equal to a third to a half of your first year's tax savings. To find one, check the Yellow Pages under "Tax Consultants." Since these advisers are not accredited by any professional organization, you'll have to judge their ability by checking references from at least three taxpayers they have worked with in the past.

Unfortunately, some assessors may discount the consultant's testimony as tainted by self-interest. One solution: Hire an appraiser, for a fee of $150 to $300, who may be able to beat your town's assessor at his own game. The best candidates are members of the Appraisal Institute.

Whether you do it yourself or with the help of a hired gun, odds are that you'll win. There are no national statistics on how many taxpayers triumph, but experts estimate that you have an 80% chance of winning a tax reduction from the assessor if your case is well documented. The odds are in your favor even if you have to appeal to a higher authority. For example, in Milwaukee, which is probably typical, the city's review board reduced 41% of such second-stage appeals in 1988.

Save Money: Do Your Own Return

Most taxpayers could hammer out their own income taxes in no more than a few hours without so much damage as a battered thumb. But, first, they have to overcome their fear.

Congress played a bitter joke on taxpayers back in 1986 when it promised simplification but then passed the Tax Reform Act—a tangle of rules that sometimes rivals the Talmud. No wonder only half of all taxpayers do their own taxes; the rest hire often expensive professional helpers. Americans fear dealing with the IRS. They are so terrified of making a mistake— even in their favor—that they pay a tax preparer to do work they could easily do themselves.

The truth is, such terror is simply not justi-fied in nearly all cases. Fully 34% of the 113 million U.S. taxpayers use one of the simple, short tax forms—the 1040EZ or the 1040A. The rest file the two-page 1040. And 60% of those taxpayers take the standard deduction ($5,450 in 1991 for a married couple filing jointly) instead of itemizing deductions. Of all taxpayers, only one in four files an itemized tax return. Thus, Congress' complicated tricks don't affect most taxpayers. There are fewer brackets, fewer deductions, and the IRS instruc-tions in the 1040 booklet are actually clearer than in the past. Indeed, according to the IRS, the number of returns that are not itemized has increased 25% since 1985, the year before reform.

Whether you're ready to take on your own tax return depends on two factors: how fearful you are of going it alone and the complexity of your tax situation. Let's say you are too nervous to file solo, or you have better ways to use the 45 minutes to 4 hours the task takes. Then your tax preparer's fee—from $13 for the simplest return to more than $1,000 for highly compli-cated ones—is well spent. Similarly, if your taxes are unquestionably convoluted, leave them to an expert. You should turn to a pro, for instance, when you are taking a lump-sum retirement distribution and need to consider the different approaches to forward averaging.

Short of such prickly challenges, you can probably prepare your own return. Start by choosing one of the three forms described here, beginning with the simplest:

1040EZ. You qualify for this basic, self-help form if you are single with no dependents, have wages subject to withholding and less than $400 in interest income, and your taxable income does not exceed $50,000. You can't use this form if you receive dividend income, are over 65, or claim any tax credits. Typical completion time: 45 minutes. If a pro does the return for you, expect to pay as much as $25.

1040A. A high school student can breeze through this next-simplest, two-page form. Taxpayers of any filing status—single, head of household, or married—may use the 1040A if their taxable income doesn't top $50,000. You may also file the 1040A if you report dividend, interest, unemployment, or tax-exempt in-come. You can file a 1040A even if you claim a write-off for an Individual Retirement Account contribution and tax credits for child and elderly care. These declarations are made on one-page forms called schedules. Retirees can use the 1040A to report pension, annuity, and IRA income and taxable Social Security benefits. Typical completion time: three hours. Cost if a pro does it: $25 to $200.

1040. This standard tax form may be used by anyone, and the experience can be fairly swift and uneventful, assuming you keep it simple. Or the 1040 can involve many hours of mind-melting work, complicated by its eight attendant schedules—from Schedule A for itemizing deductions to Schedule SE for computing Social Security self-employment tax. Not to mention the 1040's 79 ancillary forms, such as Form 4952 for investment interest deductions and Form 3903 for moving expenses. If one or more of these additional documents is called for, however, you shouldn't give up automatically. Even such formidable obstacles as figuring a casualty-loss deduction or capital gains on mutual-fund withdrawals involve fairly straightforward calculations. Typical completion time for the 1040 alone: 3 to 4 hours. Cost if a pro does it for you: $35 to $500.

Whatever form you use, a step-by-step regimen will produce the best results. Start here:

First, read your last three tax returns carefully, line by line. If you can follow most of the entries with the help of IRS Publication 17, *Your Federal Income Tax*, that's an encouraging sign. (You can order a copy of this free guide by calling 800-TAX-FORM.) Write down what you don't understand, along with details such as boxes to be checked off, schedules filled out, and deductions claimed.

Second, spend a few hours reading a tax guide, perhaps—but not necessarily—in tandem with computer tax software. The best tax guides

The Best Sources of Help for the Do-It-Aloner

If you are thinking of going accountantless into the cold night of tax preparation, forearm yourself with one of the easy-to-follow books and perhaps a computer program listed below. Each can guide you through every line, schedule, and form in your tax return. They all contain basically the same material: thorough indexes, clear explanations of changes in the tax law, worksheets for calculating deductions and other items, tips for organizing tax records, and sample copies of the key IRS forms. First, the books:

Consumer Reports Books Guide to Income Tax Preparation (Consumers Union): Two-color printing separates filing tips from explanations of tax rules.

Ernst & Young's Arthur Young Tax Guide 1991 (Ballantine,): Exceptionally detailed. Reprints IRS Publication 17, *Your Federal Income Tax*, together with examples and legal interpretations that can point you to write-offs.

J.K. Lasser's Your Income Tax 1991 (J.K. Lasser Institute): The most authoritative of the guides, it offers buyers a free 24-hour hotline.

Your 60-Minute Tax Return 1991 (J.K. Lasser Institute): This guide skips the tax code explanations and goes straight to the how-to, including "accountant alerts" to situations best handled by a pro. Recommended for, but not limited to, 1040EZ and 1040A filers.

If you are even slightly proficient with a personal computer, consider one of the following tax programs. They make tax preparation simple with question-and-answer formats, automatically do all the math, and even print out your completed return and check it for errors.

All the software requires that your computer have a hard disk with 512 K of memory. The programs can be run on IBMs and IBM-compatibles unless otherwise noted:

Personal Tax Preparer (Parsons Technology): The best for the money. Covers federal forms completely, but doesn't do state returns.

TurboTax (ChipSoft): Most comprehensive. Add-ons are available for 44 states. It also comes in a Macintosh version.

Andrew Tobias' TaxCut (Meca Software): Clearest Q&A format and most complete tax advice. Add-ons for 10 states.

Macintosh owners might consider *MacInTax* (Softview), which actually reproduces forms on the screen and has supplements for returns in 13 states. A version can be used on IBMs and IBM-compatibles equipped with the Windows 3.0.

proceed logically through the 1040 in sequence and cover most of what you need to know to fill out a complicated return, maybe even alerting you to write-offs you would otherwise overlook. The guides can also answer the questions that came up when you read through your old returns.

Third, get free IRS help with items you still don't understand. While the agency's taxpayer assistance service is far from impeccable, it has been improving. (In a May 1991 test, IRS advisers answered 91% of questions correctly.) To boost your odds of getting the right answer, try to make your questions specific. Example: "Can I deduct the points on the mortgage for my vacation home?" instead of merely "Can I deduct points?"

The taxpayer assistance service has national toll-free phone numbers: for information, call 800-829-1040; for forms or publications on a wide variety of tax subjects, 800-829-3676 (to speed your order, use the publication numbers printed in the back of the 1040 instruction booklet); and for recorded tax information messages, 800-829-4477 (code numbers for 140 topics are listed in the instruction booklet).

Fourth, be careful. When you fail to check off a box, such as the one for filing status, or when you forget to give your Social Security number, the computer at the IRS processing center automatically shunts aside your return—and that holds up your refund check. Best way to catch oversights: Don't mail the return right off; put it aside for a day or two and then review it line by line with a fresh eye.

And how about folks who push off smartly on their tax-preparation adventure, paddle into midstream, and then, for whatever reason, decide to hire a navigator? Even if you rough out your taxes in pencil and then go to a preparer, you may wind up paying less because your materials are better organized. Tax preparers often charge extra if a client brings in a shoebox crammed with papers. More important, working through your return will make you a better tax planner in years to come.

How to Avoid Costly Tax Errors

Eliminate missed exemptions, incorrect filing status, and other goofs.

In 1991, 12.3% of the 54.8 million U.S. taxpayers who prepared their own federal returns made simple, easily avoided mistakes that cost them hundreds of dollars or even more. Consider the price you pay for making a goof or two on your 1040: If your mistakes result in a substantial underpayment—the greater of $5,000 or more than 10% of the proper tax—you may be liable for a penalty of 20% of the underpayment plus interest of 10% a year, compounded daily, on both the penalty and the amount due. Your flubs can delay any refund you're owed by several weeks. That could be a considerable inconvenience. Most

ominously, certain triggers—such as high itemized deductions—can shunt your 1040 toward an audit, which could raise the discomfort to a wallet-sapping level. Average recommended tax and penalties for 1989 audits: $4,290. To help you keep your return on the straight and narrow, *Money* questioned more than a dozen tax experts, including ones at the IRS, to identify the most common—and costly—mistakes made by individual taxpayers.

The agency pinpointed four trouble spots that account for more than 25% of the taxpayer errors caught each year by its computers. Few *Money* readers would encounter the most common failing of all—miscalculating or overlooking the earned-income credit, a special write-off for households with adjusted gross incomes below $21,250 in 1991.

The next three mistakes that top the list, however, involve issues that might cause many of us to pause and chew our pencils: For example, can Donald Trump claim his children as exemptions even though they live with their mom, Ivana? On the other hand, can Ivana qualify for head-of-household status? If you turned 65 last year, does it make more sense to claim the bigger standard deduction to which you're entitled or to itemize your deductions? The 10 other entries on the list come from knowledgeable tax professionals drawing on years of experience in filing returns for taxpayers whose income and financial circumstances make them much like *Money*'s readers. Here, then, are a baker's dozen of costly mistakes— and how you can avoid them in doing your tax return:

Claim all your exemptions. Each one was worth $2,050 in 1991, which translated into a tax saving of $308 to $677, depending on your bracket. Taxpayers often overlook dependent exemptions for elderly parents, especially if they don't all live under the same roof. As a parent yourself, you are generally entitled to an exemption if you furnish more than half the support and if your child is under 19 at the end of the tax year, or under 24 if a full-time student. Warning: The kids can't also claim the exemption on their own tax returns.

Let's say your dependent 18-year-old daughter files her own 1040. Instead of taking an exemption for herself, she must check the box on line 33b. If you're divorced, the custodial parent is generally entitled to the exemption unless a written agreement states otherwise. (Donald Trump couldn't take the exemption because no such agreement exists so far, says a C.P.A. who works for Ivana.)

Your parent usually qualifies as your dependent if you contribute more than 50% of total support and his or her taxable income is less than $2,050. When the amount is over the limit but income is mostly from investments, you still may have room to maneuver. One strategy:

Your parent might liquidate securities and reinvest the proceeds in Series EE bonds. Since the interest is not included in income so long as the owner holds the bond—up to 30 years after purchase—you could claim the exemption in the interim.

Don't overlook the higher standard deduction for age or blindness. An additional standard deduction of $800 for singles ($650 per spouse for joint filers) is allowed to nonitemizing taxpayers who are blind or aged 65 or older; the elderly blind may take double that amount. Many of those eligible enter the figure on the appropriate line but forget to check the accompanying box on line 33a of the 1040 form, or vice versa.

The IRS will generally write to point out the mistake, but correcting it requires needless paperwork. More damaging, many of those eligible overlook the tax break altogether, through ignorance or confusion. If this might apply to your parent, look over his or her return before it's filed.

Double-check your filing status. While you aren't likely to forget a marriage or divorce, it's easy to slip in or out of head-of-household status without realizing it. The definition is sufficiently complicated that even the pros have to review the technical rules occasionally. You're a likely candidate if you're single, have a child or other dependent relative living with you, and pay more than half of the cost of keeping the home. The rewards can be substantial: Filing as head of household would give a parent with a taxable income of $50,000 a tax saving of $1,579. (And, yes, Ivana probably would qualify, because alimony and other income permit her to pay more than half the cost of maintaining her household.)

Calculate your own underpayment. If you paid at least 90% of your current tax liability or 100% of what you owed the previous year, you're in the clear. But if you fell short and owe $500 or more in taxes, then you are required to pay a penalty—11% annually for the period of underpayment. You could just let the IRS figure the penalty and send you the bill. Or better still, you could use Form 2210 to determine how much you owe. The IRS computes the penalty as if you had received the income throughout the year. But if you got most of the income in the last quarter of the year, you would owe a smaller penalty.

Check out the new wage basis for the self-employment tax deduction. If you work for yourself, you must pay a self-employment tax. For 1991, this tax was 15.3% on income minus expenses, with 12.4% of that going to Social Security and the remaining 2.9% going to Medicare. The maximum amount of self-employment income subject to Medicare tax was $125,000, and to Social Security tax, $53,400. Included are two new breaks. First, you may deduct half of your self-employment tax from gross income; enter the amount on line 25 of your Form 1040. Second, net income from self-employment (as reported on line 31 of Schedule C) can be reduced by 7.65% of the

Taking Advantage of the Tax Breaks That Are Left

Tax-cutting prescriptives aren't as easy to come by this filing season as they were before the 1986 tax law, when write-offs seemed to fall at taxpayers' feet like fiscal plums. Full deductibility of sales tax and consumer loan interest? Income averaging? Fat tax shelters? All are gone. But some tax breaks endure. You just have to know where to look. To help you in doing your Form 1040, *Money* asked leading tax pros to share their most useful tips for five types of taxpayers: employees, retirees, self-employeds, homeowners, and investors:

For employees. Scrutinize your W-2s so that you don't bypass major write-offs recorded there. Also be sure that the numbers match those on your year-end pay stubs. If you have a 401(k) account, for example, your gross salary should have been reduced by the amount of your tax-deferred contributions. Further advice:

If you worked part of the year at a temporary location, now you can deduct commuting costs between your home and the temporary worksite as a miscellaneous itemized deduction.

Job-hunting expenses are also deductible as a miscellaneous expense. You needn't have found a new position, but you must have looked in the same field.

For retirees. Retired taxpayers should consider filing the 33-line Form 1040A, even if they haven't in the past. It can be used to report pension and annuity income, IRA distributions, taxable Social Security benefits, the credit for the elderly, and estimated tax payments. More advice: If you turned 70 by last July 1, begin making withdrawals from your IRA before April 1. You can determine the minimum required with the help of IRS Publication 575, *Pension and Annuity Income*, which you can obtain free by calling 800-829-3676. Otherwise, you will owe Uncle Sam 50% of the shortfall.

If you moved to a new state, check whether you owe state taxes on income from pensions, profit-sharing plans, and IRAs. Many states don't tax this income.

For self-employeds. Entrepreneurs should report as many write-offs as they can on Schedule C rather than Schedule A. On Schedule A, miscellaneous expenses can be deducted only to the extent that they exceed 2% of your gross income. But all self-employment expenses reported on Schedule C are 100% deductible. Some further advice: You have until April 15—later if you get a deadline extension to August 15 by filing Form 4868—to set up a simplified employee pension plan (SEP). It's like a super-IRA in which you can stash, tax deferred, the lesser of $30,000 or 13.04% of business income minus allowable business expenses.

For homeowners. Lenders must now report to the IRS on Form 1098 whether points on a first mortgage were paid out of the borrower's pocket—and are, thus, deductible in the first year of the loan. Points paid from borrowed money must be deducted over the life of the loan. If you wrongly deduct points, the IRS will send you a notice. Points for a refinanced mortgage or one on a second home must be deducted over the term of the loan no matter how they are paid. Some additional tips: If you bought a home this year, comb your escrow

self-employment tax on your Schedule SE. The aim: to give the self-employed the same tax breaks as others.

Chase that refund check. While you have no legal obligation to inform the IRS of a move, it pays to stay in touch. In 1989, more than 72,000 refund checks totaling $41 million were returned to the IRS because they could not be delivered. In 1990, the IRS introduced a formal change-of-address notice, Form 8822. You can

papers for overlooked deductions, like payment to the seller for your prorated share of real estate taxes.

What if you have sold a home and don't know whether you will buy another? Declare the sale on Form 2119 and check the box indicating that you plan to replace the house. If you later decide not to, file an amended Form 2119 for the year of the sale, and pay what you owe.

For investors. Parents shouldn't automatically report a dependent child's income on their own 1040. You are allowed to do just one filing only if your child is under 14, has interest and dividend income of $500 to $5,000, and has no federal income tax withheld. You must also attach Form 8814. But if you do a single filing, you will boost your adjusted gross income, and you could be pushed into a higher state or local tax bracket, since those returns are usually based on your federal 1040. In addition, a higher taxable income reduces federal write-offs that are computed as a percentage of your adjusted gross income. Examples: medical and miscellaneous expenses and casualty losses. Also: Subtract from gross income any penalty you paid for cashing in a CD early. Typically, it's one to three months' interest on the amount withdrawn and it's reported to you on your 1099. Enter the amount on line 28 of your 1040.

Don't forget to deduct any interest you paid in buying bonds. If you bought a bond in September, say, that pays $400 interest each June and December, you paid accrued interest of $200 to the seller at the time of sale. Enter the full $400 as interest, but subtract the $200 in accrued interest on Schedule B.

get it at your local IRS office or simply by calling 800-829-3676. (If you think you're owed a refund from past years, call 800-829-1040.)

Don't ignore the dreaded AMT. You probably imagine that the alternative minimum tax—a labyrinthine levy that in 1990 had a rate of 21%—is reserved for fiscal fat cats, not the likes of you. But don't be too sure. Only 88,000 taxpayers were caught by the AMT in 1988, but the number rose to 130,000 in 1989 and was projected to hit 317,000 in 1991. One reason: The AMT climbed to 24% in 1991, closer to normal tax rates, making it easier to trigger.

Among the taxpayers most at risk are large itemizers, including residents of high-tax states, and self-employed people with substantial depreciation write-offs. For example, the AMT is a threat to joint filers with four exemptions if their taxable income exceeds $50,000 and they have about 60% in adjustments (like hefty state and local income taxes) and tax preference items (like large charitable donations of appreciated property). If income hits $100,000, a mere 40% or so in adjustments and preferences raises a red flag. When in doubt, figure out what your tax would be under the AMT, using Form 6251. You pay the higher sum, the amount calculated for regular tax or the AMT.

Follow the rules about deducting state and local taxes. Although confusion is rife on this one, the basic rule is relatively simple. Itemized deductions are allowed for three classes of taxes—income (state, local, or foreign), real property, and personal property—in the year they are paid. For example, people who owed $10,000 in state tax for 1991, but had only $6,000 withheld, might think they are entitled to deduct the full $10,000. In fact, they can deduct only $6,000 for 1991. They can deduct the remaining $4,000 for 1992.

Don't overstate your capital gain from a mutual-fund sale. If you calculate the tax basis (the cost on which your capital gain or loss is based) of your shares and come up with a round number like $5,000, you've probably made an error in Uncle Sam's favor. The reason is that almost everyone reinvests dividends and capital-gains distributions in new shares of the fund. Because you've paid taxes on those sums in previous years, the reinvestments raise your basis.

To arrive at your correct cost, tot up your original investment plus the reinvested distributions reported on the final fund statement for each year you owned the shares. Add any amounts reported to you annually on Form 2439 by the fund as undistributed capital gains that you were required to report as income. Then, subtract any nontaxable dividends that represented a return of your investment. The answer is your tax basis. Subtract it from the sale price to figure the taxable gain that you should report.

Make sure you round up all of your fund transactions. To avoid a letter from the IRS accusing you of negligence, carefully review all your 1099 forms. Reason: You may have more gains or losses than you think. Writing a check on an income fund is a redemption of principal and, therefore, a taxable event. You're also realizing gains or losses each time you pick up the phone and switch from, say, an equity fund to a Ginnie Mae fund in the same family.

Don't take what looks like a loss on a muni bought at a premium. When interest rates decline after a bond has been issued, its value increases so it trades at a premium. An investor may pay $55,000 for a muni with a face value of

Don't Let the Tax Man Get Too Much of Your Paycheck

If you expect a refund from the Internal Revenue Service this spring, stop smiling—you goofed on last year's taxes. Yes, *goofed*. By overpaying taxes during the year, you actually lost money. Here's why: Uncle Sam doesn't pay interest on amounts overwithheld. So if you were entitled to a $902 refund, you lost the $55 that you could have earned if you had instead stashed $35 from each biweekly paycheck in an average-yielding money-market mutual fund.

Before you begin arguing that overwithholding is the only way you can save, consider this: If your employer is among the 100,000 who offer automatic savings plans, you can shunt the money that is otherwise unnecessarily set aside for taxes into a savings account with the same out-of-sight, out-of-mind ease as withholding.

To match this year's withholding more closely to your expected tax bill, ask your payroll office for a Form W-4. Using your last year's tax return, updating figures as needed, complete the form's three worksheets to determine your correct number of allowances. And bear these pointers in mind: In addition to claiming an allowance for each exemption you take on your return, you are eligible for extra ones if you have only one job, file as head of household, or take a dependent-care credit against at least $1,500 of expenses. You can usually take additional allowances if you report

itemized deductions like mortgage interest or non-itemized adjustments, such as tax-deductible Keogh contributions. (People with complex deductions, six-figure salaries, or nonwage income should consult IRS Publication 505, *Tax Withholding & Estimated Tax*, available free by calling 800-829-3676.) If you moonlight or your spouse also holds a job and your total earnings are at least $46,000 for joint filers or $27,000 for singles, you must complete the "Two-Earner/Two-Job" worksheet to keep from having too little withheld.

Submit the W-4 form's detachable withholding certificate with your new number of allowances to your payroll department. Two-earner couples and taxpayers with more than one job can divvy up the allowances as they wish, although taking all of them against the highest-paying job is usually the most accurate approach. When you get your first paycheck reflecting the changes, check it carefully. Multiply the tax withheld by the number of pay periods left in the year; then add the result to the tax that was deducted from paychecks earlier in the year.

To avoid an underpayment penalty, you must fork over at least as much as you owed last year or 90% of your current tax bill. If you fall short, fill out another W-4 reflecting higher withholding. Or make quarterly estimated tax payments to cover your liability.

$50,000, for example, because it pays higher income than a bond that sells at face value. When the muni matures, many investors then try to deduct a $5,000 loss. No dice. The premium is considered to have been paid back to you as part of the higher interest you received.

Figure out your Keogh contributions correctly. You may put 25% of your net earnings (gross income minus allowable business expenses) from self-employment, up to a maximum of $30,000, into a so-called money-purchase Keogh retirement plan. For figuring contributions, net earnings must be reduced by the deductible contribution and by half your self-employment tax, so your effective contribution would be lower than 25%. The hitch is that a money-purchase Keogh requires a fixed-dollar contribution each year. An alternative: a profit-sharing Keogh plan, in which you deposit a variable percentage of your net earnings.

The drawback in this case is that your maximum contribution is only 15% of your net earnings, or an even lower actual rate after reducing earnings by your allowable contribution. For maximum flexibility, you can elect a combination of both plans, with some professional help from a bank or other trustee.

Do sweat the small stuff. Ignoring the filing mechanics can delay your refund, trap you in endless loops of correspondence with the IRS, and cost you money: For example, $50 for failing to report Social Security numbers for your dependents aged 1 and over; $50 if you fail to fill out Form 8606 for a nondeductible contribution to your Individual Retirement Account; at least $100 if your return is more than 60 days late and you have a balance due of more than $100. So double-check your math; make sure names and numbers match.

Like the combination to a lock, your return should be arranged with every form and schedule in a precise order. Faulty sequencing, as the IRS calls it, means the whole package must be taken apart and restapled by a clerk at the processing center—giving gremlins a great chance for mischief. Form 1040 is always on top, followed by the necessary schedules—A through SE—in alphabetical order. Next come numerical forms, which—surprise!—do not follow numerically, but according to their so-called attachment sequence numbers, marked in the upper right-hand corner. For example, Form 2106 carries a sequence number of 54; Form 2441 is 21, so it comes earlier in the roll call. Then come statements or unofficial documents—descriptions of the clothing that you gave Goodwill, for instance.

Finally, if you're married and filing jointly, decide whose name will be on top—and keep it that way. "I had clients who always filed with the wife's name on top; then they went to a tax preparer and he reversed it," says one accountant. "It generated miles of red tape and took us five years to straighten out."

I just got wonderful news from my real estate agent in Florida. They found land on my property. — Milton Berle

Protecting Your Biggest Investment

For millions of American homeowners brought up to believe that the foundation of personal wealth was in home ownership, the free-falling home prices of recent years have been unsettling. The real winners in today's market are buyers. Mortgage rates are low and real estate prices in some areas have been driven down by 30% or more since 1988.

Still, while many housing markets are more affordable now than at any time in the past decade, buying a home today remains much more difficult than it was 30, 20, or even just 15 years ago. That's particularly true for cash-strapped younger households. Fortunately, there are numerous private and government programs that offer first-timers a helping hand with their down payments. For example, Fannie Mae's Community Home Buyers Program allows first-time buyers to put down as little as 5% of a home's purchase price (and two percentage points of that may be a gift), compared with the 10% to 20% most lenders now require.

Current homeowners looking to trade up face challenges of a different sort. If you are among them, understand this: While you probably won't get a 1980s-size price for the mid-size or smaller dwelling you live in now, you may more than make up for a lower-than-anticipated profit by nabbing a true luxury-home bargain. Higher-end houses have borne the brunt of the real estate slump of the past few years.

Whether you're a first-time buyer or already own your home, the current housing market can offer unique opportunities (see the story on page 104). If you bought your home at the peak of the 1980s house-price frenzy, however, there may be no way to avoid a painful loss if you sell now, and you may be better off renovating your house to get what you want (see page 110).

This chapter also tells you how to protect your home against burglary. While you may think you're an unlikely target, more than 3 million Americans a year are victimized. To find out how to burglarproof your home, turn to the story on page 111.

Making the Most of the Housing Market's Split Personality

With home prices and mortgage rates at enticing lows, now may be the time to buy. But, first, gauge the trends in your area.

The housing market played Jekyll and Hyde in 1991, showing signs of stability in the spring, then in the fall taking a vicious turn for the worse as sales plummeted. Consumer concern about the economy was credited with the decline. Earlier, realtors had been touting a revival following an increase in existing home sales nationwide. In Boston, for example, pending sales—that is, deals in which a bid has been accepted but the sale hasn't closed— zoomed 52% in the first 10 weeks of 1991, compared with the same period in 1990. However, by September 1991, sales nationwide had plummeted 12.9%, the largest single month drop in 3 years.

Despite the market's shifting personality, now is a good time to buy a house. With mortgage rates and prices at historically low levels (at an average 9.01%, 30-year mortgage rates in September 1991 were the lowest in 14 years), houses in many areas are the most affordable they've been in a decade. And few experts foresee a meaningful rise in prices. For example, the WEFA Group, an economics consulting firm in Bala Cynwyd, Pennsylvania, forecast an after-inflation rise in home prices of just 2.5% by 1993 (for city-by-city projections, see the table beginning on page 106). Says WEFA's housing economist John Savacool: "I wouldn't hold my breath waiting for a boom."

This story will tell you how to turn this housing market to your advantage, whether you are a first-time buyer, a homeowner with a mind to trade up, or a shopper looking for a vacation retreat. Even if you plan to stay put, there are opportunities to be seized. Now may be a terrific time to renovate, for example. Though building contractors are finally emerging from their worst slump since 1982, many are still discounting their rates by as much as 10%. (You'll find a thorough look at home-renovation strategies in the story beginning on page 110.) As always, however, it is dangerous to extrapolate from national data to your own market. To gauge the trend in home values in your area, ask your local real estate board for figures on sales volume. If the number of sales is headed up—or down—from quarter to quarter, prices should eventually follow. You should also check the number of days that the average house sits on the market before selling. If that number is heading down, sales and eventually prices should rebound.

Here's a rundown of ways in which you can capitalize on the housing market:

Buying your first home. At the end of 1990, the National Association of Realtors' affordability index for first-time buyers hit its highest level since Jimmy Carter sat in the Oval Office. According to the index, anyone with the median income of young families currently renting—$24,428 a year—has 81.5% of the income needed to buy the median-priced starter home costing $77,900. In 1981, by contrast, the typical young renter had less than half the necessary income. The combination of low mortgage rates, soft prices, and sellers' willingness to make concessions are giving first-time buyers a window of opportunity, says Peter

G. Miller, author of *Buy Your First Home Now* (HarperCollins).

For most first-time buyers, however, the biggest problem is to come up with the cash for the down payment and closing costs. According to the 1990 Chicago Title & Trust Company survey of home buyers, only 78% of the average first-timer's down payment came from his or her own savings. Loans or contributions from relatives made up most of the rest.

One solution: Find a low-down-payment mortgage. Despite tighter scrutiny by lenders since the S&L debacle, many lenders will gladly loan 90% or more of a home's purchase price. Federal Housing Administration guaranteed loans, for example, require a down payment of only 3% of the first $25,000 of the sales price and 5% of the rest. Though FHA mortgages are available nationwide, the maximum loan amount ranges from $67,500 to $124,875, depending on the level of home prices in your area.

Trading up to a larger house. When the Washington, D.C. housing market fell in 1990, the prices of trade-up houses costing $250,000 or

Inspect Before You Buy a New Home

The 18-foot cathedral ceiling in the master bedroom hooked you on the house. But how sure are you that those romantic rafters won't come crashing down during the next storm—or that the heating and plumbing systems won't conk out 10 minutes after you move in? Whether you know it or not, you need a home inspector. For $150 to $350, an inspector will check out the plumbing, heating, and electrical systems and scrutinize your home for structural defects.

But finding one who's capable and reputable takes homework. Start your search in the Yellow Pages under "Building Inspection Services." Demand someone who's been doing inspections in your area for at least three years and who can furnish references from a minimum of four customers. Membership in the American Society of Home Inspectors, a professional organization whose members have completed at least 250 paid inspections, is also a plus. To get names of ASHI inspectors in your area, call 703-524-2008. Make sure the inspector carries liability insurance, which can reimburse you for damages from defects he fails to detect.

Accompany the inspector during his tour and ask questions. Don't expect him to tell you whether you're getting the house at a good price. While the inspector may estimate repair costs— and you should factor those costs into any offer— he should never solicit work for himself or others. If he does, find another inspector.

A thorough inspection should cover at least the following items:

Structural components. The inspector should check for water stains or cracks that could indicate damage in walls, floors, and the roof. He should also examine window casings, doors and frames, stairs, and the attic for signs of structural damage.

Electrical system. Safety is the major issue here. The inspector should examine the main electrical panel for aluminum circuit wiring that could cause fires and also see whether outlets are firmly attached to walls and properly grounded. If the house has a fuse box, he should make sure that the fuses have the proper amperage. Otherwise, an electrical fire could occur.

Plumbing. Fixtures such as toilets and sinks should be in working order. He should also check for adequate water pressure and signs of leaks.

Heating and cooling. He should see that the systems deliver adequate heat, cooling, and air flow to all rooms.

Foundation and basement. He'll look for cracks and signs of water seepage in basement and foundation walls that could signal structural damage. Most inspectors will also test for radon, asbestos, or formaldehyde, gauge the quality of your drinking water, and make sure the septic tank is operating properly. The cost: $50 to $100 per test. To check for termites and other wood-destroying pests, hire a termite inspector, who'll probably charge less than $100.

more were hammered down 20% in many areas—about twice the price drop on less expensive starter homes. Many other cities witnessed a similar pattern as potential buyers of more expensive properties, unable to sell their present houses, couldn't come up with large enough down payments. As a result, trade-up homes constitute some of this market's best bargains. But there's an obvious catch-22: You may be unable to unload your current homestead without selling at a discount. If that's what's holding you back, rethink your situation. Chances are, what you save on the price of a trade-up may more than compensate for any price cut you take on your present home.

Bottom fishing in repos. Intrepid home shoppers can search for bargains among the huge inventory of repossessed homes owned by the U.S. government. The Department of Housing and Urban Development has more than 40,000 homes for sale, for example, and the Resolution Trust Corporation (RTC)—the federal agency that sells off houses once owned by insolvent thrifts—is currently peddling more than 13,800 single-family homes and 5,300 condominiums. While not every property in the federal inventory is a bargain, careful shoppers can grab a home at a discount.

Keep in mind that buying at an RTC auction involves several risks. If your bid wins, you must immediately hand over a cashier's check for around $2,000. If you change your mind or fail to get financing, you forfeit the money. Most often, the Feds take no responsibility for the home's condition either. The RTC also sells houses as other sellers do—by listing them with brokers. Although the RTC may seem to be unwilling to dicker, don't believe it. "You should negotiate with them just as you would with any other motivated seller," says Carolyn Janik, co-author of *How You Can Profit from the S&L Bailout* (Bantam).

To find out about government-owned houses for sale in your area, call the RTC at 800-782-3006 or the HUD field office nearest you. Check your local newspapers as well for notices of banks, S&Ls, and developers selling homes at auction.

Midwestern Cities Promise Greatest Increase in House Prices

The White Sox's controversial Comiskey Park wasn't the only new-home story in Chicago last season. The Windy City topped 49 other major metropolitan areas in *Money*'s 1991 ranking of projected house-price changes over the next two years. According to the WEFA Group, a Bala Cynwyd, Pennsylvania economic forecasting firm, the median price of an existing single-family home in Chicago will rise to $139,200 by the first quarter of 1993, which works out to a total gain of 5.2% after inflation.

Although 5.2% sounds rather modest, it stands out in a national housing market expected to be as flat as an Illinois beanfield. The median U.S. home is expected to appreciate only 2.5% after inflation to $103,700 by 1993. Though no region appears particularly strong, Midwestern cities took six of the 15 top spots, thanks in part to their sturdy export-oriented economies. In Chicago, for example, roughly three new professional or managerial jobs are expected to be created for each new worker over the next five years.

Most of the other metro areas where housing looks comparatively healthy, such as New Orleans, Anaheim, California, and Middlesex County in New Jersey, are bouncing back from previous slumps. The big comeback market, though, is No. 2-ranked Oklahoma City. In the four years through 1989, the oil bust drove prices there down 32% after inflation; now a rebound in energy prices and service industries figures to boost the median Oklahoma City homestead to $62,300 by early 1993, a 5.1% gain after inflation. Still, prices would remain 3.7% below their 1985 peak of $64,700.

The losers include several of the once hot markets of the West. For example, in Seattle, the darling of 1989 (up 13% after inflation that year), the median price of an existing home fell 3% through the first quarter of 1991 and may barely keep pace with inflation through 1993. Riverside/San Bernardino, California also figures to burn out. After a sizzling 12.2% gain in 1989, prices in that metro area 50 miles east of Los Angeles dropped 4.1% in 1990 and could be headed for a 2.3% after-inflation dip by 1993, the worst projected performance on the table. The three-year slide, triggered by defense industry cutbacks, would wipe out more than half of the area's 1989 gain.

Metropolitan area (ranking)	Median house price[1]	Annual income needed to buy median house		% gain or loss from March 1990 to March 1991[3]	% total projected gain or loss through first quarter 1993[4]
		10% down payment	20% down payment[2]		
Anaheim, CA (3)	$240,900	$86,550	$76,950	-6.9%	+3.9%
Atlanta (48)	87,000	31,250	27,800	-3.8	-0.4
Baltimore (38)	108,900	39,150	34,800	-0.5	+1.2
Bergen/Passaic Counties, NJ (8)	189,200	68,000	60,450	-6.9	+3.1
Birmingham (5)	83,800	30,100	26,750	+2.3	+3.3
Boston (47)	174,600	62,750	55,750	-7.3	-0.3
Buffalo (26)	78,400	28,150	25,050	-4.4	+1.9
Charlotte, NC (16)	96,600	34,700	30,850	+2.0	+2.5
Chicago (1)	123,800	44,500	39,550	+4.4	+5.2
Cincinnati (21)	82,600	29,700	26,400	+0.5	+2.1
Cleveland (27)	84,900	30,500	27,100	+4.3	+1.9
Columbus, OH (19)	83,300	29,950	26,600	-1.9	+2.2
Dallas (22)	92,600	33,250	29,600	-2.7	+2.0
Dayton (30)	73,100	26,250	23,350	+3.1	+1.7
Denver (23)	89,200	32,050	28,500	-0.2	+2.0
Detroit (9)	78,400	28,150	25,050	-2.0	+3.1
Fort Lauderdale (18)	94,500	33,950	30,200	-0.6	+2.4
Hartford (34)	159,300	57,250	50,900	-4.4	+1.5
Houston (24)	73,900	26,550	23,600	-1.3	+2.0
Indianapolis (10)	76,900	27,650	24,550	-0.7	+3.1
Kansas City, MO (11)	76,500	27,500	24,450	-2.3	+2.9
Los Angeles (44)	212,500	76,350	67,850	-5.3	+0.5
Louisville (13)	63,300	22,750	20,200	+0.9	+2.8
Memphis (12)	81,000	29,100	25,850	-1.8	+2.9
Miami (39)	92,000	33,050	29,400	-3.6	+1.1
Middlesex/Somerset Counties, NJ (4)	166,200	59,700	53,100	-4.3	+3.8
Milwaukee (17)	85,800	30,850	27,400	-0.9	+2.5
Minneapolis (31)	89,000	32,000	28,450	-4.4	+1.7
Nashville (37)	83,500	30,000	26,650	-2.5	+1.3
Nassau/Suffolk Counties, NY (28)	164,600	59,150	52,550	-6.0	+1.9
New Orleans (7)	70,200	25,200	22,400	-2.1	+3.2
New York City (36)	179,600	64,550	57,350	-3.0	+1.4
Oklahoma City (2)	55,500	19,950	17,750	+3.9	+5.1
Orlando (46)	85,300	30,650	27,250	+1.0	+0.1
Philadelphia (25)	120,200	43,200	38,400	+20.2	+2.0
Phoenix (45)	86,900	31,250	27,750	-0.2	+0.2
Pittsburgh (6)	74,400	26,750	23,750	+2.7	+3.3
Portland, OR (41)	84,600	30,400	27,000	+6.6	+1.0
Providence (33)	130,500	47,000	41,700	-3.0	+1.6
Riverside, CA (50)	132,600	47,650	42,350	-4.1	-2.3
Rochester, NY (42)	82,800	29,750	26,450	-1.0	+1.0
Sacramento (29)	146,100	52,500	46,650	+8.6	+1.8
Salt Lake City (20)	72,500	26,050	23,150	-1.2	+2.2
San Antonio (35)	66,800	24,000	21,350	+0.9	+1.5
San Diego (49)	186,300	66,950	59,500	-3.6	-1.2
San Francisco (40)	263,600	94,700	84,200	-5.3	+1.1
Seattle (43)	139,900	50,250	44,700	-3.0	+0.9
St. Louis (15)	83,500	30,000	26,650	+2.6	+2.6
Tampa/St. Petersburg (32)	73,100	26,250	23,350	-5.5	+1.7
Washington, D.C. (14)	153,800	55,250	49,100	+0.3	+2.7
U.S. Median	**94,500**	**33,950**	**30,200**	**-6.8**	**+2.5**

[1] Projected median price for the first quarter of 1991. [2] Assumes a 9.4%, 30-year fixed-rate mortgage and mortgage payments equal to 25% of the buyer's gross income. [3] After subtracting 5.8% inflation. [4] After subtracting 7.2% inflation. **Source:** The WEFA Group

Shopping for vacation-home bargains. The recession, overbuilding, and a 1986 tax law that made it tougher to write off rental losses have created a red-tag sale on second homes, knocking down prices as much as 20% in vacation areas from Maine to Arizona. Though most analysts expect the slump in second homes to continue for the next couple of years, many see demand picking up again after that. One compelling reason: The same baby boomers who triggered the 1970s housing boom are now getting into prime second-home buying age—45 to 54 years old. During the 1990s, the number of households in this age group will jump 43% to 20.7 million. But there are no guarantees that the aging of the boomers will translate into a rebound in second-home prices. So you should buy a second home only because you want to enjoy it or eventually retire to it—not because you think it will yield fabulous returns. To increase the likelihood of appreciation, focus on the part of the vacation-home market that's likely to see the strongest demand: year-round resort areas within two or three hours of a large city. Says Kenneth Bleakly, a manager at Arthur Andersen Real Estate Services group in Atlanta: "People want a getaway they can escape to a few weekends a month, not just once a year on vacation."

Refinancing your mortgage. In 1991, when interest rates on 30-year fixed-rate mortgages hit the 9% range—which was their lowest level in a decade—thousands of homeowners

Taking a Break on Your Home Sale

You can realize a big tax break from selling your home. But you have to know the basics. You can get a once-in-a-lifetime exclusion from taxes on as much as $125,000 in capital gains—$62,500 if you're married and file separately—if you are 55 or older and owned the house and lived in it as your principal residence for at least three of the past five years. If you and your spouse file jointly, only one of you must meet the tests to claim the exclusion.

A seller who doesn't qualify for the exclusion but is buying another principal residence usually gets tax deferral of his gains. But you must buy or build the new house within two years before or after the sale and your new house must cost at

1. SALES PRICE _____

2. SELLING EXPENSES
(including broker's commission and legal fees) _____

3. NET SALES PROCEEDS
(line 1 minus line 2) _____

4. NET INVESTMENT IN THE HOME YOU'RE SELLING

a. Purchase price plus nondeductible closing costs _____

b. Cost of improvements _____

c. Add lines 4a and 4b _____

d. Deferred gain, if any, from previous home sales _____

e. Insurance reimbursements for casualty losses _____

f. Tax write-offs for casualty losses _____

g. Residential energy credits claimed through 1985 _____

h. Add lines 4d through 4g _____

i. Line 4c minus line 4h _____

5. YOUR CAPITAL GAIN
(line 3 minus line 4i) If zero or less, stop here. You have no gain or a nondeductible loss. _____

rushed to refinance. A smart move? Not necessarily. While it's easy to get caught up in the euphoria of falling rates, you shouldn't jump in unless they meet certain criteria. The reason: To recoup closing costs out of the savings from your new, lower mortgage payments within five years, you generally need to refinance at a rate at least two percentage points below your current one. Still, refinancing may make sense in some cases even if your new rate is not that much lower. If you have an adjustable-rate mortgage, for example, you should consider switching to a fixed loan if you can lock in a rate of less than 10%.

You might also consider refinancing if you have borrowed substantially against a home-equity line of credit. Since many home-equity lines now carry interest rates of prime plus two percentage points, you can save on interest costs and monthly payments by refinancing with a lower-rate mortgage. One caveat: If you are a recent buyer, don't be surprised if a lender is unwilling to refinance. The reason: Much of your equity may have vanished. "We're turning down some people who bought with small down payments in the past year or two because the new appraisals are coming in at or below the original mortgage level," says Jim Masters, head of residential lending at the Federal Savings Bank in Waltham, Massachusetts. If you are in that unfortunate situation, your best hope is that brokers' claims of a comeback in home values will turn out to be true soon.

least as much as the so-called adjusted sales price of your old one.

As the worksheet shows, to calculate the gain accurately, you have to factor in such things as closing costs and home improvements. Use the worksheet to figure out how much, if any, of your house-sale profits will be taxed and how much of any capital gain you must defer. If you claimed a home-office deduction over the years, fine-tune the numbers with your tax preparer so they will reflect the percentages of your house allocated to residential and business uses. The worksheet presumes you meet the tests for deferring gains discussed here.

6. ONE-TIME EXCLUSION
If you elect the one-time tax exclusion for a seller aged 55 or older, enter the amount on line 5 or $125,000, whichever is less, and continue to line 7. If not, enter zero and skip to line 8. _____

7. ADJUSTED CAPITAL GAIN
(line 5 minus line 6) If the result is zero or less, stop. You owe no tax. If the result is greater than zero, you owe taxes on this amount unless you are buying another principal residence. In that case, move on to the next steps to see how much tax you can defer on the gain. _____

8. FIX-UP EXPENSES ON THE HOME YOU'RE SELLING
Enter the cost of repairs you make within 90 days of signing a sales contract and pay for within 30 days after the sale. _____

9. ADJUSTED SALES PRICE
(line 3 minus line 8) _____

10. COST OF NEW HOME
(down payment, mortgage, and closing costs) _____

11. TAXABLE GAIN
(line 9 minus the total of line 10 plus line 6) If the result is zero or less, enter zero and proceed to line 12. If it is greater than zero, enter either that amount, the figure on line 5, or—if you elected the exclusion— the number on line 7, whichever is less. _____

12. AMOUNT OF CAPITAL GAIN YOU MUST DEFER
(line 5 minus line 11 or, if you elected the exclusion, line 7 minus line 11) _____

Remodeling Tips That Can Save You Time and Money

With contractors cutting their prices, homeowners can get rooms renovated for a lot less these days.

Since 1983, remodeling expenditures in the U.S. have risen 115% to $106 billion in 1991. Lots of people are spending lots of bucks to turn house into home. Yet, there's nothing like renovation to dissolve not only your solvency but your sanity. Getting past the most common pitfalls—cost overruns, missed deadlines, or shoddy workmanship—means taking some precautions. For advice, *Money* interviewed dozens of professional and civilian renovation veterans. Here are 10 tips to prevent your project from becoming a money pit:

Spare your savings. The best financing solution is usually a home-equity loan (paid in a lump sum) or a home-equity line of credit, which you draw down as you need it. A loan going for about 10.5%, for example, means an after-tax cost of only 7.15% to a homeowner in the 33% bracket. Your savings should earn a point or two more than that. Remember, you can deduct interest on a loan of as much as $100,000.

Get the help you need. Big jobs usually call for professionals. A contractor is appropriate for straightforward improvements—for example, replacing kitchen cabinets. But if you plan dramatic change, a skilled architect or designer will likely get you better space for the buck. Expect to pay 8% to 12% of estimated construction costs for working drawings. If you want the architect to supervise the job, you may have to pay 5% more.

Don't rely on a license alone. "Licensing gives consumers a false sense of security," Patchan warns. Some states don't even require it. Talk personally with former clients of any professional and walk through at least one project his company has completed.

Suit yourself. There's little point in designing for the next owner. Except for kitchens and baths, remodeling has limited paybacks. And Bryan Patchan at the Remodelors Council of the National Association of Home Builders advises against projects that raise your home's value more than 20% above similar local houses.

Define your dream. You can afford $85-a-foot granite counters—if, for instance, you choose inexpensive vinyl for the floor. Remember: Price varies enormously in every category.

Work in phases. If your budget won't stretch to cover your wish list, consider delayed gratification. A carpenter could put in skylight frames and then return, maybe six months later, to cut the hole and install the glass. Don't skimp on insulation, windows, or the heating, electrical, and plumbing systems, however.

Be honest about your budget. Most architects or designers will not charge for an initial hour or so to discuss your ideas. Once you find a serious contender, be open about the budget. Some owners worry that if they mention a

$25,000 ceiling, they'll get an $18,000 job with padded costs. Maybe. But if you don't trust the designer, you shouldn't hire him.

Plan for the inevitable hitches. Even the best-laid plans can be derailed by surprises lurking inside walls. Ask the contractor how he will handle problems. After an approved plan, any deviation will cost you money. Change orders should be in writing. Set aside at least 10% of your budget for unexpected costs.

Get the contract right. It should spell out the work to be done, materials to be used, and who buys what. Set up a payment schedule, reserving at least 10% that you pay only when the project is completed to your satisfaction. For $5.95, the American Homeowners Foundation (1724 South Quincy Street, Arlington, VA 22204) will provide an eight-page model agreement.

Avoid the naked-lady syndrome. Most rooms look better dressed. Reserve money for high-profile finishing details, such as special moldings, doorknobs, and other hardware. Without these accoutrements, even the best design will fall flat.

How to Burglarproof Your Home

Having your home broken into can be traumatic. Take steps to protect your family and property now.

In 1991, more than 3 million American families discovered just how devastating a burglary can be. It is the one serious crime that you are most likely to suffer, outnumbering the 1.8 million car thefts each year and the 1.1 million robberies (only larcenies—thefts such as pickpocketing that do not involve entry, damage, or injury—are more common at 9 million). Daylight is no protection: Some 49% of all break-ins occur during the day. Statistics on reported burglaries nationwide place your risk of being hit at between 2% and 3% a year, but the odds exceed 5% in many cities. More-over, Justice Department surveys suggest that better than half of all burglaries go unreported. The thieves' annual take: $3.4 billion.

Don't think of burglary as just a crime against property, either. In fully 13% of break-ins, crooks encounter someone at home; a third of those confrontations end in assault; more than half the assaults include rape. And there are often lingering emotional scars.

"After a burglary, the psyche heals slowly," says Joe Mele of the National Crime Prevention Institute (NCPI) at the University of Louisville. "Either people are afraid to go home again or they adopt a fortress-like mentality and they won't go out." In only 14% of break-ins is the culprit ever caught.

What draws a burglar to a particular house? Evidence of affluence and the lack of an alarm system; houses with alarms are struck only a third as often as those without them. Your locale counts, too, and not just whether you live in a high-crime neighborhood. Burglars are like real estate agents; they think location, location, and location. A study of Philadelphia suburbs found that burglars strike 40% more often within three blocks of major thorough-fares, which offer easy escape, than elsewhere. Crooks also prefer corner houses; nationwide, roughly four out of 10 burglaries happen at corner homes, because two of their closest neighbors are across the street.

In 95% of break-ins, burglars case the joint first. That's easy enough when the crook is a neighbor (often a teenager), as is true about 25% of the time. But professional burglars may pose as joggers so they can spend time in your neighborhood; appear at your door pretending to be salesmen or fund raisers, like the bumbling bandits in the movie "Home Alone;" or befriend maids and workmen to find out when you're gone. "Burglars are shy people

A Burglar's Crime-Stopping Tips

Forget Cary Grant's elegant cat burglar in "To Catch a Thief." The real burglar who raids your home is likely to be the criminal equivalent of a working stiff, as *Money*'s interview with one such pro reveals. Active intermittently since 1974 (except for 10 years in prison on three burglary convictions), the subject says he's looted over 250 homes—sometimes working alone, sometimes with his girlfriend—in the medium-size Sunbelt city where he lives. He's netted close to $1 million but has never gotten rich: "I spend half the money on drugs and the rest on living expenses, so I have nothing to show for it."

Q. How do you select targets?
A. We like rural homes because they're secluded, but we hit city houses, too, if they're surrounded by trees or anything that blocks a neighbor's view. Whenever we burglarize a place, we keep our eyes out for other homes to hit. A few weeks later, we come back and rob them, too.

Q. What types of people do you hit?
A. Middle income or higher. We want to go places where we can make a solid score. We're looking for homes with guns, VCRs, and two or three TV sets.

Q. How do you operate?
A. My girlfriend knocks on the door. If somebody answers, she asks for directions or acts as if she went to the wrong address. But if nobody's home, we park in the garage, close the garage door, and then break down the door leading to the home. Once inside, my girlfriend looks in closets, dressers, and under mattresses for jewelry, cash, and guns. I grab microwave ovens, television sets, VCRs, and stereo equipment. We never stay longer than 10 minutes.

Q. What time of day do you work?
A. Mostly the morning. It's simpler than at night, since the kids are in school and the parents are at work.

Q. What if someone comes home?
A. Once my girlfriend and I were in the driveway of a house we'd burgled when the owner drove up behind us. My girlfriend tried to convince her she was looking for someone. But then the woman spotted me, got scared, and took off. She got my license plate number, though. That was one time I got caught.

Q. What happens to the property?
A. I sell it to fences. Many of them are also drug dealers. Sometimes they resell it to average citizens but mostly they trade it for drugs. A lot of it winds up in Mexico. One fence I used to work for would load the stolen merchandise into a dump truck, cover it with dirt, and pretend to be hauling dirt to Mexico for road construction.

Q. How much do you get paid?
A. For a 19-inch television, anywhere from $75 to $100; for a VCR, about $100. For a .38 special or .22 pistol, the fence won't give you more than $30. But if you get a .44 Magnum or a nine millimeter, you can get $150.

Q. What would deter you?
A. A high-quality alarm system. Most burglars, if they see an alarm, they'll go to another house; why bother trying to bypass an alarm when there are so many homes without them? Dogs are noisy and threatening, but you can usually stop them with a piece of meat or, if that doesn't work, shooting them—although I don't usually go in with a gun. Neighborhood watch programs are another story. I try to stay away from neighborhoods like that.

Q. Were you ever burglarized?
A. Once, in 1986. They stole a VCR and some jewelry. I felt mad—the same way the people I robbed must have felt when they came back to an empty place. But I guess what goes around comes around.

who don't like surprises," observes Paul Cromwell, director of the Criminal Justice Program at the University of Miami, a city with a high burglary rate in 1990. "They like to arrive when nobody else is home." Since summer is vacation time for so many Americans, it is also prime burglary season (break-ins peak in August, when 9.3% of them occur).

Money offers the following advice from police, security experts, criminologists, and even a former burglar (see the box at left) on protecting your property and recovering quickly if you do suffer a loss.

Securing Your Home

First, be sure your house is protected. Experts recommend five strategies:

Reinforce all entrances. Despite their reputation as second-story men, burglars enter on the ground floor 80% of the time. And they get in quickly: According to the NCPI, the average burglar spends no more than 60 seconds breaking in. "The trick is to delay them for 90 seconds or longer so they may get nervous and leave," says NCPI's Mele. Among the tips: fortify exterior doors with deadbolt locks (about $40 to $80 each) in which the bolt extends at least 1½ inches into the door frame; reinforce sliding glass patio doors with a locking metal rod ($10 to $20) that prevents the door from being opened; and limit pet doors to no more than six inches across, because some burglars use a child to slip inside and unlock the door. In high-crime areas, consider putting steel security shutters ($120) on first- and second-floor windows and bars ($30) on basement windows. And to keep burglars out of your garage, drill a hole in the track that holds the sliding door and insert a pin or padlock to keep the door from being lifted. Most important, once you've installed these safeguards, remember to use them: 40% of burglars get in without using any force at all.

Keep your home visible to neighbors. The privacy that many homeowners seek from high fences and shrubs works against them when it comes to break-ins. The experts' advice is to limit greenery to no more than two feet in height, if practical, and build fences of the see-through variety so that burglars can't use them to hide. For protection at night, place floodlights all around your house and leave porch and garage lights on while you are asleep.

Install an alarm. Although these are practically standard equipment on new homes costing $350,000 or more, nine out of 10 American residences lack them. That's unfortunate, since several companies—including ADT and Brink's Home Security Service—install basic systems for as little as $400 to $600 (a more elaborate system for a large suburban home would run $2,000 to $3,000). Besides sounding a siren when tripped, the best alarms automatically place a telephone call to a 24-hour-a-day monitoring service (cost: $20 to $30 a month). The attendant calls you to make sure it's not a false alarm—as 98% are, thanks to homeowner carelessness—and then phones the police. Many insurers will give you 5% to 15% off your homeowners policy premiums for putting in such a system. And renters can qualify, too, by installing a wireless alarm, like AT&T's System 8000 ($1,200 and up). Regardless of what system you choose, put decals on windows and doors and a small sign on the lawn announcing its presence; otherwise, the system has no value as a deterrent.

Form a neighborhood watch group. Since nosy neighbors are your best protection, enlist their support through a block or neighborhood club whose members keep an eye out for trouble. About 1 million Americans belong to such programs, usually organized with the help of the police or sheriff's department. "They promote a better rapport between the community and the police," says Pamela Matsuda, program coordinator of Safety Awareness for Everyone (SAFE), a nonprofit association that helped set up some 2,500 watch groups in the San Francisco area. That kind of cooperation often slows crime in surprising ways. In Tulsa, for example, police began in September 1990 helping school officials fight truancy by visiting the homes of habitually absent students. Within six months, the truancy rate dropped 50% and daytime burglaries fell off an impressive 27%. "We're fighting the social ills that breed crime," says Tulsa Police Chief Drew Diamond.

Don't advertise your travels. Arrange things so that would-be crooks think you're home. "One of the biggest mistakes people make is to stop delivery of mail and newspapers—burglars may know the people who handle those services and find out you're leaving," says David Wacker, a former deputy sheriff and the author of *The Complete Guide to Home Security* (Betterway Publications). Wacker suggests that you ask a neighbor to pick up your mail and papers; use timers ($10 to $35) to turn on lights and radios every evening; and make sure to lower the ring volume on your phones so they can't be heard from the street. He also says to put your business address, not your home address, on luggage tags, so that baggage handlers won't know where you live. "That seems a bit paranoid," Wacker admits, "but a little paranoia can be healthy."

Insuring Your Possessions

Besides minimizing the risk of burglary, you should also make sure your home is properly insured. For instance, don't buy any homeowners policy that is less comprehensive than a so-called HO-3, or open-perils policy, which protects you against burglary, theft, fire, wind, and other such hazards. Expect to pay $300 to $600 a year for $100,000 of coverage with a $250 deductible, though you can bring the price down by raising the deductible (hiking it to $500 shaves the cost by 10%). The face value should equal at least 80% of what it would cost to rebuild your home from the ground up; your belongings will normally be covered for half that amount.

Since such policies do not usually reimburse you for the full cost of replacing stolen goods, only for their depreciated value, you should also consider a rider that provides replacement-value coverage. That will add about 15% to the premium. You should add another rider to cover furs, watches, jewelry, silver, and other valuables that exceed the conventional limit of $1,000 to $2,500 (cost: $100 a year for each additional $1,000 of coverage). If your valuables include fine art, hire an appraiser to judge its worth. You can find appraisers either through your insurance agent or the American Society of Appraisers (800-272-8258); fees range from $100 to $300 an hour.

Renters need insurance protection, too, though the Insurance Information Institute, a New York City-based trade association, estimates that three out of four of them lack it. Basic tenants insurance—known as HO-4—runs about $75 to $225 for a $25,000 policy with a $250 deductible. Most renters don't realize that their landlord's insurance covers only the building itself, not their possessions. They find out the hard way, after the burglary.

With all insurance, keep a complete list of your property—including serial numbers of appliances and electronic gear, so police can track it—plus receipts for all purchases. It is also a good idea to take photographs of the more valuable items, or even to make a room-by-room videotape that can serve as a visual inventory. Keep the list some place where it can't be stolen or destroyed by fire.

Coping with a Break-In

Even with the greatest precautions, there is still the possibility your home will be hit. Here's what to do then:

If you wake up and hear an intruder in your home, don't confront him directly. "Burglars are like wild animals," says Jim Rodriguez, a crime-prevention expert with the San Antonio police. "They're most likely to fight if they feel trapped." The best strategy, says Rodriguez, is to get yourself and your family out of the house fast; if that's not practical, scream or blow a compressed-air horn (about $25) while your spouse phones the police. In the nightmarish event that you wake to find someone in your room, pretend to be asleep. The experts say you still have the odds on your side: Most burglars won't attack unless frightened.

Similarly, if you return home and find your house broken into, don't go inside unless you are sure the thieves have left. Once you do go inside, be careful not to touch anything until the police have finished searching for evidence. Don't give the cops a list of stolen property off the top of your head; sit down and make a detailed inventory, since the list you give the police will serve as the basis for your insurance claim. Get a copy of the police report, and take photos of any damage before cleaning up.

Call your insurance company within a day or two and fill out its claim form carefully. Submit copies of receipts not only for lost goods but also for the cost of repairs. After reviewing the document, a company claims adjuster will propose a settlement. If you don't like the offer, you have several courses of action: you can haggle directly with the adjuster for a better deal; you can hire a private adjuster (commission: 10% to 15% of any settlement) to negotiate for you; if your contract allows, you can take the case to binding arbitration (typical cost: $150 to $350); or you can complain to your state insurance commissioner. For more information on each of these options, telephone the National Insurance Consumer Hotline at 800-942-4242.

Meanwhile, check for ancillary insurance: some credit cards, for instance, automatically insure goods charged to the card against theft, loss, or accidental damage for 90 days after purchase. Notify banks or issuers immediately of any stolen checks or credit cards. And if your insurance fails to compensate you fully, find out whether you can deduct some of the loss from your taxes. Federal tax rules let you write off that portion of a loss that exceeds the sum of any insurance money you get plus 10% of your adjusted gross income plus $100. "You won't get much of a deduction except for a major theft," says Mary Sprouse, a former Internal Revenue Service auditor and author of *Sprouse's Income Tax Handbook.* "But any deduction is better than none."

Finally, keep your eye out for clues the police might have overlooked.

The nicest thing about money is that it never clashes with anything I wear. — comedian Myron Cohen

SPENDING

Money-Saving Secrets of the Supershoppers

When was the last time you earned 134% on an investment? Not lately, we'll bet. But that, in effect, is the return Tinker Simmons got when she bought $1,734.41 worth of clothes for $741.57 during one of her well-planned shopping forays. In this chapter, you'll find out how Tinker and other very serious bargain hunters regularly save hundreds of dollars using "roboshopping" tactics.

Because looking for a bargain has become something of a national pastime in a tough economy, retail stores have increasingly turned to "sales" to lure customers. The stories in this chapter tell you how to discover and take advantage of super savings, as well as how to recognize and avoid come-ons that don't deliver. The table on pages 122-123 gives the inside story on those non-bargains, from women's and men's apparel to home furnishings to electronics and appliances.

Then there's everybody's least-favorite shopping experience: hunting for a new car. Despite significant price increases over the last decade, car dealers are feeling a pinch of their own from recalcitrant shoppers. The result is that you don't have to put up with high prices, manipulation, and sleazy salesmen anymore. It's a buyer's market. Find out how to get a great value on your next car (page 124), how to get the best deal on a rental (page 125), whether it makes more sense to lease or purchase (pages 126-127), and what salesmen *really* think of customers (page 128). Also, take advantage of *Money*'s exclusive Car Cost Ratings (beginning on page 153) to compare the suggested retail price, the dealer's cost, and your target price on 522 models.

If you're on the road a lot, you're interested in savings on hotels and flights, as well as ways to get the most from travel agents and tour operators. A package of stories beginning on page 129 outlines the traveler's bill of rights and points you toward the best deals.

No matter what you're in the market for, it pays to be informed and to shop around. These days, some of the easiest money you'll make is the money you don't spend.

The Year of the Roboshoppers

As hard times spread, a new breed of educated consumer is proving that smart shopping can often earn you far more than investing.

Tinker Simmons always snares her bargain. She employs surveillance: She stalks unsure shoppers in her favorite outlet stores and, when they put back a sale item, she moves in. Plus counterintelligence: She chats up salespeople to glean inside information about future sales. And she attacks: She demands discounts on discounts, talking down the price of what she prizes to store managers. During a recent Christmas season, Simmons, an office manager from Paducah, Kentucky with a household income of $40,000, shopped the local Hess and Elder Beerman department stores, bringing home $741.57 worth of high-quality clothing, cosmetics, and housewares that she calculates would have amounted to $1,734.41 retail—for a 57% saving.

"My friends are so jealous of my finds," she crows. Simmons deserves to boast. Have you tried making 134% in the stock market lately? In effect, that's what she did by shopping smart.

Tinker Simmons is just one of a growing number of killer shoppers who take on bargain hunting as determinedly as Schwarzenegger takes on punks. Says Sue Goldstein, author of 50 U.S. bargain sourcebooks, including *The Underground Shopper* (Ballantine): "Consumers today want things at half-price or they'll walk right out of a store."

Why now? Because between 1989 and 1990 alone, inflation jumped from an annual rate of 4.6% to 6.4%, and many families, already stretched, are facing a steep rise in consumer costs. Because a struggling economy has resulted in a sharp decline in consumer spending

and personal income, which is causing ailing retailers to drum up business. Because, explains Sharyn Brooks, vice president of consumer research at Management Horizons, a Dublin, Ohio consulting firm, "More people than ever want to beat retailers at their own game." After the spend-happy 1980s, the demand for bargains has become intense, and off-price has gone mainstream. According to a Fall 1990 survey of 4,000 households by Management Horizons, 68% considered sales the single most important reason to enter a store, up from 45% just four years before. Shopping methods that were once considered loony or low end are now viewed as just plain smart.

For the vigilant new consumers, preparation counts. They routinely mount reconnaissance trips to nearby discount stores. They do advance work for advertised sales by, yes, collecting coupons and comparing prices. And they take utmost advantage of rebates, frequently challenging store managers to match lower prices that might be found at rival stores.

Call them roboshoppers. Or call them fanatics. But the returns on such investments of time often hit 65% to 90% off retail prices on nearly anything you can name—fashionable clothing, electronics, food, furnishings, and more—which equates to sizable change in your pocket or, as one roboshopper calculates it: "The money we save lets us take $4,000 skiing trips to Colorado for free."

A common denominator among the new vulture shoppers is the time spent snaring bargains. In Lilburn, Georgia, for example, roboshopper Donna Tallent, a receptionist with an engineer husband and three children, recently upped her bargain searching from 10 to 14 hours a week. She wanted more out of the family's $60,000 annual income. Before her daily expeditions, Tallent equips herself with lunch provisions and a prime selection of discount coupons culled from the four shoeboxes she's stuffed over the past 15 years. Local cashiers watch for her arrival the way farmers track a tornado on the horizon.

Tallent's techniques? She sweeps shelves for mismarked items and pesters companies when dissatisfied with products, which often results in more rebates. She also keeps tabs on high-ticket items until they're priced just right, recently acquiring a Smith-Corona electric typewriter, for instance, after it was marked down from $269 to $89. On average, Tallent nets $300 worth of free housewares and food on a major shopping trip—or, typically, 60% savings that add up to roughly $9,000 a year.

There's no doubt that the economic gloom is fueling bargain fever, but attitude, too, is key. Shopping skirmishes have turned to all-out war. Madelyn Miller of Dallas can easily afford the luxury of retail prices and services on a combined family income of $200,000. Married to a doctor, she has two kids and owns her own advertising agency. Yet, she willingly devotes more than 10 hours a week to bargain hunting and spends approximately $8,400 on goods—but reaps savings of more than $33,000 a year. Does she like a deal? "Do the Osmonds have teeth?" she replies. Miller, who calls herself a "bargain athlete," adds: "I treat bargain hunting like training."

Miller's bargain biceps pump up to an average of 75% off retail prices. She recently purchased 25 settings of Studio Nova china for $125 (retail, $312.50) and a hand-painted Mexican chest from the Horchow Collection for $100 (originally $500). Like many killer shoppers, she gets on every mailing list she can find. She haunts Loehmann's, Marshalls, Tuesday Morning (a local discount warehouse), Macy's, and Neiman-Marcus. She reviews bargain days at the start of every month "just like business appointments." And she prefers to shop sales the night before, targeting items for the next morning's buying trip.

The time roboshoppers like Miller and Tallent spend on sales isn't excessive in this crowd; some bargain hunters will sacrifice months to seal a deal. Take, for example, Barbara Helfgott, a freelance book reviewer for the *New York Times* with a $40,000 annual income. Not long ago, she fell hard for a set of Ralph Lauren linens that she saw at Bloomingdale's, but balked at the $600-plus price tag. A pillowcase alone was $60. "Certain merchandise sings," says Helfgott. After a fruitless five-month search for a discount, she began to lose her patience—but not her desire. Red-blooded roboshopper that she is, Helfgott

How to Become a Roboshopper

A 1990 poll of 300 *Money* subscribers revealed that 54% are more concerned about finding bargains now than they were the year before. In fact, 51% said they would go 15 minutes out of their way to save $10, and 79% would invest half an hour or more to save $50. If you're ready to roboshop, here's how:

Timing. Go shopping in foul weather, such as during an unexpected snow- or rainstorm. With the faint of heart at home, you'll not only have the run of the store but optimum bargains. The best months to shop: frigid January and sweltering August, when items are also drastically reduced to make room for fresh goods.

Networking. It pays to establish relationships with managers in your favorite stores. Once you're on friendly terms, ask them what they consider buys at that moment. Many will offer you tips on your next visit as well.

Complaining. If a store has run out of an advertised item, try negotiating the same low price for a similar item. Be reasonable, but assert yourself. Simply say: "I came in for this advertised item, yet there are no more. I want this item instead at the same discount."

Treasure hunting. Most discount stores are not famous for service or neatness. If you can't see the color or size you want, keep checking the racks.

took a job at Bloomingdale's as a full-time salesclerk making $6 an hour, and after two months she qualified for the 15% employee discount. Then, after lucking into a 10%-off sale as well, she paid about $400 for the Lauren linens—and promptly quit.

Other roboshoppers are more time-efficient. In Delavan, Illinois, nursing assistant Judy Hilt and husband John, a machine repairer, make one grocery trip for staples every year, spending $600 and saving close to $1,200. On a recent expedition, the Hilts hauled home 80 grocery bags in two pickup trucks—and had a 10-foot-long register receipt. "We've been doing this for 15 years, so we've got it down to an art," explains John. Not surprisingly, this operation rivals a space shuttle launch. The

Hilts usually buy four newspapers every Sunday in order to hoard discount coupons. They notify the grocery store to prepare for their visit. Once there, the couple purchase canned goods, pounds and pounds of sugar, coffee, flour, pasta, and dried vegetables, beans, and rice. Back home, they restock their basement, and "if we're hungry," brags Hilt, "we don't need to run out to the store."

Like other bargain hunters, Hilt always negotiates prices. Recently, he was able to get a Quasar 13-inch color TV reduced from $269 to $159 at K Mart by employing a technique common to roboshoppers: the strategic complaint. "I convince store managers to knock down a price by saying I saw the item for less at another store," he says.

Sorting Out a Sale from a Scam

While everybody is slashing prices, few are really offering bargains. Here's how to recognize the difference.

Few who lived through a Crazy Eddie commercial could forget the message, shrieked at TV audiences by a half-crazed-looking pitchman for the now defunct New York-area discounter: "Our prices are insane!" Fewer still suspected that Eddie was a prophet in his own time. Today, not long after Eddie's screams were stilled by liquidation, every retailer from Bangor to Burbank seems certifiably mad. Once haughty, high-priced department stores like Lord & Taylor, Bullock's, and Neiman-Marcus are down in the dirt with the discounters, shredding price tags and luring shoppers with the promise of fabulous bargains. Marvin Rothenberg, a Fair Lawn, New Jersey retail consultant, estimates that 75% of all department store items are being sold at discount prices, compared with 40% a decade ago. So crazily competitive is the market that stately

firms like debt-ridden Bloomingdale's and Jordan Marsh are in Chapter 11, and others like B. Altman have disappeared altogether. As tough times and consumer uncertainty make selling even harder, there is no sign that the sale epidemic will do anything but spread.

Retailers' pain doesn't automatically mean shoppers' gain either. That's because much of the department store price-cutting is as deceptive as a cat's grin. They're manipulating prices madly. Nationwide, names like Sears, J.C. Penney, and the May Department Stores have been charged with price manipulation. The department stores' basic scam is to elevate the "original price" to an unreal level, then announce what appears to be a dramatically deep discount. Variations abound, but the heart of darkness is unquestionably private-label goods, which department stores order directly from manufacturers, affixing a proprietary label and the highest markups in the store.

Robert Kahn, editor of the newsletter *Retailing Today*, observes that during the past four years or so, department stores have been moving more heavily into private label, which accounts for as much as 40% of women's, men's, and kids' apparel, up from 30% in the early 1980s. Add markups running as high as 80%, and there is endless opportunity to play price games.

Just how wide a berth the stores have to mislead you and how shoppers can counter the disinformation are revealed in the accompanying table on pages 122-123. It guides you through all of the major department store lines plus electronics and appliances, which are now sold primarily by discounters.

Most retailers stonewalled our efforts to elicit this information from them. ("You're talking about educating the consumer about markdowns," said Julian Taub, a Bloomingdale's senior vice president. "For us, that would be self-defeating.") So we turned to retailing analysts, marketing consultants, and industry groups like the National Retail Federation. Here, reading from the left, is how to use the table:

Typical markup is the difference between the price the store pays for an item and what it sells it for. The lower the initial markup, the less the chance of pricing shenanigans. Conversely, because private-label goods and imports carry the highest markups, they are able to sustain the largest number of price cuts and, thereby, blow the most smoke in shoppers' eyes. So don't be impressed by a 30%-off price tag on a private-label item. Tomorrow, the same item could be 50% off—and still not amount to much of a bargain.

Percent of goods sold at a markdown refers to the proportion of all goods sold by department stores in 1990 at a discount. The more markdowns, the more the chance for deception. Retail experts estimate more than 60% of private-label men's and women's apparel is sold at reduced prices, compared with 25% of branded apparel.

Promotional sales are the short-term price reductions, typically of 20% to 30% or so. At least one item, for example, is on promotional sale in a typical store's home furnishings department every week of the year. If you see a promotional sale advertised—they usually bear such labels as "three days only" or "special event"—it may be worth your while to check it out. Usually the merchandise will rise in price again within days.

Clearance sales generally last until the goods are gone—from 10 to 12 weeks. The discounts tend to be higher than those for promotional sales—more on the order of 30% to 50% or more. Two reasons: The goods are often odd sizes and unpopular styles (apparel and shoes fall heavily into this class), and the store needs to move them in order to make way for new merchandise.

Misleading sales are the new kid on the selling floor: giveaways that last too long (like four weeks) or occur too frequently (like twice a month) to be real and often appear at a time when many other goods in that category are fully priced. A telling clue: Private-label apparel that is discounted early in the season probably was never intended to be sold at a nonsale price.

Grade, based on interviews with retailing experts, gives you a shorthand tip on how wary you should be when shopping each category of goods. It is no coincidence that private label dominates the D, or danger, grade.

What to look for or avoid flags some of the details that point to a product's value—or away from it. The cosmetics department, which has the most unmolested prices and moderate markups in the entire department store, is one area with little to avoid.

Comments pulls together the most useful shopping tips we could find on each category of merchandise listed. One rule to remember: If you are unconvinced that an item is a bargain, you can safely assume that it's overpriced. Look elsewhere.

How to Tell When a Bargain Is Really No Bargain

	Typical markup *	% of goods sold at a markdown	Number or length of promotional sales a year	Number of clearance sales a year	Number of misleading sales a year	Grade
WOMEN'S APPAREL						
BRAND NAME	50%-60%	25%	Weekly/3 to 4 days	5	5 or fewer	B
PRIVATE LABEL	60%-80%	Over 60%	Weekly/up to 7 days	5	Up to 52	D
HIGH FASHION	60%-70%	Over 50%	Weekly/7 to 10 days	5	N.A.	N.A.
MEN'S AND BOYS' APPAREL						
BRAND NAME	50%-60%	25%	Weekly/3 to 4 days	3 men's	5 or fewer	A
PRIVATE LABEL	60%-80%	Over 60%	Weekly/up to 7 days	4 boys'	Up to 52	C
HOME FURNISHINGS (LINENS, COOKWARE, PORCELAIN)						
BRAND NAME	45%-50%	15%-20%	Weekly/4 to 7 days	2	20 or fewer	B
PRIVATE LABEL	60%-75%	Over 50%	Weekly/up to 7 days	N.A.	Up to 52	A to D
WOMEN'S ACCESSORIES (COSTUME JEWELRY, HANDBAGS, SCARVES)						
BRAND NAME	50%-70%	15%-25%	Monthly/3 to 4 days	2	5 or fewer	D
PRIVATE LABEL	50%-70%	15%-25%	Monthly/3 to 4 days	N.A.	20 to 25	D
WOMEN'S SHOES						
BRAND NAME	50%	25%	Twice monthly/3 to 4 days	2	5 or fewer	B to C
PRIVATE LABEL	60%-70%	25%	N.A.	N.A.	20 to 25	C
INFANTS' AND CHILDREN'S CLOTHING						
BRAND NAME	45%-55%	25%	Weekly/5 to 7 days	4	N.A.	A
PRIVATE LABEL	60%-70%	Over 50%	N.A.	N.A.	N.A.	C
COSMETICS (MAKEUP, SKIN CARE, FRAGRANCES)						
ALL TYPES	40%-60%	N.A.	Gift-with-purchase, purchase-with-purchase; twice monthly/3 to 4 days	N.A.	N.A.	A
ELECTRONICS AND APPLIANCES						
ALL TYPES	26%-28%	10%	Weekly/7 days	N.A.	N.A.	C

* As a percentage of retail price; N.A. Not applicable

What to look for or avoid	Comments
LOOK FOR: natural buttons of shell or horn, pockets that lie smooth. **AVOID:** mismatched plaids, sloppy stitching, loose seams.	Stay with brand-name labels that you like, since the quality is unlikely to vary. When it comes to private-label merchandise, unless you've got a sharp eye for value, you're on your own. To beat stiff prices on high fashion, seek out off-price retailers such as Loehmann's or Marshalls that specialize in designer imports.
LOOK FOR: fully lined suit coats and jackets, deep pockets, securely stitched cuffs and trousers. **AVOID:** crooked collars.	The range in prices in men's and boys' wear is much narrower than for women's, so shopping for value is easier. When comparing brand and private labels, check fiber content (natural fabrics breathe better but are costlier) and make sure buttons are firmly affixed.
LOOK FOR: linens with uniformly stitched edges. **AVOID:** private-label cutlery and bakeware lacking adequate instructions for care.	Private-label cookware such as Macy's can be a good value, with well-made, sturdy, useful features. Decorative European ceramics (vases, candlesticks, and the like) are generally hand-painted. Ceramics from the Orient generally use decals (and don't disclose it).
LOOK FOR: secure clasps, thick, tightly knotted strings. **AVOID:** gold plating that isn't even.	Bags and scarves: especially check the quality of fabrics, leather, construction. It's practically impossible to make a value judgment about costume jewelry. Prices depend almost totally on the trendiness of a style or the prestige of a brand.
LOOK FOR: soles made of leather. **AVOID:** poorly glued shoes, colors that don't match.	Brand shoemakers distribute different styles to different stores, so comparison shopping can be difficult. Stick with a retailer you trust and wait for sales. To get good value in private-label footwear, stay away from shoes that have seams on the sides (a mark of inferior leather).
LOOK FOR: durable, washable fabrics. **AVOID:** zippers and lace that scratch around neck and arms.	Beware misleadingly labeled "playwear." It's designed to resemble sleepwear but does not retard flames. Also check clothing proportions carefully. The legs on some garments are too long or short for toddlers' bodies. The best-wearing kids' fabric: 80% cotton/20% poly denim.
LOOK FOR: purchase-with-purchase sales, large sizes of everything.	While the larger sizes in cosmetics pay off, the cash outlay may give you pause. You get a 15% discount on a 1.75-ounce bottle of Advanced Night Repair by Estée Lauder, for example, but it costs you $70; the 0.87-ounce size is a less daunting $40.
LOOK FOR: manufacturer's warranty. **AVOID:** extended-service warranties, unless the retailer offers to throw one in for free.	Appliances: For competitive prices, stick with big discounters or Sears' and Montgomery Ward's appliance departments. The only way to be sure you get a good deal on electronics is by comparison shopping. Stick to reputable retailers with their own service departments.

Get a Great Value on Your Next Car

Sticker prices are higher, but sales continue to skid. When it comes to negotiating a deal, you are in the driver's seat.

After a decade in which prices of new cars increased 84%—a discouraging 25% more than the median family's income—sticker shock has become a routine part of the new-car buying experience.

But dealers who expect buyers to submit quietly may be in for a shock of their own. Today's auto shoppers are willing to do whatever it takes to get the best value, from ferreting out the wholesale cost (and refusing to pay more than 2% to 6% over that amount) to shunning new cars altogether, in favor of low-mileage former rental cars. Now it's the customers who are making the rules. Buyer's market or not, though, today's best deals will still go to the savviest shoppers and steeliest bargainers. So here, step by step, is advice on how to save on the purchase of your next new automobile:

Narrow your choices to no more than four models before you go near a dealer. If you wander into a showroom with only a vague idea of the car you want, a salesman could easily hustle you into the highest-priced model on the floor. To gauge the selection in the price range you have in mind, scan the tables beginning on page 153. For more detailed data on cars that catch your fancy, consider ordering a *Money Auto Cost Comparison,* a customized report that compares specifications, standard and optional features, dealer costs, retail prices, and complete ownership costs for any two models. (To order, call 800-777-1880; the report costs $19.95.) Pay close attention to your car's expected resale value. Depreciation

Hire a Pro to Kick the Tires of a Used Car

The trouble with buying a used car is that you rarely know what shape it's really in. But, now, you can enlist an independent professional to help you steer clear of lemons. For $100 or less, two burgeoning franchised companies, Auto Critic of Dallas and Car Checkers of America in Bridgewater, New Jersey, will send out a technician within 24 hours to make a curbside, engine-to-exhaust-pipe inspection for you.

Since these diagnostic car pros aren't affiliated with garages, they have no built-in incentive to recommend repairs. And with approximately 18 million used automobiles sold last year, the inspection franchises are spreading rapidly. Auto Critic now has 21 franchises in 14 states, including Florida, New York, and Texas. Car Checkers has 35 outlets in California, Georgia, Massachusetts, and 14 other states.

At Auto Critic, which charges $54 to $89 (the fee varies by location) for its 90-point analysis, mechanics accompany prospective buyers on test drives. "Because we can tell him about a car's shortcomings, we find that the average customer saves about $600 off the originally negotiated price after using our service," says president Pat Ludwick.

Car Checkers' work costs $75 to $100 and relies on diagnostic equipment that analyzes more than 3,500 auto components. A technician also inspects the car with an ultrasound device that reveals rust invisible to the naked eye and measures paint thickness to detect bodywork the seller...uh...forgot to mention.

counts for 57% of the typical car's total costs during its first five years on the road, according to transportation cost specialist Runzheimer International. As a result, if you plan to trade in your car within five years, as most owners do, lean toward Japanese and European makes, which tend to hold their value better than domestics.

If you plan to keep your car longer than five years, however, an American nameplate may be a better buy. Resale values matter less as your car ages, and U.S. car makers have made dramatic improvements in quality and durability in recent years. According to the widely followed J.D. Power Initial Quality Survey, U.S. car makers are down to an average of 1.5 defects per car, compared with 1.2 for the Japanese and 1.7 for the Europeans. "The imports' edge in resale value is largely a matter of image," says Ashly Knapp, chief executive of the national car-buying service AutoAdvisor. "Domestics are built almost as well and last just as long."

Check to see whether the model you want is available as a slightly used rental car. While a former rental car lacks the cachet of a factory-fresh automobile, millions of buyers are concluding that program cars are good buys nonetheless. They typically come loaded with desirable options like air conditioning, cruise control, and stereo radios. Far from being abused in rental service, most were washed every few days and scrupulously maintained. Best of all, they often have less than 10,000 miles on the odometer, particularly General Motors and Chrysler models. Low-mileage Fords are harder to come by since the company recently ordered rental fleets to keep cars for at least six months or 15,000 miles.

Today's Best Deals on Rented Wheels

Auto manufacturers aren't the only ones in the car business confronting the problems of a still sluggish economy and overstocked lots. So are car-rental firms. Because of an aggressive $45 billion buying program over the past three years, there are more than 1 million cars in the rental fleet now—nearly 26% more than in 1988. But rental demand is up only 12%. There are too many cars chasing too few people.

The result: a smorgasbord of special packages that can save travelers as much as 20% or more on weekly rentals. Other deals eliminate those $10 to $200 drop-off fees for renting your car at one location and returning it to another. Still others sweeten rentals with discount coupons.

When renting, remember:

Book special rates the moment you see them advertised. Car-rental companies have begun to use the computerized yield-management techniques perfected by the airlines. Computer software enables firms to instantaneously tailor price to fluctuating demand. Prompt action gives you a better shot at limited offers.

Travel over a weekend. Off-peak weekend rates can save you 30% in most cities. Hertz, for instance, now offers promotions as low as $19 a day for subcompacts—Ford Escort or Toyota Tercel—if you keep the car over a Saturday night.

Don't overlook the little guys. Feisty competitors like Alamo, Thrifty, and General are sometimes 10% to 20% cheaper than Hertz or Avis. The drawback is that these firms are often located several miles from the airport. Small, independent companies, found in local Yellow Pages, also provide good deals and services, though they lack drop-off facilities.

Plan flight arrivals and departures for the same time of day. That way you avoid hourly overtime charges that can quickly climb as high as your day rate.

Beware of added insurance fees. Commonly called the collision damage waiver, this $8- to $14-a-day option is banned in New York and Illinois altogether. Chances are good that your own auto insurance policy already covers you on rentals. Many credit cards also carry some collision coverage when you charge rental bills. Best advice: Know the terms of your policies before you accept or decline the additional coverage.

Keep in mind, though, that getting a fair price on a program car is still a matter of hard bargaining. Insist that the dealer show you a copy of the car's title to prove that it was indeed a rental. Then shoot for a price 20% to 30% less than the original sticker.

While most former rentals are standard American sedans, you can also occasionally find minivans, sports utility vehicles, and imports.

Arrange your financing and determine the value of your old car before going to the dealer. If you try to negotiate your new-car price, your trade-in, and your financing all at once, you only give the dealer more chances to stick you with hidden expenses. So handle each transaction separately. If you don't plan to pay cash, for example, get a car loan approved in advance from your bank or credit union. Once you've negotiated the price of your new car, you can then see whether the dealer's financing terms are better than the deal offered by the bank or credit union. (Don't count on it.)

Get a fix on the value of your old car by checking a price guide such as *Edmund's Used Car Prices* (available on newsstands). Spiff the car up with the supercleaning job known as detailing ($100 to $150 at auto detailers, listed in the Yellow Pages), then take it to the used-car departments of several dealers who sell the same make and ask for bids. Expect offers to be around trade-in value, 20% less than the retail price you'd expect to get in a private sale. You may, however, be able to get a bid within 10% of the retail prices cited in the guides. If you can't do better than trade-in value, it's probably worth the trouble to sell it privately yourself.

Bargain up from the dealer's cost, not down from the sticker price. New-car list prices invariably build in fat 5% to 25% profits—so that you can get a seemingly generous discount from retail and still overpay. Experts say that you should instead start from the dealer's cost, or "invoice" price, and aim to pay just 2% to 3% more than that for cars listing under $20,000 and 5% to 6% for those over $20,000.

To find out the dealer's cost, check the tables beginning on page 153 for the exact model you want, or consult a pricing guide,

When You Should Lease, Not Buy

See that bright red Status Cruiser gleaming in the showroom? How would you like to drive one of those babies home for almost nothing down and with monthly payments as much as a third lower than a loan? All you need is a lease, purrs today's thoroughly modern car salesman.

That kind of pitch is proving irresistible to a growing number of U.S. car consumers. Leasing got a boost when Congress phased out the tax deduction for consumer interest, putting loan payments and lease payments on equal tax footing. Moreover, as climbing sticker prices hike new-car financing costs, those low monthly lease payments tend to look even more tempting than in the past.

Despite low payments, however, leasing is generally more expensive over the long run than buying an identical car with a conventional loan. (Paying cash, of course, is always cheaper than either leasing or conventional financing because you pay no interest.) On the other hand, it isn't necessarily a bamboozle, either. The overall cost of leasing (see the table at right) tends to cost a few hundred dollars a year more than financing, provided that: you would not keep a car for longer than a normal lease term of two to four years even if you owned it; and you negotiate the implicit selling price of the car you lease just as doggedly as if you were purchasing. And if you locate one of the promotional lease deals occasionally floated by manufacturers—the offers are easy to spot in local ads—then you may get a deal that beats buying.

How long you plan to keep the car is crucial. If you plan to drive it longer than four years or so, buying is almost always far less expensive, thanks to those payment-free years after you pay off the loan.

The "price" you pay for the leased car is also decisive. Lease payments are lower than those on a loan because you don't finance the car's entire value, just the difference between its implicit selling price and its residual value, or its projected worth at the end of the lease. If you don't negotiate, however, the selling price is likely to be list or higher. Under those circumstances, leasing, bluntly put, is a sucker's game. If you buy, your reflex is to haggle. Unfortunately, few people think to do so when leasing a car. If you do decide to lease, however, you'll have to take some precautions. For starters, get a closed-end agreement. In this kind of contract, the residual value is set at the outset of the lease. That way, if the car turns out to be worth less than expected at the end of the lease, it's the dealer's or leasing company's worry, and not yours.

Make sure that the agreement doesn't hold you to fewer miles than you normally drive. Most leases require you not to put more than 15,000 miles a year on the car. Go over the limit, and you'll owe a penalty, typically 10¢ to 15¢ a mile.

Also keep in mind that you are on the hook for repairs if you return the car in what the lessor claims is substandard condition. To protect yourself, have the contract specify exactly in what condition the car must be returned.

You will also need gap insurance to supplement your regular auto policy, especially during the early years of the lease when the car is depreciating rapidly. In case of theft or a serious accident, gap coverage makes up the difference between the car's depreciated market value (the most your regular policy will pay) and what you still owe on the lease. Any reputable dealer or leasing company can provide you with a gap policy. Expect to pay a total of $400 to $500, either in a lump sum when you sign the contract or in installments added to your payments.

The Real Costs of Three Alternatives

Use the table as a guide in comparing the costs of buying and leasing. First, total the various costs for each acquisition method. Then subtract the car's anticipated resale value, which your bank's loan officer can estimate for you.

In the example, paying cash for an $18,202 Ford Taurus LX is at least $1,000 cheaper than either financing the same car with a 12.3% loan from Ford Motor Credit Corporation or leasing it. That's true even after taking into account the income you could have earned by leasing the car and investing your down payment at 6.5%. To calculate foregone investment income, you should multiply your initial cash outlay (line 3) by 0.09 for a two-year lease, by 0.14 for a three-year lease, or by 0.19 for a four-year lease.

	CASH	FINANCING	LEASING
1. INITIAL PAYMENT	$18,202	$1,820[1]	$949[2]
2. SALES TAX	+910	+0[3]	+0[3]
3. TOTAL INITIAL CASH OUTLAY	19,112	1,820	949
4. MONTHLY PAYMENTS OVER 36 MONTHS	+0	+20,772	+16,590
5. TOTAL CASH OUTLAY	19,112	22,592	17,539
6. FOREGONE INVESTMENT INCOME[4]	+2,676	+255	+133
7. CASH OUTLAY PLUS OPPORTUNITY COST	21,788	22,847	17,672
8. RESALE VALUE	-6,975	-6,975	-475[5]
9. TOTAL COST	$14,813	$15,872	$17,197

[1] 10% down payment. [2] Includes $475 security deposit and first month's payment. [3] Included in payments. [4] Assumes that the initial payment was invested at 6.5% before 31% federal taxes. [5] Refund of security deposit. **Sources:** Ford Motor Credit Corporation and *Automotive Lease Guide*

such as *Edmund's New Car Prices* or *Edmund's Import Car Prices,* or a mail-order pricing service, such as the *Money Auto Cost Comparison* mentioned earlier, or Car/Puter (800-765-2277). Add up the invoice costs of the standard model and any options you want, plus the shipping or "destination" charge, which appears on the new car's sticker. That will give you the dealer's total cost for the car and options.

You can save yourself some bother and probably lower your purchase price by shopping several dealers by phone. Call the first on your list and make an offer slightly below your target. Don't waver if the salesman swears that your calculation understates his wholesale costs. Even if your bid were under invoice, the dealer's *true* cost is sure to be lower. Invoice figures omit the "holdback"—an extra margin of up to 3% that manufacturers pay dealers—as well as bonuses dealers earn for exceeding car makers' sales quotas. Also, find out ahead of time whether there is a rebate on the car (the trade magazine *Automotive News,* available in many libraries, tracks rebates and other promotions weekly). If there is, remember that the manufacturer pays it, not the dealer. Don't let the dealer treat the rebate as a concession that he made.

Whether you get your target price in the end will depend as much on the car's popularity and availability as on your bargaining skills. But in today's depressed market, dealers are often desperate to sell, particularly since they must pay inventory costs of as much as 1.5% of the car's retail price every month a car sits on their lot. If you're willing to be flexible on color and options—and don't mind if some dealers hang up on you when they hear your offer—then you have a good shot at getting your target price on all but the hottest-selling models.

When you are finally ready to buy, don't be talked into last-minute add-ons that you don't

---

A Salesman's Tips for Car Buyers

Last time we looked it up, car salesmen were among the least trusted people around, even below stockbrokers, politicians, and journalists. But that may change. Faced with tough times and smarter consumers, a new breed is showing up in the showrooms.

Meet Craig Harris, the experienced assistant sales manager of DiFeo BMW of Edgewater, New Jersey. Harris offers these candid tips on how you can avoid being taken by hard-nosed car salesmen:

Don't dress like Elmer Fudd. "Some people think that if they wear a funny hat with floppy ears, or dress down some other way, I'll drop the price," says Harris. "Instead, I don't take them seriously." And don't try to impress the salesman either. "When a customer waves a pay stub at me, I know I'm looking at a credit risk." His advice: Be yourself.

Walk in, don't crawl in. "Do enough research by reading magazines and talking to car owners to narrow your model choices before you go to a dealership," says Harris. "Otherwise, you're at the salesman's mercy. He'll size you up as a laydown—a sucker—and treat you like one."

Leave your spouse at your house. "If the salesman pressures you, you have the perfect out: 'I have to check with my wife,' " says Harris. "When I see a couple and their kids, I figure I can close the deal in that visit."

Test-drive the dealership. "Stick to dealers noted for honesty and good service departments," says Harris. Start by asking friends for names of three or four located near you.

Let the salesman make a buck. "Not a hundred dollars, but a dollar," says Harris. Some buyers reveal their ignorance by offering less than the automotive dealer's cost. "They've got a price in their head," he says. "But they're not going to get a car that low unless the salesman baits them into another model or fast-talks them into a lease with fine print that'll cost them thousands of extra dollars in the end."

And lastly, don't be a wannabe. "If the car costs as much as you make in a year, forget it," says Harris. "In most cases, you should earn around twice the car's price."

need, like rustproofing (about $200) and fabric treatments ($75 to $100). Most of today's cars already have rust-resistant metal, and you can buy a can of fabric guard in the hardware store for just $2.

If you hate haggling, use a broker. For car buyers who are fed up with dickering and high-pressure salesmanship, auto brokers are an increasingly popular alternative. Because they present dealers with ready buyers who know exactly what they want (which cuts a dealer's selling cost), brokers can often get your car at a price at least as good as you could negotiate on your own. You simply stipulate the model and options you want and leave the camel-trading to the broker. If you don't like the price the broker gets, you don't have to take it.

One of the best ways to find a reliable broker in your area is to check with your credit union. These institutions often have broker services of their own or tie-ins with local brokers. You can't

find brokers everywhere, however. In Texas and Maryland, for example, dealers' lobbies succeeded in having them banned by state law.

National brokers, though, skirt many state bans by having the cars delivered through dealers. One such firm, AutoAdvisor in Seattle (800-326-1976), will order your car from the factory for a fee of $329 (you take delivery from a dealership near you) or, for $399, will find the car in a nearby dealer's inventory. Chief executive Knapp says that his firm can get most models below invoice. Reason: Sales to his clients often help a dealer to qualify for manufacturers' volume bonuses.

If you are in a hurry, however, you may not want to wait for a broker. AutoAdvisor's factory orders take six to 12 weeks, for example, and its dealer search four weeks. Also, while brokers can get most models at a good price, they can't work miracles. If you want one of today's hottest models, you'll have to pay close to list no matter who does the negotiating.

A Guide to Low-Cost, No-Hassle Travel

By standing up for your rights, you can get everything you are entitled to from resorts, hotels, travel agents, and tour operators.

All travelers may have undeniable rights to the comfort and convenience they pay for, but that hardly means suppliers automatically deliver. "You must assert yourself," says San Francisco travel attorney Alexander Anolik. "The squeaky wheel, in this case, will get better lodging—or a refund."

All too often, people who vigilantly guard their consumer rights at home turn into wimps on the road. They don't complain enough. The American Society of Travel Agents, the trade group for 20,000 firms nationwide, receives a mere 85 complaints a month from customers and travel representatives involving

bungled reservations, shoddy service, or misleading advertising.

No one should settle for second-rate service. Your best protection is to take the initiative, be specific about your requirements, and, then, upon arrival, politely demand fulfillment of every promise you received.

To give you more clout, we queried industry experts, trade groups, and attorneys to draft this bill of rights. Here is how to get what you deserve:

Get the room you booked, not the room they want to give you. Basically, hotels should be made to honor your reservations. Start by learning about the hotel's policies. Ask specific questions, because reservation clerks rarely volunteer information on booking procedures or services. They won't tell you, for instance, that hotels often overbook to compensate for the one out of every seven reserved guests who typically doesn't show up.

Specify the kind of room you want: non-smoking, quiet, near the lobby—or whatever. Ask for written confirmation. Keep in mind,

though, that if you request a special feature, like a view, it could cost 5% to 10% more.

For the best results, make an effort to arrive as close to check-in time as possible, usually around noon. Your chances of negotiating a preferred room or better rate are 25% to 50% greater during the day than at night.

Get the best rates. One way is to be flexible about the date. A looser schedule permits you to take advantage of travel clubs and discount

Avoid Rip-Offs When You're Away from Home

Too often, travelers seem to leave their street smarts at home. "There aren't any new scams," says Bob Louden of New York City's police force who trains cops at John Jay College of Criminal Justice. "There are only new victims."

"Don't let down your guard just because you're on vacation," cautions Ann Waigand of the *Educated Traveler* newsletter ($65 a year; 703-471-1063). She and others warn, in particular, about robbers who stage planned distractions in crowded places, such as airports or theaters. Therefore, stay alert for engineered mishaps like these:

• Some stranger spills ketchup all over your suit and, as you or he frantically wipes it off, he lifts your wallet and maybe your luggage.

• A real nice guy offers to snap a picture of you and your family on vacation and, as you back up, he disappears with your camera.

• A pedestrian jumps in front of your car and falls down. When you get out to help the poor guy, he runs around, slips behind the wheel, and drives off.

Hotels are not necessarily safer ground. "The oldest scam in the book," points out Roland Boisvert, security director at Royal Sonesta Hotel in Cambridge, Massachusetts, "is hanging out at the front desk, overhearing the guest's name and room number, and then using it to gain entry later."

Keep these hotel safety procedures in mind:

• Make sure the clerk hands over your key without loudly announcing your room number. If he does,

demand another room and, this time, be sure he keeps it quiet.

• Check all locks thoroughly as soon as you enter any room. Request another if you're dissatisfied. By the way, those new coded electronic cards are safer than ordinary key locks.

• Always call the front desk for verification when a caller asks you to leave the room. It could be a crook's ruse.

• Do keep valuables in hotel safes, but remember: The hotel's liability varies with state law and can be as low as $50.

• If a clerk makes an imprint of your credit card when you check in but you pay in cash, make certain the imprint is destroyed. An employee could pocket your cash and put the bill on your card. Since even the most careful traveler can become a victim, always leave the numbers of your passport, credit cards, and traveler's checks at home just in case you need to replace them.

Most victims are too embarrassed, too cynical, or simply too busy to report cash or credit-card thefts to the police. They just replace what they can and continue traveling. Even so, in 1990, reports of luggage and pickpocket thefts at New York City's Kennedy Airport totaled 1,060. And in Orange County, California, home to Disneyland and Knott's Berry Farm, almost 25% of the emergency cases that were handled by the Traveler's Aid centers were crime-related. So be careful.

coupon books offering such tempting deals as 50% off or a second night's free stay.

Even with ironclad dates, you may turn up discounts of 20% to 50% on air/hotel packages. Many large travel agencies (and consortiums of smaller ones) negotiate preferred rates at hotels where they frequently book clients.

Just like airline agents, hotel clerks will rarely volunteer information—you have to ask the right questions. To negotiate on your own, try these approaches:

• Call the specific hotel, not some central reservation system. If rooms are going begging, an ambitious assistant manager may find a deal just right for you.

• Ask about special deals. Weekend packages may be extended to begin on Thursday or stretch to Tuesday. Request the corporate rate when calling. At check-in, don't worry about your business cards: no "proof" is necessary, say Hilton and other chains.

• Play one against the other. If the Bankbox Hotel quotes a $90 room but you prefer the Sheltering Arms, ask the Arms manager to match it.

• Join the club. Membership in the American Automobile Association, for example, can mean discounts of 10% to 25%. Rates may hit 50% off if you belong to the American Association of Retired Persons. Always make a final effort at check-in. Politely say: "I made this reservation two weeks ago. Can you do any better now?" With hotel taxes rising, every dollar counts. In New York City, for example, a $20 savings means $23.85 in your pocket.

Make the hotel liable. Unlike the airline and rail industries, hotels, resorts, inns, and other lodging establishments are not regulated by federal or state laws nor by an industrywide code of ethics. Still, you can ensure the hotel's contractual obligation by mailing or faxing a short, binding agreement to the general manager, confirming what you've been told. The manager or assistant manager will usually reply.

To avoid hassles at check-in time, bring along copies of both letters.

Attorney Alexander Anolik writes a shorthand agreement on the back of his personal checks. "The returned check," explains Anolik, "serves as a valid contract." Here's his format: "This is in (full or partial) payment for (list specific travel services and the range of chosen dates). Any disputes involving these services shall be heard by the courts of (list your hometown and state)."

Specifying your local jurisdiction requires the hotel owner (or whomever) to travel to settle the problem. That way, you avoid round-trip expenses. Besides, you may not face the most receptive judge in some resort town. Anolik says that plaintiffs have come out ahead in roughly 90% of cases involving contracts similar to his.

The hotel should solve problems, not shelve them. Start at the top. Don't discuss mishaps or mistakes with any hotel employee who ranks lower than assistant manager. Only managers are responsible for maintaining the hotel's standards and reputation. Therefore, if your room is a floor below a noisy nightclub, take the problem to management.

Be firm—not hostile. "Be willing to negotiate, especially in a foreign hotel," says Deborah Hill, author of *Travel Tips International* (Renaissance Publications). "In most cases, it's a question of a hotel manager's honor to satisfy a guest."

Don't settle for any accommodations or services below the quality you were originally promised. And don't resign yourself to misrepresentations—for example, a resort that promotes two elegant restaurants though one is merely a bar.

If the manager can't explain discrepancies between what you see and what you read in an ad or brochure, switch to another hotel if you can, or pack up and go home. Don't endure it. Upon your return, send a detailed letter and photos, if possible, to the president of the hotel or resort company stating the reasons why you should receive a refund. Explain that you will inform the Better Business Bureau, local chamber of commerce, the national tourist board (if applicable), and the press about the false ads if you don't receive an adequate response. Remember, if you grit your teeth and stay, it will be tougher for you to justify a refund later.

Take another case. Let's say your guaranteed room is given to another guest because of overbooking. If so, demand that the hotel pay for comparable lodging elsewhere. Most hotels will provide alternative accommodations. For

Fly to Terrific Destinations at a Discount

Want to fly round trip from Washington D.C. to Rome for $500? It would cost $800 to $1,229 on TWA. Or how about New York to Paris for just $380? Tempting, huh?

Welcome to the world of consolidators, or air-travel discounters. Operating legally in the U.S. since airline deregulation in 1978, about 100 consolidators can be found across the country. Most specialize in foreign travel, but some also sell domestic tickets.

Consolidators are still battling a bad rap left over from the days of fly-by-night companies and tickets on Mystery Airlines. Yet, in New York City, home of most consolidators, the state attorney general's office has found no grounds to investigate the industry.

Here's how consolidators work: When airlines can't fill seats, they sell them to a consolidator at a big discount. In turn, the consolidator offers them at about 20% to 50% below normal prices to travel agents, other consolidators, or directly to you through newspaper ads.

Discount tickets, like all bargains, require some trade-offs. Usually, the tickets are nonrefundable and cannot be changed. And if the flight's delayed, you probably won't rate meals or other compensation. To avoid surprises, ask for the consolidator's policies in writing.

Some companies put your ticket payment into an escrow account until your departure, which protects you should the consolidator or airline go under.

Perhaps the biggest hitch is the consolidators' widespread reluctance to name their airlines, which makes people nervous. Most consolidators simply promise "a major scheduled carrier," because, says David Kols of St. Louis-based UniTravel, "75% of our contracts state that the name of the carrier must not be released until ticketing."

Airlines fear the information could undermine their fare structures. Smaller carriers don't impose the same restrictions, and many need to fill seats between U.S. cities and European stopovers en route to home countries. If you're uncomfortable dealing with consolidators, find a travel agent. Most consolidator tickets are sold by agents.

Tips for shopping:

Read the fine print of consolidator ads—"OW" fares, for example, are often one way but based on a round-trip purchase.

Get your tickets from the consolidator as soon as possible, perhaps by overnight mail. That way, you'll have time to correct any scheduling errors. Also, make sure there are no alterations (flight times or dates covered with revalidation stickers, for instance).

Ask about add-ons. Weekend travel may cost $25 extra each way. And don't forget the standard $26 departure tax on international flights.

Pay by plastic—even if it's more expensive—so you can cancel payment if problems aren't corrected. If the firm refuses cards, you're probably better off elsewhere.

These consolidators are among the oldest and most reliable. All do business nationwide, and all sell seats on major carriers:

• Council Charter (800-800-8222), based in New York City, handles popular international routes and holds your payments in escrow until departure.

• Travac (800-872-8800), with offices in New York City, Los Angeles, San Francisco, and Orlando, also uses escrow accounts and will tell you what airline you'll fly before you commit for your tickets.

• UniTravel (800-325-2222) of St. Louis provides free overnight ticket delivery via Federal Express and also puts your payments in escrow.

• Sunline Express Holidays (800-SUN-LINE in California; 415-541-7800 everywhere else) of San Francisco will also disclose the carrier you'll be flying.

instance, Radisson Hotels has an estimated two to three overbookings a month at each of its 270 hotels. When that happens, the hotel will arrange to take you to another hotel and pay for a night's stay and phone calls. The next day, a Radisson representative will drive you back and give you an upgraded room at no charge.

Travel agents are accountable for full disclosure. Since travel agents make 25% of domestic hotel reservations, and 85% of international hotel bookings, and advise roughly half of their customers on where to go, the courts have started to impose legal standards on agents.

According to Thomas Dickerson, a New York City attorney and author of the treatise *Travel Law* (Law Journal Press): "Travel agents are the fiduciaries of your trip. They should know the financial condition of the hotel, resort, or tour operator that they recommend and everything about the destination, from your chances of getting sick to the likelihood of terrorist activity."

Marcus vs. Zenith Travel, which was decided in 1990 in New York State Supreme Court, is one of the most recent precedents. In that case, Sam Marcus and his wife, Renee, of Great Neck, New York, paid about $13,000 for a 16-day tour of the Far East. But when they arrived in Tokyo, they discovered that the tour operator had gone bankrupt and had not paid for their hotel. The Marcuses, in turn, sued their travel agent, Zenith, and won.

The court ruled that Zenith had breached its fiduciary duty by failing to inform the Marcuses of the tour company's financial status before their trip. Although state laws vary, courts in Illinois, New Jersey, Ohio, and Pennsylvania have recently ruled in favor of plaintiffs in similar cases. Don't trust to fate or to the courts, however. When booking through an agent, inspect your travel package thoroughly. Take notes of all conversations, and then send a letter confirming the arrangements. When you receive air tickets and other documents, scrutinize them closely. One typographical error on the date can cost you both the room and money.

If things go awry and you can document the problems, many agents will refund at least some of your money. Others may offer a free trip to make up for your troubles.

Tour operators should deliver on every part of your package. Working as wholesalers, tour operators buy blocks of hotel rooms and airline seats and tailor them into distinct travel packages. Therefore, before you commit any time or money, read every bit of fine print on brochures and pamphlets, because these serve as your contracts with the operator.

Watch for misleading language that may tip you to "bait and switch" schemes. For example, the brochure might describe lodging "at a leading hotel or similar accommodations." If the tour operator sells more packages than the reserved space at the leading hotel will accommodate, you may wind up getting dumped in an inferior location.

To check on whether the tour operator is reputable, call your local Better Business Bureau. Also call the U.S. Tour Operators Association (212-944-5727). Says Ann Waigand, publisher of the *Educated Traveler* (703-471-1063): "Ask the tour operator if such suppliers as hotels and airlines are paid through an escrow account, which will secure your money."

The best advice, besides doing your homework, is to remember to be firm: You're entitled to the best trip your money can buy. That's your basic right.

I have enough money to last me the rest of my life,
unless I buy something. — comedian Jackie Mason

Making Sure You Have the Future You Want

If you have given even a little thought to your future retirement—and, by age 40, most people have—your mental picture probably looks something like this: an attractive home, perhaps overlooking a windswept beach or a freshly mown fairway; two well-waxed cars in the garage, one late-model, the other vintage sports; and plenty of trips to exotic locations—Hawaii, the Caribbean, possibly even the south of France. And no matter where you decide to be, a cluttered social calendar.

That dream life is really not too different from the retirement fantasies of most members of your generation. But, unlike your parents' generation which basked in the glow of a succession of economic breaks during their working years, your generation can't expect the same ride. Your dream is most likely clouded by the fear that sometime after you leave work, your money will run out, leaving you destitute, a burden to your children, then, finally, a charge of the state.

Even if you are lucky enough to be covered by a generous company pension as well as secure health benefits, they won't be enough to maintain your standard of living after you retire. Today's affluent fortysomething workers will have to rely on their own investments for at least a third of their retirement income, according to the Social Security Administration. To make sure that the money will be there when you need it, you must keep it in a diversified portfolio invested for steady, long-term growth.

Fortunately, no matter what your age, you can escape an ugly future if you make the right moves—beginning now. This chapter will get you started. In the story on page 136, we help you put together a practical investment plan if you are 10 years or more from leaving work. If you don't have that long, don't despair. The story on page 141 provides a checklist of steps to take as you near retirement. Then we describe the best strategies for managing your money to make it last your lifetime and recommend two investment portfolios: the first for your early years of retirement; the second for your later years.

Starting Out Right

Saving enough for retirement is easier than you think.

In drawing up a retirement plan, you must face up to certain inescapable facts. First, to live as well as you do now, you will probably need at least 80% of your current income. While work-related costs will decline in retirement, if you retire in your fifties or sixties you are likely to sharply increase your travel and other leisure expenses; in addition, out-of-pocket medical costs will climb as you grow older. In fact, many of tomorrow's active retirees will find that their spending equals 100% of their pre-retirement income. But careful spenders may be able to get by on as little as 70%. (To calculate your own required savings, just fill out the worksheet on page 138.) Other facts to keep in mind:

You probably haven't been saving enough. A study of wage and health trends by the Urban Institute, a policy-research group in Washington, D.C., found that while Americans ages 55 to 64 in 1993 will have assets of almost $300,000 per household, workers ages 35 to 44 will amass only half that amount in 1993 dollars by the time they retire. The chief reason: Because income growth has slowed, the average savings rate dropped from 7% to 9% of after-tax income in the 1970s to as little as 3% during the 1980s, though it has recently rebounded to a slightly better rate of 4.1%.

You can't count on the equity in your house to bail you out. The house-price inflation of the mid-1980s gave homeowners a windfall beyond the home equity they would normally have accumulated during their working lives. But over the next 20 years, housing prices on average are likely to rise by only about 6% a year, one percentage point or so higher than the projected inflation rate of 5%.

An inheritance from your parents probably won't be enough to keep you comfortable. Economists estimate that the average bequest to today's 30- to 44-year-olds will be around $100,000 in 1991 dollars. If such a sum drops into your lap, be thankful. But 75% of the $100 billion in bequests each year goes to the younger members of the wealthiest U.S. families. And even if your parents are affluent, you may never see a dime—especially if one of them lives well past 80 or requires years of costly health care.

Social Security and pensions will replace only 45% of the average married man's pre-retirement income. By contrast, that replacement figure is 49% today, according to the Employee Benefit Research Institute in Washington, D.C. Reason: Generally, rising earnings will outstrip such inflation-indexed benefits.

Not everything is negative, though. You do have a great advantage your parents didn't—tax-deferred savings accounts such as Individual Retirement Accounts, Keoghs for the self-employed, profit-sharing plans, and 401(k)s. With one or more of these accounts, you can save as much as 25% of your earnings each year and have it compound tax-free until you start withdrawing money after age 59½. If a couple in their mid-forties today with joint earnings of $50,000 made the most of such accounts, they could accumulate $900,000 ($340,000 in today's dollars) by age 65.

With a typical 401(k), for example, you could contribute as much as $8,475 of your salary in 1991; the limit rises annually with inflation. In addition, many employers chip in 50¢ or more for each $1 you invest up to a set amount, usually 6% of your salary. An even more stunning fact: According to the Employee Benefit Research Institute, more than half of today's workers who get lump sums from pensions or tax-deferred savings accounts when they quit a job spend the money instead of saving it.

As difficult as saving may be, it's the only way that you can be sure of ever having the life in retirement that you deserve. If you're 20 years from retirement, you should set aside at least 5% to 10% of your annual income. The required amount could climb to 20% or more, though, if you put off saving until the last decade of your career.

Saving alone won't be enough. You will also have to invest your money wisely—by aiming for steady, long-term growth. If you put away $5,000 a year in money-market funds and it compounds tax deferred at 6% annually, you will have $183,928 after 20 years. But use stocks or equity funds to pump up the rate of compounding to an achievable 9% to 10%, and you'll have $255,801 or more.

A higher rate of return also means that you will have to set aside less to meet your goal. For example, say you want to accumulate $500,000 over 20 years. If you invest only in a money fund that beats 5% inflation by one percentage point annually, you will have to sock away $13,592 a year. But if you boost your annual return to 9%, you need put aside only $9,773 a year, or $376 per biweekly paycheck.

In aiming for a 9% return, of course, you will have to sweat out periods of stock losses. Stocks may be volatile, but they're the way to go. According to Ibbotson Associates, a Chicago investment research firm, the S&P 500-stock index has gained an average of 10% annually over the past 65 years, outrunning inflation by seven percentage points a year. By contrast, Treasury bills have provided annual inflation-adjusted returns of 1% or less.

And if you invest for 20 years or so, the volatility of top-quality stocks and equity funds isn't as worrisome as you might think. Using Ibbotson data to compare 41 different 25-year holding periods between 1926 and 1991, Pittsburgh money manager Roger Gibson found that stocks had higher returns than bonds or Treasury bills during every period. The worst 25-year return for stocks—5.9% compounded annually before inflation from 1929 through 1953—was only 1.5 percentage points lower than the best 25-year annualized return for any of the other assets.

Gibson's finding might strike you as heresy—especially if you grew up in a home where an investment in savings bonds was viewed as the outer limit of speculation. And it is true that stocks are risky over shorter time spans. For example, the S&P 500 suffered losses of 1% to 48.6% during seven of the five-year holding periods studied by Gibson. By contrast, the worst five-year performance among other holdings was a 10.6% loss for corporate bonds from 1964 through 1969. The lesson of his research for most people: Keep 30% to 40% of your assets in bonds and cash investments. You can then expect to earn an average of around 10% a year without sleepless nights.

The pie charts in the box on page 139 show two portfolios that can offer such returns. The first option: Invest 60% of your holdings in blue chips and large-company growth stocks, and divide the rest between high-quality bonds and cash. This simple portfolio may be the only practical approach for investors who have the bulk of their retirement savings in a 401(k), because such plans usually offer only three or four investment options. According to data from Bailard Biehl & Kaiser, an investment firm in San Mateo, California, such a basic portfolio would have delivered a compound annual return of 10.4% over the past two decades, compared with 11.1% for the S&P 500—with only two-thirds of the S&P's volatility.

Investors with more varied 401(k) choices at work or a substantial amount of retirement savings outside of tax-deferred plans might consider this second strategy: Put 70% of your money in a mix of large-company growth stocks, small-company stocks, value stocks, and foreign stocks. Invest 20% in bonds and 10% in

Figuring Out How Much You Need to Save

This worksheet will help you decide how much to save each year for retirement. It assumes that your savings will grow 8% a year—three points above the expected 5% annual inflation rate. Even if part of your savings is in taxable accounts, you should be able to clear 8% with a conservative mix of stocks, bonds, and cash. The worksheet also assumes that you will live a full 10 years beyond the average 17-year life expectancy of a 65-year-old and that you don't plan to leave much to your heirs. All amounts are in today's dollars. To be sure of staying on track, update this worksheet each year.

1. **Annual income needed when you retire** (80% of current income) _____

2. **Probable Social Security and pension benefits** (Call 800-772-1213 for your projected income from Social Security; ask your employee-benefits counselor to estimate your pension in today's dollars.) _____

3. **Annual retirement income needed from investments** (line 1 minus line 2) _____

4. **Amount you must save before retirement** (line 3 times factor A, below) _____

5. **Amount you have saved already,** including IRAs, corporate savings plans, and other investments _____

6. **Projected value of your current retirement savings at the time you retire** (line 5 times factor B) _____

7. **Amount of retirement capital still needed** (line 4 minus line 6) _____

8. **Annual savings needed to reach your goal** (line 7 times factor C) _____

9. **Total you must save each year** (line 8 minus annual employer contributions to savings plans) _____

AGE AT RETIREMENT	55	56	57	58	59	60	61	62	63	64	65	66	67
Factor A:	23.3	22.9	22.6	22.2	21.8	21.4	21.0	20.5	20.1	19.6	19.2	18.7	18.2

YEARS TO RETIREMENT	5	7	9	11	13	15	20	25	30
Factor B:	1.15	1.22	1.29	1.36	1.44	1.53	1.76	2.02	2.33
Factor C:	0.188	0.131	0.099	0.079	0.065	0.054	0.038	0.028	0.022

Source: Moss Adams, Seattle

cash. Such a portfolio's broad diversification will keep risk within reasonable bounds, and you can expect to beat the simpler portfolio's annual return by a percentage point or so.

In general, investment advisers recommend that you earmark money you have in tax-sheltered accounts for the bond and cash portions of your retirement portfolio. The reason: You can defer taxes on the interest income that you earn. Stocks are better suited for holdings outside of tax-sheltered accounts, because you don't have to pay taxes on your gains until you sell.

About one in three 401(k) plans offers a bond fund; most others limit fixed-income investors to short-term assets such as guaranteed investment contracts (GICs), which are roughly comparable to bank CDs that mature in one or two years. With IRAs, of course, you can invest in almost any fixed-income fund.

If you must keep the bulk of your money outside of a tax-deferred account, you might consider Treasury or government agency issues for the fixed-income part of your savings. They are backed by the federal government or its agencies, so there is no risk of default. Issues that mature in three to 10 years are among the most attractive choices. Over the past 25 years, such intermediate-term bonds have delivered annual total returns of 8.3%—compared with 6.9% for long-term bonds—while offering about 40% less price volatility.

Alternatively, investors in the 28% federal tax bracket or higher (taxable income above $35,800 for married couples filing jointly; $21,450 or more for singles) might consider tax-exempt bonds. At yields of about 6.3%, for example, intermediate-term munis offer the equivalent of 8.7% or more from a taxable bond. As a rule, you need at least $25,000 for a diversified portfolio of individual bonds. Or you can invest in munis through mutual funds that hold issues with credit ratings of A or better.

For cash investments, most 401(k)s offer little choice. Only one in three includes a money fund. If possible, choose a government money fund. Such funds run virtually no risk of

Getting the Most Growth

When your retirement is still 10 or more years away, you should be willing to take reasonable risks to make your principal grow steadily. The simple approach outlined in the top chart is particularly well suited for 401(k)s and other retirement plans that limit you to a handful of investment options. This basic diversified portfolio could deliver average gains of about 9% a year during the next decade.

If you have the time and skill to set up and monitor a more complex portfolio, you can boost your average annual return by a percentage point or two. To do that, you should divide your money among the six investment categories shown in the lower chart, buying either individual issues or mutual funds. While this mix includes some potentially volatile assets, such as small-growth stocks and foreign issues, they are counterbalanced by more secure investments such as high-quality bonds and money funds. As a result, you can expect this portfolio to deliver a higher return without exposing your savings to significantly more risk.

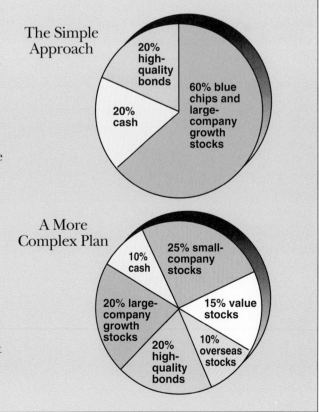

The Simple Approach

20% high-quality bonds

20% cash

60% blue chips and large-company growth stocks

A More Complex Plan

10% cash

25% small-company stocks

15% value stocks

10% overseas stocks

20% high-quality bonds

20% large-company growth stocks

default because they invest in Treasury bills and the short-term securities of government agencies. The funds are wise choices outside of a 401(k) as well because they are typically exempt from state and local taxes, which can add the equivalent of half a percentage point to your yield.

The trickiest part of building a retirement fund on your own is picking individual stocks. Therefore, novice investors or those with less than $25,000—not counting money in a 401(k)—often lean toward mutual funds. As you become more experienced and your assets grow, however, you can consider assembling shares of five to 10 individual stocks in different industries. Brokerage commissions will run about 1.5% of each purchase or sale. But if you hold shares for at least three years, that total 3% transaction cost amounts to the same or less than what you would pay a typical no-load fund with annual expenses of 1% or so. Here's a quick look at the key equity categories:

Blue chips. These are shares of industry leaders with strong finances, well-established products, and a history of rising earnings and dividends. Chuck Carlson, editor of the newsletter *Dow Theory Forecasts* in Hammond, Indiana, recommends companies that pay dividend yields of around 3% and can sustain annual earnings gains of 10% or so over the next five years. That works out to a projected total return of 13% or more. In addition, he advises sticking to blue chips that trade at price/earnings ratios below 17, the average P/E for the S&P 500.

Within a 401(k), you can probably invest in blue chips through a diversified equity fund. Outside such a plan, you can buy blue chips through large growth and income funds such as Fidelity Growth & Income (2% load; minimum investment, $2,500; 800-544-8888) or no-load Selected American Shares ($1,000 minimum; 800-553-5533).

Large growth stocks. These include the shares of companies with strong brands in fast-growing domestic and overseas markets. Typically, such stocks yield less than 3%, but they can deliver earnings growth of at least 15% a year. Carlson recommends those with P/Es of 16 or

less. Within a 401(k), you may be able to invest in these shares through a growth or aggressive growth fund. For other fund investors, Ken Gregory, editor of the *L/G No-Load Fund Analyst* newsletter in San Francisco, recommends Twentieth Century Select Investors (no minimum; 800-345-2021) or Vanguard World—U.S. Growth ($3,000 minimum; 800-662-7447).

Small-company growth stocks. Despite their volatility, the shares of these companies, typically those with annual sales of less than $500 million, have returned an average of 11.6% annually over the past 65 years, compared with 10.1% for the S&P 500.

Elliott Schlang, an executive vice president with Prescott Ball & Turben in Cleveland, recommends that conservative investors stick to shares of companies with annual revenues of at least $200 million, strong market niches, and solid finances. Among small-company funds, Gregory recommends GIT Equity—Special Growth ($2,500 minimum; 800-336-3063) and Nicholas Limited Edition ($2,000 minimum; 414-272-6133).

Value stocks. These issues trade at steep discounts to the estimated value of their assets or earnings prospects. From 1984 through April 1991, value stocks gained only 14.1% annually, compared with 17.7% for the S&P 500, according to Trinity Investment Management in Cambridge, Massachusetts. But Charles Brandes, a money manager in San Diego, notes that value stocks typically rebound sharply from periods of mediocre performance. His choices include shares of firms that have conservative balance sheets and have recently traded at P/Es under 12. Among top value-oriented funds, Ken Gregory favors Windsor II ($3,000 minimum; 800-662-7447) and Lindner Fund ($2,000 minimum; 314-727-5305).

Foreign stocks. Diversifying overseas will reduce your risk and could boost your long-term returns. Indeed, international stocks have outperformed all other major asset categories during nine of the past 20 years, according to Bailard Biehl & Kaiser. Among international funds, Don Phillips, editor of the newsletter

Mutual Fund Values, recommends two favorites with strong performance records: Harbor International ($2,000 minimum; 800-422-1050) and Scudder Global (minimum of $1,000; 800-225-2470).

Once your portfolio is in place, check the mix once a year and rebalance your holdings when sharp price moves for stocks or bonds shift your allocations by five percentage points or more. For example, after a 20% rise in stock prices, you should transfer enough money into bonds and cash to restore the original balance. In addition, redo the calculations in the retirement-planning worksheet on page 138 every year to see whether your portfolio is growing quickly enough to meet your target. If you fall behind schedule, increase your savings or rethink your goals. An occasional minor adjustment is a small price to pay for a retirement that's free of regrets.

Getting Set for Life

Good money management is still important after you retire.

You've scrimped, saved, and schemed for decades, and now retirement is less than five years away. If you are like most of the 6% of American workers on the brink of retiring, you probably think there are just a few final adjustments to make. Among them: switching most of your money into secure income investments so that you can live off the interest for the rest of your life. Nothing could be simpler or safer, right?

Wrong. That strategy may have worked for your grandparents, but it will cut your income by a third in just 10 years. The villain, of course, is inflation. The moment you retire, you lose your stoutest protection against price hikes— regular salary increases that have probably exceeded inflation by one or two percentage points annually over the past 40 years. If you invest your money in retirement solely for income, you could become a candidate for the poorhouse or, worse yet, end up financially dependent on your children.

Most people approaching retirement—or already there—are well aware that inflation is a threat. According to a recent poll by the National Taxpayers Union Foundation in Washington, D.C., 70% of retirees worry that price rises will reduce their standard of living. Their fears stem mainly from an error that they made in their final working years—and one you can easily avoid. The mistake: They underestimated how long they were likely to live in retirement.

Today, people aged 62 should count on living for another 25 years or more. Moreover, the longer you live, the longer you are likely to live. That is, as you grow older, the odds improve of your beating the U.S. average life expectancy (71.4 years for men and 78.3 for women). When a man hits 75, for instance, he has a fifty-fifty chance of making it to 84; a woman of that age can expect to reach 86. As welcome as that news might be, the financial implications may make you wince: With inflation at 5%, for example, an income of $50,000 would be worth less than $15,000 in 25 years.

Thus, as you approach your last days at your job, check the inflation resistance of your major sources of retirement income and take steps to compensate for those that are found wanting. Consider the following:

Social Security. However inadequate your benefits may seem to you, they will rise in step with living costs.

Pensions. Ask your benefits department whether your pension will be adjusted periodically for inflation. You may be among the lucky 24% of workers who can expect such adjustments. But more likely, the value of your benefits will decline steadily.

Part-time work. Until age 65, you can earn $7,440 a year (the amount rises annually with inflation) without losing any Social Security benefits; above that, benefits are reduced by 50¢ for each dollar earned. For retirees ages 65 through 69, the limit is $10,200, and the

How to Make Sure Your Savings Last

When the time comes to tap a retirement fund, most people want to withdraw a predictable amount every year without eroding the value of their principal. This is actually a lot more difficult than it sounds. First, if you keep your money in anything other than short-term income investments, such as bank CDs, your returns will vary unpredictably from year to year. Second, your true objective should be to preserve your portfolio's purchasing power, not its nominal value in dollars. That means you will have to add to your principal periodically to keep it even with inflation.

Here are the most popular ways to determine how much to spend each year:

Never touch principal. The strategy of spending only dividends and interest made perfect sense 50 years ago when consumer prices were relatively stable. Since the 1960s, though, inflation has chugged along at an annual average rate of 5%—fast enough to halve the purchasing power of your principal every 14 years.

Investors who follow the traditional approach generally try to maximize their income, which often causes them to concentrate on bonds and to underemphasize growth-oriented stocks. Assume, for example, that you want to spend about 7% of your portfolio each year. To earn that average yield with long-term Treasury bonds paying 8.2% and blue-chip stocks yielding 3.5%, you would have to put nearly three-quarters of your money in bonds. The trouble is, bonds offer no growth and, therefore, no protection against the erosion of your purchasing power, so the 25% of your money in stocks would have to grow at an unlikely 20% year after year to keep your overall holdings even with 5% inflation.

By contrast, you could put two-thirds of your money in blue-chip stocks, which would have to

grow by only 7.5% for your portfolio to match 5% inflation. The average yield, however, would be just a bit above 5%—hardly a generous income.

Make sure your principal is inflationproof. Each year, figure your total return—capital gains plus dividends and interest. Then invest enough of your after-tax income to offset the corrosive effects of inflation on your principal and spend the rest. (Remember, though, that you will have to pay taxes on the dividends, interest, and realized capital gains that you reinvest as well as on the money you spend.)

While this strategy absolutely protects your portfolio's purchasing power, your income won't be stable. Imagine, for instance, that you split a $100,000 portfolio evenly between bonds yielding 8.2% and stocks paying 3.5%. If your stocks jump 20% in value one year, the portfolio's total return will be 15.8%. With 5% inflation, you can withdraw 10.8%—or $10,800—to spend that year, leaving $105,000 ($100,000 adjusted for inflation).

Now assume that in the second year your stocks decline by 11.7%. The total return on your overall portfolio would be zero, giving you no spendable income. Further, you would have to make up for the $5,250 inflation adjustment (5% of $105,000) you missed that year by investing an extra $5,512.50 ($5,250 adjusted for inflation) in the third year.

To some extent, you could reduce the wild income swings by basing your withdrawals on several years' results. You could, for instance, take out the difference between the portfolio's average return and the average rate of inflation over the past five years. This would give you a steadier stream of income, but it wouldn't solve the entire problem.

Even over five-year periods, blue-chip-stock returns fluctuate a lot; average annual returns for

penalty on earnings above that is 33¢ on the dollar. Starting at age 70, no penalty applies.

Home equity. With the price of houses likely to outpace the annual inflation rate by a modest one percentage point or so over the next

decade or two, you might be wise to trade down to a cheaper home to reduce your monthly housing costs and free up the extra equity for investing.

Investments. Because they can outpace inflation by three to five percentage points a year, growth-oriented investments such as the ones discussed in the story "Starting Out Right," beginning on page 136, constitute your most important resource in your retirement years.

That three- to five-point real return can make an enormous difference in your future financial security, especially if you can draw on another source of income in your early retirement years and let your investments grow. Take the case of a retired couple, both aged 62, who need $50,000 in today's dollars to live comfortably and who already have an annual income of $36,000, including $14,000 from Social Security and $22,000 from a pension that does not rise with inflation. If they invest solely in the most conservative income investments and their returns outpace prices by only a percentage point or so, they will need a retirement fund of $600,000. But the couple can reduce that amount to about $420,000 if one of them earns $7,000 annually from part-time work in the first five years of retirement, and their investment portfolio beats inflation by at least three points a year.

Ideally, you should begin making final plans three to five years before you actually retire. But you can fine-tune your plan in your first months of leisure. On the eve of retiring, you can't afford to suffer big losses on your investments, because it's too late to make up for them with fresh savings. One danger you might overlook: too much money in your own company's stock. If you have an employee stock ownership plan (ESOP), such holdings can grow to 20% of your total assets—well above the maximum 5% to 10% that investment advisers say you should keep in the shares of any one company. Fortunately, your employer must allow you to move money into other investments before you retire. (Typically, you can shift 25% after age 55 and 50% after you reach age 60.)

---

these investments over five-year periods have ranged from 2% to 24% during the past 50 years.

Spend a set percentage. This year-in, year-out approach may be the best overall solution, since it reflects both long-term inflation rates and investment returns. Over the long haul—25 years or so—bond yields historically beat inflation by two to three percentage points. With 5% inflation, the average return on bonds is likely to be 7% to 8% during the 1990s. Growth-oriented stocks typically return six points or so above inflation, for a projected average return of 11% or more during the next 10 years.

If you divide your portfolio evenly between stocks and bonds, you can expect an average long-term return of around 9.5%. But if you choose your stocks wisely, you could probably achieve a long-term annual return of as much as 12%. You could then withdraw 7% of your portfolio each year and over time still keep your principal's purchasing power even with 5% inflation.

In following this strategy, you can invest your money in the mix of stocks and bonds that best fits your appetite for risk. But you will have to adjust your withdrawal rate accordingly. For example, if you are conservative and favor bonds, keep it to 5% or so; if you are willing to be more aggressive, you can go as high as 7%.

Even this strategy will not guarantee absolutely steady income from year to year. Your spending could vary by 10% or so as your portfolio's value changes. To smooth out those fluctuations, you could spend less than your set percentage in years when your stock gains are greater than 12% and a bit more in years when they are below 8%. Best of all, you can choose the investments that promise the most attractive long-term returns and still be confident that the purchasing power of your principal will be fairly well protected.

As the charts in the box, "Staying Ahead of Rising Prices," below show, the best mix of assets changes as you get older, though some of your money should always be invested for growth. You should cut back the proportion of your portfolio invested in stocks as you grow older because you will have less time to recover from severe bear market losses. Nonetheless, because inflation always remains a threat, you should keep 40% or so of your money in conservative stocks with prospects for earnings growth of 5% a year or more even 10 years after you have retired. (For specific advice on how much money you can afford to withdraw from your portfolio each year without ever running the risk of outliving your money, see the box, "How to Make Sure Your Savings Last," on pages 142-143.)

The following two portfolio allocations, recommended by experts to *Money*, offer the safest, surest ways to generate income and growth. The first is designed for your initial 10 to 15 years of retirement, the second for late retirement.

Early in Retirement

Blue chips and large growth stocks: 30%
Total-return stocks: 20%
High-quality bonds: 25%
Cash: 25%
Total-return target: 9% to 10% a year

As retirement approaches, you can lower the risk in your portfolio by adopting the mix of investments shown above. Start by reducing equities to half your portfolio, and replace some blue-chip and large-growth stocks with more conservative total-return stocks—shares of companies that offer dividend yields above that of the S&P 500.

Geraldine Weiss, editor of the newsletter *Investment Quality Trends* in La Jolla, California, recommends companies that have raised their dividends at an annual rate of 10% for the past 10 years, pay yields of nearly 4% or more, and carry price/earnings ratios of less than 15. Over a decade, such shares can deliver average total returns of as much as 14% a year.

Staying Ahead of Rising Prices

Since you should figure on living 20 years or more after you stop working, you must fully protect your portfolio against the effects of inflation during the first 10 years or so of retirement. This requires a portfolio like the one shown in the top chart. Keep at least half of your money in growth and total-return stocks (or in mutual funds that hold such issues). Over time, rising corporate profits will enable stocks to provide capital gains and higher dividends that will offset inflation.

After you turn 75, portfolio growth is less important, and you can safely cut back your equity holdings to 40% or less, as shown in the lower chart. The reason: Your reduced life expectancy makes inflation less of a threat. By boosting the amount you keep in cash and bonds or bond mutual funds and putting half your remaining stock investments into high-yield issues of income-oriented funds, you can raise your yield to as much as 7%, while still keeping sufficient inflation protection to maintain your standard of living for the rest of your life.

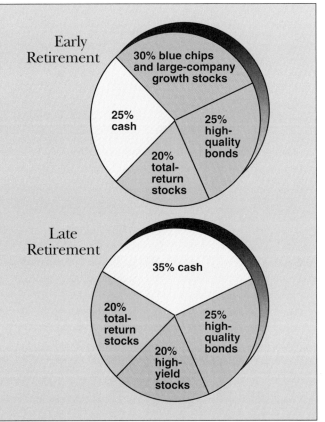

Early Retirement

30% blue chips and large-company growth stocks
25% cash
25% high-quality bonds
20% total-return stocks

Late Retirement

35% cash
20% total-return stocks
25% high-quality bonds
20% high-yield stocks

Investors who prefer mutual funds might consider no-loads that hold such stocks. Donald Phillips, editor of *Mutual Fund Values*, recommends these two: Scudder Growth & Income ($1,000 minimum investment; 800-225-2470) and T. Rowe Price Equity Income (36.6%; $2,500 minimum; 800-638-5660).

Fixed-income investments ought to account for 25% of your portfolio in the early part of your retirement; for the greatest safety, stick with Treasury issues. With $25,000, you can buy five Treasuries that will mature at regular intervals over the next decade or so—a technique known as laddering. Then, if interest rates rise, you can reinvest the proceeds of the issues that mature soonest; if rates fall, you can sell the bonds with the longest maturities at a profit.

As an alternative, you might assemble a laddered portfolio of tax-exempt municipals. A yield of 5.7% to 7.2%, for example, is equivalent to a taxable yield of 8% or better if you are in the 28% federal bracket or higher (taxable income above $35,800 for a couple filing jointly, $21,450 for singles). Mark Donohue, a senior vice president with bond dealer Gabriele Hueglin & Cashman in New York City, advises investors to buy only high-quality general-obligation municipals rated double or triple A by agencies such as Standard & Poor's. If you prefer the convenience of mutual funds, choose those that invest at least 90% of their assets in bonds rated A or better and that have expense ratios below 0.7%. Donald Phillips recommends Vanguard Municipal—Intermediate-Term Portfolio ($3,000 minimum; 800-662-7447).

Finally, keep 25% of your portfolio in cash investments to smooth out your returns. You might, for example, put $10,000 or so in a government money-market fund for emergencies and invest the rest in a short-term bond fund. Such funds buy mostly government or corporate issues with maturities of one to five years, so their share prices may fluctuate by 3% or 4% a year. But these funds offer a low-risk way to boost your income. Phillips suggests Scudder Short-Term Bond ($1,000 minimum; 800-225-2470).

Late in Retirement

Total-return stocks: 20%
High-yield stocks: 20%
High-quality bonds: 25%
Cash: 35%
Total-return target: 8% a year

As you reach your seventies, inflation is less of a concern, but your vulnerability to unexpected losses is much greater. You should, therefore, adopt the investment portfolio shown above, which carries only about a third of the risk of the overall stock market. This strategy calls for boosting your holdings of bonds and cash to 25% and 35% of your portfolio, respectively. Don't take any chances with either. With bonds, buy Treasuries that mature in five to seven years; and for safety, keep your cash in a government money fund.

Since you can expect to live for at least another decade, leave 40% of your investment money in stocks. Hang on to the total-return stocks you bought early in retirement for their combination of dividend income and growth. But reduce your overall portfolio risk by shifting from blue chip stocks and other large-company growth shares to high-yield stocks, which typically pay out 7% or more a year and can boost their dividends at least as fast as inflation.

Chuck Carlson, editor of the newsletter *Dow Theory Forecasts* in Hammond, Indiana, recommends financially strong utilities that have raised their dividends for at least 15 consecutive years. Among funds, Don Phillips recommends no-load Fidelity Utilities Income ($2,500 minimum; 800-544-8888).

By the time you reach age 75 or so, you can probably begin dipping into your capital—at least sparingly—without fear your life savings will run out before you do. And you may find that you will still have a sizable estate to leave behind to your heirs. But don't be in any hurry to make big gifts to relatives or charities while you are alive. After all, you might be whacking golf balls and quaffing vintage wines at least for another decade or two.

Stretch Your Company Benefits

Make your company's insurance, retirement, and savings plans work for you.

Everyone with benefits at work needs to take a close look at them to make sure that they are squeezing out every dollar. That's more important than ever these days for two reasons. First, companies, faced with rising bills, are shifting more of the burden of health insurance to employees by increasing the cost of coverage and cutting back on the amount that insurance reimburses.

Second, benefits plans are becoming more complicated. Many traditional plans have introduced choices, usually in health insurance and retirement savings features. Moreover, about 27% of major corporations now provide so-called flexible plans, which require employees to select benefits from a varied menu.

Yes, you will have to do some work to make your benefits work better for you. But it's worth it. By managing benefits as carefully as the rest of his or her finances, a $40,000-a-year middle manager can gain $3,500 or more in tax breaks and company subsidies.

The first step, no matter what kind of benefits plan you have at work, is the same: Make sure you know every detail of your employer's offerings. Unless you are a new recruit fresh from a benefits briefing, it's a good idea to settle in for a few hours with the latest edition of your benefits handbook—and your spouse's plan if he or she has one. You may be surprised by overlooked features or recent rule changes. After that, the specific choices you make will depend on a number of variables, including your family's size and its health and the choices your plan offers. A few basic principles apply to almost everyone, however.

Traditional Plans: More Choice Than Meets the Eye

In traditional plans, all eligible employees are given the same package of company-determined benefits. But some plans require you to take the initiative to get everything you're entitled to, most notably with these offerings:

Flexible spending accounts. About 50% of all companies with 1,000 or more workers sponsor FSAs, which are terrific tax shelters that let you set aside untaxed dollars to pay for medical expenses not reimbursed by insurance and for care of a child or disabled dependent. You can usually stash as much as $2,000 to $5,000 in a health-care FSA (your employer sets the limit) and up to $5,000 in a dependent-care account. The federal tax savings on a $3,000 contribution to either type of FSA amounts to $840 for someone in the 28% bracket (annual income above $35,800 for a couple filing jointly, $21,450 for a single person). The catch is that you must determine your annual contribution in advance, and you can't get back any money you don't use.

Savings plans. If your employer offers a tax-deferred retirement savings plan—90% of large and medium-size companies (those with more than 500 workers) have them—and you're not enrolled in it, you're passing up free money. For example, whatever you contribute to the most common type, a 401(k), up to the federal limit of $8,475 in 1991, reduces your taxable income dollar for dollar. In addition, most employers kick in 50¢ or more for every $1 you save, up to a company-set maximum, typically 6% of pay. And the money in your account grows tax deferred. Here's the payoff: If you're in the 28% federal tax bracket and contribute $1,000 to your 401(k), you'll save $280 on taxes. In addition, if your company matches your contribution with $500 and the account earns 8% a year, you'll have gained $900, for an unbeatable annual investment return of 90%.

Life insurance. Even traditional plans may offer several levels of life insurance, usually starting with coverage equal to a year's salary at no cost to you. Often you can buy more at the company's group rate, typically 5¢ to $1.50 a month for each $1,000 of coverage, depending on your age. For singles with no dependents,

the minimum is more than enough. But as the head of a family, you may want to buy more. Before stepping up your coverage, however, compare your company's rates with term insurance you can buy on your own.

Flexible Plans: Try for a Custom Fit

Getting the most out of a flexible plan can seem like a full-time job in itself. First of all, the advice we have just given for people with traditional plans also applies to you. But that's only the beginning. Flex plans can operate in a variety of ways, though, in general, each worker gets an allotment of credits with which to buy medical, dental, life, and disability coverage. There will often be several levels of each. If you exceed your allotment, the money comes out of your paycheck. If you use less, you can take

Guaranteed Investments That Aren't

If you've got money in your company's retirement savings plan, chances are you've put some of it in guaranteed investment contracts—or GICs. After all, about 65% of the more than $289 billion in 401(k)-type savings plans are in GICs, which are portfolios of fixed-income securities sold and backed by insurance companies. Now there's a new GIC coming, called a separate account GIC, that unfortunately is not nearly as guaranteed as its name suggests. These GICs get their name because, unlike in a traditional GIC, the securities underlying the contract are not held by the insurance company in its own account, but are deposited in a separate account controlled by your retirement plan's sponsor. Thus, if the insurer standing behind your GIC goes under (as 56 companies have in the past three years), your plan's assets are still safe.

The catch: Again unlike traditional GICs, which guarantee a set yield for as long as 10 years, a separate account GIC does not. If one of the contract's issues goes bust, the insurer is not bound to maintain the interest rate it initially paid. So much for guarantees. "Unless a separate account GIC is loaded with squeaky-clean stuff like U.S.

government securities," warns David Schupp, a principal at the Hartford insurance research firm Townsend & Schupp, "employees who put their money in it are probably less safe than they were in a conventional GIC."

So, are the new GICs—or the old ones, for that matter—a lousy deal? Not necessarily. GICs generally do return at least two-thirds of a percentage point more than Treasuries of comparable maturities, at relatively little extra danger. That can make them attractive, especially when you consider that they are the least risky option in many retirement plans.

But to be sure your GICs are among the best, you should phone your benefits department to find out which insurers stand behind its GIC portfolio. If you work for a big company with 5,000 or more employees, it should have contracts with at least five to 10 providers. You should also make certain that the GICs your plan owns are with insurers rated double A or better by rating services such as Moody's and Standard & Poor's. And to protect against low yields, you should check the payout each year. If it lags that of Treasuries or the potential return on equities, it's time to get out.

the surplus in cash or put it into a savings plan or flexible spending account or, in some cases, use it to buy extra vacation. The following elements, common to almost all flexible plans, are especially tricky:

Health insurance. You may have to choose among as many as five levels of coverage. For instance, AT&T offers three: the minimum, with a $2,500 deductible, pays 70% of medical bills and requires an employee to pay no more than $3,000 of his bills (in addition to the deductible); the standard plan, in which the deductible equals $200 to $350, depending on salary, reimburses 80% of bills and limits out-of-pocket payments to $2,000; and the high-benefits plan, with a deductible of $150 to $300, based on salary, reimburses 80% to 100%, depending on the procedure, and has a $1,000 out-of-pocket maximum. Another option: Employees can join a health maintenance organization (HMO).

If the choice sounds difficult or confusing, that's because it is. To work through the options, sit down with your past three years of medical bills and figure out what you would have paid under each type of coverage; that exercise will help you find your best deal. In general, single people who visit the doctor only once or twice a year should consider the least expensive option. Chances are, it will not be worth the extra money just to get a lower deductible; your annual expenses might not even meet the low deductible, so you would be paying for coverage you don't need. Yet, you'll still be protected if you suffer a major accident or health problem, thanks to the out-of-pocket maximum, which represents the most you would have to pay for covered expenses in any one year. As long as you can raise enough cash to cover your out-of-pocket maximum, relax. You need insurance for catastrophes, not routine expenses. You can put a few dollars into an FSA to cover the routine expenses you are likely to incur.

Large families with frequent bills, on the other hand, tend to come out ahead by choosing the so-called managed-care option, such as an HMO. With managed care, as much as 100% of your medical expenses will be covered,

though the insurance premiums may be high. And you must agree to patronize only those doctors and hospitals approved by your managed-care plan.

Long-term disability insurance. Traditional plans generally pay benefits of 60% or 65% of your pretax salary, with no annual maximum. Flex plans, however, may offer a basic benefit as low as 45%. If you want more coverage, you must pay for it. Heads of household and single people with no other means of support almost certainly should take the extra coverage. Further, if the option is available, pay for it with taxable dollars rather than credits; that way any benefits you might collect would come to you tax-free. Disability benefits are considered taxable income by the Internal Revenue Service if your employer pays for the insurance policy or if you pay for it with tax-free credits under a flex plan.

Two-Income Couples: Get Coordinated

Today, 44% of the U.S. work force consists of two-income couples (although not all of them have company benefits). The rule for couples with a choice of benefits plans sounds simple: Go for the one that gives you the most value at the least cost. However, applying that rule is, as you might suspect, difficult. These examples may help you do it:

Health insurance. If one spouse has free family coverage and the other must pay to protect dependents, the choice of whose coverage to use may seem obvious. But you and your spouse must do more than look at up-front cost. You must also weigh the deductibles, premiums, and expenses covered. Another factor two-plan couples must consider is that many companies have eliminated 100% coordination of benefits, under which the second insurer pays the remainder of eligible claims not covered by the primary insurer. Your best approach is to review last year's health bills carefully to determine what each different option would have cost you.

Flexible spending accounts. If both husband and wife are eligible for FSAs and one spouse earns more than $55,500 while the other earns less, the lower-earning spouse should fund the account. That way you can shave another few dollars off your tax bill. Here's why: If the lower-paid spouse puts in the money, it will escape not only federal and local income taxes, but also the 6.2% Social Security tax levied on incomes up to $55,500; the better-paid spouse will pay the maximum annual Social Security tax in any case.

Savings plans. If you and your spouse can't afford to make the maximum contributions to two savings plans, direct your dollars to the one that is eligible for the most generous company matching policy or the most attractive choice of investments. One drawback is that all your company retirement savings will be in one partner's name. If you divorce, that partner may have a greater claim on the assets. On the other hand, if you're still speaking to each other after the ordeal of sorting out your benefits, staying married should be a snap.

How to Find the Safest Annuities

Misleading sales pitches and the collapse of some insurers have turned once staid fixed annuities into riskier investments.

Step right up, folks! I've got a remedy here that is going to cure, I say cure, everything that ails you financially. Did I hear you say you want a safe investment costing as little as $1,500? One with high yields and no taxes? Lemme tell you about this miracle product that gives you all this and more. The name of this wondrous, fabulous financial concoction? Annuities. I'll say it again. Annuities!

No, the fast-talking Professor Harold Hill from "The Music Man" hasn't switched from marching bands to financial services. But he may as well have. In cities across the land, a growing army of salesmen at insurance agencies, banks, and brokerage houses is flogging fixed-rate annuities with resounding success. And frequently, the salesmen are using snake-oil pitches that would make the professor proud. Typical of the dubious ploys being used these days to woo savers: touting the annuities as tax-sheltered substitutes for federally insured bank CDs—even as newspapers are filled with stories about financially shaky life insurers;

promising "bonus" rates that supposedly boost yields to 15% or higher; and pushing schemes that pay initial rates of, say, 9% but drop to 6% before you can say "76 trombones."

Even some insurance executives fear that the public is being misled. "We see brochures using terms like 'tax-deferred certificates' that never mention the word annuity," says Kerry Geurkink, a consultant to Minnesota Mutual Life. "This kind of smokescreen is bad for consumers and bad for insurers."

Strip away the obfuscation and you'll find that fixed annuities are essentially simple investments. You hand over a lump sum—usually $5,000 or more—to a salesman who passes it along to the insurer issuing the annuity contract. The insurer pays a specific fixed interest rate, usually for a year, though some companies lock in rates for as long as 10 years. (Returns on variable annuities, by contrast, fluctuate with stock and bond prices.) When the rate comes up for renewal, you can reinvest at the rate then offered by the company, switch to another insurer, or take your money out.

As with an Individual Retirement Account, interest grows tax-free until you withdraw your money, typically at retirement. At that point, you can pull all your money out, withdraw a little at a time, or annuitize—that is, turn the account's value into a monthly income stream that can run for the rest of your life. (For advice on annuity withdrawals, see below.) Upon withdrawal, you owe federal income tax on the earnings—plus a 10% tax penalty if you're younger than 59½.

There are no front-end fees on annuities; the salesman's 4% to 7% commission is factored into the annuity's interest rate. But most annuities charge sizable fees for substantial withdrawals. The surrender charges are as high as 15% of your accumulated earnings for a withdrawal made in the first year of the contract and drop by about one percentage point

What You Should Know Before Taking Money Out

With most investments, you shop around once—then you buy. But annuity investors should go through the exercise twice: when they purchase the contracts and when they're ready to cash out. That's because annuities are portable. Once surrender charges have expired, you can take your money, without penalty, out of the company that built up your account's value and move it to another company that may offer a more generous or flexible payout.

Before embarking on your second shopping expedition, it's essential to understand your withdrawal options. You can simply pull your money out of the annuity in a lump sum, but you'll immediately owe taxes on all your earnings. There are two ways, however, to postpone that tax bite and turn your annuity account into a reliable income stream.

One is annuitizing—an irrevocable decision to turn over the accumulated value of your annuity to the insurer in return for a fixed monthly income, typically for the rest of your life. Annuitizing has a distinct tax advantage: It lets you postpone paying taxes on some of the earnings you've accrued. Each check is only partly earnings; the rest is your original principal.

The other option is setting up a systematic withdrawal plan. With this method, *you* tell the insurance company how much cash to send you from your account each month. Systematic withdrawal offers flexibility; at any time you can raise, lower, or stop the payments as well as annuitize. But unlike annuitization, your account could run out of money someday. What's more, cash paid out in a systematic plan is usually fully taxable until you have drained all your earnings from the account. Since the tax law governing annuities is quite complex, however, you should consult a financial planner or tax adviser before going ahead with either withdrawal option.

You'll want to annuitize if you prefer the certainty of getting a specific income each year. By choosing a standard life annuity, you guarantee yourself a lifetime income, but since the payments expire when you do, you're also betting on how long you will live. By settling for 5% or so less each month, you can instruct the insurer to make sure your spouse or another dependent will get income after you die. Ask your agent for a joint-and-survivor annuity, which pays out as long as you or your beneficiary is alive, or a life-with-period-certain annuity, which assures you of a lifetime income but also guarantees payments for a period of time, usually 10 years. If you die within that time, your beneficiary collects the remaining payments.

If you decide to annuitize, compare the payments offered by several insurers. Recently, a 65-year-old man with a $100,000 annuity could convert it to $809 a month for life with Travelers. But by taking the same sum to Northwestern Mutual, he could get $906 a month. "Never assume that the company whose annuities build the most value will be the one offering the most generous payments when you annuitize," says Joe Rosanswank, editor of *Comparative Annuity Reports Newsletter.*

Not all insurers offer systematic withdrawal plans, though several financially sound companies, such as Lincoln Benefit Life and Safeco, do. Of course, the more income you take out, the quicker you'll deplete your stash. Assuming your $100,000 balance earns 8% a year, a $1,000 monthly draw would bleed your account dry within 14 years. If you limit withdrawals to your annuity's annual earnings, however, you can keep your principal stable. Any money left in the account when you die goes to your beneficiary.

each year until they disappear, typically in seven to 10 years. Many insurers, however, let you withdraw 10% of your account's value each year without penalty.

The best candidates for fixed annuities are conservative investors who are at least 50 years old and are willing to lock up their money for 10 or more years before drawing on it for retirement. But many fee-hungry salesmen are peddling annuities to younger people who would be better off in investments offering potential long-term capital growth. A 1990 survey of annuity buyers by the Life Insurance Marketing and Research Association shows that 37% of fixed annuities are bought by people under 50.

If a fixed annuity appeals to you, expect to sift through a lot of marketing mendacity to find the right one. There are two main types of hype today: exaggerations of safety and of investment returns.

Safety claims. Although salesmen like to point out that an annuity's value is "guaranteed," that promise is only as strong as the insurer making it. An annuity is backed by the insurer's investment portfolio, which, nowadays, may contain junk bonds and troubled real estate investments. In the first half of 1991 alone, five large annuity marketers collapsed, jeopardizing more than 500,000 annuity holders: First Capital Life, Fidelity Banker's Life, two subsidiaries of First Executive Life, and Mutual Benefit Life.

If your insurer fails, you may become just another creditor hoping to be paid back. In July 1991, for example, when the New Jersey insurance department took over Mutual Benefit Life, the state froze the accounts of annuity holders, preventing them from withdrawing money unless they could prove a significant financial hardship.

To woo conservative savers who prefer the rock-solid security of bank accounts, banks and insurance companies have begun touting so-called CD annuities and certificates of annuity. The most popular of these beguiling innovations offer a one-year term, usually paying a half to a percentage point more than a comparable bank CD, with no surrender charges if you withdraw at the end of the term.

But don't be fooled by the name. No annuities, even those sold in bank lobbies, are federally insured. Bear in mind, too, that unlike a bank CD, if you withdraw money from a CD annuity before age 59½, you'll pay the 10% tax penalty. This pinch can pretty much wipe out the yield advantage over genuine bank CDs. And even though one-year CD annuity yields beat bank CDs, they often lag yields of conventional annuities by a half to a full percentage point or more. Says Glenn Daily, author of *The Individual Investor's Guide to Low-Load Insurance Products* (International Publishing): "You're giving up a lot of yield for the privilege of being able to get out every year."

There's no way to be absolutely certain an insurer won't founder, but you can tilt the odds in your favor by staying with companies that get high safety ratings from at least two companies that monitor insurers' financial health. Stick to insurers that get an A+ rating from A.M. Best and at least an AA from Standard & Poor's, Moody's, or Duff & Phelps. You may also want to check the safety ratings of Weiss Research, a tough though controversial grader. Your insurance agent can provide you with an annuity issuer's ratings.

Rate-of-return claims. Some annuity marketers inflate their yields by playing games with the way they calculate them; others advertise sumptuous rates that have more strings attached than a marionette. If somebody's yield is way out of line, you know they're either sacrificing the quality of their investments or restricting your ability to get at your money.

The most widespread form of rate deception today is the bonus annuity, in which insurers tack on as much as eight percentage points to their current interest rate, boosting the first-year yield to 15% or higher. But many of these alluring bonuses can be illusory. The 1991 sales brochure for Life USA's "Excelerator" annuity, for instance, touts a "guaranteed" first year 8% bonus on top of its 7.25% rate. But you'll get the bonus on your accrued earnings only if you eventually annuitize and take the money in monthly installments over a period of at least 10 years. If you ask Life USA for your cash in a lump sum, the insurer will retroactively subtract the 8% bonus, plus the interest that compounded on the bonus—*and* you'll be charged a 15% penalty on your original investment.

Tiered-rate annuities—so named because they have two levels of interest rates—are even more insidious. They ballyhoo an above-average rate of, say, 9%. But, as with their bonus-rate cousins, the accrued earnings in your account will reflect this so-called accumulation rate only when you annuitize. A straight withdrawal will knock you down to a "surrender value" rate as low as 6% for every year you've invested.

Other insurers simply resort to the time-dishonored practice of luring customers with lofty initial rates that are lowered at renewal time. But gravitating toward annuities paying blimpish rates—no matter how an insurer juices up its yield—can be a big mistake; such annuities are frequently lousy performers over the long haul.

An A.M. Best survey of the renewal rates paid each year to annuity holders by 69 insurers from 1985 to 1990 shows that you are generally better off opting for a competitive rate, but not necessarily the highest. In 1985, Federal Kemper Life touted a 12.25% first-year rate on its annuities, while Aetna Life & Annuity was paying a more realistic 10.5%. Three years later, however, Federal Kemper had dropped its rate to 8%, while Aetna was paying 9%. Result: After five years, $10,000 invested with Federal Kemper was worth $14,621, net of surrender charges—$496 less than the $15,117 value of Aetna's annuity.

To avoid being sucked in by a lossleader rate, compare the annuity's initial rate to that of its competitors. The bimonthly newsletter *Annuity & Life Insurance Shopper* ($20 an issue; 800-872-6684) publishes current rates of approximately 150 fixed annuities. Then ask the annuity salesman for the insurer's renewal rates over the past three to five years. It's okay if renewal rates have gone down, provided they've moved in tandem with some proxy of what insurers hold in their portfolio, such as the yield onfive-year corporate bonds. Two

insurance companies with an attractive history of renewal rates, according to Glenn Daily, are John Alden Life and USAA Life.

Many insurers say they'll protect you against low renewal rates with what's known as a bailout provision. A bailout lets you out of an annuity without surrender charges if the renewal rate slips by, say, one percentage point or more below your initial rate. You're better off without the bailout, though. For one thing, it's expensive. Annuities with bailouts typically pay initial rates a half to a percentage point below those without teaser rates and escape clauses. What's more, a bailout really protects you only against a company ripping you off through arbitrarily lowering its rates. If interest rates drop overall and you bail out, you probably won't be able to reinvest in another annuity at a higher rate anyway.

Overstating the value of tax deferral is another way some marketers make their returns look impressively high. For example, in its 1991 promotional material for its customers, Citibank boasts that its Nationwide Life annuity offers "an easy way to make 7% worth 11%," implying that a 7% return on its tax-deferred annuity is like an 11% pretax return on a taxable investment. Citibank's annuity brochure shows how someone in a 39% combined federal and state income tax bracket investing $25,000 would wind up with $49,178 in an annuity, versus $37,978 in a taxable investment. But that return is tax *deferred*, not tax-free. You do eventually have to pay taxes on those annuity earnings.

If you withdrew the money and paid taxes, the $49,178 would drop to $39,749, giving you a 4.8% annual return. If you owed the 10% tax penalty, your sum would dwindle to $37,332—$646 less than the taxable investment, and a piddling 4.1% annual return.

At the end of "The Music Man," Professor Hill mends his ways, but don't expect the same from annuity salesmen. "People want high rates and salesmen want commissions," says Ted Charles, president of a Topsfield, Massachusetts firm that markets annuities to insurance agents and financial institutions. "So I think we're going to see more gimmicks as long as interest rates remain low."

Money's Car Cost Ratings

When it comes to getting a great value on a new car, the purchase price is only part of the story. The crucial second part is what you pay after you drive off the dealer's lot—in gasoline, maintenance, insurance, and, most of all, depreciation. "By the time the typical car is five years old, the cost to own and operate it will exceed its original purchase price," explains Peter Levy, president of IntelliChoice, a San Jose research firm that analyzes automobile ownership costs. "In the long run," he says, "those costs can be more important than purchase price in determining the value you get in a car."

Compare, for example, the Buick Regal Custom and the Honda Accord EX, both mid-size four-door sedans. At the 1992 price of $18,245, the Honda costs $1,400 more to buy. But when you add up the costs of owning the Honda over five years, you get a total ownership expense of under $26,000 versus more than $28,000 for the Buick.

Because the true cost of a car isn't obvious, *Money* teamed up with IntelliChoice to develop the all-new *Money*'s Car Cost Ratings. The ratings combine various expenses to determine which models really cost the least to own. In the table on page 154, we identify the winners in each of eight categories of cars and light trucks, including the vehicles with the lowest total five-year cost, best gas mileage, least costly maintenance, and best resale value. Then in the 10 pages that follow, we give total ownership expenses for 522 models of cars, trucks, vans, and utility vehicles, ranging from the $6,600 Daihatsu Charade to the $127,000 Mercedes-Benz 600 SEL.

In addition to steering you to the best values, the tables also provide the information you need to negotiate a great buy, including 1992 **suggested retail price** (or an estimate, in the case of models for which 1992 prices were not available at press time), **dealer's cost**, and a **target price**. Our target prices reflect the sluggishness of today's market, in which you can often bargain to within 2% to 6% of the dealer's cost.

Keep in mind that our prices include standard equipment only. If you want optional features, you can adjust your target price with the help of the figures under **options cost**. Say, for example, you have your eye on a Chevrolet Lumina, on which air conditioning comes as part of an options package listing for $1,020. According to the table, the dealer's cost for options on Chevrolets is 85% of the retail price, which works out to roughly $870 for air conditioning. Thus, to keep cool in a Lumina, you should aim to pay $900 or so—$870 plus a 3% profit margin—over the car's target price of $11,980.

In calculating total ownership expenses, we assumed that you put 14,000 miles on the car per year and paid average insurance premiums, loan interest, and gasoline prices. We then added up estimates for each model's five-year depreciation (purchase price minus resale value), financing, fuel and insurance costs, state fees, and anticipated outlays for **maintenance** and **repairs**. All our projections are based on data from the 1991 model-year. For cars redesigned in 1992, we based our estimates on the record of the car's predecessor or closest automotive kin, if any.

The Best in Their Categories

Lowest Total Cost

Except for the Suzuki, none of the cars or trucks below carries the lowest sticker price in its category. But when you calculate the true costs of ownership over five years—which includes depreciation, financing, maintenance, insurance, and repairs—each of the vehicles is a standout value.

Best Mileage

The entries below get the farthest in their category per gallon of gas. Among the winners, mileage ranges from a high of 50 highway miles per gallon for the three-cylinder Geo Metro to a low of 28 for the four-cylinder Toyota Celica GT convertible. Over five years, every extra mile per gallon will save you about $200.

Maintenance

The cost of keeping these vehicles in peak mechanical health is the lowest in their categories, based on the estimated cost of following each model's maintenance schedule and making other common repairs. Over five years, maintenance on the Chrysler Imperial, for example, runs as much as $2,000 less than competitors.

Best Resale

Honda and Mercedes excel in resisting depreciation, the most important ownership cost. In good condition, both companies' top models figure to fetch close to 70% of their original list price in a private sale five years hence. The strongest American entries, a Dodge minivan and a Chevy pickup, would get a similar percent.

Lowest Total Cost	Best Mileage	Maintenance	Best Resale
Under $10,000 **Honda Civic two-door hatchback**	Under $10,000 **Geo Metro hatchback**	Under $10,000 **Isuzu Stylus S**	Under $10,000 **Honda CRX**
$10,000 to $15,000 **Honda Civic DX four-door sedan**	$10,000 to $15,000 **Honda Civic four-door sedan**	$10,000 to $15,000 **Dodge Daytona**	$10,000 to $15,000 **Honda Accord DX**
$15,000 to $20,000 **Geo Prizm LSi four-door sedan**	$15,000 to $20,000 **Geo Prizm LSi four-door sedan**	$15,000 to $20,000 **Dodge Dynasty LE**	$15,000 to $20,000 **Honda Prelude Si**
$20,000 to $30,000 **Volvo 240 four-door sedan**	$20,000 to $30,000 **Toyota Celica GT Convertible**	$20,000 to $30,000 **Chrysler Imperial**	$20,000 to $30,000 **Mercedes-Benz 190 E 2.3**
Over $30,000 **Mercedes-Benz 190 E 2.6 four-door sedan**	Over $30,000 **Mercedes-Benz 300 D 2.5**	Over $30,000 **Lincoln Town Car Signature**	Over $30,000 **Mercedes-Benz 300 E**
Small Pickups **Ford Ranger Sport**	Small Pickups **Ford Ranger**	Small Pickups **Isuzu Spacecab LS**	Small Pickups **Chevrolet C 1500 Extended Cab**
Sport Utility Vehicles **Suzuki Samurai JA**	Sport Utility Vehicles **Suzuki Samurai Convertible**	Sport Utility Vehicles **GMC Jimmy two-door 4WD**	Sport Utility Vehicles **Toyota 4Runner SR5 V6 4WD**
Minivans **Dodge Caravan SE**	Minivans **Plymouth Voyager**	Minivans **Plymouth Voyager LE AWD**	Minivans **Dodge Grand Caravan SE AWD**

Under $10,000

Make and model	Suggested retail price	Est. dealer's cost	Your target price	Options cost (% of retail)[2]	Five-year resale value	Miles per gallon (city/hwy.)	Cost to insure[3]	Five-year costs Mainte-nance[4]	Repairs[5]	Total ownership expense[6]
Chevrolet Cavalier RS 2dr	$9,999	$9,279	$9,465	85%	$3,300	25/36	High	$4,110	$155	$22,708
Chevrolet Cavalier VL 2dr	8,899	8,436	8,605	85	2,759	25/36	High	4,110	155	22,398
Chevrolet Cavalier VL 4dr	8,899	8,531	8,702	85	2,848	25/36	Average	4,110	155	22,268
Daihatsu Charade SE 2dr hatch	6,621[1]	6,157	6,280	86	2,119	38/42	Very high	4,179	N.A.	N.A.
Dodge Colt 2dr hatch	7,302	6,933	7,072	83	2,483	29/35	Very high	4,236	95	18,941
Dodge Colt GL 2dr hatch	8,122	7,682	7,836	83	2,599	29/35	Very high	4,347	95	20,257
Dodge Shadow America 2dr hatch	7,984	7,433	7,582	85	2,874	26/32	High	3,604	184	19,908
Dodge Shadow 4dr hatch	9,646	8,831	9,008	85	3,473	26/32	High	3,604	184	20,867
Eagle Summit 2dr hatch	7,302	6,933	7,072	86	N.A.	31/36	Very high	4,179	N.A.	N.A.
Eagle Summit 4dr	8,981	8,481	8,651	86	3,413	29/35	High	4,179	N.A.	N.A.
Eagle Summit ES 4dr	9,998	9,368	9,555	86	3,699	29/35	High	4,290	N.A.	N.A.
Ford Escort LX 2dr hatch	9,055	8,179	8,343	85	3,079	30/37	Very high	3,729	201	20,139
Ford Escort LX 4dr	9,795	8,838	9,015	85	N.A.	30/37	Very high	N.A.	N.A.	N.A.
Ford Escort 2dr hatch	8,355	7,723	7,877	92	2,757	32/40	Very high	3,729	201	19,675
Ford Festiva GL 2dr hatch	7,839	7,375	7,523	85	2,822	35/41	Very high	3,832	114	18,470
Ford Festiva L 2dr hatch	6,911	6,512	6,642	85	2,488	35/41	Very high	3,767	114	17,755
Ford Tempo GL 2dr	9,963	8,992	9,172	85	3,387	23/33	Average	4,313	331	23,871
Geo Metro 2dr hatch	6,999	6,474	6,603	88	2,800	46/50	Very high	4,151	N.A.	N.A.
Geo Metro 4dr hatch	7,399	6,844	6,981	88	3,034	46/50	Very high	4,151	N.A.	N.A.
Geo Metro LSi convert.	9,999	9,249	9,434	88	N.A.	41/46	Very high	4,233	N.A.	N.A.
Geo Metro LSi 2dr hatch	8,199	7,584	7,736	88	3,034	46/50	Very high	4,151	N.A.	N.A.
Honda Civic 2dr hatch	7,308[1]	6,577	6,709	90	5,042	42/48	High	4,095	85	15,850
Honda Civic DX 2dr hatch	9,188[1]	7,810	7,966	85	5,421	35/40	High	4,169	85	17,846
Honda CRX 2dr hatch	9,955[1]	8,462	8,631	85	7,367	32/36	Very high	4,171	85	20,750
Hyundai Excel 2dr hatch	6,595	6,133	6,256	93	1,976	30/36	Very high	3,939	181	19,073
Hyundai Excel 4dr	7,695	7,156	7,299	93	2,403	30/36	Very high	3,912	181	19,926
Hyundai Excel GS 2dr hatch	7,599	6,763	6,898	89	2,571	29/36	Very high	4,072	181	20,153
Hyundai Scoupe 2dr	8,799	7,919	8,077	90	N.A.	26/34	High	N.A.	N.A.	N.A.
Hyundai Scoupe LS 2dr	9,999	8,799	8,975	88	N.A.	26/34	High	N.A.	N.A.	N.A.
Isuzu Stylus S 4dr	9,521[1]	8,569	8,740	85	N.A.	31/37	High	3,399	N.A.	N.A.
Mazda 323 2dr hatch	6,999	6,509	6,639	80	2,870	29/37	Very high	3,807	79	18,040
Mazda 323 SE 2dr hatch	8,299	7,469	7,618	80	3,403	29/37	Very high	3,827	79	18,614
Mazda Protege DX 4dr	9,999	8,899	9,077	80	4,200	28/36	Very high	3,706	79	19,942
Mercury Tracer 4dr	9,773	8,828	9,005	85	N.A.	30/37	Very high	N.A.	194	N.A.
Mitsubishi Mirage 4dr	8,939	8,045	8,206	82	3,355	29/35	Very high	3,893	303	19,907
Mitsubishi Mirage VL 2dr hatch	7,319	6,614	6,746	82	2,708	31/36	Very high	3,893	303	18,705
Mitsubishi Precis 2dr hatch	6,695[1]	6,093	6,215	80	2,008	29/33	Very high	4,244	N.A.	N.A.
Nissan Sentra E 2dr	8,495	7,971	8,130	85	3,738	29/37	Very high	3,958	89	20,310
Nissan Sentra E 4dr	9,550	8,475	8,645	85	4,489	29/37	High	3,958	89	19,330
Nissan Sentra XE 2dr	9,880	8,768	8,943	85	3,853	29/39	Very high	4,324	89	21,701
Plymouth Colt 2dr hatch	7,302	6,933	7,072	83	2,556	31/36	Very high	3,998	95	18,660
Plymouth Colt GL 2dr hatch	8,122	7,682	7,836	83	2,599	29/35	Very high	4,110	95	20,214
Plymouth Sundance America 2dr hatch	7,984	7,433	7,582	85	2,794	26/32	High	3,475	184	19,503
Plymouth Sundance 4dr hatch	9,646	8,831	9,008	85	3,665	26/32	High	3,475	184	20,560
Pontiac LeMans Aerocoupe 2dr hatch	8,050	7,446	7,595	85	2,657	28/37	Very high	4,074	327	20,845
Pontiac LeMans SE 4dr	9,465	8,755	8,930	85	3,123	31/41	Very high	4,318	327	22,631
Pontiac Sunbird LE 2dr	9,620	8,927	9,106	85	3,367	25/35	High	4,522	217	24,660
Pontiac Sunbird LE 4dr	9,720	9,020	9,200	85	3,499	25/35	Average	4,522	217	24,268
Saturn SL 4dr	8,195	7,294	7,440	89	N.A.	28/38	Average	N.A.	N.A.	N.A.
Saturn SL1 4dr	8,995	8,006	8,166	89	N.A.	28/38	Average	N.A.	N.A.	N.A.
Subaru Justy 2dr hatch	6,645	6,113	6,235	92	2,192	33/37	High	4,234	113	18,049
Subaru Justy GL 4WD 4dr hatch	8,949	8,054	8,215	90	2,601	28/32	Very high	4,334	113	20,341
Subaru Loyale 4dr	9,799	8,824	9,000	89	3,528	25/32	High	4,340	113	21,467
Suzuki Swift GA 2dr hatch	6,899	6,209	6,333	90	N.A.	39/43	Very high	4,049	N.A.	N.A.
Suzuki Swift GS 4dr	9,099	8,007	8,167	87	N.A.	39/43	Very high	4,027	N.A.	N.A.

[1]Estimate [2]Dealer's average cost as a percentage of suggested retail price. [3]Compared with other models in its class. Actual costs will vary, depending on your location, the number and age of drivers and so forth. [4]Includes scheduled maintenance, as well as replacement of tires, brake pads, batteries and other parts. [5]Average five-year repair costs not covered by warranty. [6]Includes depreciation, financing, maintenance, repairs, state taxes and registration fees, insurance and fuel. Sources: IntelliChoice Inc., AutoAdviser Inc., Insurance Services Office and the manufacturers.

Under $10,000

Make and model	Suggested retail price	Est. dealer's cost	Your target price	Options cost (% of retail)[2]	Five-year resale value	Miles per gallon (city/hwy.)	Cost to insure[3]	Mainte-nance[4]	Repairs[5]	Total ownership expense[6]
Toyota Corolla 4dr	$9,418	$8,382	$8,550	80%	$4,426	28/33	High	$4,186	$97	$19,097
Toyota Tercel 2dr	6,998	6,402	6,530	80	2,799	32/37	Very high	4,823	97	18,626
Toyota Tercel Deluxe 4dr	8,528	7,675	7,829	80	3,155	29/36	High	4,860	97	N.A.
Toyota Tercel LE 4dr	9,908	8,520	8,690	80	3,963	29/36	High	4,860	97	20,909
Volkswagen Fox 2dr	7,670	7,096	7,238	86	3,452	25/32	Very high	4,355	180	18,899
Volkswagen Fox GL 4dr	8,890	8,086	8,248	86	3,912	25/32	Very high	4,485	180	19,831
Volkswagen Golf GL 2dr hatch	9,640	8,668	8,841	86	4,916	25/32	Very high	4,642	136	21,295
Volkswagen Golf GL 4dr hatch	9,950	8,945	9,124	86	5,174	25/32	High	4,642	136	21,407

◆ $10,000 to $15,000

Make and model	Suggested retail price	Est. dealer's cost	Your target price	Options cost (% of retail)[2]	Five-year resale value	Miles per gallon (city/hwy.)	Cost to insure[3]	Mainte-nance[4]	Repairs[5]	Total ownership expense[6]
Acura Integra LS 4dr	14,990[1]	12,592	12,969	84	8,342	24/28	High	4,685	137	24,713
Acura Integra RS 2dr hatch	12,463[1]	10,469	10,783	84	8,100	24/28	High	4,685	137	21,901
Buick Century Custom 2dr	14,550	12,629	13,008	85	4,074	22/31	Low	4,655	275	27,879
Buick Century Custom 4dr	14,755	12,807	13,191	85	4,574	22/31	Very low	4,644	275	26,982
Buick Century Special 4dr	13,795	12,250	12,618	85	3,863	22/31	Very low	4,655	275	27,879
Buick Skylark 2dr	13,560	12,611	12,989	85	4,068	19/29	Low	N.A.	197	N.A.
Buick Skylark 4dr	13,560	12,611	12,989	85	4,204	19/29	Low	N.A.	197	N.A.
Chevrolet Beretta 2dr	10,999	9,877	10,075	85	3,740	25/34	High	4,248	198	26,073
Chevrolet Beretta GT 2dr	12,575	11,292	11,631	85	4,150	19/28	High	4,360	198	27,744
Chevrolet Camaro RS 2dr	12,075	10,843	11,168	85	4,709	17/27	Very high	4,310	137	30,296
Chevrolet Cavalier RS 4dr	10,199	9,465	9,654	85	3,366	25/36	Average	4,110	155	22,673
Chevrolet Cavalier RS 4dr wgn	11,199	10,393	10,705	85	3,808	23/31	Average	4,300	155	24,544
Chevrolet Cavalier VL 4dr wgn	10,099	9,574	9,765	85	3,232	23/31	Average	4,110	155	22,807
Chevrolet Cavalier Z24 2dr	12,995	11,670	12,020	85	4,288	20/28	High	4,452	155	26,786
Chevrolet Corsica LT 4dr	10,999	9,877	10,075	85	3,630	25/34	Average	4,484	198	24,975
Chevrolet Lumina 2dr	13,200	11,458	11,802	85	5,676	21/28	Low	5,092	N.A.	N.A.
Chevrolet Lumina 4dr	13,400	11,631	11,980	85	5,762	21/28	Low	5,092	N.A.	N.A.
Chrysler LeBaron 2dr	13,488	11,975	12,334	85	4,586	23/27	Low	3,704	236	25,189
Chrysler LeBaron 4dr	13,798	12,224	12,591	85	4,001	23/27	Low	4,022	236	27,810
Dodge Daytona 2dr hatch	10,469	9,487	9,772	85	3,245	23/31	Very high	3,375	278	23,080
Dodge Daytona ES 2dr hatch	11,510	10,414	10,725	85	3,338	23/31	Very high	3,470	278	24,422
Dodge Daytona IROC 2dr hatch	12,805	11,566	11,913	85	3,714	19/28	Very high	3,470	278	24,422
Dodge Dynasty 4dr	14,277	12,355	12,726	85	5,568	22/28	Very low	3,655	232	23,852
Dodge Monaco LE 4dr	14,354	12,451	12,825	85	N.A.	18/26	Low	4,206	N.A.	N.A.
Dodge Shadow ES 2dr hatch	10,912	9,971	10,170	85	3,928	23/31	High	3,965	184	24,705
Dodge Shadow convert.	13,457	12,261	12,629	85	N.A.	23/31	High	3,604	184	N.A.
Dodge Spirit 4dr	11,470	10,264	10,572	90	4,015	23/31	Low	3,952	236	24,146
Dodge Spirit ES 4dr	14,441	12,878	13,264	85	4,766	21/27	Low	4,024	250	28,169
Eagle Talon TSi Turbo 2dr	14,963	13,697	14,108	85	N.A.	21/28	High	5,518	268	N.A.
Ford Escort GT 2dr hatch	11,871	10,685	11,006	85	4,630	26/31	Very high	4,144	201	23,871
Ford Escort LX 4dr wgn	10,067	9,080	9,262	85	3,322	30/37	Very high	3,729	201	20,792
Ford Mustang LX 2dr hatch	11,229	10,164	10,469	85	4,492	22/30	Very high	4,029	111	26,983
Ford Mustang LX 2dr	10,723	9,714	9,908	85	4,182	22/30	Very high	4,029	111	26,307
Ford Mustang LX 5.0L Sport 2dr hatch	14,734	13,283	13,681	85	5,894	17/24	Very high	5,057	111	31,634
Ford Mustang LX 5.0L Sport 2dr	13,949	12,584	12,962	85	5,440	17/24	Very high	5,057	111	31,082
Ford Probe GL 2dr hatch	12,141	10,970	11,299	85	5,828	24/31	High	4,634	N.A.	N.A.
Ford Probe GT 2dr hatch	14,741	13,284	13,683	85	6,339	21/27	High	5,221	N.A.	N.A.
Ford Probe LX 2dr hatch	13,141	11,860	12,216	85	6,045	19/26	High	4,586	N.A.	N.A.
Ford Taurus L 4dr	14,913	12,851	13,237	85	5,369	20/29	Very low	4,543	345	24,264
Ford Tempo GL 4dr	10,113	9,125	9,308	85	3,540	23/33	Low	4,313	331	23,517
Ford Tempo GLS 2dr	12,628	11,364	11,705	85	4,041	21/28	Average	4,313	331	24,699
Ford Tempo GLS 4dr	12,776	11,495	11,840	85	4,344	21/28	Low	4,313	331	24,414
Ford Tempo LX 4dr	11,091	9,996	10,196	85	3,549	23/33	Low	4,313	331	24,836

[1]Estimate [2]Dealer's average cost as a percentage of suggested retail price. [3]Compared with other models in its class. Actual costs will vary, depending on your location, the number and age of drivers and so forth. [4]Includes scheduled maintenance, as well as replacement of tires, brake pads, batteries and other parts. [5]Average five-year repair costs not covered by warranty. [6]Includes depreciation, financing, maintenance, repairs, state taxes and registration fees, insurance and fuel. Sources: IntelliChoice Inc., AutoAdviser Inc., Insurance Services Office and the manufacturers.

$10,000 to $15,000

Make and model	Suggested retail price	Est. dealer's cost	Your target price	Options cost (% of retail)[2]	Five-year resale value	Miles per gallon (city/ hwy.)	Cost to insure[3]	Five-year costs Mainte-nance[4]	Repairs[5]	Total ownership expense[6]
Geo Prizm 4dr	$10,125	$9,366	$9,553	85%	$3,848	28/33	High	$4,385	$70	$21,232
Geo Prizm GSi 4dr	13,770	12,737	13,119	85	5,233	25/31	High	4,765	70	24,798
Geo Storm 2+2 2dr	11,330	10,254	10,562	85	N.A.	30/36	Very high	4,992	59	N.A.
Honda Accord DX 2dr	13,025	10,941	11,269	84	8,857	24/30	Average	4,645	85	20,413
Honda Accord DX 4dr	13,225	11,109	11,442	84	8,596	24/30	Low	4,645	85	20,741
Honda Civic DX 4dr	10,555	8,971	9,240	85	6,333	35/40	High	4,169	85	18,104
Honda Civic EX 4dr	13,575	11,538	11,884	85	7,195	29/36	High	4,289	85	20,374
Honda Civic LX 4dr	11,385	9,677	9,967	85	6,376	35/40	High	4,169	85	19,242
Honda Civic Si 2dr hatch	10,784[1]	9,166	9,441	85	6,255	29/36	High	4,570	85	19,862
Honda CRX Si 2dr hatch	11,747[1]	9,985	10,285	85	8,458	28/33	High	4,167	85	22,091
Hyundai Sonata 4dr	11,150	9,924	10,121	80	N.A.	20/27	High	5,372	N.A.	N.A.
Isuzu Stylus RS 4dr	11,694[1]	10,291	10,600	83	N.A.	28/33	High	3,798	N.A.	N.A.
Mazda 626 DX 4dr	13,025	11,397	11,739	80	5,601	24/31	High	4,477	79	25,013
Mazda 626 LX 4dr	14,595	12,625	13,004	80	5,984	24/31	High	4,481	79	26,645
Mazda MX-5 Miata convert.	14,800	12,876	13,262	80	N.A.	24/30	High	4,306	N.A.	N.A.
Mazda MX-6 DX 2dr	13,265	11,474	11,818	80	6,102	24/31	Very high	4,463	79	25,636
Mazda MX-6 LX 2dr	14,585	12,470	12,844	80	6,417	24/31	Very high	4,431	79	26,737
Mazda Protege Luxury 4dr	11,699	10,295	10,604	80	4,914	25/30	Very high	4,023	79	21,347
Mercury Topaz GS 2dr	10,487	9,469	9,658	85	3,461	23/33	High	4,489	329	24,665
Mercury Topaz GS 4dr	10,653	9,617	9,809	85	3,622	23/33	Low	4,489	329	24,229
Mercury Topaz LS 4dr	12,033	10,844	11,169	85	3,490	23/33	Low	4,489	329	26,084
Mercury Topaz LTS 4dr	14,220	12,791	13,175	90	3,839	21/28	Low	4,489	329	26,736
Mercury Tracer 4dr wgn	10,794	9,737	9,932	85	N.A.	30/37	Very high	N.A.	194	N.A.
Mitsubishi Eclipse 2dr	11,259	9,852	10,049	82	N.A.	23/32	High	4,326	221	N.A.
Mitsubishi Expo LRV 3dr wgn	11,169	10,055	10,357	N.A.	N.A.	23/29	N.A.	N.A.	N.A.	N.A.
Mitsubishi Expo LRV Sport 3dr wgn	11,989	10,434	10,747	N.A.	N.A.	23/29	N.A.	N.A.	N.A.	N.A.
Mitsubishi Galant 4dr	11,699	10,529	10,845	79	4,690	20/26	Average	4,414	515	24,618
Mitsubishi Galant LS 4dr	14,809	12,588	12,965	80	5,949	20/26	Average	4,448	515	25,555
Mitsubishi Mirage GS 4dr	10,899	9,591	9,783	82	3,801	23/28	Very high	4,337	303	22,828
Nissan 240SX 2dr	14,515	12,881	13,267	85	6,241	22/27	Very high	5,033	89	30,422
Nissan NX 1600 2dr	11,300	10,143	10,447	85	N.A.	28/38	High	N.A.	N.A.	N.A.
Nissan Sentra GXE 4dr	12,950	11,426	11,769	85	4,533	29/39	High	4,069	89	23,059
Nissan Sentra SE 2dr	10,560	9,317	9,503	85	3,379	29/39	Very high	4,069	89	22,671
Nissan Sentra SE-R 2dr	11,850	10,455	10,769	85	3,792	24/32	Very high	4,384	89	24,577
Nissan Sentra XE 4dr	10,565	9,376	9,564	85	3,909	29/39	High	4,324	89	21,469
Oldsmobile Achieva S 2dr	12,275[1]	11,048	11,379	85	4,541	22/29	N.A.	4,184	167	24,617
Oldsmobile Achieva S 4dr	12,375[1]	11,138	11,472	85	4,578	22/29	N.A.	4,372	167	25,117
Oldsmobile Cutlass Ciera S 4dr	12,755	11,837	12,192	85	4,464	22/31	Very low	4,652	223	26,230
Oldsmobile Cutlass Cruiser S 4dr wgn	13,860	12,862	13,248	85	4,297	21/28	Average	4,648	223	27,469
Plymouth Acclaim 4dr	11,470	10,264	10,572	85	3,785	23/31	Low	3,639	236	24,058
Plymouth Colt Vista 4dr wgn	11,397	10,447	10,760	83	4,559	23/29	Low	4,160	280	23,561
Plymouth Colt Vista 4WD 4dr wgn	13,469	12,312	12,681	83	5,792	22/26	Low	4,092	280	23,591
Pontiac Firebird 2dr	12,505	11,229	11,566	85	4,877	17/27	Very high	4,208	172	29,227
Pontiac Grand Am 2dr	11,889	11,057	11,388	85	4,070	22/29	High	4,585	157	23,470
Pontiac Grand Am 4dr	11,999	11,159	11,494	85	3,942	22/29	Low	4,585	157	23,537
Pontiac Grand Prix LE 4dr	14,890	13,222	13,619	85	5,360	19/27	Low	5,070	123	26,810
Pontiac Sunbird GT 2dr	12,820	11,512	11,857	85	3,846	19/28	High	4,593	217	28,001
Pontiac Sunbird SE 2dr	10,380	9,321	9,507	85	3,633	25/35	High	4,568	217	25,991
Pontiac Sunbird SE 4dr	10,480	9,411	9,599	85	3,563	25/35	Average	4,436	217	22,426
Saturn SC 2dr	11,875	10,569	10,886	89	N.A.	24/33	High	N.A.	N.A.	N.A.
Saturn SL2 4dr	10,395	9,252	9,437	89	N.A.	24/33	Average	N.A.	N.A.	N.A.
Subaru Legacy L 4dr	12,428	11,805	12,159	88	N.A.	23/30	Average	5,042	N.A.	N.A.
Subaru Legacy L 4WD 4dr wgn	13,728	12,953	13,342	88	N.A.	21/26	Average	5,119	N.A.	N.A.
Subaru Loyale 4dr wgn	10,649	9,580	9,772	89	3,834	25/30	High	4,274	113	22,166
Subaru Loyale 4WD 4dr wgn	12,149	10,912	11,239	89	4,252	24/29	High	4,527	214	23,812

[1]Estimate [2]Dealer's average cost as a percentage of suggested retail price. [3]Compared with other models in its class. Actual costs will vary, depending on your location, the number and age of drivers and so forth. [4]Includes scheduled maintenance, as well as replacement of tires, brake pads, batteries and other parts. [5]Average five-year repair costs not covered by warranty. [6]Includes depreciation, financing, maintenance, repairs, state taxes and registration fees, insurance and fuel. Sources: IntelliChoice Inc., AutoAdviser Inc., Insurance Services Office and the manufacturers.

$10,000 to $15,000

Make and model	Suggested retail price	Est. dealer's cost	Your target price	Options cost (% of retail)[2]	Five-year resale value	Miles per gallon (city/ hwy.)	Cost to insure[3]	Five-year costs		
								Mainte-nance[4]	Repairs[5]	Total ownership expense[6]
Toyota Camry Deluxe 4dr	$14,368	$12,213	$12,579	80%	$7,328	22/29	Very low	$4,904	$97	$25,187
Toyota Celica ST 2dr	13,378	11,438	11,781	80	7,358	25/32	High	4,921	97	26,266
Toyota Corolla Deluxe 4dr	10,408	8,950	9,129	80	4,996	28/33	High	4,465	97	19,938
Toyota Corolla Deluxe 4dr wgn	11,078	9,526	9,717	80	5,207	28/33	High	4,465	97	20,669
Toyota Corolla Deluxe All-Trac 4dr wgn	12,688	10,910	11,237	80	6,471	22/27	High	4,465	141	22,226
Toyota Corolla LE 4dr	12,598	10,796	11,120	80	6,047	26/33	High	4,465	97	21,118
Volkswagen GTI 2dr hatch	11,110	9,983	10,183	86	5,555	25/32	Very high	4,939	136	22,629
Volkswagen GTI 16V 2dr hatch	13,910	12,281	12,649	86	6,677	21/28	Very high	5,225	136	25,739
Volkswagen Jetta Carat 4dr	12,930	10,943	11,271	86	8,017	25/32	Very high	5,154	136	23,012
Volkswagen Jetta GL 4dr	11,370	10,045	10,346	86	7,277	25/32	Very high	5,102	136	21,909

◆ $15,000 to $20,000

Make and model	Suggested retail price	Est. dealer's cost	Your target price	Options cost (% of retail)[2]	Five-year resale value	Miles per gallon (city/ hwy.)	Cost to insure[3]	Five-year costs		
								Mainte-nance[4]	Repairs[5]	Total ownership expense[6]
Acura Integra GS 4dr	17,144[1]	14,401	14,833	84	9,600	24/28	High	4,685	137	25,937
Buick Century Custom 4dr wgn	15,660	13,593	14,001	85	5,951	21/28	Very low	4,644	275	27,521
Buick Century Limited 4dr	15,695	13,623	14,032	85	4,709	22/31	Very low	4,644	275	28,061
Buick Century Limited 4dr wgn	16,395	14,231	14,658	85	5,410	21/28	Very low	4,644	275	29,031
Buick LeSabre Custom 4dr	18,695	16,227	16,714	87	7,478	18/28	Very low	5,042	475	28,720
Buick Regal Custom 2dr	16,610	14,417	14,850	85	6,146	19/27	Low	5,127	161	28,291
Buick Regal Custom 4dr	16,865	14,639	15,078	85	6,409	19/27	Low	5,127	161	28,390
Buick Regal Gran Sport 2dr	18,600	16,145	16,629	N.A.	N.A.	18/28	Low	N.A.	N.A.	N.A.
Buick Regal Gran Sport 4dr	19,300	16,752	17,255	N.A.	N.A.	18/28	Low	N.A.	N.A.	N.A.
Buick Regal Limited 2dr	17,790	15,442	15,905	85	6,582	19/27	Low	5,155	161	29,030
Buick Regal Limited 4dr	18,110	15,719	16,191	85	6,701	19/27	Low	5,127	161	29,503
Buick Skylark Gran Sport 2dr	15,555	14,000	14,419	90	4,511	19/29	Low	4,502	197	27,135
Chevrolet Beretta GTZ 2dr	15,590	14,000	14,420	85	5,301	19/28	High	4,690	198	N.A.
Chevrolet Camaro RS convert.	18,055	16,213	16,699	85	8,666	17/27	Very high	3,940	137	35,891
Chevrolet Camaro Z28 2dr	16,055	14,417	14,850	85	6,904	17/26	Very high	4,255	216	33,824
Chevrolet Caprice 4dr	17,300	15,016	15,466	85	6,055	18/26	Very low	3,976	164	27,020
Chevrolet Caprice 4dr wgn	18,700	16,232	16,719	85	6,545	17/25	Very low	4,016	164	29,188
Chevrolet Caprice Classic 4dr	19,300	16,752	17,255	87	7,913	18/26	Very low	3,969	164	27,538
Chevrolet Lumina Euro 2dr	15,600	13,541	13,947	85	6,708	19/27	Low	4,885	N.A.	N.A.
Chevrolet Lumina Euro 4dr	15,800	13,714	14,125	85	6,794	17/26	Low	4,899	N.A.	N.A.
Chevrolet Lumina Z34 2dr	18,400	15,971	16,450	85	N.A.	17/27	Low	5,010	N.A.	N.A.
Chrysler LeBaron GT convert.	18,985	16,757	17,260	88	6,265	18/27	Average	3,821	265	31,582
Chrysler LeBaron GT 2dr	16,164	14,303	14,732	85	4,526	20/28	Low	3,821	265	30,061
Chrysler LeBaron Landau 4dr	15,510	13,714	14,125	N.A.	N.A.	20/27	Low	N.A.	N.A.	N.A.
Chrysler LeBaron LX 2dr	16,094	14,242	14,669	85	4,989	20/27	Low	3,914	236	28,902
Chrysler LeBaron LX 4dr	15,087	13,346	13,746	N.A.	N.A.	20/27	Low	N.A.	N.A.	N.A.
Chrysler New Yorker Salon 4dr	18,649	16,112	16,595	85	6,714	19/25	Very low	4,071	232	27,571
Dodge Dynasty LE 4dr	15,967	13,792	14,206	85	6,706	20/27	Very low	3,675	232	25,351
Dodge Monaco ES 4dr	17,203	14,873	15,319	85	N.A.	18/26	Very low	4,234	N.A.	N.A.
Dodge Spirit R/T 4dr	18,674	16,603	17,101	85	N.A.	19/26	Very low	4,321	250	N.A.
Dodge Stealth 2dr	17,155	15,436	17,155	83	N.A.	18/24	High	N.A.	N.A.	N.A.
Dodge Stealth ES 2dr	19,028	17,085	19,028	83	N.A.	19/24	High	N.A.	N.A.	N.A.
Eagle Premier ES 4dr	18,057	15,598	16,065	85	6,320	18/26	Low	4,621	N.A.	N.A.
Eagle Premier LX 4dr	15,716	13,609	14,017	85	5,658	18/26	Low	4,556	N.A.	N.A.
Ford Crown Victoria 4dr	18,728	16,154	16,639	86	6,555	18/25	Very low	3,863	164	29,254
Ford Crown Victoria LX 4dr	19,543	16,846	17,351	86	6,058	18/25	Very low	3,863	164	30,777
Ford Mustang GT 2dr hatch	15,717	14,159	14,584	85	7,230	17/24	Very high	5,063	168	31,893
Ford Mustang LX convert.	16,788	15,112	15,565	85	7,890	22/30	Very high	4,015	111	30,744
Ford Mustang LX 5.0L Sport convert.	19,921	17,900	18,437	85	8,765	17/24	Very high	5,057	111	37,230
Ford Taurus GL 4dr	15,213	13,106	13,499	85	5,781	20/29	Very low	4,617	345	26,842
Ford Taurus GL 4dr wgn	16,101	13,861	14,277	85	7,245	20/29	Very low	4,386	345	25,558

[1]Estimate [2]Dealer's average cost as a percentage of suggested retail price. [3]Compared with other models in its class. Actual costs will vary, depending on your location, the number and age of drivers and so forth. [4]Includes scheduled maintenance, as well as replacement of tires, brake pads, batteries and other parts. [5]Average five-year repair costs not covered by warranty. [6]Includes depreciation, financing, maintenance, repairs, state taxes and registration fees, insurance and fuel. Sources: IntelliChoice Inc., AutoAdviser Inc., Insurance Services Office and the manufacturers.

$15,000 to $20,000

Make and model	Suggested retail price	Est. dealer's cost	Your target price	Options cost (% of retail)[2]	Five-year resale value	Miles per gallon (city/ hwy.)	Cost to insure[3]	Five-year costs		
								Mainte-nance[4]	Repairs[5]	Total ownership expense[6]
Ford Taurus L 4dr wgn	$15,824	$13,626	$14,035	85%	$6,646	20/29	Very low	$4,386	$345	$25,908
Ford Taurus LX 4dr	17,434	14,994	15,444	85	6,102	20/29	Very low	4,386	345	28,301
Ford Taurus LX 4dr wgn	19,024	16,346	16,836	85	7,990	18/28	Very low	4,365	345	28,585
Ford Thunderbird 2dr	16,268	14,033	14,454	85	6,833	20/27	Low	4,716	159	28,560
Ford Thunderbird LX 2dr	18,702	16,102	16,585	85	7,107	20/27	Low	4,716	159	31,373
Ford Thunderbird Sport Coupe 2dr	18,470	15,904	16,381	N.A.	N.A.	17/24	Low	N.A.	N.A.	N.A.
Geo Prizm LSi 4dr	16,398	14,842	15,287	85	6,231	28/33	High	4,366	70	23,467
Honda Accord EX 2dr	18,045	15,158	15,613	84	9,744	24/30	Average	4,979	85	26,320
Honda Accord EX 4dr	18,245	15,325	15,785	84	9,487	24/30	Low	4,979	85	25,881
Honda Accord EX 4dr wgn	19,900	16,716	17,217	84	N.A.	22/27	Low	4,895	85	N.A.
Honda Accord LX 2dr	15,625	13,125	13,518	84	8,906	24/30	Average	4,673	85	24,191
Honda Accord LX 4dr	15,826	13,293	13,692	84	8,071	24/30	Low	4,673	85	24,431
Honda Accord LX 4dr wgn	17,450	14,658	15,098	84	N.A.	22/27	Low	4,895	85	N.A.
Honda Prelude Si 2dr	19,250	16,170	16,655	84	12,512	22/26	High	4,850	85	27,994
Infiniti G20 4dr	18,300	14,640	15,079	80	N.A.	24/32	High	N.A.	N.A.	N.A.
Mazda MX-6 GT 2dr	16,905	14,454	14,888	80	6,762	21/28	Very high	4,663	85	30,616
Mercury Cougar LS 2dr	16,385	14,123	14,547	85	6,718	20/27	Low	4,857	208	29,434
Mercury Grand Marquis LS 4dr	19,789	17,061	17,573	85	7,916	18/25	Very low	3,904	194	29,415
Mercury Sable GS 4dr	16,351	14,089	14,512	85	6,213	20/29	Very low	4,212	245	26,038
Mercury Sable GS 4dr wgn	17,329	14,920	15,368	85	7,625	20/29	Very low	4,212	245	25,989
Mercury Sable LS 4dr	17,301	14,896	15,343	85	6,401	20/29	Very low	4,212	245	27,046
Mercury Sable LS 4dr wgn	18,328	15,769	16,242	85	8,248	20/29	Very low	4,212	245	26,439
Mitsubishi Diamante 4dr	19,939	16,749	17,251	80	N.A.	18/25	N.A.	N.A.	N.A.	N.A.
Mitsubishi Eclipse GS Turbo 2dr	17,109	14,886	15,333	82	N.A.	21/28	High	5,374	234	N.A.
Mitsubishi Eclipse GSX Turbo 4WD	18,849	16,402	16,894	82	N.A.	20/25	High	5,374	N.A.	N.A.
Mitsubishi Expo SP AWD 4dr wgn	15,839	13,626	14,035	N.A.	N.A.	19/24	N.A.	N.A.	N.A.	N.A.
Mitsubishi Galant GS 4dr	15,179	12,902	13,289	80	5,932	20/26	Average	5,394	515	27,478
Mitsubishi Galant GSX 4dr 4WD	17,729	15,070	15,522	80	7,044	19/25	Average	5,411	N.A.	N.A.
Nissan 240SX LE 2dr fast	18,725	16,617	17,116	85	7,865	22/27	Very high	5,033	89	33,742
Nissan 240SX SE 2dr	16,690	14,810	15,254	85	7,177	22/27	Very high	5,033	89	31,902
Nissan 240SX SE 2dr fast	16,885	14,984	15,434	85	7,261	22/27	Very high	5,033	89	32,076
Nissan Maxima GXE 4dr	19,695	17,135	17,649	87	8,863	21/26	Low	4,890	251	30,500
Nissan Stanza GXE 4dr	17,070	15,022	15,472	85	5,803	22/29	High	4,568	89	28,280
Oldsmobile Achieva SL 2dr	16,050[1]	14,445	14,878	85	5,135	22/29	N.A.	4,282	167	29,362
Oldsmobile Achieva SL 4dr	16,150[1]	14,535	14,971	85	5,168	22/29	N.A.	4,455	167	28,095
Oldsmobile Cutlass Ciera SL 4dr	16,895	14,665	15,105	85	6,082	19/26	Very low	4,323	223	26,884
Oldsmobile Cutlass Cruiser SL 4dr wgn	17,395	15,099	15,552	85	5,566	19/26	Average	4,329	223	27,904
Oldsmobile Cutlass Supreme S 2dr	15,695	13,623	14,032	N.A.	N.A.	19/27	Low	N.A.	N.A.	N.A.
Oldsmobile Cutlass Supreme S 4dr	15,795	13,710	14,121	N.A.	N.A.	19/27	Low	N.A.	N.A.	N.A.
Oldsmobile Eighty-Eight Royale 4dr	18,495	16,054	16,536	87	7,213	18/28	Low	4,824	190	28,528
Pontiac Bonneville SE 4dr	18,599	16,144	16,628	87	5,394	18/28	Very low	5,037	150	33,484
Pontiac Firebird convert.	19,375	17,399	17,921	85	N.A.	17/27	Very high	N.A.	N.A.	N.A.
Pontiac Firebird Formula 2dr	16,205	14,552	14,989	85	6,482	17/26	Very high	5,157	172	32,593
Pontiac Firebird Trans Am 2dr	18,105	16,258	16,746	85	7,242	17/26	Very high	4,045	193	35,506
Pontiac Grand Prix SE 2dr	15,390	13,359	13,760	85	5,694	19/27	Low	5,070	123	26,588
Pontiac Grand Prix SE 4dr	16,190	14,053	14,475	85	5,828	19/27	Low	5,068	123	27,454
Pontiac Sunbird SE convert.	15,345	13,780	14,193	85	N.A.	25/35	High	4,522	217	N.A.
Saab 900 2dr hatch	19,395	16,389	16,881	85	10,279	20/27	High	5,513	385	30,940
Saab 900 4dr	19,995	16,895	17,402	84	10,397	20/27	High	5,513	385	31,506
Subaru Legacy L 4WD 4dr	15,028	14,075	14,497	88	N.A.	21/26	Average	5,119	N.A.	N.A.
Subaru Legacy LS 4dr	18,428	16,505	17,000	87	N.A.	23/30	Average	5,061	N.A.	N.A.
Subaru Legacy LS 4dr wgn	18,928	16,484	16,979	87	N.A.	23/30	Average	5,061	N.A.	N.A.
Subaru Legacy LS 4WD 4dr	19,928	17,371	17,892	87	N.A.	21/26	Average	5,119	N.A.	N.A.
Subaru Legacy LSi 4dr	19,828	17,345	17,865	87	N.A.	23/30	Average	5,061	N.A.	N.A.
Subaru Legacy Sport 4WD 4dr	18,928	16,553	17,050	87	N.A.	19/25	Average	5,422	N.A.	N.A.

[1]Estimate [2]Dealer's average cost as a percentage of suggested retail price. [3]Compared with other models in its class. Actual costs will vary, depending on your location, the number and age of drivers and so forth. [4]Includes scheduled maintenance, as well as replacement of tires, brake pads, batteries and other parts. [5]Average five-year repair costs not covered by warranty. [6]Includes depreciation, financing, maintenance, repairs, state taxes and registration fees, insurance and fuel. Sources: IntelliChoice Inc., AutoAdviser Inc., Insurance Services Office and the manufacturers.

$15,000 to $20,000

Make and model	Suggested retail price	Est. dealer's cost	Your target price	Options cost (% of retail)[2]	Five-year resale value	Miles per gallon (city/hwy.)	Cost to insure[3]	Mainte-nance[4]	Repairs[5]	Total ownership expense[6]
Toyota Camry LE 4dr	$16,998	$14,448	$14,881	80%	$8,669	21/27	Very low	$5,220	$97	$26,613
Toyota Camry XLE 4dr	18,848	15,832	16,307	N.A.	N.A.	21/27	Very low	N.A.	N.A.	N.A.
Toyota Celica GT 2dr	15,708	13,352	13,753	80	7,854	22/29	High	4,931	97	28,951
Toyota Celica GT 2dr lift	15,838	13,462	13,866	80	8,394	22/29	High	4,931	97	28,863
Toyota Celica GT-S 2dr lift	17,328	14,642	15,081	80	8,144	22/29	High	5,617	97	31,737
Toyota MR2 2dr	16,048	13,561	13,968	80	N.A.	22/28	High	4,175	N.A.	N.A.
Volkswagen Cabriolet convert.	17,320	15,368	15,829	86	N.A.	25/32	Very high	4,676	136	N.A.
Volkswagen Cabriolet Carat convert.	18,950	16,811	17,315	86	N.A.	25/32	Very high	4,676	136	N.A.
Volkswagen Corrado 2dr	19,860	17,517	18,043	86	N.A.	20/28	Very high	5,574	N.A.	N.A.
Volkswagen Jetta GLI 16V 4dr	15,480	13,663	14,073	86	9,907	21/28	Very high	5,350	136	25,345
Volkswagen Passat GL 4dr	17,550	15,484	15,949	86	N.A.	21/30	Low	5,562	N.A.	N.A.
Volkswagen Passat GL 4dr wgn	17,970	15,853	16,329	86	N.A.	21/30	Low	5,550	N.A.	N.A.

◆ $20,000 to $30,000

Make and model	Suggested retail price	Est. dealer's cost	Your target price	Options cost (% of retail)[2]	Five-year resale value	Miles per gallon (city/hwy.)	Cost to insure[3]	Mainte-nance[4]	Repairs[5]	Total ownership expense[6]
Acura Legend 4dr	28,204[1]	23,127	24,283	82	15,794	18/26	Very low	5,696	115	33,640
Audi 80 Quattro 4dr 4WD	26,496[1]	22,787	23,926	84	9,008	18/24	High	5,348	356	39,327
BMW 318 i convert.	28,870	24,828	26,070	85	15,878	22/27	Average	4,290	N.A.	N.A.
BMW 325 i 4dr	27,990	22,895	24,040	82	15,115	18/26	Average	4,952	424	35,328
Buick LeSabre Limited 4dr	20,775	18,033	18,935	87	7,271	18/28	Very low	5,042	475	30,793
Buick Park Avenue 4dr	25,285	21,695	22,779	85	10,367	18/27	Very low	5,049	475	34,285
Buick Park Avenue Ultra 4dr	28,780	24,693	25,928	85	10,073	17/27	Very low	5,049	475	38,174
Buick Riviera 2dr	25,415	21,806	22,896	85	9,404	18/27	Very low	4,858	250	34,466
Buick Roadmaster 4dr	21,865	18,979	19,928	87	N.A.	16/25	Very low	N.A.	N.A.	N.A.
Buick Roadmaster Estate 4dr wgn	23,040	19,999	20,999	83	6,451	17/25	Very low	4,134	N.A.	N.A.
Chrysler Imperial 4dr	28,253	24,073	25,277	85	9,041	19/25	Very low	3,968	49	38,212
Chrysler New Yorker Fifth Avenue 4dr	21,874	18,933	19,880	85	7,000	19/25	Very low	3,991	152	32,431
Dodge Stealth R/T 2dr	25,500	22,780	23,919	85	N.A.	19/24	High	N.A.	N.A.	N.A.
Ford Mustang GT convert.	20,548	18,457	19,380	85	10,274	17/24	Very high	5,077	168	36,359
Ford Taurus SHO 4dr	23,772	20,381	21,400	85	8,320	18/26	Very low	4,315	N.A.	N.A.
Infiniti M30 2dr	25,000	20,000	23,750	80	N.A.	19/25	Low	N.A.	N.A.	N.A.
Lexus ES 300 4dr	25,250	20,705	25,250	80	N.A.	19/26	Average	N.A.	N.A.	N.A.
Mazda 929 4dr	27,800	23,352	24,520	84	11,398	19/24	Low	4,918	N.A.	N.A.
Mercedes-Benz 190E 2.3 4dr	28,950	23,160	24,318	80	19,686	20/28	Low	4,753	224	31,200
Mitsubishi Diamante LS 4dr	25,135	20,611	21,642	80	N.A.	18/24	N.A.	N.A.	N.A.	N.A.
Nissan Maxima SE 4dr	20,815	18,109	19,014	87	8,742	19/26	Low	4,800	251	32,679
Oldsmobile Custom Cruiser 4dr wgn	20,995	18,224	19,135	87	6,299	17/25	Very low	4,063	316	34,452
Oldsmobile Cutlass Supreme convert.	21,995	19,092	20,047	87	8,138	19/27	Average	5,288	N.A.	N.A.
Oldsmobile Cutlass Supreme Intl. 4dr	21,895	19,005	19,955	85	7,444	17/26	Low	5,397	N.A.	N.A.
Oldsmobile Eighty-Eight Royale LS 4dr	21,395	18,571	19,500	87	7,916	18/28	Very low	4,824	190	30,225
Oldsmobile Ninety-Eight Regency 4dr	26,195	22,737	23,874	85	9,430	18/27	Very low	4,900	448	34,739
Oldsmobile Ninety-Eight Touring 4dr	28,995	25,168	26,426	85	9,568	18/27	Very low	4,957	448	41,384
Oldsmobile Toronado 2dr	24,695	21,435	22,507	85	8,149	18/27	Very low	4,983	229	36,523
Pontiac Bonneville SSE 4dr	23,999	20,831	21,873	87	9,600	18/28	Very low	4,982	150	35,740
Pontiac Firebird Trans Am GTA 2dr	25,880	23,240	24,402	90	8,799	17/25	Very high	5,368	193	44,993
Pontiac Grand Prix STE 4dr	21,635	18,779	19,718	85	6,491	19/27	Low	4,840	123	33,438
Saab 900 S 2dr hatch	23,395	19,768	20,756	84	10,060	20/27	High	5,577	385	36,014
Saab 900 S 4dr	23,995	20,275	21,289	84	10,078	20/27	High	5,577	385	36,473
Saab 9000 S 4dr hatch	28,095	23,235	24,397	83	9,833	20/26	Low	6,283	317	40,283
Subaru Legacy LS 4WD 4dr wgn	20,428	17,807	18,697	87	N.A.	21/26	Average	5,119	N.A.	N.A.
Subaru Legacy LSi 4WD 4dr	21,328	18,682	19,616	87	N.A.	21/26	Average	5,061	N.A.	N.A.
Toyota Celica All-Trac Turbo 2dr lift	22,048	18,631	19,563	80	10,363	19/24	High	5,389	149	37,598
Toyota Celica GT convert.	20,468	17,398	18,268	80	10,643	22/28	High	4,763	97	32,617
Toyota Cressida 4dr	23,488	19,260	20,223	80	10,335	19/24	Low	4,683	224	31,906

[1]Estimate [2]Dealer's average cost as a percentage of suggested retail price. [3]Compared with other models in its class. Actual costs will vary, depending on your location, the number and age of drivers and so forth. [4]Includes scheduled maintenance, as well as replacement of tires, brake pads, batteries and other parts. [5]Average five-year repair costs not covered by warranty. [6]Includes depreciation, financing, maintenance, repairs, state taxes and registration fees, insurance and fuel. Sources: IntelliChoice Inc., AutoAdviser Inc., Insurance Services Office and the manufacturers.

$20,000 to $30,000

Make and model	Suggested retail price	Est. dealer's cost	Your target price	Options cost (% of retail)[2]	Five-year resale value	Miles per gallon (city/hwy.)	Cost to insure[3]	Five-year costs Mainte-nance[4]	Repairs[5]	Total ownership expense[6]
Toyota Supra 2dr	$25,280	$20,730	$21,767	80%	$10,618	18/23	High	$5,773	$224	$41,181
Toyota Supra Turbo 2dr	28,750	23,575	24,754	80	12,075	18/23	High	6,054	238	45,032
Volvo 240 4dr	20,800	18,720	19,656	82	11,232	21/28	Very low	4,637	194	27,298
Volvo 240 4dr wgn	21,320	19,188	20,147	90	12,152	22/28	Very low	4,554	194	27,321
Volvo 740 4dr	24,285	21,371	22,439	88	10,685	20/28	Very low	5,079	194	32,130
Volvo 740 4dr wgn	24,965	21,969	23,067	88	10,734	20/28	Very low	5,079	194	32,827

◆ Over $30,000

Make and model	Suggested retail price	Est. dealer's cost	Your target price	Options cost (% of retail)[2]	Five-year resale value	Miles per gallon (city/hwy.)	Cost to insure[3]	Five-year costs Mainte-nance[4]	Repairs[5]	Total ownership expense[6]
Acura Legend LS 4dr	35,242[1]	28,898	30,632	82	19,388	18/26	Very low	5,696	115	38,410
Acura NSX 2dr	64,170[1]	52,619	55,776	82	N.A.	19/24	High	N.A.	N.A.	N.A.
Alfa Romeo 164 S 4dr	33,176[1]	27,204	28,836	82	N.A.	17/25	Average	N.A.	N.A.	N.A.
Audi 100 CS 4dr	32,900	27,307	28,945	N.A.	N.A.	17/25	Low	N.A.	N.A.	N.A.
Audi V8 Quattro 4dr 4WD	52,300	43,654	46,273	83	N.A.	14/20	Low	6,957	N.A.	N.A.
BMW 325 i convert.	36,320	30,146	31,954	82	20,702	18/26	High	4,918	424	34,897
BMW 525 i 4dr	35,600	29,192	30,944	82	17,101	17/25	Low	4,863	424	42,693
BMW 535 i 4dr	44,350	36,367	38,549	82	21,021	16/22	Low	5,658	424	51,737
BMW 735 i 4dr	52,990	43,452	46,059	82	23,690	15/21	Low	5,927	424	61,022
BMW 750 iL 4dr	77,584[1]	62,067	73,704	80	35,689	12/18	Low	7,417	N.A.	N.A.
BMW 850 i 2dr	80,808[1]	64,646	76,767	80	N.A.	12/19	Average	7,607	N.A.	N.A.
BMW M5 4dr	59,904[1]	49,121	56,908	82	N.A.	12/23	N.A.	6,695	N.A.	N.A.
Cadillac Allante convert.	58,470	50,352	53,373	86	18,126	15/22	High	6,460	N.A.	N.A.
Cadillac Brougham 4dr	31,740	27,233	28,867	84	11,426	17/25	Very low	4,423	142	41,613
Cadillac Coupe DeVille 2dr	31,740	27,233	28,867	84	12,696	16/25	Low	5,072	210	41,708
Cadillac Eldorado 2dr	32,470	27,839	29,509	84	12,014	15/25	Very low	5,128	233	44,051
Cadillac Fleetwood 2dr	36,360	31,197	33,069	84	13,090	16/25	Low	5,072	142	48,030
Cadillac Fleetwood 4dr	36,360	31,197	33,069	84	13,817	16/25	Very low	5,072	142	45,901
Cadillac Sedan DeVille 4dr	31,740	27,233	28,867	84	13,966	16/25	Very low	5,072	210	40,054
Cadillac Seville 4dr	34,975	30,009	31,810	84	13,291	15/25	Very low	5,128	249	45,431
Chevrolet Corvette convert.	40,145	34,043	36,086	85	18,467	17/25	High	7,147	206	57,388
Chevrolet Corvette 2dr	33,635	28,522	30,233	85	15,808	17/25	High	7,147	206	49,979
Dodge Stealth R/T Turbo 2dr 4WD	30,885	27,519	29,170	85	N.A.	18/24	High	N.A.	N.A.	N.A.
Infiniti Q45 4dr	42,000	33,169	35,159	79	N.A.	16/22	Very low	N.A.	N.A.	N.A.
Jaguar XJS convert.	67,500	55,350	58,671	82	31,800	13/18	High	6,423	1,347	77,767
Jaguar XJ6 4dr	44,500	37,380	39,623	84	23,650	17/22	Low	6,322	1,347	46,845
Lexus LS 400 4dr	42,200	33,760	42,200	80	N.A.	18/23	Low	N.A.	N.A.	N.A.
Lexus SC 300 2dr	31,100	25,502	31,100	N.A.	N.A.	18/22	N.A.	N.A.	N.A.	N.A.
Lincoln Continental Signature 4dr	34,337	29,188	30,939	84	12,705	17/25	Very low	6,207	282	43,813
Lincoln Mark VII LSC 2dr	31,699	26,972	28,590	84	11,412	17/24	Low	4,265	211	42,747
Lincoln Town Car Signature 4dr	34,588	29,414	31,179	84	12,452	17/23	Very low	4,175	135	44,301
Maserati Spyder convert.	51,500[1]	N.A.	N.A.	N.A.	N.A.	16/22	High	8,320	N.A.	N.A.
Mercedes-Benz 190E 2.6 4dr	34,000	27,200	28,832	80	22,780	19/27	Low	4,862	224	35,201
Mercedes-Benz 300 CE 2dr	60,400	48,320	51,219	80	35,032	17/23	High	5,608	224	58,708
Mercedes-Benz 300 D 2.5 4dr	42,950	34,360	36,422	80	23,623	26/31	Very low	4,888	N.A.	N.A.
Mercedes-Benz 300 E 4dr	49,500	39,600	41,976	80	30,195	18/23	Very low	5,099	224	46,703
Mercedes-Benz 300 E 4Matic 4dr 4WD	57,100	45,680	48,421	80	32,547	17/20	Very low	5,099	224	54,436
Mercedes-Benz 300 SD Turbo 4dr	69,400	55,900	59,254	80	N.A.	22/25	Low	N.A.	N.A.	N.A.
Mercedes-Benz 300 SE 4dr	69,400	55,900	59,254	80	40,946	16/20	Low	4,988	224	53,512
Mercedes-Benz 300 SL convert.	82,500	66,000	69,960	80	N.A.	16/23	Average	6,684	N.A.	N.A.
Mercedes-Benz 300 TE 4dr wgn	53,900	43,120	45,707	80	31,262	17/21	Very low	5,053	224	51,662
Mercedes-Benz 300 TE 4Matic 4dr wgn	53,900	48,880	51,813	80	30,184	16/20	Very low	5,053	224	57,983
Mercedes-Benz 400 E 4dr	55,800	44,640	47,318	N.A.	N.A.	N.A.	Very low	N.A.	N.A.	N.A.
Mercedes-Benz 500 E 4dr	79,200	63,360	75,240	N.A.	N.A.	N.A.	Very low	N.A.	N.A.	N.A.
Mercedes-Benz 500 SL convert.	97,500	78,000	92,625	80	N.A.	14/18	Average	6,824	N.A.	N.A.

[1]Estimate [2]Dealer's average cost as a percentage of suggested retail price. [3]Compared with other models in its class. Actual costs will vary, depending on your location, the number and age of drivers and so forth. [4]Includes scheduled maintenance, as well as replacement of tires, brake pads, batteries and other parts. [5]Average five-year repair costs not covered by warranty. [6]Includes depreciation, financing, maintenance, repairs, state taxes and registration fees, insurance and fuel. Sources: IntelliChoice Inc., AutoAdviser Inc., Insurance Services Office and the manufacturers.

Over $30,000

Make and model	Suggested retail price	Est. dealer's cost	Your target price	Options cost (% of retail)[2]	Five-year resale value	Miles per gallon (city/hwy.)	Cost to insure[3]	Five-year costs Mainte-nance[4]	Repairs[5]	Total ownership expense[6]
Mercedes-Benz 600 SEL 4dr	$127,800	$102,790	$121,410	N.A.	N.A.	N.A.	Low	N.A.	N.A.	N.A.
Mitsubishi 3000GT VR-4 2dr 4WD	32,800	26,848	28,459	82%	N.A.	18/24	High	N.A.	N.A.	N.A.
Nissan 300ZX Turbo 2dr	35,780[1]	31,129	32,997	87	$11,450	18/24	High	$6,316	$158	$59,484
Porsche 911 Carrera 2 2dr	63,900	53,676	56,897	84	41,483	17/25	High	8,849	231	65,898
Porsche 911 Carrera 4 Targa convert.	77,380	64,999	68,899	84	N.A.	15/23	High	8,849	N.A.	N.A.
Porsche 911 Turbo 2dr	98,875	83,056	88,038	84	N.A.	13/21	High	9,732	244	N.A.
Porsche S4/928 GT 2dr	77,500	64,095	67,941	83	37,200	13/19	Average	7,706	621	94,534
Saab 9000 CD 4dr	30,195	24,972	26,470	83	10,266	17/25	Low	6,304	317	42,530
Saab 9000 CD Turbo 4dr	36,695	30,346	32,167	83	13,577	17/24	Low	7,626	539	48,293
Volvo 960 4dr	33,975	29,558	31,332	87	11,146	20/28	Very low	5,686	207	46,844
Volvo 940 Turbo 4dr wgn	31,475	27,383	28,752	87	10,733	19/22	Very low	6,011	207	43,358

◆ Small Pickups

Make and model	Suggested retail price	Est. dealer's cost	Your target price	Options cost (% of retail)[2]	Five-year resale value	Miles per gallon (city/hwy.)	Cost to insure[3]	Five-year costs Mainte-nance[4]	Repairs[5]	Total ownership expense[6]
Chevrolet C1500 ext. cab	14,045	12,191	12,557	85	10,253	17/23	Low	4,028	195	23,795
Chevrolet C1500 reg. cab	13,095	11,366	11,707	85	9,036	17/23	Low	3,944	195	23,007
Chevrolet C1500 Work Truck reg. cab	10,600	9,519	9,709	85	N.A.	17/23	Low	3,652	N.A.	N.A.
Chevrolet K1500 ext. cab 4WD	16,298	14,144	14,568	85	11,898	16/20	Low	4,607	309	26,423
Chevrolet K1500 reg. cab 4WD	15,345	13,319	13,719	85	10,742	16/20	Low	4,570	309	26,104
Chevrolet K1500 Work Truck reg. cab	13,615	12,226	12,593	85	N.A.	16/20	Low	4,275	N.A.	N.A.
Chevrolet S-10 reg. cab	9,858	8,852	9,029	85	5,126	23/27	High	3,836	181	20,700
Chevrolet S-10 4WD reg. cab	13,424	12,055	12,417	85	6,712	16/20	High	3,993	239	25,177
Chevrolet S-10 Maxi-Cab ext. cab	11,358	10,199	10,505	85	N.A.	23/27	High	4,274	181	N.A.
Dodge Dakota reg. cab	10,705	9,600	9,792	85	5,031	21/26	Low	3,690	150	22,346
Dodge Dakota 4WD reg. cab	14,194	12,670	13,050	85	6,813	15/20	Low	4,125	N.A.	N.A.
Dodge Dakota S reg. cab	8,995	8,455	8,624	85	4,587	21/26	Low	3,653	150	19,005
Dodge Dakota Sport reg. cab	9,464	8,698	8,872	85	4,353	21/26	Low	3,509	150	24,317
Dodge Power Ram 50 reg. cab 4WD	11,130	10,235	10,542	N.A.	4,563	19/22	High	3,994	91	21,821
Dodge Ram 50 SE reg. cab	9,298	8,657	8,830	86	4,184	19/24	High	3,965	91	21,097
Dodge Ram D150 reg. cab	13,083	11,341	11,681	85	7,588	15/19	Average	3,932	146	27,104
Dodge Ram D150 Club Cab ext. cab	15,165	13,110	13,503	85	9,251	13/17	Average	4,155	146	28,524
Dodge Ram W150 reg. cab 4WD	15,549	13,437	13,840	85	9,174	13/17	High	4,155	171	30,303
Ford F150 reg. cab	12,868	11,123	11,457	85	9,008	15/19	Low	3,848	196	22,779
Ford F150 4WD reg. cab	14,954	12,896	13,283	85	10,169	15/18	Low	4,176	313	26,013
Ford F150 Supercab ext. cab	14,137	12,201	12,567	85	10,037	15/19	Low	4,050	196	24,263
Ford Ranger reg. cab	10,147	9,064	9,245	85	5,175	23/28	High	3,824	126	19,770
Ford Ranger 4WD reg. cab	13,351	11,884	12,241	85	6,408	21/26	High	4,017	220	25,144
Ford Ranger Sport reg. cab	8,930	8,351	8,518	85	5,715	23/28	High	3,824	126	18,146
Ford Ranger Supercab ext. cab	11,568	10,315	10,624	85	5,437	23/28	High	3,871	126	23,252
GMC C1500 ext. cab	14,283	12,398	12,770	85	10,284	17/23	Average	4,202	195	24,221
GMC C1500 reg. cab	13,333	11,573	11,920	85	9,200	17/23	Average	4,138	195	23,244
GMC K1500 ext. cab 4WD	16,536	14,354	14,785	85	N.A.	15/19	Average	4,495	195	N.A.
GMC K1500 reg. cab 4WD	15,583	13,526	13,932	85	N.A.	15/19	Average	4,776	195	N.A.
GMC Sonoma reg. cab	8,790	7,911	8,069	85	4,747	23/27	High	4,369	181	20,729
GMC Sonoma 4WD reg. cab	12,362	11,126	11,460	85	6,181	16/20	High	4,246	239	25,106
Isuzu Pickup S reg. cab	8,349	7,715	7,870	85	3,924	22/24	High	3,499	79	20,777
Isuzu Spacecab LS ext. cab	13,119	11,312	11,652	85	5,379	22/24	N.A.	3,387	79	23,117
Jeep Comanche reg. cab	9,329	8,871	9,048	85	4,478	21/23	Average	3,920	140	20,797
Jeep Comanche 4WD reg. cab	12,346	11,059	11,391	85	6,420	20/22	Average	3,964	296	22,380
Mazda B2200 reg. cab	8,495	7,646	7,799	81	5,352	21/26	High	3,670	68	18,677
Mazda B2200 Cab Plus ext. cab	9,995	8,896	9,074	81	5,397	21/26	High	3,736	68	20,428
Mazda B2600i reg. cab	9,120	8,117	8,279	81	5,381	19/23	High	3,749	68	19,732
Mazda B2600i 4WD reg. cab	11,495	10,346	10,656	81	6,092	18/20	High	3,866	119	22,060
Mitsubishi Mighty Max reg. cab	8,079	7,271	7,417	80	3,467	19/24	High	3,702	125	21,095

[1]Estimate [2]Dealer's average cost as a percentage of suggested retail price. [3]Compared with other models in its class. Actual costs will vary, depending on your location, the number and age of drivers and so forth. [4]Includes scheduled maintenance, as well as replacement of tires, brake pads, batteries and other parts. [5]Average five-year repair costs not covered by warranty. [6]Includes depreciation, financing, maintenance, repairs, state taxes and registration fees, insurance and fuel. Sources: IntelliChoice Inc., AutoAdviser Inc., Insurance Services Office and the manufacturers.

Small Pickups

Make and model	Suggested retail price	Est. dealer's cost	Your target price	Options cost (% of retail)[2]	Five-year resale value	Miles per gallon (city/hwy.)	Cost to insure[3]	Five-year costs		Total ownership expense[6]
								Mainte-nance[4]	Repairs[5]	
Mitsubishi Mighty Max 4WD reg. cab	$12,289	$10,814	$11,138	80%	$5,391	19/22	High	$4,097	$184	$24,158
Nissan Pickup reg. cab	8,844[1]	8,313	8,479	85	5,306	23/27	High	4,211	75	20,224
Nissan Pickup 4WD reg. cab	11,882[1]	10,931	12,238	85	7,129	19/22	High	4,446	124	24,276
Toyota Pickup reg. cab	8,998	8,098	8,260	90	5,129	22/26	High	3,856	75	19,135
Toyota Pickup Deluxe reg. cab	9,868	8,733	8,908	82	5,427	22/26	High	3,856	75	20,043
Toyota Pickup Deluxe 4WD reg. cab	12,818	11,216	11,552	82	7,050	19/22	High	4,149	115	25,328

◆ Utility Vehicles

Make and model	Suggested retail price	Est. dealer's cost	Your target price	Options cost (% of retail)[2]	Five-year resale value	Miles per gallon (city/hwy.)	Cost to insure[3]	Mainte-nance[4]	Repairs[5]	Total ownership expense[6]
Chevrolet S-10 Blazer 4WD 2dr wgn	16,583	14,892	15,339	85	8,955	16/20	High	4,060	289	27,012
Chevrolet S-10 Blazer 4WD 4dr wgn	17,953	16,122	16,606	85	10,054	16/20	High	4,060	289	28,044
Daihatsu Rocky SE convert. 4WD	11,692[1]	10,523	10,839	85	N.A.	23/23	Low	4,710	N.A.	N.A.
Dodge Ramcharger AD150 2dr wgn	18,764	16,199	16,685	85	9,570	13/16	Low	4,125	144	30,042
Dodge Ramcharger AW150 2dr wgn	19,595	16,906	17,413	85	10,581	11/14	Low	3,946	176	31,117
Ford Bronco Custom 2dr wgn 4WD	18,843	16,266	16,754	85	12,248	14/17	Very low	4,156	169	26,300
Ford Bronco Eddie Bauer 2dr wgn 4WD	23,191	19,963	20,961	86	14,842	14/17	Very low	4,707	N.A.	N.A.
Ford Explorer Eddie Bauer 2dr wgn	21,918	19,528	20,504	85	N.A.	17/21	Very low	3,919	N.A.	N.A.
Ford Explorer Eddie Bauer 4dr wgn	23,449	20,875	21,918	85	N.A.	17/21	Very low	3,919	N.A.	N.A.
Ford Explorer Sport 2dr wgn	16,991	15,192	15,648	85	N.A.	17/22	Low	3,836	N.A.	N.A.
Ford Explorer XL 4dr wgn	16,565	14,817	15,262	85	N.A.	17/22	Low	3,836	N.A.	N.A.
Ford Explorer XL 4WD 2dr wgn	17,399	15,551	16,018	85	N.A.	17/22	Low	3,836	N.A.	N.A.
Ford Explorer XLT 4WD 4dr wgn	20,504	18,283	19,197	85	N.A.	17/22	Low	3,836	N.A.	N.A.
Geo Tracker convert.	9,995	9,495	9,685	88	N.A.	25/27	High	4,927	105	N.A.
Geo Tracker 4WD convert.	11,800	11,210	11,546	88	5,074	25/27	High	4,917	105	22,898
Geo Tracker 4WD 2dr wgn	12,200	11,468	11,812	88	5,246	25/27	High	4,917	105	23,200
Geo Tracker LSi 4WD 2dr wgn	13,500	12,690	13,071	88	5,805	25/27	High	4,917	105	23,931
GMC Jimmy 2dr wgn	15,022	13,520	13,925	85	8,112	16/20	High	4,694	330	29,144
GMC Jimmy 2dr wgn 4WD	16,803	15,123	15,576	85	9,073	17/22	High	3,472	183	24,430
GMC Jimmy 4dr wgn 4WD	18,173	16,356	16,846	85	10,176	16/20	High	3,992	289	28,045
Isuzu Amigo S convert.	11,099	10,024	10,325	85	N.A.	19/21	High	3,481	N.A.	N.A.
Isuzu Amigo XS 4WD convert.	15,349	13,541	13,947	85	N.A.	16/20	High	3,901	N.A.	N.A.
Isuzu Rodeo LS 4WD 4dr wgn	17,849	15,917	16,394	85	N.A.	15/19	N.A.	N.A.	N.A.	N.A.
Isuzu Rodeo S 4dr wgn	13,859	12,473	12,847	85	N.A.	18/22	N.A.	N.A.	N.A.	N.A.
Isuzu Rodeo XS 4WD 4dr wgn	17,529	15,633	16,102	85	N.A.	15/19	N.A.	N.A.	N.A.	N.A.
Isuzu Trooper LS 4dr wgn 4WD	18,339[1]	16,138	16,622	85	11,370	15/17	N.A.	4,028	175	24,915
Isuzu Trooper S 4dr wgn 4WD	14,489[1]	12,750	13,133	85	9,997	15/17	N.A.	4,058	175	22,127
Jeep Cherokee 2dr wgn	14,346	12,919	13,307	85	9,755	19/24	Low	3,890	N.A.	N.A.
Jeep Cherokee 4WD 2dr wgn	15,832	14,227	14,654	85	10,449	19/23	Low	4,009	351	23,614
Jeep Cherokee Briarwood 4dr wgn	24,799	22,118	23,224	85	14,631	15/19	Low	4,042	351	30,524
Jeep Cherokee Laredo 4dr wgn	15,357	13,809	14,223	85	8,907	18/22	Low	3,811	N.A.	N.A.
Jeep Cherokee Laredo 4WD 2dr wgn	15,832	14,227	14,654	85	9,499	17/21	Low	3,767	351	27,400
Jeep Cherokee Limited 4WD 4dr wgn	25,334	22,589	23,718	85	14,947	15/19	Low	4,191	351	32,209
Jeep Cherokee Sport 2dr wgn	14,346	12,919	13,307	85	N.A.	18/22	Low	N.A.	N.A.	N.A.
Jeep Cherokee Sport 4WD 2dr wgn	15,832	14,227	14,654	85	9,183	17/21	Low	3,857	351	24,659
Jeep Cherokee Sport 4WD 4dr wgn	16,842	15,116	15,569	85	10,105	17/21	Low	3,857	351	25,448
Jeep Wrangler convert. 4WD	12,839	11,523	11,869	85	8,089	18/20	High	3,992	134	22,779
Mazda Navajo DX 2dr wgn	15,795	13,584	13,992	86	N.A.	17/22	Low	N.A.	N.A.	N.A.
Mitsubishi Montero LS 4dr wgn 4WD	19,767[1]	16,407	16,899	79	N.A.	15/18	Average	4,127	190	N.A.
Nissan Pathfinder SE-V6 4WD 4dr wgn	21,980	19,393	20,362	89	14,946	15/18	Average	4,362	124	28,378
Nissan Pathfinder XE-V6 4dr wgn	17,265	15,233	15,690	85	12,258	15/19	Average	4,299	75	25,724
Oldsmobile Bravada 4dr wgn 4WD	24,595	22,086	23,190	90	N.A.	16/21	Average	4,578	N.A.	N.A.
Range Rover County 4dr wgn 4WD	48,956[1]	41,123	43,590	84	N.A.	13/16	High	N.A.	N.A.	N.A.
Suzuki Samurai JA convert.	6,299	6,110	6,232	97	2,079	28/29	High	3,996	105	18,622
Suzuki Samurai JL convert. 4WD	8,199	7,379	7,527	90	N.A.	28/29	High	3,977	105	N.A.

[1]Estimate [2]Dealer's average cost as a percentage of suggested retail price. [3]Compared with other models in its class. Actual costs will vary, depending on your location, the number and age of drivers and so forth. [4]Includes scheduled maintenance, as well as replacement of tires, brake pads, batteries and other parts. [5]Average five-year repair costs not covered by warranty. [6]Includes depreciation, financing, maintenance, repairs, state taxes and registration fees, insurance and fuel. Sources: IntelliChoice Inc., AutoAdviser Inc., Insurance Services Office and the manufacturers.

Utility Vehicles

Make and model	Suggested retail price	Est. dealer's cost	Your target price	Options cost (% of retail)[2]	Five-year resale value	Miles per gallon (city/hwy.)	Cost to insure[3]	Five-year costs		Total ownership expense[6]
								Maintenance[4]	Repairs[5]	
Suzuki Sidekick JLX 4dr wgn 4WD	$13,699	$11,918	$12,276	87%	N.A.	24/27	High	$4,377	N.A.	N.A.
Suzuki Sidekick JX convert. 4WD	11,999	10,799	11,123	90	N.A.	25/27	High	4,377	N.A.	N.A.
Suzuki Sidekick JX 4dr wgn 4WD	13,349	10,874	11,200	87	N.A.	24/27	High	4,377	N.A.	N.A.
Toyota 4Runner SR5 V6 4dr wgn	19,198	16,222	16,709	80	$14,399	17/21	High	4,162	$75	$24,509
Toyota 4Runner SR5 V6 4WD 2dr wgn	20,428	17,670	18,553	80	14,300	15/18	High	3,708	141	26,925
Toyota 4Runner SR5 V6 4WD 4dr wgn	19,928	16,839	17,344	80	15,145	15/18	High	3,765	141	25,375

◆ Minivans

Make and model	Suggested retail price	Est. dealer's cost	Your target price	Options cost (% of retail)[2]	Five-year resale value	Miles per gallon (city/hwy.)	Cost to insure[3]	Maintenance[4]	Repairs[5]	Total ownership expense[6]
Chevrolet Astro CS 3dr	13,995	12,568	12,945	85	9,097	16/21	Very high	3,813	201	23,047
Chevrolet Astro CS AWD 3dr	16,325	14,660	15,100	85	11,101	15/20	Very high	3,813	201	24,092
Chevrolet Astro CS Extended 3dr	15,875	14,288	14,717	85	10,636	15/20	Very high	3,823	201	24,790
Chevrolet Astro CS Extended AWD 3dr	17,885	16,097	16,580	85	11,983	15/20	Very high	3,823	201	24,790
Chevrolet Lumina APV 2dr	15,570	13,982	14,401	85	N.A.	18/23	High	4,746	N.A.	N.A.
Chevrolet Lumina APV CL 2dr	17,355	15,585	16,053	85	N.A.	18/23	High	4,746	N.A.	N.A.
Chrysler Town & Country 3dr	24,469	21,903	22,998	89	14,069	17/23	Low	3,845	300	36,429
Dodge Caravan LE 3dr	20,245	18,065	18,837	85	12,463	19/23	Very low	4,139	300	24,734
Dodge Caravan LE AWD 3dr	22,347	19,915	20,780	89	13,544	15/20	Very low	3,972	300	26,862
Dodge Caravan SE 3dr	15,529	13,915	14,469	85	10,975	18/24	Very low	4,139	300	21,358
Dodge Grand Caravan LE 3dr	20,965	18,699	19,502	89	13,743	19/23	Very low	3,915	300	24,478
Dodge Grand Caravan LE AWD 3dr	22,965	20,459	21,350	89	15,063	15/20	Very low	3,915	300	25,957
Dodge Grand Caravan SE 3dr	17,511	15,660	16,130	85	12,783	18/24	Very low	3,915	300	21,800
Dodge Caravan SE AWD 3dr	18,737	16,739	17,241	85	13,116	15/20	Very low	3,972	300	23,031
Ford Aerostar Eddie Bauer 3dr	21,140	18,803	19,743	89	11,627	17/22	Low	4,274	591	27,689
Ford Aerostar Eddie Bauer Ext. 3dr	22,327	19,848	20,840	89	11,833	17/22	Low	4,274	591	28,716
Ford Aerostar Eddie Bauer 4WD 3dr	23,813	21,155	22,213	89	13,097	15/19	Low	4,274	N.A.	N.A.
Ford Aerostar XL 3dr	14,001	12,521	12,897	85	8,961	17/22	Low	4,196	591	23,570
Ford Aerostar XL 4WD 3dr	17,185	15,323	15,783	85	11,514	15/19	Low	4,274	N.A.	N.A.
Ford Aerostar XL Extended 3dr	15,672	13,991	14,411	85	10,030	17/22	Low	4,274	591	23,996
Ford Aerostar XL Extended 4WD 3dr	18,104	16,131	16,615	85	N.A.	15/19	Low	4,274	N.A.	N.A.
Ford Aerostar XLT 3dr	17,267	15,395	15,857	90	11,051	17/22	Low	4,274	591	24,500
Ford Aerostar XLT Extended 3dr	18,165	16,185	16,671	89	11,626	17/22	Low	4,274	591	24,834
Ford Aerostar XLT Plus 4WD 3dr	19,678	17,516	18,041	89	12,987	15/19	Low	4,274	N.A.	N.A.
GMC Safari SLE 3dr	17,129	15,416	15,879	85	10,963	16/21	Very low	3,902	201	23,258
GMC Safari SLE AWD 3dr	19,209	17,288	17,807	85	12,678	16/19	Very low	3,902	201	24,622
GMC Safari SLE Extended 3dr AWD	19,829	17,846	18,381	85	13,682	15/20	Very low	3,911	201	25,541
GMC Safari SLX 3dr	15,404	13,863	14,279	85	10,013	16/21	Very low	3,902	201	22,527
GMC Safari SLX AWD 3dr	17,484	15,736	16,208	85	11,714	16/19	Very low	3,902	201	23,886
GMC Safari SLX Extended AWD 3dr	18,104	16,293	16,782	85	11,949	15/20	Very low	3,911	201	24,276
Mazda MPV 3dr	15,165	13,194	13,590	82	8,189	18/24	Low	4,396	N.A.	N.A.
Mazda MPV 4WD 3dr	20,135	17,517	18,393	82	10,873	16/19	Low	4,296	N.A.	N.A.
Oldsmobile Silhouette 3dr	19,095	17,147	17,661	82	N.A.	18/23	Low	5,132	N.A.	N.A.
Plymouth Grand Voyager LE 3dr	20,773	18,530	19,457	89	13,710	18/24	Very low	3,865	293	24,312
Plymouth Grand Voyager LE AWD 3dr	22,773	20,290	21,305	89	15,030	16/20	Very low	3,865	293	25,833
Plymouth Grand Voyager SE 3dr	17,511	15,660	16,130	85	12,783	19/23	Very low	3,865	293	21,478
Plymouth Voyager LE 3dr	19,964	17,818	18,353	90	12,178	20/28	Very low	3,825	293	24,377
Plymouth Voyager LE AWD 3dr	22,155	19,746	20,733	90	13,293	16/20	Very low	3,753	293	26,549
Plymouth Voyager SE 3dr	15,679	14,048	14,469	85	8,780	20/28	Very low	3,779	293	23,397
Pontiac Trans Sport GT 3dr	20,935	18,800	19,740	85	N.A.	18/23	Low	5,260	N.A.	N.A.
Pontiac Trans Sport SE 3dr	16,225	14,570	15,007	85	N.A.	18/23	Low	5,260	N.A.	N.A.
Toyota Previa All-Trac Deluxe 3dr 4WD	19,128	16,259	16,747	80	N.A.	17/20	Low	4,459	N.A.	N.A.
Toyota Previa All-Trac LE 3dr 4WD	24,058	17,015	17,866	85	N.A.	17/20	Low	4,446	N.A.	N.A.
Toyota Previa Deluxe 3dr	16,518	14,123	14,547	80	N.A.	18/22	Low	4,364	N.A.	N.A.
Toyota Previa LE 3dr	21,448	18,231	19,143	80	N.A.	18/22	Low	4,351	N.A.	N.A.

[2]Dealer's average cost as a percentage of suggested retail price. [3]Compared with other models in its class. Actual costs will vary, depending on your location, the number and age of drivers and so forth. [4]Includes scheduled maintenance, as well as replacement of tires, brake pads, batteries and other parts. [5]Average five-year repair costs not covered by warranty. [6]Includes depreciation, financing, maintenance, repairs, state taxes and registration fees, insurance and fuel. Sources: IntelliChoice Inc., AutoAdviser Inc., Insurance Services Office and the manufacturers.

Money's College Value Rankings

Contemplating an expensive college diploma, many parents may well wonder: Can we pay less and still get a quality education? And if we do scrape the money together for a high-priced elite school, can we be sure the sacrifice will be worth every penny?

You'll find answers to those questions on page 166 in the list of 100 top schools at all price levels that more than justify their cost. The schools were chosen from the 1,011 accredited four-year colleges—that welcome students of all creeds—listed in the tables that start on page 167.

The top 100 schools are a remarkably varied lot. They include 56 private and 44 public institutions. Some are academic powerhouses like Princeton, Stanford, the University of Chicago, and Yale, which are easily worth the annual $16,000-plus required of those gifted enough to get in. Others are solid state schools like Trenton State College and Texas A&M, both of which charge less than $5,000 for out-of-state students. You can find schools that impose structured course requirements, like Hendrix College, or ones where students plot their own courses of study, like the New College of the University of South Florida. There are science centers like Caltech and MIT, humanities havens like Barnard and Pomona, and megacampuses that offer something for everyone, like the University of Wisconsin at Madison.

The value rankings are only one criterion to consider as you search for a school. No single formula can tell you which college will be right for your child.

In the Top 100, the aim is not to designate the best schools in America, because we believe that no one school can be considered best for all students. Instead, we explore the relationship between price and quality—what a school charges and what it delivers—and how that relationship varies from one institution to another. Establishing the price side of the equation is fairly simple. We use the schools' full stated charges for tuition and mandatory fees. To compensate for the fact that state schools receive taxpayer subsidies, we use nonresident tuitions for public schools, even though most students attending them pay the much lower resident charges. We believe it's fair to compare public and private schools, despite the different ways they are funded, because we are looking at them from the perspective of the people who are paying the bills. We ignore financial aid in the calculation of the Top 100 because it varies so greatly from student to student.

Measuring educational quality is trickier. After discussions with dozens of higher education experts, we decided to base the rankings on 12 factors: student/faculty ratio; faculty strength (the number of full-time faculty and the number of Ph.D.s available to teach undergraduates); library resources; instructional and student service expenditures; entrance exam results; class rank in high school; acceptance rate (out of those who applied for admission); freshman retention rate (the percentage of freshmen who return); graduation rate; percentage of graduates who go on to earn graduate or professional degrees; percentage of graduates who earn doctorate degrees; and business success (the number of top corporate executives who are alumni).

Using a statistical model, we then compared each school's tuition with our measures of educational strength, discarding institutions scoring below average on most indicators. The top 100 colleges proved to have the lowest tuitions relative to their quality scores.

In the tables that begin on page 167, we included some—but not all—of the statistics from the study that produced our Top 100. Here is a description of each statistic listed after the names of the schools in the tables:

Percent of need met. Actual need among students who qualify for financial aid varies with the price of the school and the amount a student's family is judged able to pay. This figure tells you how much of the eligible students' need was met with grants, loans, and work/study jobs in 1990.

Tuition and fees. Provided by each college for the 1991-92 academic year; nonresident tuition is given for public schools. Some schools, indicated with a footnote, had not set their tuitions by press time.

Room and board. These charges may vary; the number listed is either the typical charge or, where indicated, the minimum.

Percent with high test scores. The portion of the 1990 freshman class that scored 500 and above on the verbal SAT or 21 and above on the ACT. Two versions of the ACT were given in 1990. Schools that reported scores from the new version are indicated with a footnote.

Top 100

The schools listed below deliver the best education for the money. We ranked them using data from Peterson's Guides of Princeton, New Jersey and other sources.

1. Rice University
2. New College of U. of S. Fla.
3. Trenton State
4. University of Virginia
5. U. of Ill.—Urbana-Champaign
6. Calif. Inst. of Technology
7. SUNY—Binghamton
8. University of Washington
9. U. of N.C.—Chapel Hill
10. University of Texas—Austin
11. SUNY—Albany
12. Auburn University
13. Hanover College
14. Texas A&M
15. New Mexico Inst. of Mining
16. Yale University
17. St. Mary's of Maryland
18. Spelman College
19. Fisk University
20. Princeton University
21. Trinity University
22. Centenary of Louisiana
23. Mary Washington College
24. Ohio University
25. Johns Hopkins University
26. SUNY—Buffalo
27. University of Florida
28. SUNY—Genesco
29. Hendrix College
30. Georgia Inst. of Tech.
31. U. of Wisconsin—Madison
32. SUNY—Stony Brook
33. Rutgers College
34. Michigan Technological
35. University of Georgia
36. Wake Forest University
37. Baylor University
38. James Madison University
39. Douglass College
40. Samford University
41. North Carolina State
42. Notre Dame of Maryland
43. U. of California—Berkeley
44. Chestnut Hill College
45. Pomona College
46. SUNY—Potsdam
47. Bellarmine College
48. Wabash College
49. Purdue University
50. Florida Southern College
51. University of Iowa
52. U. of South Carolina
53. Erskine College
54. Swarthmore College
55. Iowa St. Science and Tech
56. Washington and Lee U.
57. Emory and Henry College
58. Incarnate Word College
59. Kentucky Wesleyan C.
60. Virginia Polytechnic Inst.
61. Centre College
62. Harvey Mudd College
63. University of Tulsa
64. Case Western Reserve U.
65. Miami University (Ohio)
66. Cook College
67. UCLA
68. William and Mary
69. University of Chicago
70. Rosemont College
71. Westminster College (Mo.)
72. St. Joseph's C. (Maine)
73. Clemson University
74. Columbia University
75. Furman University
76. Michigan State University
77. Shenandoah University
78. Wesleyan College (Ga.)
79. Lenoir-Rhyne College
80. University of Pittsburgh
81. St. Bonaventure U.
82. Davidson College
83. Creighton University
84. John Carroll University
85. U. of Missouri—Rolla
86. Agnes Scott College
87. Benedictine College
88. Stanford University
89. St. John's University (N.Y.)
90. University of Dallas
91. Southwestern U. (Texas)
92. Barnard College
93. Claremont McKenna C.
94. University of Connecticut
95. MacMurray College
96. Hillsdale College
97. LeMoyne College
98. MIT
99. St. Louis University
100. U. of Md.—College Park

Percent who graduate in five years. The average percentage of incoming freshmen in 1984, 1985, and 1986 who had received bachelor's degrees by the spring semester of 1990.

Percent from top half of class. The portion of the 1990 freshman class that ranked in the top half of their high school graduating class.

Student/faculty ratio. This figure refers to undergraduates only.

Average grant per student with need. This counts only money given by the school itself, not funds from the government or other sources.

Finally, we included phone numbers for each college admissions office—or the school's main phone number—so that you can get more information from colleges and universities that interest you. Most schools will send you a package full of facts to answer your questions.

1,011 Colleges

College name and location	Tuition and fees	Room and board	% of need met	Avg. grant per student with need	Student/ faculty ratio	% who graduate in five years	% with high test scores	% from top half of class	Telephone
Adams State (Colo.)	$4,157	$2,804	80	$283	20:1	40	38(A)	79	719-589-7712
Adelphi (N.Y.)	10,420	5,530	63	861	13:1	71	41(S)	89	516-877-3050
Adrian (Mich.)	9,420	3,000	95	2,591	15:1	44	61(A)	90	517-265-5161
Agnes Scott (Ga.)[1] 86	11,070	4,515	100	3,938	8:1	62	73(S)	97	404-371-6285
Alabama A&M	3,000	2,036	81	0	16:1	31	N.A.	N.A.	205-851-5245
Alabama State	2,428	1,910	N.A.	N.A.	22:1	9	5(A)[2]	58	205-293-4291
Alaska Pacific	6,330	4,050[3]	75	658	15:1	N.A.	N.A.	N.A.	907-564-8248
Albany State (Ga.)	4,260	2,370	80	455	14:1	40	2(S)	56	912-430-4650
Albertus Magnus (Conn.)	9,980	4,930	85	1,639	12:1	70	20(S)	76	203-773-8527
Albion (Mich.)	11,064	4,064	100	4,148	13:1	65	73(S)	96	517-629-0321
Albright (Pa.)	13,520	4,015	93	5,669	11:1	80	61(S)	96	215-921-7512
Alcorn State (Miss.)	2,882	1,900	N.A.	N.A.	20:1	50	13(A)	35	601-877-6147
Alderson-Broaddus (W.Va.)	8,667	2,665	92	1,618	13:1	55	N.A.	78	304-457-1700
Alfred (N.Y.)	13,960	4,470	97	4,737	12:1	67	61(S)	96	607-871-2115
Alice Lloyd (Ky.)	3,240	2,750	92	3,188	15:1	34	N.A.	65	606-368-2101
Allegheny (Pa.)	14,850	4,120	100	7,356	10:1	67	51(S)	92	814-332-4351
Allentown–St. Francis de Sales (Pa.)	8,000	4,150	90	3,246	14:1	58	31(S)	85	215-282-4443
Alma (Mich.)	10,635	3,878	100	4,621	15:1	70	84(A)[2]	96	517-463-7139
Alvernia (Pa.)	6,962	3,600	73	199	14:1	70	14(S)	80	215-777-5411
American (D.C.)	13,716	5,972	100	8,096	15:1	65	80(S)	97	202-885-6000
American International (Mass.)	8,060	4,132	90	1,122	16:1	59	34(S)	67	413-747-6201
Amherst (Mass.)	16,755	4,800	100	10,143	10:1	94	96(S)	100	413-542-2328
Angelo State (Texas)	4,669[4]	3,490	N.A.	N.A.	25:1	31	58(A)[2]	90	915-942-2041
Anna Maria (Mass.)	9,855	4,380	92	2,836	16:1	70	15(S)	63	508-757-4586
Antioch (Ohio)	13,370	2,880	100	4,085	8:1	50[5]	63(S)	N.A.	513-767-6400
Appalachian State (N.C.)	6,315	2,300	95	285	15:1	60	33(S)	97	704-262-2120
Aquinas (Mich.)	8,960	3,950	100	3,949	15:1	50	47(A)	81	616-732-4460
Arizona State	7,058	3,668	90	900	22:1	38	31(S)	80	602-965-7788
Arkansas College	7,040	3,140	92	3,960	12:1	23	67(A)	88	501-793-9813
Arkansas State[6]	2,670	2,040	80	N.A.	24:1	40	50(A)	N.A.	501-972-2031
Arkansas Tech	2,920	2,200	N.A.	N.A.	18:1	40	32(A)	50	501-968-0343

Footnotes are on page 188.

Grants Galore

SCHOOLS THAT PROVIDE THE BIGGEST
AVERAGE GRANTS OUT OF THEIR OWN
FUNDS TO STUDENTS WITH NEED

Stanford University	**$11,711**
Tulane University	**11,095**
Swarthmore College	**10,701**
Bowdoin College	**10,663**
Mount Holyoke College	**10,298**
Scripps College	**10,152**
Amherst College	**10,143**
Bennington College	**9,646**
California Inst. of Technology	**9,374**
Smith College	**9,353**

College name and location	Tuition and fees	Room and board	% of need met	Avg. grant per student with need	Student/ faculty ratio	% who graduate in five years	% with high test scores	% from top half of class	Telephone
Armstrong State (Ga.)	$4,047	$2,994	70	$281	17:1	40	N.A.	48	912-927-5275
Ashland (Ohio)	9,966	4,119	98	4,026	15:1	60	58(A)	65	419-289-5052
Assumption (Mass.)	9,835	5,050	100	N.A.	16:1	85	27(S)	85	508-752-5615
Auburn (Ala.) 12	4,788	3,603[6]	81	379	16:1	64	84(A)[2]	80	205-844-4080
Augsburg (Minn.)	10,245	3,832	90	2,515	15:1	N.A.	37(S)	71	612-330-1001
Augustana (Ill.)	11,175	3,666	N.A.	N.A.	14:1	62	79(A)	95	309-794-7341
Augustana (S.D.)	9,330	2,946	85	N.A.	14:1	65	79(A)[2]	94	605-336-5516
Austin (Texas)	9,465	3,745	100	3,705	14:1	61	58(S)	90	903-813-2387
Austin Peay State (Tenn.)	4,992	2,450	70	6	18:1	30	25(A)	N.A.	615-648-7661
Averett (Va.)	8,750	4,200	87	659	16:1	60	35(S)	78	804-791-5660
Babson (Mass.)	13,853	5,228	100	6,816	10:1	83	39(S)	93	617-239-5522
Baker College of Muskegon (Mich.)[6]	4,800	1,575[7]	65	145	24:1	75	N.A.	N.A.	616-726-4904
Baker College of Owosso (Mich.)[6]	5,000	1,575[7]	65	442	26:1	70	N.A.	18	517-723-5251
Baker U. (Kans.)	7,050	3,450	95	N.A.	15:1	53	62(A)	89	913-594-6451
Baldwin-Wallace (Ohio)	9,945	3,450	100	3,433	15:1	70	59(A)	87	216-826-2222
Ball State (Ind.)	5,360	2,970	90	0	17:1	45	19(S)	74	317-285-8287
Barat (Ill.)	8,780	3,300	100	613	12:1	73	27(A)	69	708-234-3000
Barber–Scotia (N.C.)[8,6]	4,000	2,487	75	115	13:1	70	N.A.	45	704-786-5171
Bard (N.Y.)	17,110	5,565	90	6,113	11:1	70	N.A.	N.A.	914-758-7472
Barnard (N.Y.)[1] 92	15,874	6,892	100	8,438	12:1	88	93(S)	100	212-854-2014
Baruch College–City U. of N.Y.	4,275	No dorms	93	353	22:1	50	N.A.	80	212-447-3754
Bates (Maine)	21,400[9]	N.A.	100	7,840	12:1	90	92(S)	99	207-786-6000
Baylor (Texas) 37	6,060	3,658	75	1,087	17:1	71	46(S)	94	817-755-1811
Beaver (Pa.)	10,960	4,750	95	4,666	13:1	64	28(S)	75	215-572-2910
Bellarmine (Ky.) 47	7,160	2,500	99	1,219	15:1	74	82(A)[2]	99	502-452-8131
Belmont Abbey (N.C.)	7,870	3,804	92	1,807	17:1	40	17(S)	53	704-825-6665
Beloit (Wis.)	13,050	3,300	100	6,150	12:1	59	N.A.	91	608-363-2500
Bemidji State (Minn.)	3,760	2,703	100	44	20:1	36	45(A)	73	218-755-2040
Benedict (S.C.)[8,6]	4,884	2,492	N.A.	N.A.	17:1	65	N.A.	N.A.	803-256-4220
Benedictine (Kans.) 87	7,930	3,300	N.A.	N.A.	13:1	51	50(A)	70	913-367-5340
Bennett (N.C.)[1,8]	5,400	2,600	N.A.	N.A.	11:1	30	6(S)	N.A.	919-370-8624
Bennington (Vt.)	19,400	3,800	100	9,646	9:1	70	74(S)	85	802-442-6349
Bentley (Mass.)	11,390	4,768	100	4,157	19:1	75	22(S)	88	617-891-2244
Berry (Ga.)	6,990	3,360	100	1,520	15:1	45	48(S)	N.A.	404-236-2215
Bethany (Kans.)	7,028	3,127	87	1,619	14:1	38	N.A.	76	913-227-3311
Bethany (W.Va.)	11,710	4,000	99	5,494	14:1	68	38(S)	80	304-829-7611
Bethel (Tenn.)	4,350	2,400	N.A.	N.A.	15:1	40	29(A)[2]	73	901-352-1000
Birmingham-Southern (Ala.)	9,550	3,760	85	4,968	15:1	73	94(A)[2]	88	205-226-4686
Black Hills State (S.D.)	3,322	2,140	76	N.A.	25:1	40	23(A)[2]	60	605-642-6343

Footnotes are on page 188.

College name and location	Tuition and fees	Room and board	% of need met	Avg. grant per student with need	Student/ faculty ratio	% who graduate in five years	% with high test scores	% from top half of class	Telephone
Blackburn (Ill.)	$7,750	$1,000	100	$2,040	14:1	40	43(A)	79	217-854-3231
Bloomfield (N.J.)	7,450	3,700	83	N.A.	13:1	65	N.A.	N.A.	201-748-9000
Bloomsburg U. of Pennsylvania	4,532[10]	2,466	70	181	17:1	67	28(S)	94	717-389-4316
Bluffton (Ohio)	8,100	3,324	90	1,899	12:1	55	60(A)[2]	81	419-358-3000
Boise State (Idaho)	3,304	2,830	N.A.	N.A.	19:1	N.A.	41(A)[2]	N.A.	208-385-1156
Boston College (Mass.)	13,964	6,150[3]	80	3,878	15:1	85	80(S)	99	617-552-3100
Boston University (Mass.)	16,190	6,320	100	8,538	15:1	66	71(S)	98	617-353-9814
Bowdoin (Maine)	16,380	5,590	100	10,663	10:1	90	95(S)	100	207-725-3100
Bowling Green State (Ohio)	6,724	2,686	75	177	20:1	60	88(A)[2]	92	419-372-2086
Bradford (Mass.)	11,885	5,875	94	5,512	12:1	64	N.A.	41	508-372-7161
Bradley (Ill.)	9,098	3,960	100	3,730	18:1	77	77(A)[2]	86	309-677-1000
Brandeis (Mass.)	16,484	6,250	100	8,631	6:1	79	N.A.	98	617-736-3500
Brescia (Ky.)	5,615	2,434	75	957	14:1	40	55(A)	95	800-284-1962
Briar Cliff (Iowa)	8,760	3,147	98	2,851	14:1	41	47(A)[2]	61	712-279-5200
Bridgewater (Va.)	9,195	4,295	100	3,441	15:1	55	N.A.	87	703-828-2501
Bridgewater State (Mass.)	6,606	3,550[3]	90	0	17:1	40	21(S)	76	508-697-1237
Brooklyn College–City U. of N.Y.	4,155[4]	No dorms	85	N.A.	13:1[11]	N.A.	N.A.	N.A.	718-780-5011
Brown (R.I.)	16,727	5,219	100	7,743	9:1	92	95(S)	99	401-863-2378
Bryant (R.I.)	10,933	5,935	92	3,886	17:1[11]	88	23(S)	87	401-232-6000
Bryn Mawr (Pa.)	15,600	5,850	100	9,131	9:1	85	93(S)	99	215-526-5152
Bucknell (Pa.)	15,650	3,825	100	5,569	13:1	86	79(S)	97	717-524-1101
Buena Vista (Iowa)	10,900	3,110	89	2,650	14:1	54	75(A)	93	712-749-2235
Butler (Ind.)	10,570	3,740	95	4,623	13:1	58	56(S)	92	317-283-9255
Cabrini (Pa.)	8,830	5,510	90	1,783	19:1	65	21(S)	65	215-971-8552
California Inst. of Technology 6	14,205	4,333	100	9,374	3:1	75	100(S)	100	818-356-6341
California Lutheran	9,950	4,600	75	1,956	15:1	60	22(S)	75	805-493-3135
California Polytechnic–San Luis Obispo	7,098	4,025	N.A.	N.A.	16:1	55	36(S)	N.A.	805-756-2311
California State–Bakersfield	8,460	3,599	N.A.	N.A.	16:1	45	25(S)	N.A.	805-664-2160
California State–Chico	6,748[4]	3,720	81	21	14:1	45	20(S)	N.A.	916-898-6324
California State–Fresno	8,454[10]	3,824	65	143	18:1	63	16(S)	N.A.	209-278-2191
California State–Fullerton	8,488	3,249[7]	65	0	19:1	31	14(S)	N.A.	714-773-2350
California State–Long Beach	8,925	4,672	90	41	20:1	N.A.	N.A.	N.A.	213-985-4141
California State–Northridge	7,688	4,990	76	86	17:1	45	17(S)	N.A.	818-885-3700
California State–Sacramento	8,440[10]	4,170	N.A.	N.A.	18:1	40	23(S)	95	916-278-3901
California State–San Bernardino	8,961	3,928	N.A.	N.A.	18:1	N.A.	13(S)	N.A.	714-880-5202
California State Polytechnic–Pomona	8,904	4,233	80	0	18:1	26	16(S)	N.A.	714-869-3422
California U. of Pennsylvania	4,682[4]	2,490	89	203	19:1	52	8(S)	58	412-938-4404
Camden College–Rutgers U. (N.J.)	6,894	4,018	83	N.A.	15:1	22	38(S)	82	609-757-6104
Cameron (Okla.)	3,305	2,252	80	N.A.	18:1	40	33(A)[2]	32	405-581-2238
Canisius (N.Y.)	8,830	4,650	92	1,819	17:1	47	39(S)	85	716-888-2200
Capital (Ohio)	11,085	3,700	98	3,826	14:1	73	67(A)[2]	94	614-236-6101
Carleton (Minn.)	16,296	3,324	100	6,173	11:1	84	95(S)	99	507-663-4190
Carnegie Mellon (Pa.)	15,350	5,110	N.A.	N.A.	9:1	70	75(S)	97	412-268-2082
Carroll (Mont.)	6,625	3,230	90	1,748	13:1	50	66(A)	65	406-442-3450
Carroll (Wis.)	11,068	3,560	93	5,305	14:1	65	67(A)	89	414-524-7220
Carthage (Wis.)	10,640	3,350	98	3,611	15:1	60	39(A)[2]	55	414-551-6000
Case Western Reserve (Ohio) 64	13,710	4,930	100	8,818	8:1	68	75(S)	97	216-368-4450
Castleton State (Vt.)	7,226	4,290	95	160	15:1	N.A.	16(S)	63	802-468-5611
Catawba (N.C.)	7,700	3,700	85	1,617	14:1	53	10(S)	54	704-637-4402
Catholic U. (D.C.)	11,876	5,686	86	N.A.	12:1	65	64(S)	95	202-319-5305
Centenary of Louisiana 22	7,210	3,060	91	2,538	11:1	66	69(A)[2]	89	318-869-5131
Central Connecticut State	6,144	3,830	100	704	17:1	50	12(S)	70	203-827-7548
Central Methodist (Mo.)	6,710	3,270	95	2,836	13:1[11]	43	35(A)[2]	62	816-248-3391
Central Michigan	5,560[10]	3,500[3]	90	288	19:1	50	47(A)	90	517-774-3076
Central Missouri State	3,570	2,800[3]	N.A.	N.A.	19:1	44	28(A)	61	816-429-4810
Central U. of Iowa	9,293	3,417	98	3,630	15:1	65	73(A)	91	800-458-5503

Footnotes are on page 188.

Bucks for Brains

SCHOOLS THAT OFFER THE BIGGEST
AVERAGE MERIT-BASED SCHOLARSHIPS

Trinity College (Conn.)	**$15,120**
Bard College	**15,000**
Holy Cross	**14,200**
Tulane University	**14,200**
U. of the Pacific	**12,000**
Catholic University	**10,860**
Colorado College	**10,100**
Duke University	**10,100**
Providence College	**10,000**
Boston University	**9,983**

College name and location	Tuition and fees	Room and board	% of need met	Avg. grant per student with need	Student/ faculty ratio	% who graduate in five years	% with high test scores	% from top half of class	Telephone
Central Washington	$6,033	$3,332	92	N.A.	20:1	49	25(S)	99	509-963-3001
Centre (Ky.) 61	10,110	3,930	100	$5,491	11:1	69	94(A)	99	606-236-6064
Chadron State (Neb.)[6]	2,375	2,350	100	133	22:1	45	N.A.	60	308-432-6263
Chaminade U. of Honolulu (Hawaii)	7,500	3,840[3]	N.A.	N.A.	16:1	N.A.	15(S)	70	808-735-4735
Chapman (Calif.)	12,625	5,004	100	6,943	14:1	40	N.A.	N.A.	714-997-6711
Chatham (Pa.)[1]	11,065	4,490	100	4,484	9:1	56	N.A.	74	412-365-1290
Chestnut Hill (Pa.)[1] 44	8,250	4,080	100	3,817	11:1	78	46(S)	72	215-248-7001
Cheyney U. of Pennsylvania[6,8]	5,322	2,956	70	0	13:1	30	N.A.	N.A.	215-399-2275
Chicago State (Ill.)	5,168	No dorms	N.A.	N.A.	24:1	N.A.	N.A.	N.A.	312-995-2513
Christ College (Calif.)	8,790	2,430[7]	N.A.	N.A.	18:1	31	21(S)	90	714-854-8002
Christian Brothers (Tenn.)	7,540	2,960[3]	100	N.A.	12:1	45	76(A)[2]	71	901-722-0205
Christopher Newport (Va.)	4,260	No dorms	65	12	19:1	33	30(S)	78	804-594-7015
The Citadel, Military College of S.C.[12]	11,945[13]	N.A.	N.A.	N.A.	13:1	69	38(S)	71	803-792-5230
City College–City U. of N.Y.	4,145	No dorms	64	152	15:1	28	N.A.	81	212-650-6977
Claflin (S.C.)[8]	4,223	2,910	71	N.A.	15:1	50	1(S)	N.A.	803-534-2710
Claremont McKenna (Calif.) 93	14,810	5,180	100	6,728	8:1	81	90(S)	99	714-621-8088
Clarion U. of Pennsylvania	4,888[10]	2,600[3]	74	32	19:1	70	11(S)	84	814-226-2306
Clark (Mass.)	15,380	4,500	100	7,732	13:1	70	N.A.	98	508-793-7431
Clark Atlanta (Ga.)[8]	6,970	3,268	65	N.A.	15:1	41	10(S)	N.A.	404-880-8018
Clarkson (N.Y.)	13,675	4,732	85	3,553	16:1	75	53(S)	95	315-268-6479
Clemson (S.C.) 73	6,858	2,966	87	718	20:1	67	40(S)	95	803-656-2287
Cleveland State (Ohio)[6]	5,364	3,213[3]	60	218	19:1[11]	N.A.	27(A)	50	216-687-3755
Coe (Iowa)	10,380	3,840	100	4,841	12:1	65	85(A)[2]	93	319-399-8540
Coker (S.C.)	8,309	3,818	90	15,985	10:1	60	28(S)	78	803-383-8050
Colby (Maine)	15,710	5,350	100	6,703	10:1	84	89(S)	100	207-872-3168
Colby-Sawyer (N.H.)	12,525	4,715	95	N.A.	11:1	60	14(S)	57	603-526-2010
Colgate (N.Y.)	16,150	5,070	99	7,825	12:1	81	90(S)	97	315-824-7401
College of Boca Raton (Fla.)[6]	12,200	4,700	58	N.A.	20:1	65	N.A.	80	407-994-0770
College of Charleston (S.C.)	4,650	2,800	77	110	20:1	N.A.	34(S)	92	803-792-5671
College of Idaho	9,200	2,700[3]	98	4,511	11:1	40	75(A)	59	208-459-5425
College of Mount Saint Vincent (N.Y.)	9,810	4,900	80	3,077	12:1	57	19(S)	74	212-549-8000
College of New Rochelle (N.Y.)[1]	8,480	4,220	75	1,241	12:1	57	24(S)	69	914-654-5452
College of Notre Dame (Calif.)	10,165	4,500	73	2,940	10:1	32	N.A.	61	415-508-3533
College of St. Benedict (Minn.)[1]	10,135	3,750	100	2,199	14:1	65	66(A)[2]	88	612-363-5308
College of St. Francis (Ill.)	7,980	3,580	100	2,582	11:1	62	80(A)[2]	89	815-740-3400
College of the Atlantic (Maine)	11,625	3,295	95	984	10:1	56	80(S)	81	207-288-5015
College of William and Mary (Va.) 68	10,450	3,746	88	1,816	17:1	81	85(S)	99	804-221-3999
College of Wooster (Ohio)	13,410	4,240	100	N.A.	12:1	65	53(S)	85	216-263-2000
Colorado College	13,665	3,645	98	6,589	13:1	77	75(S)	98	719-389-6344

Footnotes are on page 188.

Costly Credits

SCHOOLS THAT CHARGE THE HIGHEST
FEES FOR TUITION, ROOM AND BOARD

Bennington College	$23,200
Sarah Lawrence College	23,150
Barnard College	22,766
Brandeis University	22,734
Bard College	22,675
Cornell University	22,558
Boston University	22,510
Tulane University	22,485
Tufts University	22,479
New York University	22,394

College name and location	Tuition and fees	Room and board	% of need met	Avg. grant per student with need	Student/ faculty ratio	% who graduate in five years	% with high test scores	% from top half of class	Telephone
Colorado School of Mines	$10,315	$3,680[3]	99	$2,320	12:1	65	100(A)	100	303-273-3220
Colorado State	6,812	3,915	75	223	15:1	50	85(A)[2]	90	303-491-6909
Columbia (Ill.)[6]	7,000	No dorms	66	N.A.	15:1[11]	33	N.A.	N.A.	312-663-1600
Columbia (Mo.)	6,824	3,082	70	2,007	15:1	19	46(A)[2]	35	314-875-7352
Columbia (S.C.)[1]	8,725	3,255	91	959	14:1	50	6(S)	70	803-786-3646
Columbia Christian (Ore.)[6]	8,170	2,710	92	1,250	10:1	30	18(A)	90	503-257-1202
Columbia U. (N.Y.) 74	15,858	6,122	100	N.A.	8:1	93	91(S)	99	212-854-2521
Columbus (Ga.)	5,416	4,536	73	135	20:1	49	10(S)	N.A.	404-568-2035
Concord (W.Va.)	3,622	2,894	100	38	22:1	55	26(A)	N.A.	304-384-5248
Concordia (Minn.)	8,690	2,710	N.A.	2,546	15:1	68	67(A)[2]	91	218-299-3004
Connecticut College	16,270	5,370	100	8,325	10:1[11]	85	89(S)	94	203-439-2200
Converse (S.C.)[1]	10,368	3,000	100	1,519	9:1	62	54(S)	88	803-596-9040
Cook College–Rutgers U. (N.J.) 66	7,742	4,018	79	N.A.	16:1	43	44(S)	93	908-932-3770
Cooper Union (N.Y.)	300	3,650[7]	100	1,153	7:1	84	72(S)	100	212-353-4120
Cornell College (Iowa)	12,350	4,190	99	5,474	14:1	60	84(A)	90	319-895-4477
Cornell U. (N.Y.)	16,204	6,354	100	4,600	8:1[11]	84	88(S)	99	607-255-5241
Creighton (Neb.) 83	8,996	3,798	N.A.	2,532	14:1	64	73(A)	84	402-280-2703
Culver-Stockton (Mo.)	6,500	2,600	95	2,723	16:1	54	67(A)	86	314-288-5221
Cumberland (Tenn.)[6]	4,700	2,830	75	250	14:1	30	28(A)[2]	70	615-444-2562
Curry (Mass.)	11,900	4,800[3]	80	2,844	15:1	44	5(S)	49	800-669-0686
Daemen (N.Y.)	7,920	3,950	70	1,308	15:1	N.A.	12(S)	N.A.	716-839-1820
Dakota State (S.D.)	1,840	2,116[3]	100	480	14:1	62	39(A)	49	605-256-5139
Dakota Wesleyan (S.D.)	6,250	2,530	85	1,673	15:1	36	39(A)[2]	57	605-995-2650
Dana (Neb.)	7,370	2,770	95	9,286	11:1	34	35(A)	37	402-426-7222
Daniel Webster (N.H.)	10,440	4,312	90	1,687	15:1	53	19(S)	63	603-883-3556
Dartmouth (N.H.)	16,335	5,379	100	8,535	12:1	92	93(S)	99	603-646-2875
Davidson (N.C.) 82	13,680	4,160	100	4,428	12:1	89	87(S)	98	704-892-2230
Davis & Elkins (W.Va.)	7,710	3,930	95	1,453	15:1	48	5(S)	41	304-636-5850
Defiance (Ohio)	8,690	3,290	100	1,832	14:1	45	30(A)	75	419-784-4010
Delaware State	3,770	3,330	60	N.A.	13:1	N.A.	N.A.	55	302-739-4917
Delaware Valley (Pa.)	10,120	3,900	93	2,552	14:1	65	33(S)	70	215-345-1500
Delta State (Miss.)	3,462	2,000	100	270	19:1	51	44(A)	75	601-846-4655
Denison (Ohio)	14,700	3,980	100	N.A.	13:1	76	49(S)	87	614-587-6627
DePaul (Ill.)	9,342	4,000	100	N.A.	17:1	58	68(A)	87	312-362-8300
DePauw (Ind.)	12,288	4,420	100	6,174	12:1	77	71(S)	97	317-658-4006
Dickinson (Pa.)	15,565	4,530	100	6,766	13:1	86	75(S)	98	717-245-1231
Dickinson State (N.D.)[6]	4,256	1,850	100	794	17:1	38	34(A)	55	701-227-2331
Dillard (La.)[8]	5,800	3,250	N.A.	N.A.	14:1	58	N.A.	74	504-283-8822
Doane (Neb.)	8,320	2,600[3]	95	3,378	12:1	45	66(A)	84	402-826-2161

College name and location	Tuition and fees	Room and board	% of need met	Avg. grant per student with need	Student/ faculty ratio	% who graduate in five years	% with high test scores	% from top half of class	Telephone
Dominican of San Rafael (Calif.)	$10,390	$5,150	89	$4,171	12:1	30	35(S)	N.A.	415-485-3204
Douglass College–Rutgers U. (N.J.)[1] 39	7,006	4,018	89	N.A.	17:1	62	46(S)	93	908-932-3770
Drake (Iowa)	11,040	4,295	100	4,391	17:1	73	86(A)	88	515-271-3181
Drew (N.J.)	16,512	4,850	66	8,660	13:1	74	74(S)	93	201-408-3739
Drexel (Pa.)	11,059	5,800	85	N.A.	15:1	55	37(S)	83	215-895-2400
Drury (Mo.)	7,510	3,184	70	3,845	13:1	50	83(A)	92	417-865-8731
Duke (N.C.)	15,101	5,050	100	4,693	12:1	92	95(S)	100	919-684-3214
Duquesne (Pa.)	9,600	4,318	99	2,476	17:1	64	35(S)	87	412-434-6220
Earlham (Ind.)	13,479	3,726	100	4,721	12:1	75	76(S)	89	317-983-1600
East Carolina (N.C.)	5,672	4,200	100	N.A.	15:1	45	11(S)	71	919-757-6640
East Central (Okla.)	3,150	1,982	N.A.	N.A.	23:1	30	38(A)[2]	81	405-332-8000
East Stroudsburg U. of Pennsylvania	4,672	2,705	80	0	19:1	55	19(S)	83	717-424-3542
East Tennessee State	4,829	3,000	91	244	22:1	33	29(A)	68	615-929-4213
East Texas State	4,340[10]	4,974	N.A.	N.A.	21:1	55	N.A.	N.A.	903-886-5101
East-West (Ill.)[6,8]	5,985	No dorms	100	N.A.	12:1	30	25(A)	43	312-939-0111
Eastern Connecticut State	6,136	3,464	100	N.A.	18:1	38	18(S)	71	203-456-5286
Eastern Illinois	5,544	2,690	N.A.	N.A.	18:1	59	54(A)	84	217-581-2223
Eastern Kentucky[6]	4,040	2,796	85	2,525	18:1	36	16(A)	N.A.	606-622-2106
Eastern Michigan	4,512	2,600	80	N.A.	21:1	65	49(A)[2]	N.A.	313-487-0193
Eastern Montana	3,585	2,760	85	303	19:1	34	37(A)[2]	88	406-657-2303
Eastern New Mexico	4,248	2,188	N.A.	N.A.	22:1	30	28(A)[2]	75	505-562-2178
Eastern Oregon State	1,764	2,880	85	630	11:1	N.A.	15(S)	N.A.	503-962-3672
Eastern Washington	5,970	3,330	82	305	20:1	29	15(S)	N.A.	509-359-2397
Eckerd (Fla.)	13,040	3,210	86	4,988	12:1	70	54(S)	86	813-864-8331
Edinboro U. of Pennsylvania	4,624[4]	2,904	N.A.	N.A.	19:1	49	N.A.	N.A.	814-732-2761
Elizabeth City State (N.C.)	5,261[10]	2,554	76	1,150	16:1	32	5(S)	66	919-335-3000
Elizabethtown (Pa.)	11,650	3,950	96	4,334	14:1	62	49(S)	95	717-367-1151
Elmhurst (Ill.)	8,460	3,498	100	2,307	15:1	55	35(A)	60	708-617-3400
Elmira (N.Y.)	11,380	3,700	95	3,703	13:1	75	23(S)	76	607-734-3911
Elms (Mass.)[1]	9,250	4,400	100	3,141	14:1	75	23(S)	85	413-592-3189
Elon (N.C.)	7,520	3,350	90	811	18:1	53	16(S)	65	919-584-2370
Emerson (Mass.)	13,325	6,700	100	5,052	20:1	63	52(S)	83	617-578-8600
Emmanuel (Mass.)[1]	10,245	5,420	100	N.A.	12:1	68	N.A.	57	617-735-9715
Emory (Ga.)	14,780	4,532	100	8,687	9:1	80	75(S)	90	404-727-6036
Emory & Henry (Va.) 57	7,270	3,956	86	1,877	14:1	60	28(S)	88	800-848-5493
Emporia State (Kans.)[6]	4,004	5,390	98	N.A.	20:1	40	32(A)	75	316-343-1200
Erskine (S.C.) 53	9,615	3,300	95	2,324	11:1	66	35(S)	73	803-379-8832
Eugene Lang–New School (N.Y.)	11,944	7,166[3]	85	4,249	9:1	70	72(S)	88	212-741-5665
Eureka (Ill.)	9,425	3,160	95	3,068	11:1	59	37(A)	76	309-467-5350
Evergreen State (Wash.)	5,649	3,384	N.A.	N.A.	24:1	37	60(S)	86	206-866-6824
Fairfield (Conn.)	12,920	5,350	90	N.A.	15:1	81	64(S)	94	203-254-4100
Fairleigh Dickinson (N.J.)	9,856	5,106	N.A.	2,686	14:1	55	12(S)	64	201-460-5267
Fairmont State (W.Va.)	3,454	2,720	90	14	24:1	45	19(A)	39	304-367-4141
Fayetteville State (N.C.)	6,322	2,250[3]	N.A.	N.A.	13:1[11]	40	5(S)	61	919-486-1371
Ferris State (Mich.)	4,896[10]	3,318	90	124	17:1	N.A.	26(A)[2]	N.A.	616-592-2100
Ferrum (Va.)	7,400	3,400	90	987	15:1	23	4(S)	65	703-365-4290
Fisk (Tenn.)[8] 19	5,015	3,050	62	N.A.	10:1	64	N.A.	41	615-329-8665
Fitchburg State (Mass.)	6,848	3,166	75	88	16:1	50	17(S)	79	508-345-2151
Flagler (Fla.)	4,550	2,840	80	331	25:1	52	44(S)	92	904-829-6481
Florida A&M	5,720	2,342[3]	N.A.	425	16:1	30	N.A.	N.A.	904-599-3115
Florida Inst. of Technology	10,335	3,465	69	2,464	15:1	55	50(S)	94	407-768-8000
Florida Southern 50	6,600	4,200	85	1,231	15:1	70	N.A.	81	813-680-4131
Florida State	5,,630	4,000	100	584	18:1	55	58(S)	N.A.	904-644-6200
Fontbonne (Mo.)	7,470	3,560[3]	93	2,640	12:1	53	29(A)[2]	68	314-889-1400
Fordham (N.Y.)	11,070	6,525[3]	70	4,412	17:1	75	57(S)	90	212-579-2133
Fort Hays State (Kans.)[6]	4,061	2,628	85	N.A.	18:1	33	46(A)	N.A.	913-628-4187

Footnotes are on page 188.

In Search of... Men

COED LIBERAL ARTS COLLEGES WITH
THE HIGHEST PERCENTAGE OF MEN

Unity College	**78%**
Tri-State University	**71**
Cooper Union	**69**
Drexel University	**69**
Carnegie Mellon University	**68**
U. of New Haven	**67**
U. of Wisconsin–Plateville	**66**
Westminster College (Mo.)	**66**
Lees–McRae College	**65**
Washington and Lee University	**65**

College name and location	Tuition and fees	Room and board	% of need met	Avg. grant per student with need	Student/ faculty ratio	% who graduate in five years	% with high test scores	% from top half of class	Telephone
Fort Lewis (Colo.)	$5,504	$3,020[3]	95	$27	21:1	35	42(A)[2]	60	303-247-7184
Fort Valley State (Ga.)	4,230	2,310	N.A.	N.A.	14:1	26	N.A.	N.A.	912-825-6307
Framingham State (Mass.)	5,404	3,160	N.A.	N.A.	16:1	55	14(S)	75	508-626-4500
Francis Marion (S.C.)	4,280	3,010	90	N.A.	18:1	11	N.A.	72	803-661-1232
Franklin and Marshall (Pa.)	20,885[9]	N.A.	100	4,002	12:1	80	80(S)	93	717-291-3951
Franklin College of Indiana	8,860	3,410	82	2,491	12:1	60	35(S)	86	317-738-8062
Franklin Pierce (N.H.)	11,040	4,160	85	3,357	17:1	41	12(S)	38	603-899-4055
Friends (Kans.)	7,155	2,460	N.A.	N.A.	14:1	48	52(A)	N.A.	316-261-5842
Frostburg State (Md.)	4,040	3,870[3]	80	39	18:1	41	24(S)	90	301-689-4201
Furman (S.C.) 75	10,922	3,728	80	2,757	13:1	75	75(S)	95	803-294-2034
Gannon (Pa.)	8,744	3,500	90	2,284	16:1	60	43(S)	46	814-871-7240
George Mason (Va.)	7,464	4,750	N.A.	N.A.	17:1	N.A.	49(S)	76	703-323-2100
George Washington (D.C.)	14,902	6,230	95	8,130	8:1	50	70(S)	91	202-994-6040
Georgetown (D.C.)	15,652	6,584	100	7,780	17:1	87	87(S)	99	202-687-3600
Georgia College	4,143	2,298[3]	71	292	9:1	75	19(S)	N.A.	912-453-5234
Georgia Inst. of Technology 30	6,279	3,855	N.A.	N.A.	19:1	66	69(S)	100	404-894-4154
Georgia Southern	5,095	2,100[3]	N.A.	N.A.	22:1	36	12(S)	N.A.	912-681-5531
Georgia Southwestern	4,275[4]	2,372	85	N.A.	17:1	36	14(S)	N.A.	912-928-1273
Georgian Court (N.J.)	7,180	3,750	44	1,256	10:1	55	17(S)	85	908-367-4440
Gettysburg (Pa.)	16,500	3,470	100	7,794	13:1	78	78(S)	99	717-337-6100
Glassboro State (N.J.)	3,533	4,425	N.A.	N.A.	18:1	55	28(S)	81	609-863-5346
Glenville State (W.Va.)	3,450	2,780	67	105	18:1	52	40(A)[2]	75	304-462-7361
GMI Eng. & Mgt. Inst. (Mich.)	9,482	2,840	85	437	13:1	75	96(A)	98	313-762-7865
Goddard (Vt.)	12,330	4,120	90	3,445	16:1	N.A.	90(S)	N.A.	802-454-8311
Gonzaga (Wash.)	10,335	3,700	94	3,333	16:1	53	34(S)	86	509-484-6484
Goucher (Md.)	12,885	5,600	100	5,997	9:1	75	53(S)	67	301-337-6100
Graceland (Iowa)	7,850	2,650	92	2,308	13:1	38	58(A)[2]	77	515-784-5118
Grambling State (La.)[6]	3,328	2,636	60	N.A.	21:1	70	N.A.	N.A.	318-274-2487
Grand Valley State (Mich.)	4,910	3,500[3]	100	N.A.	24:1	50	48(A)	86	616-895-2025
Grand View (Iowa)[6]	7,750	2,900	80	736	15:1	19	27(A)	54	515-263-2810
Green Mountain (Vt.)	7,890	4,880	88	1,876	14:1	70	21(S)	58	802-287-9313
Greensboro (N.C.)	6,820	3,280	90	1,199	15:1[11]	40	20(S)	57	919-271-2211
Grinnell (Iowa)	13,742	3,868	100	5,973	10:1	79	88(S)	97	515-269-3600
Grove City (Pa.)	4,630	2,670	95	830	20:1	77	60(S)	96	412-458-2100
Guilford (N.C.)	10,470	4,300	99	3,064	14:1	70	N.A.	70	919-292-5511
Gustavus Adolphus (Minn.)	11,900	2,900	100	3,988	14:1	72	88(S)	91	507-931-7676
Hamilton (N.Y.)	16,650	4,550	100	9,080	11:1	87	80(S)	98	315-859-4421
Hamline (Minn.)	11,725	3,631	100	3,386	15:1	58	99(A)	99	612-641-2207
Hampden-Sydney (Va.)[12]	11,556	4,205	98	5,463	13:1	76	59(S)	75	804-223-4388

Footnotes are on page 188.

College name and location	Tuition and fees	Room and board	% of need met	Avg. grant per student with need	Student/ faculty ratio	% who graduate in five years	% with high test scores	% from top half of class	Telephone
Hampshire (Mass.)	$17,460	$4,560	100	$7,571	13:1	60	N.A.	95	413-549-4600
Hampton (Va.)[8]	6,550	3,000	N.A.	N.A.	18:1	59	14(S)	N.A.	804-727-5328
Hanover (Ind.) 13	6,700	2,700	100	2,407	14:1	60	76(S)	98	812-866-7000
Hartwick (N.Y.)	13,450	4,350	100	5,219	13:1	66	33(S)	81	607-431-4150
Harvard (Mass.)	16,560	5,520	100	7,403	8:1[11]	95	98(S)	100	617-495-1551
Harvey Mudd (Calif.) 62	14,910	5,890	100	5,271	8:1	72	99(S)	100	714-621-8011
Hastings (Neb.)	8,090	2,910	81	2,649	13:1	60	61(A)	75	402-461-7315
Haverford (Pa.)	16,150	5,400	100	8,004	11:1	90	92(S)	100	215-896-1350
Hawaii Loa	8,400	4,800	86	3,524	12:1	40	33(S)	70	808-235-3641
Hawaii Pacific	5,150	3,990[7]	80	899	20:1	35	27(S)	80	808-544-0212
Heidelberg (Ohio)	11,680	3,730	95	3,491	14:1	62	68(A)	81	419-448-2330
Henderson State (Ark.)	2,420	1,900	75	13	22:1	60	22(A)	35	501-246-5511
Hendrix (Ark.) 29	7,153	2,775	100	1,949	15:1	65	94(A)[2]	97	501-329-6811
High Point (N.C.)	6,710	3,200	85	1,213	17:1	39	17(S)	53	919-841-9216
Hillsdale (Mich.) 96	9,610	4,000	75	5,138	14:1	73	79(A)	85	517-437-7341
Hiram (Ohio)	11,950	3,780	N.A.	N.A.	12:1	70	52(S)	93	216-569-5169
Hobart (N.Y.)[12]	16,277	5,166	98	7,893	14:1	75	62(S)	95	315-781-3623
Hofstra (N.Y.)	9,790	5,780	75	855	17:1	60	43(S)	97	516-463-6700
Hollins (Va.)[1]	11,600	4,600	100	5,806	10:1	69	N.A.	68	703-362-6401
Holy Cross (Mass.)	14,605	5,400	100	5,902	14:1	88	86(S)	98	508-793-2443
Holy Names (Calif.)	8,510[4]	4,150	N.A.	3,034	10:1	45	N.A.	N.A.	415-436-1321
Hood (Md.)	12,078	5,675	100	5,044	14:1	65	42(S)	88	301-663-3131
Hope (Mich.)	10,086	3,688	100	3,199	15:1	63	79(A)[2]	94	616-394-7850
Howard (D.C.)[8]	6,405	3,580	N.A.	N.A.	6:1	38	N.A.	N.A.	202-806-2750
Humboldt State (Calif.)	8,968	3,916	75	0	16:1	N.A.	37(S)	100	707-826-4101
Hunter College–City U. of N.Y.	4,143[10]	No dorms	N.A.	N.A.	17:1	15	N.A.	N.A.	212-772-4479
Huntingdon (Ala.)	6,500	3,200	100	1,520	13:1	45	69(A)[2]	78	205-834-3300
Husson (Maine)[6]	7,330	3,770	90	1,975	20:1	N.A.	8(S)	N.A.	207-947-1121
Idaho State	3,350	2,790	N.A.	N.A.	16:1	N.A.	34(A)	N.A.	208-236-3277
Illinois Benedictine	8,980	3,605	100	3,400	15:1	55	61(A)	75	708-960-1500
Illinois College	6,600	3,250	98	1,002	15:1	68	63(A)[2]	80	217-245-3030
Illinois Inst. of Technology	12,730	4,350	N.A.	N.A.	9:1	50	75(A)	97	312-567-3025
Illinois State	6,030	2,648	100	99	19:1	62	53(A)	73	309-438-2181
Illinois Wesleyan	11,115	3,695	N.A.	N.A.	13:1	78	100(A)	100	309-556-3031
Incarnate Word (Texas) 58	7,200	3,600	85	605	15:1	70	N.A.	88	512-829-6005
Indiana State	5,490	3,211	43	423	14:1	45	10(S)	67	812-237-2121
Indiana U. Bloomington	7,758	3,370	100	294	18:1	59	36(S)	99	812-855-0661
Indiana U. of Pennsylvania	4,645[4]	2,476	89	279	19:1	75	32(S)	93	412-357-2230
Iona (N.Y.)	8,970	4,760[3]	83	3,467	20:1	60	11(S)	N.A.	914-633-2502
Iowa State Science and Technology 55	6,406	2,720	N.A.	N.A.	18:1	62	86(A)[2]	96	515-294-5836
Iowa Wesleyan	7,800	3,000	100	2,242	14:1	45	23(A)	53	319-385-6231
Ithaca (N.Y.)	11,946	5,104	90	4,636	13:1	67	56(S)	86	607-274-3124
Jackson State (Miss.)	2,968[10]	2,620	N.A.	N.A.	28:1	N.A.	14(A)	72	601-968-2100
Jacksonville (Fla.)	8,450	3,880	N.A.	N.A.	17:1	60	N.A.	82	904-744-3950
Jacksonville State (Ala.)	2,130	2,350	N.A.	N.A.	26:1	60	23(A)	N.A.	205-782-5000
James Madison (Va.) 38	6,650	4,102	70	16	18:1	76	56(S)	97	703-568-6147
Jamestown (N.D.)	6,670	2,980	100	5,504	17:1	45	68(A)	73	701-252-3467
Jersey City State (N.J.)	3,203	4,650	100	0	16:1	60	10(S)	71	201-547-3234
John Carroll (Ohio) 84	9,280	5,050	90	3,874	14:1	75	75(A)	89	216-397-4294
Johns Hopkins (Md.) 25	16,000	6,120	100	6,943	11:1	87	95(S)	98	301-338-8171
Johnson C. Smith (N.C.)[8]	5,876	2,158	80	361	15:1	35	2(S)	47	704-378-1010
Johnson State (Vt.)	6,954	4,290	73	115	16:1	33	16(S)	50	802-635-2356
Juniata (Pa.)	12,470	3,690	96	4,486	14:1	70	43(S)	97	814-643-4310
Kalamazoo (Mich.)	12,669	4,053	100	4,827	12:1	70	98(A)[2]	98	616-383-8408
Kansas State[6]	5,376	2,640	90	447	10:1	55	57(A)	87	913-532-6250
Kean College (N.J.)	3,000	3,275	80	84	18:1	40	34(S)	71	908-527-2195

Footnotes are on page 188.

Doors to Diversity

SCHOOLS FROM MONEY'S TOP 100 WITH
THE LARGEST PERCENTAGE MINORITY
ENROLLMENTS, EXCLUDING
HISTORICALLY BLACK COLLEGES

UC Berkeley	**52%**
UCLA	**52**
Incarnate Word College	**51**
Stanford University	**37**
MIT	**36**
Columbia University	**29**
Kentucky Wesleyan University	**29**
Pomona College	**29**
Rutgers College	**29**
Claremont McKenna College	**28**

College name and location	Tuition and fees	Room and board	% of need met	Avg. grant per student with need	Student/ faculty ratio	% who graduate in five years	% with high test scores	% from top half of class	Telephone
Keene State (N.H.)	$6,575	$3,612	99	$874	19:1	53	20(S)	78	603-358-2276
Kendall (III.)	7,005	4,473	76	226	15:1	35	20(A)	65	708-866-1305
Kent State (Ohio)	6,570	3,188	80	N.A.	21:1	40	41(A)	74	216-672-2444
Kentucky State	3,986	2,468[3]	94	467	13:1	22	15(A)	64	502-227-6813
Kentucky Wesleyan 59	6,690	3,760	97	353	11:1	58	80(A)	95	502-926-3111
Kenyon (Ohio)	16,050	3,375	93	8,122	11:1	84	82(S)	99	614-427-5776
Keuka (N.Y.)	8,120	3,850	95	N.A.	12:1	60	17(S)	86	315-536-4411
King's (N.Y.)	8,310	3,820	90	2,873	10:1	45	22(S)	79	914-944-5653
King's (Pa.)	8,740	4,120	90	2,231	17:1	68	32(S)	81	717-826-5858
Knox (III.)	12,609	3,675	100	5,529	13:1[11]	74	92(A)	96	309-343-0112
Knoxville (Tenn.)[6,8]	5,270	3,600	100	N.A.	17:1	40	N.A.	60	615-524-6525
Kutztown U. of Pennsylvania	4,514[4]	2,548	80	N.A.	19:1	55	20(S)	79	215-683-4060
La Salle (Pa.)	10,300	4,500	80	N.A.	15:1	82	71(S)	93	215-951-1500
Lafayette (Pa.)	15,475	4,900	99	8,008	12:1	88	75(S)	99	215-250-5100
LaGrange (Ga.)	5,601	3,165	72	1,157	12:1	55	26(S)	N.A.	404-882-2911
Lake Erie (Ohio)	7,840[4]	3,900	N.A.	N.A.	14:1	65	43(A)	75	216-352-1561
Lake Forest (III.)	13,895	3,155	100	6,561	11:1	73	62(S)	86	708-234-3100
Lake Superior State (Mich.)	4,932	3,625	90	266	19:1	47	40(A)	N.A.	906-635-2613
Lamar U.–Beaumont (Texas)	4,020[4]	2,500	90	304	24:1	19	15(S)	73	409-880-8353
Lambuth (Tenn.)	4,630	3,000	100	1,644	14:1	43	40(A)	68	901-425-3223
Lander (S.C.)	3,740	2,480	72	131	14:1	45	N.A.	80	803-229-8307
Lane (Tenn.)[8]	4,357	2,473	97	N.A.	16:1	35	3(A)	45	901-424-4600
Langston (Okla.)	3,271	2,420	N.A.	N.A.	25:1	44	N.A.	48	405-466-2231
Lawrence (Wis.)	14,685	3,363	100	8,186	11:1	70	92(A)[2]	97	414-832-6500
Lawrence Technological (Mich.)	5,679	2,088	80	463	19:1	N.A.	54(A)[2]	91	313-356-0200
Le Moyne (N.Y.) 97	9,190	4,020	95	2,132	15:1	74	37(S)	90	315-445-4300
Lebanon Valley (Pa.)	11,750	4,325	90	3,101	11:1	75	25(S)	70	717-867-6181
Lees-McRae (N.C.)	6,148	3,102	86	1,028	15:1	N.A.	3(S)	36	704-898-6698
Lehigh (Pa.)	15,650	5,140	98	7,498	13:1	83	68(S)	98	215-758-3100
LeMoyne–Owen (Tenn.)[6,8]	3,650	No dorms	76	N.A.	13:1	60	N.A.	55	901-942-7302
Lenoir-Rhyne (N.C.) 79	8,239	3,326	98	1,594	12:1	62	25(S)	95	704-328-7300
Lesley (Mass.)[1]	10,750	4,862	90	4,110	15:1	45[5]	22(S)	46	617-349-8800
Lewis (III.)	8,502	3,620[3]	98	2,000	16:1	42	55(A)[2]	52	815-838-0500
Lewis and Clark (Ore.)	13,470	4,328[3]	99.5	6,247	14:1	65	56(S)	92	503-768-7040
Lewis-Clark State (Idaho)	3,224	2,432[3]	80	202	16:1	30	29(A)	N.A.	208-799-2210
Lincoln (Mo.)[6]	2,956	2,728[3]	80	N.A.	20:1	N.A.	6(A)	N.A.	314-681-5022
Lincoln (Pa.)[8]	3,760[4]	2,715	100	1,727	14:1	60	4(S)	56	215-932-8300
Lincoln Memorial (Tenn.)	4,780	2,430[3]	85	N.A.	18:1	43	62(A)[2]	80	615-869-3611
Lindsey Wilson (Ky.)	5,168	3,332	80	1,635	18:1	32	30(A)	65	502-384-2126

Footnotes are on page 188.

College name and location	Tuition and fees	Room and board	% of need met	Avg. grant per student with need	Student/ faculty ratio	% who graduate in five years	% with high test scores	% from top half of class	Telephone
Linfield (Ore.)	$11,250	$3,500	95	$4,047	13:1	56	47(S)	93	503-472-4121
Livingston College–Rutgers U. (N.J.)	7,059	4,018	85	N.A.	17:1	28	30(S)	93	908-932-3770
Lock Haven U. of Pennsylvania	5,155[10]	3,144	96	105	18:1	60	26(S)	90	717-893-2027
Long Island U.–Brooklyn (N.Y.)	7,504	3,310[3]	82	1,018	18:1	36	45(S)	30	718-403-1011
Long Island U.–C. W. Post (N.Y.)	10,010	4,500	80	1,669	12:1	53	N.A.	75	516-299-2413
Long Island U.–Southampton (N.Y.)	10,050	4,420[3]	70	4,255	17:1	47	30(S)	75	516-283-4000
Longwood (Va.)	6,790	3,404[3]	90	0	19:1	49	25(S)	82	804-395-2060
Loras (Iowa)	9,115	3,110[3]	100	2,638	13:1	55	55(A)	60	319-588-7235
Louisiana State and A&M	5,243	2,050[3]	80	245	19:1	41	75(A)[2]	N.A.	504-388-1175
Louisiana State–Shreveport[6]	3,690	No dorms	N.A.	N.A.	19:1	8	26(A)	N.A.	318-797-5249
Louisiana Tech[6]	2,996	2,015	98	612	23:1	40	51(A)[2]	80	318-257-3036
Loyola (Md.)	10,670	5,400[3]	97	3,886	16:1	70	62(S)	86	301-532-5012
Loyola Marymount (Calif.)	11,441	5,400	88	2,536	16:1	68	44(S)	94	213-338-2750
Loyola U. of Chicago (Ill.)	9,400	4,000[3]	96	1,236	10:1	60	75(A)	90	312-915-6500
Loyola U. of New Orleans (La.)	9,350	4,670[3]	95	3,927	15:1	N.A.	89(A)	74	504-865-3240
Luther (Iowa)	10,600	3,300	97	3,265	13:1	77	83(A)[2]	91	319-387-1287
Lycoming (Pa.)	11,200	3,980	94	4,152	14:1	65	27(S)	74	717-321-4026
Lynchburg (Va.)	10,330	5,050	94	5,108	12:1[11]	58	17(S)	63	804-522-8300
Lyndon State (Vt.)	6,510	4,086	65	777	17:1	45	4(S)	60	802-626-9371
Macalester (Minn.)	13,331	3,970	100	6,528	12:1	70	88(S)	98	612-696-6357
MacMurray (Ill.) 95	8,150	3,350	96	2,213	13:1	62	44(A)	80	217-479-7056
Manchester (Ind.)	8,270	3,246	98	2,810	14:1	50	23(S)	89	219-982-5055
Manhattan (N.Y.)	11,000	5,800	93	3,636	14:1	61	38(S)	65	212-920-0200
Manhattanville (N.Y.)	12,840	5,600	92	6,043	12:1	75	40(S)	88	914-694-2200
Mankato State (Minn.)	3,755	2,181[3]	90	N.A.	20:1	50	81(A)[2]	67	507-389-1822
Mansfield U. of Pennsylvania	4,641[4]	2,490	90	100	18:1	73	12(S)	70	717-662-4243
Marian (Ind.)	7,584	3,104	91	1,339	13:1	70	13(S)	75	317-929-0321
Marian College Fond du Lac (Wis.)	7,520	2,950[3]	78	1,591	15:1	63	30(A)	70	414-923-7650
Marietta (Ohio)	11,800	3,460	98	6,317	13:1	67	31(S)	75	614-374-4600
Marist (N.Y.)	9,280	5,210	90	1,474	19:1	61	35(S)	77	914-575-3000
Marlboro (Vt.)	15,420	5,150	99	6,683	7:1	55	N.A.	85	802-257-4333
Marquette (Wis.)	9,034	4,000	85	3,025	13:1	70	93(A)[2]	91	414-288-7302
Mars Hill (N.C.)	6,650	3,250[3]	87	1,244	13:1	43	19(S)	67	704-689-1201
Mary Baldwin (Va.)[1]	9,165	6,175	100	3,586	11:1	53	29(S)	69	703-887-7019
Mary Washington (Va.) 23	6,076	4,250	50	99	17:1	66	68(S)	97	703-899-4681
Marymount (N.Y.)	10,200	5,750	85	2,718	12:1	60	N.A.	69	914-332-8295
Marymount (Va.)	9,707	4,650	100	4,135	14:1	40	N.A.	59	703-284-1500
Maryville (Tenn.)	8,400	3,595[3]	100	3,940	13:1	35	25(S)	85	615-982-6412
Marywood (Pa.)	9,020	3,800	90	1,970	11:1	63	28(S)	74	717-348-6234
Massachusetts Inst. of Technology 98	16,900	3,950	100	5,405	4:1	87	92(S)	100	617-253-4791
Mayville State (N.D.)[6]	4,305	2,196[3]	100	261	15:1	45	30(A)	44	701-786-4873
McKendree (Ill.)	6,746	3,290[3]	95	716	15:1	65	36(A)	71	618-537-4481
McMurry (Texas)	5,000	2,880[3]	85	757	15:1	27	43(A)[2]	79	915-691-6226
McNeese State (La.)[6]	3,186	1,640[3]	54	49	26:1	50	20(A)	N.A.	318-475-5145
McPherson (Kans.)	7,270	3,230	80	1,707	10:1	30	50(A)[2]	70	316-241-0731
Memphis State (Tenn.)	5,502	1,155[3]	60	187	18:1	30	64(A)[2]	N.A.	901-678-2101
Menlo (Calif.)	12,390	6,030[3]	95	7,941	10:1	65	9(S)	N.A.	415-688-3753
Mercer (Ga.)	9,450	3,780	90	4,945	17:1	42	N.A.	77	912-752-2021
Mercyhurst (Pa.)	8,700	3,175	65	1,995	17:1	63	36(S)	63	814-825-0241
Meredith (N.C.)[1]	5,720	2,820	100	754	17:1	59	25(S)	93	919-829-8581
Merrimack (Mass.)	10,350	5,700	95	3,274	17:1	72	N.A.	74	508-837-5120
Mesa State (Colo.)	4,322	2,932	100	41	23:1	40	38(A)	70	303-248-1376
Methodist (N.C.)	7,700	3,100	71	153	16:1	40[5]	14(S)	85	919-488-7110
Metropolitan State (Colo.)	4,915	N.A.	80	752	20:1	N.A.	31(A)	53	303-556-3977
Miami (Ohio) 65	8,054	3,360	76	489	21:1	73	94(A)[2]	99	513-529-2531
Michigan State 76	8,723	3,405	95	619	18:1	67	73(A)	94	517-355-8332

Footnotes are on page 188.

Comfort Zones

TOP-RANKED MID-SIZE SCHOOLS
(1,600 TO 4,000 UNDERGRADUATES)

Rice University	**2,694[1]**
Spelman College	**1,708**
Trinity University (Texas)	**2,332**
Mary Washington College	**3,395**
Johns Hopkins University	**3,042**
Wake Forest University	**3,533**
Samford University	**3,161**
Bellarmine College	**2,054**
Florida Southern College	**1,717**
Washington and Lee University	**1,647**

[1]Undergraduate enrollment

College name and location	Tuition and fees	Room and board	% of need met	Avg. grant per student with need	Student/ faculty ratio	% who graduate in five years	% with high test scores	% from top half of class	Telephone
Michigan Technological 34	$6,555	$3,390	85	$318	14:1	60	90(A)	96	906-487-2335
Middle Tennessee State	4,820	1,994	70	284	21:1[11]	40	31(A)	100	615-898-2300
Middlebury (Vt.)	21,200[9]	N.A.	100	N.A.	11:1	92	N.A.	95	802-388-3711
Midland Lutheran (Neb.)	8,110	2,550	94	3,126	13:1	46	51(A)	82	402-721-5480
Midway (Ky.)[1]	5,820	3,550	76	1,275	10:1	38	N.A.	99	606-846-4221
Midwestern State (Texas)	3,508	2,830	100	71	19:1	71	14(S)	62	817-692-6611
Miles (Ala.)[6,8]	3,760	2,300	N.A.	N.A.	13:1	76	33(A)	27	205-923-2771
Millersville U. of Pennsylvania	4,670[4]	3,080	80	345	19:1	64	36(S)	90	717-872-3371
Millikin (Ill.)	10,081	3,784	100	3,414	14:1	60	81(A)[2]	86	217-424-6210
Mills (Calif.)[1]	13,400	5,700	100	6,864	8:1	60	N.A.	92	415-430-2135
Millsaps (Miss.)	9,710	3,635	93	4,252	14:1	65	97(A)[2]	88	601-974-1050
Milwaukee School of Eng. (Wis.)	9,150	2,925	90	N.A.	17:1	50	85(A)[2]	94	414-277-7200
Minot State (N.D.)[6]	4,251	1,878	76	304	19:1	40	N.A.	N.A.	701-857-3340
Misericordia (Pa.)	8,250	4,800[3]	90	656	13:1	80	15(S)	73	717-674-6460
Mississippi State	3,685	2,800[3]	100	N.A.	13:1	48	58(A)	90	601-325-2323
Mississippi U. for Women	3,515	2,022[3]	95	1,022	16:1	44	69(A)[2]	35	601-329-7106
Missouri Southern State	2,590	2,340	100	136	21:1	39	44(A)[2]	54	417-625-9300
Missouri Valley	8,178	4,656	80	3,273	17:1	53	18(A)	79	816-886-6924
Missouri Western State[6]	3,112	2,154[3]	85	64	19:1	40	34(A)	65	816-271-4267
Molloy (N.Y.)	8,100	N.A.	85	520	11:1	60	16(S)	76	516-678-5000
Monmouth (Ill.)	12,450	3,350	100	3,778	10:1	68	84(A)	80	309-457-2131
Monmouth (N.J.)	10,530	4,590	95	3,114	15:1	53	14(S)	70	908-571-3456
Montana Mineral Science and Technology	3,900	3,340	100	387	15:1	40	55(A)[2]	85	406-496-4178
Montana State	3,994	3,058	95	63	18:1	68	56(A)	74	406-994-2452
Montclair State (N.J.)	3,688	4,248[3]	65	19	16:1	57	25(S)	97	201-893-4444
Moore of Art and Design (Pa.)[1]	11,970	4,600	66	3,406	10:1	80	29(S)	95	215-568-4515
Moorhead State (Minn.)	3,755	2,583	92	182	20:1	42	63(A)[2]	88	218-236-2161
Moravian (Pa.)	12,698	4,044	98	5,380	14:1	65	40(S)	91	215-861-1320
Morehead State (Ky.)	4,080	2,700	95	285	20:1	24	31(A)[2]	N.A.	606-783-2000
Morehouse (Ga.)[8,12]	6,692	4,734	75	N.A.	16:1	38	33(S)	99	404-681-2800
Morningside (Iowa)	9,206	2,980	99	2,764	16:1	52	58(A)	68	712-274-5111
Morris (S.C.)[6,8]	3,939	2,387	91	272	13:1	40	N.A.	41	803-775-9371
Morris Brown (Ga.)[8]	10,350	3,800	75	158	15:1	38	N.A.	N.A.	404-220-0309
Mount Holyoke (Mass.)[1]	16,050	4,900	100	10,298	9:1	80	77(S)	97	413-538-2023
Mount Marty (S.D.)	6,790	2,705	87	2,794	12:1	55	65(A)[2]	85	800-658-4552
Mount Mary (Wis.)[1]	6,950	2,447	98	1,317	11:1	50	N.A.	66	414-259-9220
Mount Mercy (Iowa)	7,750	3,060	90	704	15:1	50	50(A)	81	319-363-8213
Mount Senario (Wis.)	6,340	2,625	90	509	12:1	46	23(A)	N.A.	715-532-5511
Mount St. Clare (Iowa)	7,325	3,780	87	1,795	10:1	38	32(A)	52	319-242-4023

Footnotes are on page 188.

College name and location	Tuition and fees	Room and board	% of need met	Avg. grant per student with need	Student/ faculty ratio	% who graduate in five years	% with high test scores	% from top half of class	Telephone
Mount St. Mary (N.Y.)	$7,310	$4,300	80	$2,413	14:1	68	16(S)	72	914-561-0800
Mount St. Mary's (Calif.)	10,310	4,650	90	2,964	11:1	48	46(S)	97	213-471-9516
Mount St. Mary's (Md.)	9,875	5,700	80	1,636	16:1	72	27(S)	64	301-447-5214
Mount Union (Ohio)	11,322	3,280[3]	95	5,104	16:1	65	71(A)	90	216-821-5320
Mount Vernon (D.C.)[1]	12,610	6,090	N.A.	N.A.	13:1	40	N.A.	75	202-331-3444
Muhlenberg (Pa.)	15,115	4,165	96	7,076	12:1	76	57(S)	95	215-821-3200
Murray State (Ky.)	4,120	2,395	90	727	20:1	55	45(A)	48	502-762-3380
Muskingum (Ohio)	11,855	3,380[3]	92	6,174	15:1	65	62(A)[2]	77	614-826-8137
Nazareth College of Rochester (N.Y.)	9,080	4,246[3]	100	3,352	14:1	69	59(S)	73	716-586-2525
Nebraska Wesleyan	8,282	2,870[3]	80	2,696	13:1	42	76(A)[2]	84	402-465-2218
New College of the U. of South Florida 2	6,690	3,375	95	1,383	10:1	47	91(S)	100	813-355-2963
New England (N.H.)	11,290	4,700	95	1,990	14:1	50	9(S)	N.A.	603-428-2223
New Hampshire College	10,008	4,635	97	1,710	22:1	58[5]	N.A.	55	603-645-9611
New Jersey Inst. of Technology	8,358	5,120[3]	92	35	15:1	50	33(S)	94	201-596-3300
New Mexico Highlands[6]	4,488	1,880[3]	85	341	17:1	20	37(A)[2]	N.A.	505-454-3424
New Mexico Inst. of Mining and Tech 15	5,084	2,720[3]	97	420	11:1	55	90(A)[2]	71	505-835-5424
New Mexico State	5,290	2,346[3]	90	462	19:1	38	51(A)[2]	N.A.	505-646-3121
New York Inst. of Technology	7,140	4,480	N.A.	N.A.	12:1[11]	40	15(S)	N.A.	516-686-7520
New York University (N.Y.)	15,620	6,774	93	4,078	13:1	65	87(S)	98	212-998-4500
Newberry (S.C.)	7,400	3,000	95	N.A.	13:1	42	13(S)	79	803-321-5127
Niagara (N.Y.)	9,030	3,980	99	2,060	17:1	57	N.A.	N.A.	716-285-1212
Nicholls State (La.)[6]	3,449	2,450	97	406	22:1	29	32(A)	60	504-446-8111
North Adams State (Mass.)	6,850	3,600	N.A.	N.A.	18:1	55	13(S)	65	413-664-4511
North Carolina A&T State	5,645[4]	2,334	62	63	14:1	N.A.	5(S)	58	919-334-7946
North Carolina Central	5,545[4]	2,764	N.A.	N.A.	14:1	11	2(S)	54	919-560-6298
North Carolina State 41	5,872[4]	3,030	100	152	14:1	59	42(S)	98	919-737-2434
North Carolina Wesleyan	7,160	3,540	94	1,667	18:1	35	13(S)	60	919-977-7171
North Central (Ill.)	9,960	3,735	100	3,822	15:1	60	72(A)	94	708-420-3414
North Dakota State[6]	5,370	2,085	96	193	19:1	37[5]	48(A)	85	701-237-8643
North Georgia	4,140	2,295	N.A.	N.A.	34:1	40	N.A.	N.A.	404-864-1750
North Park (Ill.)	10,625	3,905	92	2,299	12:1	50	60(A)	73	312-583-2700
Northeast Louisiana[6]	3,209	1,950	75	N.A.	20:1[11]	28	28(A)	N.A.	318-342-5252
Northeast Missouri State	3,504	2,480	N.A.	N.A.	16:1	55	98(A)	96	816-785-4114
Northeastern (Mass.)	9,968[4]	6,375	85	1,382	22:1	41	24(S)	68	617-437-2200
Northeastern State (Okla.)	3,059[10]	2,112	90	406	21:1	48	22(A)[2]	N.A.	918-456-5511
Northern Arizona	6,242	2,776	90	243	21:1	42	46(A)	83	602-523-5511
Northern Illinois	5,974[4]	2,808	N.A.	N.A.	18:1	50	62(A)	86	815-753-0446
Northern Kentucky[6]	4,010	1,320[7]	50	202	17:1	36	48(A)	N.A.	606-572-5220
Northern Michigan	4,040	3,326	100	534	20:1	43	40(A)	N.A.	906-227-2650
Northern Montana	3,105	2,988	50	149	17:1	40	27(A)	N.A.	406-265-3704
Northern State (S.D.)	3,288	1,598	100	71	19:1	41	39(A)	95	605-622-2544
Northland (Wis.)	8,320	3,450	96	2,751	15:1	42	34(S)	74	715-682-1224
Northwest Missouri State	2,880	2,645	100	393	20:1	47	44(A)	67	816-562-1562
Northwestern (Ill.)	14,370	4,827	100	6,416	8:1	86	88(S)	100	708-491-7271
Northwestern Oklahoma State	3,048	1,784	100	N.A.	20:1	N.A.	43(A)[2]	N.A.	405-327-1700
Northwestern State of Louisiana[6]	3,467	2,143[3]	N.A.	N.A.	23:1	43	24(A)	N.A.	318-357-4503
Northwood Institute (Mich.)	8,190	3,720	100	N.A.	26:1	75	17(A)	N.A.	517-631-1600
Norwich (Vt.)	12,614	4,376	79	4,296	14:1	60	27(S)	57	802-485-2001
Notre Dame College (N.H.)	8,306	4,635	86	1,435	11:1	54	19(S)	68	603-669-4298
Notre Dame of Maryland[1]	9,500	4,800	100	3,712	15:1	64	36(S)	85	301-532-5330
Oakland (Mich.)	5,880[4]	3,000	95	939	18:1	47	69(A)	95	313-370-3364
Oakland City (Ind.)	6,456	3,480	90	N.A.	15:1	58	33(A)[2]	75	812-749-1222
Oberlin (Ohio)	16,817	5,155	100	8,186	13:1	85	90(S)	100	216-775-8411
Occidental (Calif.)	14,784	4,943	100	7,842	12:1	72	74(S)	98	213-259-2700
Oglethorpe (Ga.)	10,250	4,000	87	4,572	8:1	59	65(S)	98	404-233-6864
Ohio Dominican	7,020	3,740	87	1,056	17:1	47	N.A.	N.A.	614-253-2741

Footnotes are on page 188.

In Search of... Women

COED LIBERAL ARTS COLLEGES WITH
THE HIGHEST PERCENTAGE OF WOMEN

Villa Julie College	**85%**
Molloy College	**83**
College of Mount St. Vincent	**81**
Marywood College	**79**
Marymount University (Va.)	**78**
Notre Dame College (N.H.)	**78**
Dominican College of San Ráfael	**77**
Goucher College	**77**
Wheaton College	**77**
Queens College (N.C.)	**75**

College name and location	Tuition and fees	Room and board	% of need met	Avg. grant per student with need	Student/ faculty ratio	% who graduate in five years	% with high test scores	% from top half of class	Telephone
Ohio Northern	$12,255	$3,390	93	$4,554	13:1	57	76(A)	91	419-772-2260
Ohio State	6,942[4]	3,636	95	711	15:1	55	60(A)	85	614-292-3980
Ohio U. 24	5,805[4]	3,474	82	580	21:1	76	88(A)	95	614-593-4100
Ohio Wesleyan	13,610	4,884	100	7,297	14:1	74	59(S)	88	614-368-3024
Oklahoma City	5,425	3,520	90	1,147	20:1	55	65(A)[2]	78	405-521-5050
Oklahoma State	4,701	2,678	75	N.A.	22:1	44	73(A)[2]	86	405-744-6876
Old Dominion (Va.)	6,864	4,052	72	962	17:1	40	22(S)	90	804-683-3637
Olivet (Mich.)	7,890	2,860	N.A.	N.A.	15:1	38	19(A)	N.A.	616-749-7635
Oregon Inst. of Technology	4,301	3,315	N.A.	N.A.	16:1	60	20(S)	N.A.	503-885-1150
Oregon State	5,637	2,810	N.A.	N.A.	7:1	44	29(S)	N.A.	503-737-4411
Ottawa (Kans.)	6,450	2,998	90	N.A.	17:1	19	34(A)	64	913-242-5200
Otterbein (Ohio)	10,800	3,912	100	3,372	13:1	64	74(A)[2]	90	614-890-0004
Our Lady of the Lake (Texas)	6,586	3,130	N.A.	N.A.	17:1	39	16(S)	85	512-434-6711
Pacific (Ore.)	11,334	3,175	100	4,349	14:1	52	31(S)	95	503-357-6151
Pacific Lutheran (Wash.)	11,075	3,890	N.A.	N.A.	14:1	64	55(S)	97	206-535-7151
Park (Mo.)	6,860	3,300	98	N.A.	12:1	43	40(A)	65	816-741-2000
Pembroke State (N.C.)	5,388	4,020	N.A.	N.A.	15:1[11]	44	7(S)	73	919-521-4214
Penn State–The Behrend College	8,444[4]	3,510	N.A.	N.A.	17:1	59	23(S)	94	814-898-6100
Penn State–University Park	9,188	3,670	N.A.	N.A.	19:1	59	54(S)	96	814-865-5471
Pepperdine (Calif.)	15,290	6,070	73	N.A.	13:1	N.A.	69(S)	98	213-456-4392
Pfeiffer (N.C.)	6,620[4]	2,960	N.A.	N.A.	15:1	42	10(S)	62	704-463-1360
Philadelphia Textiles & Science (Pa.)	9,736	4,500	75	3,022	16:1	65	30(S)	76	215-951-2800
Phillips (Okla.)	8,530	2,770	85	3,062	13:1	N.A.	63(A)	85	405-237-4433
Pikeville (Ky.)[6]	4,000	2,400	79	829	16:1	40	26(A)	70	606-432-9322
Pine Manor (Mass.)[1]	14,052	5,700	90	8,450	13:1	60	10(S)	20	617-731-7104
Pittsburg State (Kans.)	3,964	2,600	85	140	17:1	22	31(A)[2]	53	316-235-4252
Pitzer (Calif.)	16,192	4,860	100	8,757	10:1	73	65(S)	99	714-621-8129
Plymouth State–U.of N.H.	6,593	3,620	99	901	19:1	43	12(S)	70	603-535-5000
Polytechnic U.–Brooklyn (N.Y.)	13,700	1,605	85	8,745	14:1	66	26(S)	93	718-260-3100
Pomona (Calif.) 45	14,930	6,150	100	8,954	10:1	90	95(S)	100	714-621-8134
Portland State (Ore.)	5,676[4]	3,709	71	150	18:1	N.A.	25(S)	N.A.	503-725-3511
Prairie View A&M (Texas)	4,388	3,150	66	80	19:1	65	12(S)	80	409-857-2618
Pratt Institute (N.Y.)	11,406	5,600	70	4,286	12:1	65	23(S)	76	718-636-3669
Presbyterian (S.C.)	10,326	3,184	92	4,317	15:1	67	54(S)	95	803-833-2820
Princeton (N.J.) 20	16570	5,311	100	7,077	5:1	95	96(S)	100	609-258-3060
Providence (R.I.)	11,840	5,300	98	4,713	16:1	84	51(S)	83	401-865-2535
Purdue (Ind.) 49	7,440	3,300	95	897	18:1	69	52(S)	94	317-494-1776
Queens (N.C.)	9,300	4,400	95	5,674	12:1	56	N.A.	93	704-337-2212
Queens College–City U. of N.Y.	4,630	No dorms	85	N.A.	10:1	42	N.A.	72	718-997-5600

Footnotes are on page 188.

College name and location	Tuition and fees	Room and board	% of need met	Avg. grant per student with need	Student/ faculty ratio	% who graduate in five years	% with high test scores	% from top half of class	Telephone
Quincy (Ill.)	$8,604	$3,440	99	$3,279	15:1	62	85(A)[2]	87	217-222-8020
Quinnipiac (Conn.)	10,350	4,990	100	2,202	15:1	64	15(S)	67	203-281-8600
Radford (Va.)	5,584	3,718	N.A.	N.A.	22:1	75	15(S)	84	703-831-5371
Ramapo College of New Jersey	3,200	3,950	N.A.	N.A.	24:1	57	45(S)	72	201-529-7600
Randolph-Macon (Va.)	10,810	4,600	90	3,318	11:1	65	44(S)	80	804-752-7305
Randolph-Macon Woman's (Va.)[1]	11,780	5,140	100	5,754	8:1	68	48(S)	83	804-846-7392
Reed (Ore.)	16,700	4,640	100	7,142	12:1	54	87(S)	97	503-777-7511
Regis (Colo.)	10,790	4,500	N.A.	N.A.	16:1	50	67(A)	60	303-458-4900
Regis (Mass.)[1]	10,550	5,200	96	3,108	11:1	69	20(S)	77	617-893-1820
Rensselaer Polytechnic Inst. (N.Y.)	15,625	5,960	100	7,223	11:1	72	70(S)	98	518-276-6216
Rhode Island College	5,604	4,660	100	1,202	17:1	50	17(S)	70	401-456-8234
Rhode Island School of Design	14,121	5,892	15	2,273	12:1	75	17(S)	87	401-331-3511
Rhodes (Tenn.)	12,958	4,516	100	5,680	11:1[11]	68	84(S)	96	901-726-3700
Rice (Texas) 1	8,018	4,900	100	5,073	9:1	88	93(S)	100	713-527-4036
Rider (N.J.)	10,060	4,330	N.A.	N.A.	16:1	65	15(S)	66	609-896-5042
Ripon (Wis.)	12,900	4,150	100	6,455	11:1	75	81(A)	84	414-748-8185
Rivier (N.H.)	8,750	4,310	99	1,637	12:1	75	28(S)	68	603-888-1311
Roanoke (Va.)	11,250	4,000	100	4,289	14:1	50	33(S)	75	703-375-2270
Robert Morris (Pa.)	5,640	3,500	83	985	23:1	57	8(S)	62	412-262-8463
Rochester Inst. of Technology (N.Y.)	12,018	5,100	100	2,601	12:1	53	39(S)	74	716-475-6631
Rockhurst (Mo.)	8,380	3,610	70	4,943	20:1	48	58(A)	84	816-926-4100
Rocky Mountain (Mont.)	7,212	3,000	78	2,110	15:1	51	43(A)	67	406-657-1026
Roger Williams (R.I.)	10,560	5,120	85	1,897	20:1	47	14(S)	48	401-254-3500
Rollins (Fla.)	13,900	4,195[3]	96	6,720	12:1	72	62(S)	87	407-646-2161
Rosary (Ill.)	9,226	4,036	N.A.	N.A.	11:1	50	N.A.	80	708-366-2490
Rose-Hulman Inst. of Technology (Ind.)[12]	10,935	3,627	76	2,247	12:1	72	66(S)	100	812-877-1511
Rosemont (Pa.)[1] 70	9,445	5,400	95	2,245	10:1	70	37(S)	60	215-525-6420
Rust (Miss.)[8]	4,152	1,948	95	254	17:1	50	5(A)	N.A.	601-252-4661
Rutgers College–Rutgers U. (N.J.) 33	7,070	4,018	89	N.A.	17:1	60	62(S)	93	908-932-3770
Sacred Heart (Conn.)	9,020	3,510	N.A.	N.A.	14:1	75	15(S)	50	203-371-7880
The Sage Colleges (N.Y.)[1]	10,470	4,240	90	2,923	9:1	78	31(S)	90	518-270-2217
Salem (N.C.)[1]	9,075	5,600	N.A.	4,170	8:1	53	39(S)	85	919-721-2621
Salem State (Mass.)	5,770	3,574[3]	90	0	19:1	60	12(S)	40	508-741-6200
Salem-Teikyo (W.Va.)	6,280	3,840	N.A.	N.A.	13:1	50	32(S)	71	304-782-5336
Salisbury State (Md.)	4,598	3,990	65	85	16:1	50	38(S)	90	301-543-6161
Salve Regina (R.I.)	11,950	5,500	93	3,044	19:1	75	N.A.	N.A.	401-847-6650
Sam Houston State (Texas)	4,120[10]	2,730	N.A.	N.A.	24:1	30	38(A)	76	409-294-1056
Samford (Ala.) 40	6,540	3,354	85	2,472	15:1	65	70(A)	95	205-870-2901
San Diego State (Calif.)	8,990	4,436	65	0	12:1	42	16(S)	N.A.	619-594-5384
San Francisco State (Calif.)	4,992	4,192	90	0	20:1	23	16(S)	N.A.	415-338-2163
San Jose State (Calif.)	8,564	4,244	98	0	16:1	25	13(S)	N.A.	408-924-2000
Sarah Lawrence (N.Y.)	16,750	6,400	100	8,837	6:1	80	81(S)	84	914-395-2510
Savannah State (Ga.)	4,215	2,145	N.A.	N.A.	16:1	54	19(S)	60	912-356-2181
Schreiner (Texas)	7,350	5,965	90	3,233	13:1	45	15(S)	71	512-896-5411
Scripps (Calif.)[1]	14,800	6,650	100	10,152	9:1	75	85(S)	98	714-621-8149
Seattle Pacific (Wash.)	10,500	3,969	100	4,477	16:1	34	42(S)	N.A.	206-281-2021
Seattle U. (Wash.)	10,710	4,300	N.A.	N.A.	14:1	52	33(S)	86	206-296-5800
Seton Hall (N.J.)	10,950	5,622	75	3,009	17:1	80	28(S)	78	201-761-9332
Seton Hill (Pa.)	9,000	3,700	92	2,730	13:1	75	32(S)	81	412-838-4255
Shawnee State (Ohio)[6]	4,465	1,565	N.A.	N.A.	13:1	40	17(A)	60	614-354-3205
Sheldon Jackson (Alaska)[6]	5,960	4,215	85	2,488	9:1	15	N.A.	N.A.	907-747-5221
Shenandoah (Va.) 77	7,800	3,500	75	1,890	7:1	60	16(S)	N.A.	703-665-4581
Shepherd (W.Va.)	4,314	3,320	95	283	18:1	67	68(S)	N.A.	304-876-2511
Shippensburg U. of Pennsylvania	4,728[4]	2,594	95	N.A.	20:1	64	26(S)	87	717-532-1231
Siena (N.Y.)	9,060	4,465	83	1,834	16:1	74	49(S)	95	518-783-2423
Sierra Nevada (Nev.)	6,750	2,200[7]	70	N.A.	15:1	34	35(S)	58	702-831-1314

Footnotes are on page 188.

Top 10 Black Colleges

HISTORICALLY BLACK SCHOOLS
THAT SCORED HIGHEST ON MONEY'S
VALUE RANKINGS

Spelman College
Fisk University
Howard University
Barber-Scotia College
LeMoyne-Owen College
Benedict College
Tuskegee University
Morehouse College
Clark Atlanta University
Hampton University

College name and location	Tuition and fees	Room and board	% of need met	Avg. grant per student with need	Student/ faculty ratio	% who graduate in five years	% with high test scores	% from top half of class	Telephone
Simmons (Mass.)[1]	$14,074	$6,000	100	$6,862	10:1	70	N.A.	84	617-738-2107
Simpson (Iowa)	8,900	3,375	93	5,311	14:1	56	94(A)[2]	93	515-961-1624
Sioux Falls (S.D.)	7,496	2,941	92	2,408	15:1	63	56(A)	65	605-331-6600
Skidmore (N.Y.)	16,000	5,090	100	7,509	11:1	93	72(S)	95	518-587-7569
Slippery Rock U. of Pennsylvania	4,702[4]	2,794	95	64	19:1	46	N.A.	97	412-738-2116
Smith (Mass.)[1]	15,770	6,100	100	9,353	9:1	84	85(S)	99	413-585-2500
Sonoma State (Calif.)	8,128	4,332	80	571	17:1	22	27(S)	N.A.	707-664-2778
South Carolina State	4,030	2,386	N.A.	N.A.	15:1[11]	21	8(S)	64	803-536-7185
South Dakota State	3,629	1,986	99	265	17:1	55	57(A)	76	605-688-4121
Southeast Missouri State	3,035	2,300	80	N.A.	17:1[11]	40	44(A)[2]	68	314-651-2255
Southeastern Louisiana[6]	3,503	2,280	N.A.	N.A.	25:1	35	17(A)	N.A.	504-549-2123
Southeastern Massachusetts	7,221	4,138[3]	100	220	14:1	50	22(S)	95	508-999-8605
Southeastern Oklahoma State	2,608	1,960	75	422	19:1	35	35(A)[2]	26	405-924-0121
Southern Arkansas[6]	1,940	3,100	100	462	18:1	41	28(A)	84	501-235-4012
Southern College of Technology (Ga.)	4,257	3,215	87	0	20:1	30	13(S)	N.A.	404-528-7281
Southern Connecticut State	5,887	4,018	100	995	19:1	48	13(S)	64	203-397-4450
Southern Illinois–Carbondale	6,559	2,780	98	54	17:1	43	48(A)[2]	68	618-453-4381
Southern Illinois–Edwardsville	6,712	2,349	90	84	16:1	N.A.	44(A)	77	618-692-2010
Southern Methodist (Texas)	11,768	4,832	N.A.	N.A.	14:1	68	94(A)	89	214-692-2058
Southern Oregon State	5,847[10]	3,100	80	100	18:1	37	N.A.	N.A.	503-552-6411
Southern Utah[6]	3,777[10]	2,370	N.A.	N.A.	22:1	48	N.A.	80	801-586-7715
Southern Vermont	7,430	3,828	100	849	17:1	41	N.A.	34	802-442-5427
Southwest Missouri State	2,834[4]	2,460[3]	90	451	20:1	35	57(A)[2]	68	417-836-5517
Southwest State (Minn.)	3,375[10]	2,400[3]	97	200	19:1	40	44(A)	74	507-537-6286
Southwest Texas State	4,410[4]	2,872	N.A.	N.A.	22:1	40	12(S)	71	512-245-2364
Southwestern (Kans.)	5,050	2,810	98	1,468	12:1	51	44(A)[2]	80	316-221-4150
Southwestern (Texas) 91	9,400	4,181	100	3,280	13:1	63	66(S)	99	512-863-1200
Southwestern Oklahoma State	3,013[4]	1,530	90	53	18:1	50	30(A)[2]	80	405-774-3778
Spelman (Ga.)[1,8] 18	6,707	4,770	65	N.A.	16:1	N.A.	38(S)	97	404-681-3643
Spring Garden (Pa.)	8,060[4]	4,000	N.A.	N.A.	11:1	70	21(S)	75	215-248-7904
Spring Hill (Ala.)	10,153[10]	4,158	93	4,047	13:1	61	69(A)	71	205-460-2028
Springfield (Mass.)	9,441	4,376	N.A.	N.A.	20:1	66	16(S)	75	413-788-3136
St. Ambrose (Iowa)	8,530	3,430	100	N.A.	16:1	65	73(A)	85	319-383-8888
St. Andrews Presbyterian (N.C.)	8,875	3,920	95	2,845	14:1	58	N.A.	N.A.	919-276-3652
St. Anselm (N.H.)	10,160	5,000	90	3,539	15:1	74	43(S)	81	603-641-7500
St. Augustine's (N.C.)[8]	4,950	3,200	80	684	21:1	50	36(S)	40	919-828-4451
St. Bonaventure (N.Y.) 81	9,067	4,376	90	2,831	14:1	68	30(S)	78	716-375-2400
St. Catherine (Minn.)[1]	10,140	3,593	98	2,134	14:1	43	65(A)	82	612-690-6505
St. Cloud State (Minn.)	3,765	2,424	95	78	25:1	45	66(A)[2]	73	612-255-2244

Footnotes are on page 188.

College name and location	Tuition and fees	Room and board	% of need met	Avg. grant per student with need	Student/ faculty ratio	% who graduate in five years	% with high test scores	% from top half of class	Telephone
St. Edward's (Texas)	$7,136	$3,596	N.A.	$3,813	16:1	50	17(S)	83	512-448-8500
St. Francis (Ind.)	7,033	3,450	77	1,824	15:1	48	14(S)	75	219-434-3244
St. Francis (N.Y.)	6,230	N.A.	69	446	17:1	35	N.A.	N.A.	718-522-2300
St. Francis (Pa.)	9,596	4,490	85	N.A.	18:1	60	35(S)	62	814-472-3100
St. John Fisher (N.Y.)	9,170	4,996[3]	92	2,211	16:1	60	31(S)	91	716-385-8064
St. John's (Md.)	14,262	4,696	100	5,362	8:1	53	N.A.	87	301-263-2371
St. John's (N.M.)	14,312	4,696	98	5,737	8:1[11]	65	84(S)	75	505-982-3691
St. John's U. (N.Y.) 89	7,530	N.A.	90	881	20:1	65	N.A.	90	718-990-6161
St. John's U. (Minn.)	9,565	3,685	98	2,998	14:1	65	76(A)	75	612-363-2196
St. Joseph (Conn.)[1]	10,400	4,050[3]	90	1,308	11:1	60	N.A.	75	203-232-4571
St. Joseph's (Ind.)	8,610	3,570	100	3,069	15:1	43	17(S)	69	219-866-6170
St. Joseph's (Maine) 72	8,500	4,300	83	2,295	13:1	72	15(S)	72	207-892-6766
St. Joseph's U. (Pa.)	10,000	4,750[3]	97	3,119	16:1	75	45(S)	70	215-660-1300
St. Lawrence (N.Y.)	15,751	5,050	100	9,155	12:1	80	53(S)	N.A.	315-379-5261
St. Leo (Fla.)	8,230	3,690	71	796	17:1	65	8(S)	45	904-588-8283
St. Louis University (Mo.) 99	9,160	4,230	N.A.	N.A.	15:1	63	72(A)	84	314-658-2500
St. Mary of the Plains (Kans.)	6,410	3,000	90	1,717	11:1	35	N.A.	60	316-225-0108
St. Mary's (Ind.)[1]	10,524	4,260	100	3,757	11:1	76	37(S)	93	219-284-4587
St. Mary's of California	11,036	5,436	85	5,005	16:1	74	59(S)	99	415-631-4224
St. Mary's of Maryland 17	4,560	4,100	80	491	16:1	49	81(S)	92	800-492-7181
St. Mary's of Minnesota	9,205	3,150	100	2,949	11:1	68	43(A)	62	507-457-1700
St. Mary's U. of San Antonio (Texas)	7,188	3,400	N.A.	N.A.	18:1	64	39(A)[2]	90	512-436-3126
St. Michael's (Vt.)	11,265	5,090	N.A.	N.A.	14:1	87	44(S)	93	802-655-2017
St. Norbert (Wis.)	10,225	3,890	100	3,520	15:1	69	83(A)	87	414-337-3005
St. Olaf (Minn.)	12,080	3,345	100	4,088	12:1	79	90(A)[2]	95	507-663-3025
St. Paul's (Va.)[8]	4,806	3,180	80	251	14:1	42	N.A.	75	804-848-3984
St. Peter's (N.J.)	6,855	1,950	90	N.A.	16:1	65	14(S)	66	201-915-9213
St. Rose (N.Y.)	8,440	3,460	80	N.A.	17:1	60	29(S)	88	518-454-5150
St. Scholastica (Minn.)	9,861	3,255	100	9,509	14:1	55	74(A)[2]	86	218-723-6046
St. Thomas (Minn.)	9,938	3,160	97	1,924	15:1	65	71(A)[2]	99	612-647-5265
St. Thomas (Fla.)	7,950	4,100	92	950	15:1	41	8(S)	56	305-628-6546
St. Thomas Aquinas (N.Y.)	6,700	2,600[7]	70	500	17:1	70	11(S)	80	914-359-9500
St. Vincent (Pa.)	8,429	3,280	85	1,874	15:1	57	N.A.	79	412-537-4540
Stanford (Calif.) 88	15,401	6,160	100	11,711	10:1	87	95(S)	99	415-723-2091
State U. of N.Y.–Albany 11	6,177	3,670	96	16	17:1	70	59(S)	99	518-442-5435
State U. of N.Y.–Binghamton 7	6,043	4,388	100	16	17:1	72	66(S)	100	607-777-2728
State U. of N.Y.–Brockport	5,261	3,620	100	100	20:1	40	21(S)	91	716-395-2751
State U. of N.Y.–Buffalo 26	6,120	4,132	85	117	19:1	55	53(S)	100	716-831-2111
State U. of N.Y.–Cortland	5,750[10]	3,410	100	30	21:1	50	18(S)	86	607-753-4711
State U. of N.Y.–Fredonia	6,003	3,560	94	46	20:1	54	36(S)	97	716-673-3251
State U. of N.Y.–Geneseo 28	6,045	3,267	67	33	19:1	66	83(S)	100	716-245-5571
State U. of N.Y.–New Paltz	5,750[10]	3,720	95	31	18:1	50	31(S)	96	914-257-3200
State U. of N.Y.–Oneonta	5,986	3,800	84	42	20:1	55	N.A.	86	607-431-2524
State U. of N.Y.–Oswego	5,750[10]	3,420	87	0	21:1	55	45(S)	98	315-341-2250
State U. of N.Y.–Plattsburgh	5,965	3,416	100	176	20:1	56	39(S)	89	518-564-2040
State U. of N.Y.–Potsdam 46	5,980	2,850	90	33	19:1	58	29(S)	86	315-267-2180
State U. of N.Y.–Purchase	5,750[10]	4,060[3]	92	201	19:1	43	37(S)	75	914-251-6300
State U. of N.Y.–Stony Brook 32	6,061	3,894	100	92	15:1	52	25(S)	97	516-632-6868
State U. of N.Y. College at Buffalo	5,685	4,264	95	N.A.	22:1	40	N.A.	80	716-878-4017
Stephen F. Austin State (Texas)	4,282[10]	2,994	N.A.	N.A.	22:1	42	9(S)	70	409-568-2504
Stephens (Mo.)[1]	11,525	4,500	N.A.	N.A.	11:1	46	49(A)[2]	53	314-876-7207
Stetson (Fla.)	10,020	3,835	90	1,386	13:1	60	47(S)	97	904-822-7100
Stevens Inst. of Technology (N.J.)	15,650	4,830	97	6,043	9:1	72	70(S)	96	201-420-5194
Stockton State (N.J.)	3,096	3,750	90	300	21:1	49	33(S)	88	609-652-4261
Stonehill (Mass.)	10,290[10]	5,366	83	2,389	12:1	74	33(S)	94	508-230-1373
Suffolk (Mass.)	8,475	5,250	88	1,263	14:1	50	17(S)	65	617-573-8460

Footnotes are on page 188.

Professional Places

COLLEGES SENDING THE HIGHEST PERCENTAGE OF GRADUATES TO MEDICAL SCHOOL

Johns Hopkins University	28%
Xavier University of Louisiana	16
City College–City U. of New York	15
Albany State College (Ga.)	15
New York University	14
Washington and Jefferson College	14
Emory University	13
Willamette University	13
Illinois Benedictine College	12
Brown University	12

COLLEGES SENDING THE HIGHEST PERCENTAGE OF GRADUATES TO LAW SCHOOL

Columbia University	24%
Duke University	23
Fisk University	20
Fordham University	20
University of Michigan	19
UCLA	18
Widener University	18
Brandeis University	17
Willamette University	17
Frostburg State University	15

College name and location	Tuition and fees	Room and board	% of need met	Avg. grant per student with need	Student/ faculty ratio	% who graduate in five years	% with high test scores	% from top half of class	Telephone
Sul Ross State (Texas)[6]	$4,305	$2,860	N.A.	N.A.	17:1	20	N.A.	52	915-837-8050
Susquehanna (Pa.)	13,950	4,040	100	$6,367	14:1	78	40(S)	85	717-372-4260
Swarthmore (Pa.) 54	16,640	5,520	100	10,701	9:1	90	98(S)	100	215-328-8300
Sweet Briar (Va.)[1]	12,625	4,850	100	5,947	7:1	60	42(S)	79	804-381-6142
Syracuse (N.Y.)	12,960	5,570	85	N.A.	11:1	78	68(S)	92	315-423-3611
Tabor (Kans.)	6,800	3,200	78	1,531	16:1	37	54(A)[2]	77	316-947-3121
Talladega (Ala.)[8]	4,449	2,364	92	631	13:1	34	6(A)	59	205-362-0206
Tarleton State (Texas)	4,204[4]	2,182	N.A.	N.A.	21:1	16	48(A)	76	817-968-9125
Teikyo Westmar (Iowa)	8,397	3,339	87	2,930	14:1	44	34(A)	48	800-352-4634
Temple (Pa.)	8,696	4,681	70	992	8:1[11]	N.A.	32(S)	78	215-787-7200
Tennessee State	4,600[4]	2,342	97	N.A.	15:1	N.A.	5(A)	N.A.	615-320-3420
Tennessee Technological	6,606[10]	2,700	91	25	21:1	49	50(A)[2]	N.A.	615-372-3888
Texas A&I	4,210[10]	2,625	80	N.A.	23:1	30	21(A)	61	512-595-2315
Texas A&M 14	4,444[10]	3,560	89	846	20:1	68	40(S)	97	409-845-1031
Texas Christian	8,166	2,160[3]	98	1,086	17:1	56	N.A.	82	817-921-7490
Texas College[6,8]	3,605[4]	2,430	100	N.A.	16:1	N.A.	2(S)	50	214-593-8311
Texas Southern	4,385	3,320	80	323	16:1	38	80(A)	50	713-527-7011
Texas Tech	4,258[10]	2,881[3]	35	99	18:1	40	18(S)	81	806-742-1493
Texas Wesleyan	5,600	3,150	89	N.A.	14:1	34	42(S)	82	817-531-4422
Thiel (Pa.)	9,142	4,250	N.A.	N.A.	13:1	50	N.A.	53	412-589-2345
Thomas (Maine)	8,050	4,150	100	1,860	21:1	64	44(S)	85	207-877-0101
Thomas Aquinas (Calif.)	11,700	4,600	100	3,509	9:1	62	78(S)	81	805-525-4417
Thomas More (Ky.)	8,160	3,600	95	3,165	10:1	55	57(A)[2]	71	606-341-5800
Tougaloo (Miss.)[8]	4,620	1,690	100	N.A.	14:1	45	12(A)	75	601-977-7700
Touro (N.Y.)	6,500	4,450[7,15]	N.A.	N.A.	14:1	60	32(S)	70	212-447-0700
Towson State (Md.)	4,380	4,310	N.A.	N.A.	17:1	57	33(S)	N.A.	301-830-2112
Transylvania (Ky.)	9,619	4,048	100	4,314	12:1	62	91(A)	85	606-233-8242
Trenton State (N.J.) 3	4,400	4,750	98	545	15:1	65	65(S)	98	609-771-2131
Tri-State (Ind.)	8,298	3,600	100	2,704	15:1	30	15(S)	77	219-665-4131
Trinity (Conn.)	16,950	4,820	100	8,208	11:1	88	84(S)	98	203-297-2180
Trinity (D.C.)[1]	10,750	6,280	95	N.A.	8:1	81	N.A.	80	202-939-5040
Trinity U. (Texas) 21	10,346	4,542	100	4,966	11:1	78	82(S)	99	512-736-7207
Troy State (Ala.)	2,272	2,631	N.A.	N.A.	22:1	55	40(A)	65	205-566-8112
Tufts (Mass.)	17,179	5,300	100	6,787	14:1	90	93(S)	98	617-381-3170
Tulane (La.)	16,980	5,505	95	11,095	14:1	80	72(S)	96	504-865-5731
Tuskegee (Ala.)[8]	6,250	2,950	74	444	13:1	40	N.A.	82	205-727-8580
U. of Akron (Ohio)[6]	6,748	3,360	100	400	23:1	70	33(A)[2]	61	216-972-7077
U. of Alabama	4,800	3,288	91	319	20:1	N.A.	68(A)[2]	N.A.	205-348-5666
U. of Alaska–Fairbanks	4,410	2,880[3]	65	N.A.	14:1	N.A.	46(A)[2]	N.A.	907-474-7521

Footnotes are on page 188.

College name and location	Tuition and fees	Room and board	% of need met	Avg. grant per student with need	Student/ faculty ratio	% who graduate in five years	% with high test scores	% from top half of class	Telephone
U. of Arizona	$6,996	$3,701	84	$1,326	16:1[11]	60	40(S)	91	602-621-3237
U. of Arkansas	4,468	3,300	78	1,524	22:1	35	N.A.	N.A.	501-575-5346
U. of Arkansas at Monticello[6]	4,528	2,130	68	692	20:1	40	24(A)[2]	N.A.	501-460-1035
U. of Arkansas at Pine Bluff	3,264	1,960	87	197	18:1	33	N.A.	N.A.	501-541-6500
U. of Bridgeport (Conn.)	12,020	5,920	90	3,232	13:1	50	23(S)	54	203-576-4552
U. of California–Berkeley 43	10,377	6,222	100	N.A.	8:1	65	74(S)	100	415-642-2316
U. of California–Davis	10,482	5,015	100	330	19:1	95	51(S)	100	916-752-2971
U. of California–Irvine	10,223	5,293	N.A.	N.A.	19:1	54	N.A.	94	714-856-6703
U. of California–Los Angeles 67	10,030	5,230	90	391	18:1	64	61(S)	N.A.	213-825-3101
U. of California–Riverside	10,090	4,935	N.A.	N.A.	13:1	69	29(S)	N.A.	714-787-3411
U. of California–San Diego	10,162	6,152	100	1,046	18:1	60	67(S)	100	619-534-4831
U. of California–Santa Barbara	10,071	5,338	N.A.	N.A.	19:1	60	50(S)	N.A.	805-893-2881
U. of California–Santa Cruz	10,272	5,109	100	1,559	19:1	49	61(S)	N.A.	408-459-4008
U. of Central Arkansas	2,740	2,306	75	651	19:1	40	N.A.	N.A.	501-450-3128
U. of Central Florida	5,268	4,000	85	71	17:1	42	40(S)	99	407-823-3000
U. of Central Oklahoma	3,392	2,150	N.A.	N.A.	24:1	28	35(A)	62	405-341-2980
U. of Chicago (Ill.) 69	16,212	5,688	100	8,459	3:1	79	92(S)	100	312-702-8650
U. of Cincinnati (Ohio)	7,386	4,197	N.A.	N.A.	14:1	42	72(A)	87	513-556-1100
U. of Colorado at Boulder	10,322	3,507	73	193	19:1	60	N.A.	94	303-492-6301
U. of Connecticut 94	9,173	4,522[3]	91	1,031	14:1	70	41(S)	96	203-486-3137
U. of Dallas (Texas) 90	8,600	4,788	96	3,282	12:1	60	67(S)	94	214-721-5266
U. of Dayton (Ohio)	9,410	3,760	100	2,736	16:1	65	85(A)[2]	79	513-229-4411
U. of Delaware	8,538	3,540	48	239	17:1	64	42(S)	91	302-451-8123
U. of Denver (Colo.)	12,852	4,206	100	5,719	13:1	67	35(S)	83	303-871-2036
U. of Dubuque (Iowa)	9,205	3,105	100	2,864	15:1	45	37(A)[2]	56	319-589-3200
U. of Evansville (Ind.)	9,771	3,750	91	3,415	13:1	60	43(S)	93	812-479-2468
U. of Findlay (Ohio)	8,984	3,930	95	N.A.	14:1	30	51(A)[2]	72	419-424-4640
U. of Florida 27	5,986	3,960	90	957	25:1	60	67(S)	N.A.	904-392-1365
U. of Georgia 35	5,520	3,105	100	178	25:1	55	45(S)	N.A.	404-542-2112
U. of Hartford (Conn.)	13,594	5,414[3]	94	5,620	12:1	50	26(S)	61	203-243-4296
U. of Hawaii at Manoa	3,978	2,848	100	74	14:1	41	N.A.	N.A.	808-956-8975
U. of Houston (Texas)	4,262	3,770	95	147	25:1	N.A.	35(S)	92	713-749-2321
U. of Idaho	3,746	2,522	N.A.	N.A.	17:1	42	67(A)	79	208-885-6326
U. of Illinois–Chicago	7,018	4,580	70	N.A.	10:1	23	48(A)	89	312-996-4350
U. of Illinois–Urbana-Champaign 5	6,827	3,902	69	44	10:1	71	93(A)	97	217-333-2033
U. of Indianapolis (Ind.)	8,280[4]	3,250	90	2,187	13:1	60	N.A.	82	317-788-3216
U. of Iowa 51	6,470	2,982	N.A.	N.A.	17:1	53	82(A)	90	319-335-3847
U. of Kansas	5,340	2,684	99	141	16:1	53	74(A)[2]	75	913-864-3911
U. of Kentucky	5,084	2,734	85	118	15:1	49	67(A)	N.A.	606-257-2000
U. of Lowell (Mass.)	8,435	4,000	N.A.	N.A.	14:1[11]	65	N.A.	70	508-934-3930
U. of Maine	6,948	4,241	88	852	16:1[11]	51	34(S)	83	207-581-1561
U. of Maine at Farmington	5,445	3,586	N.A.	N.A.	16:1[11]	60	26(S)	85	207-778-9521
U. of Maine at Fort Kent	5,310	3,545	96	347	11:1	25	21(S)	60	207-834-3162
U. of Maine at Machias	5,350	3,430	N.A.	N.A.	15:1	42	28(S)	90	207-255-3313
U. of Mary (N.D.)	5,568	2,400	100	1,782	17:1	43	46(A)[2]	74	701-255-7500
U. of Maryland–Baltimore County	7,304	4,712	87	721	14:1	42	34(S)	86	301-455-2291
U. of Maryland–College Park 100	7,297	4,990	80	288	17:1	43	54(S)	N.A.	301-314-8385
U. of Maryland–Eastern Shore	6,010	3,534	N.A.	N.A.	14:1	40	5(S)	75	301-651-2200
U. of Massachusetts at Amherst	10,120	3,700	N.A.	N.A.	18:1	55	44(S)	90	413-545-0222
U. of Miami (Fla.)	14,079	5,930	93	5,968	7:1	52	58(S)	96	305-284-4323
U. of Michigan	12,938	4,052	90	1,421	12:1	65	72(S)	99	313-764-7433
U. of Minnesota–Duluth	8,170	3,000	95	N.A.	17:1	34	64(A)	85	218-726-7500
U. of Minnesota–Morris	8,123	2,950	100	1,598	16:1	65	89(A)	100	612-589-6035
U. of Minnesota–Twin Cities Campus	8,176	3,250	91	724	9:1[11]	43	71(A)	81	612-625-2006
U. of Mississippi	3,683	3,100[3]	100	N.A.	16:1	55	55(A)	70	601-232-7226
U. of Missouri–Columbia	5,941	3,004	95	463	23:1	48	74(A)	88	314-882-7651

Footnotes are on page 188.

College name and location	Tuition and fees	Room and board	% of need met	Avg. grant per student with need	Student/ faculty ratio	% who graduate in five years	% with high test scores	% from top half of class	Telephone
U. of Missouri–Kansas City	$6,426	$3,065	90	$700	12:1	33	89(A)	90	816-276-1215
U. of Missouri–Rolla 85	7,309	3,365	70	N.A.	14:1	53	88(A)	93	314-341-4164
U. of Montana	3,546	3,128	95	277	19:1	33	48(A)	N.A.	406-243-6266
U. of Montevallo (Ala.)	3,720	2,820	89	648	19:1	60	48(A)[2]	94	205-665-6457
U. of Nebraska–Kearney	2,470	2,250	N.A.	N.A.	22:1	35	51(A)[2]	65	308-234-8526
U. of Nebraska–Lincoln	4,995	2,820	95	414	17:1	42	50(A)[2]	73	402-472-3620
U. of Nevada–Las Vegas	5,070	4,438	80	N.A.	25:1	79	32(A)	N.A.	702-739-3443
U. of Nevada–Reno	5,070	3,720	80	246	21:1	N.A.	56(A)	N.A.	702-784-6865
U. of New England (Maine)	9,770	4,525	87	925	14:1	64	15(S)	80	207-283-0171
U. of New Hampshire	10,299[10]	3,600	95	1,182	17:1	65	45(S)	99	603-862-1360
U. of New Mexico	5,520	3,028	60	431	11:1	N.A.	63(A)[2]	83	505-277-3430
U. of New Orleans (La.)	4,616	2,174	100	329	27:1	19	43(A)	N.A.	504-286-6595
U. of North Carolina–Asheville	5,610	3,000	99	321	17:1	31	34(S)	95	704-251-6480
U. of North Carolina–Chapel Hill 9	7,116	3,700	N.A.	N.A.	15:1	72	64(S)	99	919-966-3621
U. of North Carolina–Charlotte	6,203	2,900	95	136	16:1	49	22(S)	97	704-547-2045
U. of North Carolina–Greensboro	7,370	3,600	75	156	14:1	52	25(S)	86	919-334-5243
U. of North Carolina–Wilmington	6,356	3,530	64	222	16:1	36	16(S)	86	919-395-3243
U. of North Dakota[6]	5,274	2,485	100	958	19:1	N.A.	60(A)[2]	87	701-777-3821
U. of Northern Colorado	6,032	3,434	61	299	20:1	N.A.	62(A)[2]	77	303-351-2881
U. of Northern Iowa	4,982	2,326	N.A.	N.A.	14:1	51	76(A)[2]	92	319-273-2281
U. of Notre Dame (Ind.)	13,700	3,650	95	2,917	12:1	93	85(S)	99	219-239-7505
U. of Oklahoma	4,705	3,172[3]	100	270	15:1[11]	42	60(A)	N.A.	405-325-2251
U. of Oregon	7,008	3,200	N.A.	N.A.	19:1	45	42(S)	N.A.	503-346-3201
U. of Pennsylvania	15,894	6,000	100	7,677	7:1	88	89(S)	99	215-898-7507
U. of Pittsburgh (Pa.) 80	9,260	3,280	100	1,056	15:1	N.A.	N.A.	94	412-624-7488
U. of Portland (Ore.)	9,240	3,580	100	2,520	16:1	48	33(S)	80	503-283-7147
U. of Puget Sound (Wash.)	12,690	3,980	86	3,483	13:1	57	58(S)	95	206-756-3211
U. of Redlands (Calif.)	14,316	5,370	98	7,616	13:1	75	69(S)	95	714-335-4074
U. of Rhode Island	8,842	4,620	95	264	13:1	56	24(S)	80	401-792-9800
U. of Richmond (Va.)	11,695	2,865	99	4,149	14:1	75	84(S)	N.A.	804-289-8640
U. of Rio Grande (Ohio)[6]	4,845	2,850	75	N.A.	18:1	50	45(A)[2]	N.A.	614-245-5353
U. of Rochester (N.Y.)	15,511	5,750	99	8,347	8:1	72	63(S)	96	716-275-3221
U. of San Diego (Calif.)	11,700	5,630	100	4,459	18:1	60	46(S)	N.A.	619-260-4506
U. of San Francisco (Calif.)	10,960	5,216	90	2,035	15:1	56	28(S)	88	415-666-6563
U. of Santa Clara (Calif.)	11,271	5,292	97	5,543	13:1	79	53(S)	95	408-554-4700
U. of Science and Arts of Oklahoma	3,345	2,610[3]	100	N.A.	19:1	36	47(A)	40	405-224-3140
U. of Scranton (Pa.)	9,626	4,502	60	2,369	18:1	83	54(S)	94	717-941-7540
U. of South Alabama	2,700	3,150	60	0	23:1	34	46(A)	N.A.	205-460-6141
U. of South Carolina 52	6,716	3,072	N.A.	N.A.	16:1	59	30(S)	93	803-777-7700
U. of South Carolina–Coastal Carolina	5,050	2,400[3]	80	51	20:1	26	11(S)	74	803-349-2026
U. of South Dakota	3,802	2,270	75	370	18:1	65	49(A)[2]	72	605-677-5434
U. of South Florida	5,725	3,000	92	588	13:1	50	42(S)	N.A.	813-974-3350
U. of Southern California	15,435	6,040	100	4,786	4:1	55	N.A.	95	213-740-6753
U. of Southern Colorado	5,957	3,392	76	69	17:1	25	35(A)	65	719-549-2461
U. of Southern Indiana[6]	4,503	1,336[7]	63	228	20:1	40	10(S)	64	812-464-1765
U. of Southern Mississippi	3,570	2,020	78	695	17:1	37	51(A)[2]	N.A.	601-266-5555
U. of Southwestern Louisiana[6]	3,318	2,008	69	N.A.	25:1	35	N.A.	N.A.	318-231-6467
U. of St. Thomas (Texas)	6,780	3,500	N.A.	N.A.	15:1	28	38(S)	94	713-522-7911
U. of Tampa (Fla.)	10,920	3,996	85	4,002	13:1	35	N.A.	91	813-253-6228
U. of Tennessee–Chattanooga	4,922	2,672[3]	58	N.A.	18:1	35	N.A.	N.A.	615-755-4662
U. of Tennessee–Knoxville	5,152	2,966[3]	65	1,053	17:1	51	77(A)[2]	84	615-974-2184
U. of Tennessee–Martin	4,984	2,580[3]	80	1,524	19:1	38	29(A)	N.A.	901-587-7020
U. of Texas–Arlington	4,300[10]	2,700	100	167	28:1	26	24(S)	84	817-273-2119
U. of Texas–Austin 10	4,142	3,300	94	871	20:1	57	56(S)	98	512-471-1711
U. of Texas–El Paso	4,290[10]	2,600	80	0	26:1	N.A.	N.A.	71	915-747-5576
U. of Texas–Pan American[6]	4,218	2,556	50	N.A.	27:1	30	8(A)	N.A.	512-381-2209

Footnotes are on page 188.

Stellar Schools for Women

THE 10 HIGHEST-SCORING WOMEN'S
COLLEGES IN MONEY'S VALUE RANKINGS

Spelman College
Douglass College
Notre Dame of Maryland
Chestnut Hill College
Wesleyan College (Ga.)
Agnes Scott College
Barnard College
Elms College
Wells College
Scripps College

College name and location	Tuition and fees	Room and board	% of need met	Avg. grant per student with need	Student/ faculty ratio	% who graduate in five years	% with high test scores	% from top half of class	Telephone
U. of the Pacific (Calif.)	$14,546	$5,100	69	$6,926	14:1	64	25(S)	81	209-946-2211
U. of the South (Tenn.)	13,505	3,510	100	6,857	10:1	77	75(S)	99	615-598-1238
U. of Toledo (Ohio)[6]	6,531	2,988	78	N.A.	18:1	31[5]	45(A)	N.A.	419-537-2696
U. of Tulsa (Okla.) 63	8,650	3,500	95	4,056	13:1	60	83(A)	91	918-631-2307
U. of Utah	5,619	2,700	N.A.	N.A.	15:1	56	58(A)	N.A.	801-581-7281
U. of Vermont	13,500	4,556	100	1,570	16:1	72	51(S)	96	802-656-3370
U. of Virginia 4	9,564	3,312[3]	90	1,324	11:1	90	81(S)	100	804-924-7751
U. of Washington 8	6,100	3,684	91	N.A.	9:1	51	40(S)	N.A.	206-543-9686
U. of West Florida	5,601	3,825	100	N.A.	27:1	65	N.A.	50	904-474-2224
U. of Wisconsin–Eau Claire	5,687	2,590[3]	100	58	18:1	48	79(A)[2]	92	715-836-5415
U. of Wisconsin–Green Bay	5,659	2,355	100	143	20:1	30	54(A)	83	414-465-2111
U. of Wisconsin–La Crosse	5,799	2,170[3]	95	95	21:1	51	54(A)[2]	88	608-785-8067
U. of Wisconsin–Madison 31	7,167	3,087	100	704	12:1	63	88(A)	99	608-262-3961
U. of Wisconsin–Milwaukee	7,098	2,708	85	35	19:1	N.A.	55(A)	73	414-229-6164
U. of Wisconsin–Oshkosh	5,674	2,062	88	44	21:1	58	N.A.	84	414-424-0202
U. of Wisconsin–Parkside	5,716	2,840	90	40	14:1	25	44(A)	68	414-553-2573
U. of Wisconsin–Platteville	5,810	2,410	85	0	25:1	48	N.A.	80	608-342-1125
U. of Wisconsin–River Falls	5,750	2,204	78	218	18:1	45	41(A)	64	715-425-3500
U. of Wisconsin–Stevens Point	5,808	2,756	95	42	20:1	N.A.	71(A)[2]	80	715-346-2441
U. of Wisconsin–Stout	5,785	2,390	93	0	20:1	44	33(A)	55	715-232-1231
U. of Wisconsin–Superior	5,659	2,362	91	134	15:1	36	72(A)[2]	77	715-394-8230
U. of Wisconsin–Whitewater	5,768	2,168	N.A.	N.A.	15:1	52	47(A)[2]	87	414-472-1440
U. of Wyoming	4,097	3,262	90	130	19:1	40	64(A)[2]	80	307-766-5160
Union (Ky.)	5,590	2,560	100	1,397	13:1	42	38(A)[2]	76	606-546-4223
Union (N.Y.)	15,598	5,395	100	7,220	12:1	85	N.A.	98	518-370-6112
Union (Neb.)[6]	7,720	3,450	100	2,576	12:1	22	N.A.	N.A.	402-486-2504
U.S. Air Force Academy (Colo.)	0	0	100	N.A.[16]	8:1	74	94(S)	97	719-472-3070
U.S. Coast Guard Academy (Conn.)	0	0	100	N.A.[16]	9:1[11]	64	32(S)	100	203-444-8501
U.S. International (Calif.)	9,105	4,605	100	N.A.	10:1	27	25(S)	77	619-693-4799
U.S. Merchant Marine Academy (N.Y.)	0	0	100	N.A.	11:1[11]	64	21(S)	100	516-773-5000
U.S. Military Academy (N.Y.)	0	0	100	N.A.[16]	8:1[11]	72	84(S)	97	914-938-4041
U.S. Naval Academy (Md.)	0	0	100	N.A.[16]	7:1[11]	76	86(S)	96	301-267-4361
Unity (Maine)	8,300	4,400	100	1,113	14:1	52	14(S)	N.A.	207-948-3131
Upsala (N.J.)	9,800	5,000	N.A.	N.A.	17:1	50	7(S)	45	201-266-7191
Urbana (Ohio)	7,271	3,880	100	N.A.	10:1	36	16(A)[2]	49	513-652-1301
Ursinus (Pa.)	12,530	4,500	98	6,669	12:1	76	47(S)	95	215-489-4111
Utah State	4,668	2,790[3]	80	N.A.	19:1	N.A.	40(A)	N.A.	801-750-1107
Valdosta State (Ga.)	4,218	2,535	80	218	22:1	43[14]	N.A.	N.A.	912-333-5791
Valley City State (N.D.)[6]	4,257	1,905	72	674	18:1	40	24(A)	N.A.	701-845-7204

Footnotes are on page 188.

Where Pay for Profs Is Tops
...and Not So Hot

SCHOOLS PAYING THE HIGHEST AVERAGE SALARIES TO FULL PROFESSORS	
Harvard University	$89,600
California Inst. of Technology	86,000
Stanford University	83,300
Yale University	82,300
MIT	79,800
University of Chicago	78,500
University of Pennsylvania	77,400
UC Berkeley	76,500
New York University	76,200
Carnegie Mellon University	76,100

SCHOOLS PAYING THE LOWEST AVERAGE SALARIES TO FULL PROFESSORS	
Mount Marty College	$29,200
St. Paul's College	29,200
Dana College	28,800
St. Mary of the Plains College	28,600
McPherson College	28,400
Bennett College	27,800
Tabor College	27,800
Union College (Neb.)	26,600
Tougaloo College	26,200
Claflin College	23,900

College name and location	Tuition and fees	Room and board	% of need met	Avg. grant per student with need	Student/ faculty ratio	% who graduate in five years	% with high test scores	% from top half of class	Telephone
Valparaiso (Ind.)	$9,990	$2,740	N.A.	N.A.	13:1	70	48(S)	95	219-464-5011
Vanderbilt (Tenn.)	14,975	5,420	95	$8,901	8:1	76	83(S)	N.A.	615-322-2561
Vassar (N.Y.)	16,510	5,260	100	9,230	11:1	85	95(S)	99	914-437-7300
Villa Julie (Md.)	5,770	No dorms	78	1,065	15:1	52	N.A.	77	301-486-7001
Villanova (Pa.)	11,570	5,320	90	2,311	14:1	83	62(S)	97	215-645-4000
Virginia Commonwealth	8,280	4,000	90	112	12:1	41	27(S)	84	804-367-1222
Virginia Military Institute[12]	9,865	3,525	92	1,411	14:1	65	44(S)	76	703-464-7211
Virginia Polytechnic Institute 60	8,152	2,754	90	216	17:1	67	58(S)	99	703-231-6267
Virginia State	5,907	3,978	N.A.	N.A.	17:1	30	2(S)	N.A.	804-524-5902
Virginia Wesleyan	8,740	4,425	85	1,692	16:1	N.A.	26(S)	80	804-455-3208
Viterbo (Wis.)	7,960	2,900	N.A.	N.A.	12:1	52	95(A)[2]	98	608-791-0421
Wabash (Ind.)[12] 48	10,700	3,665	100	5,650	11:1	73	58(S)	95	317-364-4225
Wagner (N.Y.)	10,050	4,850	N.A.	N.A.	12:1	63	29(S)	79	718-390-3411
Wake Forest (N.C.) 36	10,800	3,900	100	3,610	12:1	78	81(S)	99	919-759-5201
Walsh (Ohio)	6,528	3,350	100	760	19:1	56	26(S)	75	216-499-7090
Warren Wilson (N.C.)[17]	8,565	812	95	831	8:1	47	48(S)	81	800-934-3536
Wartburg (Iowa)	9,640	3,080	88	2,214	16:1	63	69(A)	86	319-352-8264
Washington (Md.)	12,312	4,930	100	2,238	13:1	65	45(S)	88	800-422-1782
Washington and Jefferson (Pa.)	12,850	3,290	89	4,534	12:1	85	54(S)	93	412-223-6025
Washington and Lee (Va.) 56	11,695	4,068	100	5,615	11:1	85	99(S)	100	703-463-8710
Washington State	6,076	3,600	N.A.	N.A.	17:1	50	N.A.	N.A.	509-335-5586
Washington U. (Mo.)	16,110	5,187	97	8,113	10:1	84	80(S)	99	314-889-6000
Wayne State (Neb.)[6]	2,387	2,390	100	0	16:1	40	40(A)[2]	56	402-375-7234
Waynesburg (Pa.)	7,690	3,050	84	2,130	16:1	55	N.A.	89	412-852-3248
Webber (Fla.)	5,390	2,730	51	574	19:1	40[5]	10(S)	88	800-741-1844
Weber State (Utah)	3,954	2,670	80	N.A.	22:1	N.A.	N.A.	N.A.	801-626-6046
Wellesley (Mass.)[1]	15,966	5,657[3]	100	8,165	10:1	85	89(S)	100	617-431-1183
Wells (N.Y.)[1]	12,850	4,600	100	6,846	8:1	65	58(S)	89	315-364-3264
Wesley (Del.)	8,055	3,800	80	665	16:1	50	N.A.	54	302-736-2400
Wesleyan (Conn.)	17,180	4,640	100	7,684	11:1	92	94(S)	99	203-344-7900
Wesleyan (Ga.)[1] 78	8,075	3,500[3]	95	3,989	12:1	55	55(S)	95	800-447-6610
West Chester U. of Pennsylvania	4,562	3,520	70	182	15:1	55	21(S)	85	215-436-3411
West Georgia	4,233	2,259	100	0	17:1	N.A.	10(S)	N.A.	404-836-6416
West Liberty State (W.Va.)	3,470	2,650	100	0	18:1	49	36(A)[2]	52	304-336-8076
West Texas State	4,394	2,706[5]	85	23	22:1	36	26(S)	71	806-656-2020
West Virginia Inst. of Technology[6]	3,752	3,250	91	212	18:1	N.A.	31(A)	60	304-442-3167
West Virginia State	3,688	2,950	N.A.	N.A.	23:1	64	20(A)	N.A.	304-766-3221
West Virginia U.	5,018	3,846	88	192	17:1	50	23(S)	N.A.	304-293-2121
West Virginia Wesleyan	11,830	3,150	82	4,260	15:1	51	20(S)	74	304-473-8514

Footnotes are on page 188.

College name and location	Tuition and fees	Room and board	% of need met	Avg. grant per student with need	Student/ faculty ratio	% who graduate in five years	% with high test scores	% from top half of class	Telephone
Westbrook (Maine)	$9,800	$4,650	90	$3,131	10:1	68	N.A.	63	207-797-7261
Western Carolina (N.C.)[6]	6,387	2,234[3]	N.A.	517	16:1	41	12(S)	76	704-227-7317
Western Illinois	5,542	2,870	85	N.A.	24:1	40	34(A)	60	309-298-1965
Western Kentucky	4,040	1,020	75	0	19:1	39	53(A)[2]	N.A.	502-745-2551
Western Maryland	12,505	4,740	98	3,776	12:1	65	27(S)	100	800-638-5005
Western Michigan	5,218	3,628	95	31	20:1	43	63(A)[2]	76	616-387-2000
Western Montana–U. of Montana	3,434	3,408	95	0	25:1	70	N.A.	N.A.	406-683-7331
Western New England (Mass.)	7,982	4,900	74	848	17:1	48	9(S)	57	413-782-1321
Western New Mexico	4,352	2,030[3]	66	330	17:1	23	16(A)	66	505-538-6119
Western Oregon State	5,739	3,000	85	0	14:1	N.A.	20(S)	N.A.	503-838-8211
Western State of Colorado	5,058	3,180	100	2,674	20:1	43	41(A)	51	303-943-2119
Western Washington	5,727	3,488	100	376	19:1	N.A.	37(S)	81	206-676-3440
Westfield State (Mass.)	6,536	3,353[3]	90	0	18:1	52	18(S)	80	413-568-3311
Westminster (Mo.) 71	8,400	3,350	100	3,498	14:1	68	79(A)	78	800-252-1851
Westminster (Pa.)	10,580	3,115	100	4,768	15:1	69	35(S)	89	412-946-7100
Wheaton (Mass.)	15,760	5,480	100	7,157	12:1	68	53(S)	85	800-541-3639
Wheeling Jesuit (W.Va.)	8,550	3,840	94	N.A.	13:1	58	21(S)	71	304-243-2359
Wheelock (Mass.)	10,912	5,078	98	2,777	15:1	69	12(S)	65	617-734-5200
Whitman (Wash.)	13,345	4,340	100	5,411	12:1	75	76(S)	94	509-527-5176
Whittier (Calif.)	14,622	4,960	97	6,818	14:1	54	56(S)	89	213-907-4238
Whitworth (Wash.)	10,425	3,850	N.A.	2,861	15:1	41	35(S)	87	800-533-4668
Widener (Pa.)	10,500	4,560	96	2,654	12:1	75	50(S)	90	215-499-4124
Wiley (Texas)[6,8]	3,946	2,544	93	566	15:1	20	N.A.	8	903-927-3311
Wilkes (Pa.)	9,275	4,250	95	2,293	13:1	67	19(S)	70	717-824-4651
Willamette (Ore.)	12,480	3,950	98	3,875	13:1	68	60(S)	94	503-370-6303
William Jewell (Mo.)	8,300	2,680	95	1,480	14:1	50	71(A)[2]	88	800-753-7009
William Paterson (N.J.)	2,560	4,050	75	187	14:1	16	16(S)	80	201-595-2125
William Penn (Iowa)	9,250	2,720	98	N.A.	15:1	45	N.A.	58	800-779-7366
William Smith (N.Y.)[1]	16,077	5,166	98	7,388	13:1	82	71(S)	90	315-781-3472
William Woods (Mo.)[1]	8,140	3,560	90	2,573	13:1	57	43(A)[2]	70	314-592-4221
Williams (Mass.)	16,885	5,110	100	9,104	9:1	88	92(S)	99	413-597-2211
Wilmington (Ohio)	8,680	3,200	93	1,998	15:1	50	48(A)	70	513-382-6661
Winona State (Minn.)	3,800	2,535	98	N.A.	19:1	55	70(A)[2]	80	507-457-5100
Winston-Salem State (N.C.)	5,002	2,762	78	217	15:1	21	2(S)	66	919-750-2070
Winthrop (S.C.)	4,612	2,668[3]	90	160	17:1	43	N.A.	N.A.	803-323-2191
Wisconsin Lutheran	5,780	3,200	90	N.A.	10:1	42	59(A)[2]	72	414-774-8620
Wittenberg (Ohio)	13,491	4,044	95	N.A.	14:1	70	61(S)	90	513-327-6314
Wofford (S.C.)	9,790	4,150	95	3,593	15:1	70	59(S)	96	803-597-4130
Worcester Polytechnic Inst. (Mass.)	14,125	4,590	95	5,731	11:1	79	68(S)	100	508-831-5286
Worcester State (Mass.)	6,202	3,650	96	115	19:1	22	22(S)	59	508-793-8040
World College West (Calif.)	9,500	4,300	95	4,308	12:1	33	67(S)	90	707-765-4502
Wright State (Ohio)[6]	5,298	3,363	96	191	20:1	21	45(A)[2]	56	513-873-2211
Xavier (Ohio)	9,700	4,110[3]	N.A.	N.A.	15:1	72	34(S)	72	513-745-3301
Xavier U. of Louisiana	5,800	3,200	N.A.	N.A.	14:1	22	40(A)[2]	84	504-483-7388
Yale (Conn.) 16	16,300	5,900	100	9,211	3:1	85	97(S)	N.A.	203-432-1900
York College of Pennsylvania	4,448	3,126	98	472	19:1	65	46(S)	80	717-846-7788
Youngstown State (Ohio)[6]	4,071	3,405	N.A.	N.A.	19:1	N.A.	32(A)	58	216-742-3150

Notes and explanations: [1]Women's college. [2]Enhanced ACT. [3]Minimum plan; additional meals or different rooms available at higher cost. [4]1990 tuition. [5]Estimate. [6]Open admissions, in most cases for state residents only. [7]Room only; meals not included. [8]Predominantly black college. [9]Comprehensive tuition price also covers room and board. [10]Estimate; tuition was not set as of Aug. 7, 1991. [11]MONEY estimate of student/faculty ratio based on school's reported full-time and part-time faculty. [12]Men's college. [13]Includes freshman charges for uniforms, books and supplies. [14]1989. [15]For women; men pay $3,900. [16]Students receive stipends to cover expenses. [17]Weekly 15-hour work program required of all students. All data current as of Aug. 7, 1991.

Sources: For salary tables the American Association of University Professors. For all other data, Peterson's Guides of Princeton, N.J. and the schools.

Money's Mutual Fund Rankings

Over a long distance, the race goes not to the sprinters, but rather to the most consistent runners. So it is with mutual funds. The funds that make most investors feel comfortable, not to mention richer, are those that deliver above-average returns year after year and manage to avoid serious stumbles. The question facing investors, then, is: Out of the hundreds of mutual funds on the market, how do you pick the winners?

You can start by turning to the tables beginning on page 190 which rank the top performers in different stock and bond categories based on their five-year returns. If you want to

The *Money* 20: Superior Funds for the Long Haul

	Type	Money risk-adjusted grade	% gain (or loss) to August 1, 1991			Portfolio analysis		% maximum initial sales	Telephone
			One year	Five years	10 years	% yield	% cash		
STOCKS (ranked by five-year return)									
GROWTH									
1 AIM Weingarten	Gro	A	21.0	116.4	452.6	0.6	4.0	5.5	800-347-1919
2 Janus Twenty	Max	A	23.2	111.9	—	0.9	2.0	None	800-525-8983
3 SoGen International	Gro	A	4.9	78.9	386.2	3.9	17.0	3.75	800-334-2143
4 Nicholas II	SCG	B	18.7	76.2	—	1.4	8.8	None	414-272-6133
TOTAL RETURN									
1 Financial Industrial Income	EqI	A	21.7	106.3	455.7	3.1	11.2	None	800-525-8085
2 United Income	EqI	A	10.6	100.0	459.3	2.9	5.2	8.5	913-236-1303
3 Investment Co. of America	G&I	A	13.9	88.8	387.5	3.5	3.5	5.75	800-421-0180
4 Phoenix Balanced Series	Bal	A	15.5	76.1	429.4	4.1	12.0	4.75	800-243-4361
OVERSEAS									
1 Ivy International	Intl	A	(8.1)	118.9	—	2.6	7.6	None	800-235-3322
2 T. Rowe Price International Stock	Intl	B	(8.1)	82.7	370.1	1.6	6.5	None	800-541-8832
BONDS (ranked by five-year return)									
TAXABLE									
1 FPA New Income	USG	A	14.4	64.0	243.0	8.4	5.5	4.5	800-421-4374
2 Merrill Lynch Corporate—High Income A	HYC	A	13.7	60.4	242.7	13.6	4.8	4.0	800-637-3863
3 Vanguard Fixed Income—GNMA	MBS	A	11.7	58.5	264.4	8.5	6.7	None	800-662-7447
4 Lexington GNMA Income	MBS	A	10.7	54.6	213.8	8.8	6.0	None	800-526-0056
5 Vanguard Fixed Income—Invest. Grade	HGC	A	10.5	54.2	244.5	8.8	3.3	None	800-662-7447
6 Scudder Short-Term Bond	STT	A	11.8	51.3	—	9.1	9.0	None	800-225-2470
7 Babson Bond Trust—Long-Term Portfolio	HGC	B	9.0	48.3	230.2	8.6	2.0	None	800-422-2766
8 Scudder International Bond	WI	—	13.5	—	—	9.4	6.0	None	800-225-2470
TAX-EXEMPT									
1 Safeco Municipal Bond	HGT	A	8.6	56.2	—	6.5	5.1	None	800-426-6730
2 Financial Tax-Free Income Shares	HGT	A	8.6	53.2	—	6.2	1.5	None	800-525-8085

Source: Lipper Analytical Services

narrow your choices further, there's The *Money* 20, our own carefully selected roster of 10 stock and 10 bond funds that, above all else, have delivered superior returns, but also meet more stringent criteria than the funds on the top performers list. First compiled in 1985 and updated monthly in *Money* magazine, most of The *Money* 20 are on the list of top performers (for convenience, they are also listed in the table on page 189).

How did we choose our elite? First, we screened 592 funds, ranking them within categories according to a measure devised by Stanford University finance professor William Sharpe. Sharpe's formula rewards strong performance and penalizes funds for wide swings in price.

Next, we threw out any fund that had changed its portfolio manager or investment approach in the past five years. That eliminated such stalwarts as Fidelity Magellan—but in our view, consistency

begins at the top. We also ditched any funds that may have enjoyed a one-time boost because of a narrow investment focus (like sector funds). And because of the instability of the junk-bond market, we dropped high-yield funds from our competition, though we retained funds that merely dabble in risky paper.

Last, we eliminated funds with annual expenses significantly greater than their category averages. In cases where load and no-load funds were judged roughly comparable, we chose the less expensive no-loads.

How to Use the Fund Tables

Most mutual funds had a pleasing story to tell their investors for the first half of 1991. But one year, let alone six months, doesn't tell you if a fund has staying power. So beginning on this page, we rank the top performers in five stock and eight bond fund categories based on

THE MONEY RANKINGS: TOP TAX-EXEMPT BOND FUNDS

Ranked by five-year performance	Type	MONEY risk-adjusted grade	% gain (or loss) to July 1, 1991				% compound annual return		Five-year analysis		Lipper market-phase rating			Net assets (millions)
			1991	One year	Three years	Five years	Three years	Five years	Best quarter	Worst quarter	Current	Prior up	Prior down	
LONG-TERM TAX-EXEMPTS			4.2	8.1	28.1	45.7	8.6	7.8						
1. UST Master Tax-Exempt–Long Term	HGT	A	3.7	8.4	32.6	67.3	9.9	10.8	9.0	(2.2)	A	—	A	$38.2
2. SteinRoe High-Yield Municipals	HYT	A	4.4	8.8	33.2	55.1	10.0	9.2	9.1	(4.3)	A	C	A	353.5
3. Safeco Municipal Bond	HGT	A	4.6	8.9	31.3	54.3	9.5	9.1	9.8	(4.2)	A	A	A	330.6
4. Lord Abbett Tax-Free Income–National	HGT	A	4.2	9.1	30.3	53.5	9.2	8.9	9.5	(5.0)	A	B	A	340.5
5. United Municipal Bond	HGT	A	4.0	8.4	31.7	52.5	9.6	8.8	11.3	(6.5)	C	A	A	708.2
6. Fidelity Aggressive Tax-Free	HYT	A	4.2	8.8	29.9	52.4	9.1	8.8	9.6	(3.3)	B	—	A	561.7
7. T. Rowe Price Tax-Free–High Yield	HYT	A	4.7	8.8	30.1	52.0	9.2	8.7	9.9	(4.2)	A	—	C	514.9
8. Kemper Municipal Bond	HGT	A	4.3	9.1	29.3	52.0	8.9	8.7	9.1	(2.7)	B	B	A	2,230.1
9. Vanguard Muni–High-Yield	HYT	A	5.2	9.2	32.7	51.9	9.9	8.7	9.8	(5.9)	B	A	B	1,056.6
10. Nuveen Municipal Bond	HGT	A	4.8	8.6	30.2	51.9	9.2	8.7	10.0	(3.9)	B	D	A	1,472.5
11. Scudder Managed Muni Bond	HGT	A	3.9	9.1	30.9	51.8	9.4	8.7	6.5	(5.1)	B	D	A	728.5
12. Eaton Vance Muni Bond	HGT	A	4.4	9.0	31.6	51.5	9.6	8.7	9.8	(4.3)	A	B	A	82.3
13. Mutual of Omaha Tax-Free Income	HGT	A	3.9	8.7	30.6	51.2	9.3	8.6	10.4	(6.0)	A	A	C	369.2
14. Financial Tax-Free Income Shares	HGT	A	3.7	8.5	34.2	51.1	10.3	8.6	12.1	(7.5)	A	A	B	195.6
15. Vanguard Muni–Insured Long-Term	HGT	A	3.9	8.5	30.8	50.9	9.4	8.6	10.1	(4.6)	B	—	A	1,330.0
SHORT-INTERMEDIATE TAX-EXEMPTS			3.7	7.7	22.3	38.0	7.0	6.6						
1. Vanguard Muni–Intermediate-Term	ITT	A	4.8	9.3	29.3	49.9	9.0	8.4	7.4	(3.6)	A	A	A	1,567.0
2. UST Master Tax-Exempt–Intermed.-Term	ITT	A	3.7	8.3	23.7	45.3	7.4	7.8	9.0	(2.3)	B	—	A	122.0
3. Dreyfus Intermediate Municipal	ITT	A	4.2	8.3	25.2	42.9	7.8	7.4	6.7	(2.8)	C	B	B	1,184.5
4. USAA Tax Exempt–Intermediate-Term	ITT	B	4.3	8.5	25.7	42.5	7.9	7.3	6.5	(2.8)	C	B	A	572.9
5. Fidelity Limited Term Muni	ITT	A	4.4	9.3	24.7	41.8	7.7	7.2	7.1	(3.6)	B	A	C	490.3
Shearson Lehman Bros. municipal bond index			4.4	9.0	29.7	51.3	9.1	8.6	10.1	(2.7)				

Types: HGT-High-grade tax-exempts; HYT-High-yield tax-exempts; ITT-Short-intermediate tax-exempts   [1]Fund may impose back-end load or exit fee.

their five-year returns to July 1991. We've divided diversified domestic stock funds into two broad categories: growth-style funds that aim for capital gains, and total-return funds that mix in dividend income. Overseas, sector, and gold funds compete in separate categories.

For each fund in our tables, you will find not only the manager's name, age, and tenure at the fund but also additional significant facts about the portfolio, such as its **yield**, **price/earnings ratio** (for stock funds), and **average maturity** (for bond funds). We have also assigned each fund a **risk-adjusted grade**. *Money*'s grade compares funds within broad groupings (equity, international, gold and sectors, taxable bonds, and tax-exempt bonds), rewarding those with superior returns and punishing those with above-average risk. The funds get three other grades as well in the **Lipper market-phase ratings**. Lipper Analytical Services compares a fund's return with that of its competition during the current market phase (which, by Lipper's measure, still counts as a rising

phase for both stocks and bonds) as well as the most recent down and up phases. In both *Money*'s and Lipper's ratings, A's go to the top 20% in each grouping, B's to the next 20%, and so on.

Since low expenses tilt the odds in your favor, we give an **expense analysis** for each fund. Look especially at the **five-year expense projection**. It estimates what you would pay in total sales charges and operating expenses on a $1,000 investment that compounds at 5% a year and is withdrawn after five years.

Beginning on page 198, you'll find *Money*'s alphabetical guide to 1,020 mutual funds, with performance records for one-, three-, five-, and ten-year periods to January 1991. (For more recent data on leading funds, see the latest issue of *Money*.) As with the top-performer rankings, the information in this guide is most useful as an indicator of how individual funds measure up over the long haul. (For fund phone numbers not listed, you can call directory assistance, 800-555-1212.)

% yield	Average maturity (years)	% cash	% of assets rated at least AA	BBB	Senior fund manager, age (years managing fund)	% maximum initial sales charge	Annual expenses (% of assets)	Five-year projection	% annual portfolio turnover	Minimum initial investment	Telephone
6.8										◀**CATEGORY AVERAGE**	
5.9	18.0	1.4	88.7	99.8	Kenneth McAlley, 46 (5)	4.5	0.86	$95	197	$1,000	800-233-1136
6.9	17.1	7.9	30.3	79.3	Thomas Conlin, 37 (4)	None	0.71	40	261	1,000	800-338-2550
6.6	20.0	7.7	55.1	93.8	Stephen Bauer, 46 (9)	None	0.56	31	66	1,000	800-426-6730
6.9	24.0	3.2	73.9	99.9	Nicoletta Marinelli, 30 (3 months)	4.75	0.78	89	43	1,000	800-426-1130
6.5	22.8	2.5	51.0	97.0	John Holliday, 56 (11)	4.25	0.56	74	181	500	913-236-1303
7.7	20.4	9.0	28.9	52.1	Anne Punzak, 32 (5)	None[1]	0.66	37	46	2,500	800-544-8888
7.1	20.1	4.4	23.7	64.3	William Reynolds, 43 (6)	None	0.88	49	72	2,500	800-541-8832
6.8	20.0	2.0	73.0	100.0	Patrick Beimford, 41 (5)	4.5	0.49	71	30	1,000	800-621-1048
7.2	21.8	0.1	39.6	94.5	Ian MacKinnon, 43 (10)	None	0.25	14	82	3,000	800-662-7447
6.6	20.3	2.0	54.8	98.1	Thomas Spalding, 40 (13)	4.75	0.62	80	8	1,000	800-621-7210
6.4	11.0	4.0	84.0	100.0	Donald Carleton, 57 (5)	None	0.61	26	84	1,000	800-225-2470
7.1	24.9	1.7	58.7	90.2	Thomas Fetter, 47 (5)	4.75	0.85	96	187	1,000	800-225-6265
6.4	23.3	3.8	58.8	99.8	Mark Winter, 40 (4)	4.75	0.78	94	40	1,000	800-228-9596
6.3	25.7	2.3	41.0	99.1	William Veronda, 45 (7)	None	0.75	41	27	250	800-525-8085
6.7	20.2	0.0	99.9	99.9	Ian MacKinnon, 43 (7)	None	0.25	14	47	3,000	800-662-7447
6.1										◀**CATEGORY AVERAGE**	
6.5	10.1	3.0	66.9	99.3	Ian MacKinnon, 43 (10)	None	0.25	14	54	3,000	800-662-7447
6.3	8.0	8.7	89.4	99.8	Kenneth McAlley, 46 (5)	4.5	0.66	83	216	1,000	800-233-1136
6.8	9.3	2.2	54.0	95.0	Monica Wieboldt, 40 (6)	None	0.71	40	40	2,500	800-782-6620
6.8	8.0	2.7	49.0	97.0	Kenneth Willmann, 45 (9)	None	0.44	25	92	3,000	800-531-8181
6.6	9.5	5.3	55.9	93.3	David Murphy, 43 (1)	None	0.67	37	72	2,500	800-544-8888
6.6	**14.6**		**66.3**	**100.0**							

MONEY's grades compare long-term and short/intermediate-term tax-exempt bond funds by five-year, risk-adjusted return. The top 20% in each group receive an A, the next 20% a B and so on.

THE MONEY RANKINGS: TOP EQUITY FUNDS

Ranked by five-year performance	Type	Money risk-adjusted grade	1991	One year	Three years	Five years	Three years	Five years	Best quarter	Worst quarter	Current	Prior up	Prior down	Net assets (millions)
			% gain (or loss) to July 1, 1991				**% compound annual return**		**Five-year analysis**		**Lipper market-phase rating**			
GROWTH			**18.2**	**5.3**	**40.7**	**53.5**	**11.9**	**8.7**						
1. Delaware Group–Delcap I	Max	A	17.5	5.4	47.6	142.3	13.9	19.4	76.1	(18.5)	B	A	D	$259.3
2. IDEX II	Gro	A	22.2	8.4	91.5	123.4	24.2	17.4	22.7	(22.0)	B	A	D	94.5
3. Transamerica Capital Appreciation	Max	A	24.6	(1.8)	37.5	118.6	11.2	16.9	47.0	(29.1)	A	A	E	81.3
4. Fidelity Contrafund	Gro	A	26.2	21.0	93.3	117.8	24.6	16.9	25.0	(28.8)	A	A	B	565.4
5. IDEX Fund	Gro	A	21.3	8.0	86.6	114.5	23.1	16.5	24.2	(21.9)	B	A	D	139.9
6. Twentieth Century Ultra	Max	A	32.0	30.1	83.9	110.7	22.5	16.1	40.8	(26.7)	A	A	E	863.3
7. Gabelli Asset	Gro	A	11.1	8.4	40.8	104.2	12.1	15.4	19.5	(14.0)	E	B	A	415.4
8. Fidelity Destiny II	Gro	A	23.9	14.4	52.8	97.2	15.2	14.5	44.3	(24.8)	A	A	E	309.2
9. Kemper Growth	Gro	A	23.5	15.1	66.0	95.3	18.4	14.3	27.2	(23.1)	A	A	D	474.3
10. Janus Venture	SCG	A	20.6	11.9	72.6	93.0	20.0	14.1	22.3	(16.9)	D	B	A	535.9
11. Janus Fund	Max	A	17.1	7.4	81.7	92.0	22.0	13.9	19.1	(16.3)	C	A	B	1,752.2
12. Berger One Hundred	Gro	A	32.2	18.6	81.2	91.4	21.9	13.9	31.2	(20.6)	A	A	E	32.4
13. T. Rowe Price Capital Appreciation	Max	A	14.1	10.8	41.8	90.3	12.4	13.7	12.2	(9.8)	C	D	A	174.9
14. Franklin Growth Series	Gro	A	13.8	9.1	43.3	89.1	12.7	13.6	18.9	(12.7)	C	D	A	245.8
15. AIM Weingarten	Gro	A	17.7	10.4	68.0	88.3	18.9	13.5	23.9	(21.8)	B	A	C	1,650.4
16. Thomson Growth B	Gro	A	14.7	6.0	55.3	87.3	15.8	13.4	23.0	(21.3)	D	B	B	434.1
17. Keystone America Omega	Max	A	22.7	10.4	60.4	87.2	17.1	13.4	26.9	(19.4)	B	A	D	48.0
18. AIM Constellation	Max	A	26.5	5.6	58.6	86.9	16.6	13.3	36.1	(26.9)	A	A	E	257.9
19. IDS New Dimensions	Gro	A	18.1	12.3	63.3	85.4	17.8	13.2	26.6	(14.6)	B	B	B	1,197.2
20. Janus Twenty	Max	A	24.3	10.8	104.1	84.6	26.9	13.0	27.1	(22.2)	B	A	D	469.5
21. CGM Capital Development[1]	Gro	A	40.7	22.4	66.3	84.0	18.5	13.0	37.5	(23.2)	A	C	E	229.7
22. SteinRoe Special	Gro	A	18.4	2.8	58.4	83.5	16.6	12.9	19.3	(19.5)	D	A	C	531.7
23. Mathers Fund	Gro	A	4.7	8.6	28.2	82.5	8.6	12.8	22.4	(5.0)	E	E	A	398.7
24. Fidelity Growth Company	Gro	A	21.6	12.5	80.1	82.2	21.7	12.8	24.9	(24.0)	A	A	E	1,064.3
25. Fidelity Magellan	Gro	A	20.1	9.8	58.8	82.1	16.7	12.7	22.9	(24.7)	B	A	C	14,805.3
TOTAL RETURN			**12.3**	**6.4**	**34.9**	**52.1**	**10.4**	**8.7**						
1. FPA Paramount[1]	G&I	A	17.6	14.9	43.4	116.7	12.8	16.7	27.2	(16.0)	C	B	A	229.3
2. Cigna Value	G&I	A	15.4	2.9	59.6	94.8	16.9	14.3	22.0	(20.1)	A	A	E	110.0
3. Fidelity Growth & Income	G&I	A	24.8	14.1	57.2	90.8	16.3	13.8	29.7	(21.2)	A	A	D	2,226.5
4. AIM Charter	G&I	A	15.7	15.8	74.7	88.1	20.4	13.5	22.6	(19.0)	C	A	A	185.4
5. Financial Industrial Income	Eql	A	18.2	12.3	60.9	81.7	17.2	12.7	17.6	(17.0)	A	A	D	755.6
6. Flag Investors Telephone Income	Eql	A	6.7	4.8	54.2	79.2	15.5	12.4	13.2	(13.2)	E	A	A	196.6
7. United Income	Eql	A	17.2	4.7	47.9	78.3	13.9	12.3	22.1	(17.4)	A	A	E	1,837.8
8. IDS Managed Retirement	G&I	A	16.7	4.3	55.0	76.3	15.7	12.0	23.3	(19.5)	A	A	E	851.9
9. Nationwide Fund	G&I	A	13.2	11.9	57.7	76.1	16.4	12.0	19.4	(21.9)	B	A	B	554.7
10. Mass. Investors Trust	G&I	A	11.3	5.2	54.6	74.6	15.6	11.8	22.0	(23.1)	D	A	B	1,410.1
11. Investment Co. of America	G&I	A	11.3	8.3	49.2	74.0	14.3	11.7	16.8	(18.8)	D	B	B	6,984.8
12. Oppenheimer Premium Income	OpInc	A	16.1	4.2	19.2	73.1	6.0	11.6	19.3	(15.2)	B	D	D	213.5
13. Vanguard Index Trust–500 Portfolio	G&I	A	14.1	7.2	49.8	72.8	14.4	11.6	21.2	(22.7)	B	A	D	2,698.7
14. T. Rowe Price Equity Income	Eql	A	16.7	9.8	31.9	72.0	9.7	11.5	15.2	(13.9)	A	B	D	1,017.7
15. Putnam Fund for Growth & Income	G&I	A	9.5	8.4	43.0	71.3	12.7	11.4	15.8	(19.8)	D	B	B	2,352.1
16. IDS Stock	G&I	A	11.3	8.8	51.2	70.7	14.8	11.3	19.7	(17.4)	D	B	A	1,442.8
17. Selected American Shares	G&I	A	23.6	16.7	50.6	69.1	14.6	11.1	26.0	(19.1)	A	C	D	549.7
18. Mutual Benefit	G&I	A	13.1	5.9	45.9	68.9	13.4	11.1	16.4	(21.1)	C	A	B	42.0
19. Merrill Lynch Capital A	G&I	A	10.1	8.7	41.6	68.6	12.3	11.0	16.0	(15.9)	D	C	A	1,083.7
20. FPA Perennial	G&I	A	11.3	7.7	43.9	68.6	12.9	11.0	11.4	(16.1)	D	B	B	55.6
21. IDS Strategy–Equity	G&I	A	15.7	7.5	37.8	68.5	11.3	11.0	15.0	(14.5)	B	B	D	369.9
22. Phoenix Balanced Series	Bal	A	11.5	14.2	52.4	68.5	15.1	11.0	14.4	(8.8)	C	C	A	609.7
23. Fundamental Investors	G&I	B	15.0	3.0	40.1	67.4	11.9	10.9	20.9	(22.2)	C	A	D	939.8
24. State Street Investment	G&I	B	12.2	3.9	48.6	67.4	14.1	10.9	23.1	(22.0)	D	A	C	589.0
25. Mutual Qualified[1]	G&I	A	14.3	4.4	25.2	67.2	7.8	10.8	15.5	(16.2)	D	D	B	1,157.7
S&P 500-stock index			**14.2**	**7.4**	**50.7**	**75.6**	**14.6**	**11.9**	**14.5**	**(22.5)**				

Types: Bal-Balanced; Eql-Equity income; Gro-Growth; G&I-Growth and income; Max-Maximum capital gains; OpInc-Option income; SCG-Small-company growth
[1] Currently closed to new investors   [2] Fund may impose back-end load or exit fee.   N.A. Not available

	Portfolio analysis				Expense analysis					
% yield	P/E ratio	% cash	Largest sector (% of assets)	Senior fund manager, age (years managing fund)	% maximum initial sales charge	Annual expenses (% of assets)	Five-year projection	% annual portfolio turnover	Minimum initial investment	Telephone
1.6									◀ **CATEGORY AVERAGE**	
2.1	24.6	23.9	Consumer cyclical (26.4)	Edward Antoian, 36 (5)	4.75	1.41	$121	45	$250	800-523-4640
1.0	25.0	5.2	Consumer cyclical (35.7)	Thomas Marsico, 35 (5)	5.5	1.35	156	99	50	800-237-3055
1.0	29.2	13.6	Capital goods (27.5)	Roger Young, 45 (6)	4.75	1.54	127	152	100	800-472-3863
0.4	19.7	4.0	Consumer goods (27.9)	Will Danoff, 31 (9 months)	3.0	1.06	87	320	2,500	800-544-8888
1.0	26.0	11.3	Consumer cyclical (24.1)	Thomas Marsico, 35 (5)	8.5	1.39	155	97	50	800-237-3055
0.0	45.2	2.3	Consumer goods (84.1)	Team management	None	1.00	55	141	None	800-345-2021
4.4	23.1	23.3	Consumer cyclical (20)	Mario Gabelli, 49 (5)	None	1.20	69	56	25,000	800-422-3554
1.5	17.6	3.7	Capital goods (35.2)	George Vanderheiden, 45 (5)	9.0	0.80	N.A.	109	25	800-225-5270
0.9	31.5	6.0	Consumer goods (43.5)	Stephen Lewis, 50 (1 month)	5.75	0.89	115	194	1,000	800-621-1048
0.2	34.6	40.9	Consumer goods (24.9)	James Craig, 35 (6)	None	1.16	64	219	1,000	800-525-8983
1.9	31.0	32.6	Consumer goods (24.9)	James Craig, 35 (4)	None	1.02	56	307	1,000	800-525-8983
0.0	34.8	14.3	Consumer goods (41.9)	William Berger, 65 (17)	None	2.13	137	145	250	800-333-1001
3.4	17.3	17.7	Basic industries (20.7)	Richard Howard, 44 (2)	None	1.25	69	99	2,500	800-541-8832
2.1	20.8	27.3	Capital goods (20.3)	Jerry Palmieri, 63 (27)	4.0	0.73	79	0	100	800-342-5236
0.6	23.5	2.1	Consumer goods (48.2)	Harry Hutzler, 68 (22)	5.5	1.26	120	87	1,000	800-347-1919
0.9	25.6	8.0	Consumer goods (43.8)	Irwin Smith, 51 (5)	None[2]	1.70	112	89	1,000	800-628-1237
1.7	23.8	2.6	Capital goods (34.9)	Maureen Cullinane, 45 (2)	4.75	1.73	118	77	1,000	800-343-2898
0.0	28.4	3.0	Consumer goods (28)	Harry Hutzler, 68 (15)	5.5	1.37	137	149	1,000	800-347-1919
1.9	28.1	18.6	Consumer goods (23.9)	Gordon Fines, N.A. (4 months)	5.0	0.85	96	91	2,000	800-328-8300
1.0	33.6	5.3	Consumer goods (28.4)	Thomas Marsico, 35 (3)	None	1.32	72	228	1,000	800-525-8983
0.4	27.6	0.0	Consumer goods (86.9)	G. Kenneth Heebner, 50 (15)	None	0.94	52	254	1,000	800-345-4048
1.8	18.3	18.7	Capital goods (16.3)	Bruce Dunn, 57 (4 months)	None	1.02	56	70	1,000	800-338-2550
5.3	27.2	89.0	N.A.	Henry Van der Eb Jr., 46 (16)	None	0.98	54	303	1,000	800-962-3863
0.0	25.6	23.1	Capital goods (46.3)	Robert Stansky, 35 (4)	3.0	1.14	91	189	2,500	800-544-8888
1.6	19.3	4.4	Consumer goods (20.4)	Morris Smith, 34 (1)	3.0	1.01	87	135	2,500	800-544-8888
4.2									◀ **CATEGORY AVERAGE**	
3.9	22.4	41.9	Finance (12.4)	William Sams, 53 (10)	6.5	0.95	114	94	1,500	800-421-4374
1.6	22.7	8.4	Capital goods (18.7)	James Giblin, 46 (5)	5.0	1.21	116	131	500	800-572-4462
2.8	20.7	1.0	Capital goods (24.7)	Jeff Vinik, 32 (9 months)	2.0	0.86	67	258	2,500	800-544-8888
1.9	21.1	25.0	Consumer goods (53.8)	Julian Lerner, 66 (22)	5.5	1.35	125	215	1,000	800-347-1919
3.4	20.0	10.2	Consumer goods (25.1)	John Kaweske, 49 (6)	None	0.76	55	132	250	800-525-8085
4.4	15.7	3.7	Utilities (69.4)	Bruce Behrens, 47 (7)	4.5	0.92	95	2	2,000	800-767-3524
3.0	16.3	3.2	Consumer cyclical (16.7)	Russell Thompson, 51 (12)	8.5	0.68	120	31	500	913-236-1303
2.6	25.7	5.3	Consumer goods (26.6)	Robert Healy, N.A. (4 months)	5.0	0.90	98	78	2,000	800-328-8300
2.5	18.0	5.8	Consumer goods (38.5)	Charles Bath, 36 (6)	7.5	0.63	107	13	250	800-848-0920
3.0	17.8	7.0	Consumer goods (31.8)	Laurence Leonard, 61 (6)	5.75	0.72	95	26	1,000	800-225-2606
3.7	15.6	11.1	Consumer goods (18.4)	Multiple portfolio counselors	5.75	0.55	86	11	250	800-421-0180
9.2	19.6	4.6	Consumer cyclical (33)	Charlotte Johnson, 42 (1)	8.5	0.95	133	267	1,000	800-525-7048
3.3	18.2	0.0	Consumer goods (24.5)	George Sauter, 37 (4)	None	0.22	62	23	3,000	800-662-7447
5.4	18.8	13.2	Consumer cyclical (19.4)	Brian Rogers, 36 (6)	None	1.13	62	24	2,500	800-541-8832
5.0	15.8	19.1	Capital goods (17.3)	John Maurice, N.A. (23)	5.75	0.89	113	81	500	800-225-1581
4.0	16.5	13.2	Consumer goods (22.8)	Robert Healy, N.A. (4 months)	5.0	0.63	83	26	2,000	800-328-8300
2.7	18.9	15.0	Consumer goods (36.8)	Donald Yacktman, 49 (8)	None	1.35	74	48	1,000	800-553-5533
3.0	17.5	18.0	Consumer cyclical (24.8)	John Stone, 49 (10)	4.75	1.01	101	14	250	800-323-4726
5.1	13.7	9.0	Capital goods (10.3)	Ernest Watts, 58 (8)	6.5	0.60	96	85	250	800-637-3863
3.5	14.8	24.2	Consumer cyclical (23.4)	Christopher Linden, 41 (7)	6.5	1.14	124	29	1,500	800-421-4374
3.0	N.A.	10.3	N.A.	Thomas Medcalf, 44 (2)	None[2]	1.66	114	65	2,000	800-328-8300
4.2	24.6	39.0	Consumer goods (16.8)	Patricia Bannan, 29 (6)	4.75	0.85	105	144	500	800-243-4361
3.0	19.8	15.4	Capital goods (21.2)	Multiple portfolio counselors	5.75	0.70	94	12	250	800-421-0180
2.7	18.9	4.7	Consumer goods (28.2)	Peter Bennett, 52 (3)	4.5	0.50	72	10	250	800-882-0052
5.0	18.7	20.0	Consumer cyclical (10.9)	Michael Price, 40 (11)	None	0.89	51	73	1,000	800-448-3863
3.3	**17.7**									

Money's grades compare domestic equity, overseas, and sector funds by five-year, risk-adjusted return. The top 20% in each group receive an A, the next 20% a B and so on.

THE Money RANKINGS: TOP EQUITY FUNDS

Ranked by five-year performance	Type	MONEY risk-adjusted grade	% gain (or loss) to July 1, 1991				% compound annual return		Five-year analysis		Lipper market-phase rating			Net assets (millions)
			1991	One year	Three years	Five years	Three years	Five years	Best quarter	Worst quarter	Current	Prior up	Prior down	
OVERSEAS			**6.2**	**(8.3)**	**23.5**	**64.4**	**7.1**	**10.0**						
1. G.T. Global–Japan Growth	Intl	A	13.9	(16.9)	31.0	168.5	9.4	21.8	29.6	(28.6)	C	A	E	$63.2
2. G.T. Global–Pacific Growth	Intl	A	13.9	(0.8)	57.1	130.9	16.3	18.2	22.0	(20.9)	A	A	C	295.2
3. First Investors Global	Glo	A	6.1	(12.0)	30.8	130.2	9.4	18.1	24.9	(21.8)	D	A	D	227.3
4. Templeton Foreign	Intl	A	6.5	(5.2)	46.2	119.4	13.5	17.0	18.9	(16.8)	B	A	A	1,083.5
5. Nomura Pacific Basin	Intl	A	12.2	0.2	25.6	115.1	7.9	16.6	26.7	(20.3)	C	D	B	54.2
6. Ivy International	Intl	A	10.0	(9.1)	36.4	111.6	10.9	16.2	24.3	(22.7)	B	A	D	77.2
7. Merrill Lynch Pacific A	Intl	A	13.0	13.6	38.3	108.7	11.4	15.9	30.6	(25.9)	B	C	A	261.7
8. Vanguard Trustees' Commingled–Intl.	Intl	A	0.5	(14.5)	18.6	90.6	5.9	13.8	19.4	(18.0)	E	A	C	879.0
9. EuroPacific Growth	Intl	A	6.1	(2.4)	42.4	90.3	12.5	13.7	18.8	(19.3)	A	A	A	1,138.4
10. G.T. Global–International Growth	Intl	B	10.6	(6.4)	42.9	89.9	12.6	13.7	19.3	(23.1)	B	A	B	403.9
11. New Perspective	Glo	B	7.6	(1.2)	36.8	84.4	11.0	13.0	17.8	(18.0)	B	B	C	1,834.3
12. Japan Fund	Intl	B	8.8	(6.7)	14.2	82.6	4.5	12.8	27.8	(22.4)	D	E	B	352.3
13. T. Rowe Price International Stock	Intl	B	4.8	(9.1)	28.7	82.3	8.8	12.8	22.6	(18.7)	C	A	C	1,205.7
14. Oppenheimer Global	Glo	B	4.7	(8.6)	49.6	80.7	14.4	12.6	25.7	(32.0)	D	A	C	923.9
15. Kleinwort Benson–International Equity	Intl	B	10.0	(9.2)	27.8	74.0	8.5	11.7	24.5	(21.7)	A	B	E	79.8
16. G.T. Global–Europe Growth	Intl	B	1.0	(18.9)	30.5	71.9	9.3	11.5	15.9	(25.1)	B	A	E	1,513.3
17. Templeton Growth	Glo	B	15.5	1.1	36.5	71.5	10.9	11.4	19.5	(22.2)	A	B	D	2,667.4
18. Scudder International	Intl	C	4.5	(11.1)	30.2	71.2	9.2	11.4	19.0	(23.2)	C	A	C	911.3
19. Kemper International	Intl	C	6.0	(6.8)	26.5	68.7	8.2	11.0	18.4	(16.8)	B	B	C	202.9
20. Vanguard World–International Growth	Intl	C	1.2	(11.9)	18.3	60.9	5.8	10.0	23.3	(18.3)	D	B	B	827.1
SECTORS			**12.5**	**5.8**	**47.2**	**63.6**	**13.1**	**9.9**						
1. Financial Strategic–Health Sciences	Sec	A	32.3	41.5	183.1	201.6	41.5	24.7	33.0	(22.9)	B	A	D	349.4
2. Vanguard Special. Portfolio–Health Care	Sec	A	18.6	24.1	90.8	124.9	24.0	17.6	23.7	(25.6)	D	C	B	301.1
3. Fidelity Select–Health Care	Sec	A	33.0	44.9	135.8	121.6	33.1	17.3	34.5	(28.5)	C	D	A	646.7
4. Fidelity Select–Food & Agriculture	Sec	A	13.6	12.8	89.2	114.9	23.7	16.5	24.6	(22.5)	D	A	A	59.7
5. Vanguard Specialized Portfolio–Energy	Sec	A	2.6	(1.3)	50.0	112.6	14.5	16.3	26.2	(23.6)	C	A	A	133.6
6. Fidelity Select–Medical	Sec	A	36.2	43.3	160.8	108.4	37.7	15.8	41.6	(24.9)	A	B	D	144.1
7. Fidelity Select–Biotechnology	Sec	A	35.3	49.7	171.6	107.0	39.5	15.7	40.4	(29.1)	C	B	A	530.2
8. Fidelity Select–Telecommunications	Sec	A	8.8	(1.8)	47.3	103.0	13.8	15.2	20.6	(21.1)	E	B	A	53.9
9. Putnam Health Sciences Trust	Sec	A	19.9	22.3	97.7	97.9	25.5	14.6	25.9	(22.9)	D	D	C	498.5
10. Financial Strategic–Technology	Sec	B	24.0	4.5	51.4	86.6	14.8	13.3	34.8	(31.7)	A	A	E	61.7
11. Putnam Energy Resources	Sec	A	6.2	1.1	39.3	84.3	11.7	13.0	23.1	(21.2)	B	B	D	126.7
12. Dean Witter Natural Resources Develop.	Sec	B	6.3	(2.5)	27.6	78.2	8.5	12.3	24.6	(20.3)	B	C	E	145.2
13. United Science & Energy	Sec	B	15.9	5.8	41.6	72.6	12.3	11.5	23.9	(17.8)	D	C	A	287.9
14. Merrill Lynch Natural Resources B	Sec	B	0.6	(0.4)	13.8	71.0	4.4	11.3	30.7	(24.9)	D	E	A	350.4
15. Fidelity Select–Energy	Sec	B	(2.0)	(5.1)	33.2	68.6	10.0	11.0	22.1	(24.5)	E	B	A	90.6
16. T. Rowe Price New Era	Sec	B	9.6	2.1	21.9	64.8	6.8	10.5	26.8	(19.7)	A	D	E	767.2
17. Financial Strategic–Financial Services	Sec	B	33.9	23.5	65.9	62.2	18.4	10.2	27.7	(20.5)	A	A	B	54.0
18. Franklin DynaTech Series	Sec	B	16.9	4.7	44.6	62.1	13.1	10.1	28.5	(20.6)	D	B	A	45.1
19. N&B Selected Sectors Plus Energy	Sec	B	9.1	2.5	37.9	61.3	11.3	10.0	18.7	(22.2)	D	C	B	407.8
20. Seligman Communications & Information	Sec	C	19.5	(6.8)	35.3	61.1	10.6	10.0	35.2	(31.1)	B	A	E	46.3
GOLD			**2.2**	**(3.9)**	**(7.6)**	**57.7**	**(2.9)**	**9.2**						
1. Oppenheimer Gold & Special Minerals	Gold	A	2.0	(10.7)	(2.0)	151.0	(0.7)	20.2	44.7	(11.4)	B	A	E	145.6
2. Franklin Gold	Gold	A	7.9	0.5	17.9	124.8	5.7	17.6	58.1	(22.7)	A	A	D	251.6
3. Vanguard Special. Portfolio–Gold & PM	Gold	B	7.0	2.7	4.3	88.1	1.4	13.5	52.9	(22.6)	A	B	B	158.9
4. IDS Precious Metals	Gold	B	3.4	(3.4)	(14.7)	71.3	(5.2)	11.4	50.9	(22.2)	B	C	D	67.7
5. Van Eck–International Investors	Gold	C	9.3	1.4	11.7	66.4	3.8	10.7	52.9	(21.8)	A	B	C	579.8
S&P 500-stock index			**14.2**	**7.4**	**50.7**	**75.6**	**14.6**	**11.9**	**14.5**	**(22.5)**				

Types: Glo-Global; Intl-International; Sec-Sector   [1] Figure reflects borrowing to boost investments.   [2] Fund may impose back-end load or exit fee.   N.A. Not available

% yield	P/E ratio	% cash	Largest sector (% of assets)	Senior fund manager, age (years managing fund)	% maximum initial sales charge	Annual expenses (% of assets)	Five-year projection	% annual portfolio turnover	Minimum initial investment	Telephone
1.9									◀ **CATEGORY AVERAGE**	
0.0	N.A.	4.9	Japan (84)	Marshall Auerback, 32 (10 months)	4.75	2.25	$162	138	$500	800-824-1580
2.7	N.A.	16.0	Hong Kong (24)	Christian Wignall, 35 (4)	4.75	2.14	157	75	500	800-824-1580
0.0	N.A.	1.9	Japan (30.1)	Jerry Mitchell, 52 (4 months)	6.9	1.88	172	116	2,000	800-423-4026
3.4	N.A.	20.4	United Kingdom (12.6)	John Templeton, 78 (8)	8.5	0.77	124	17	500	800-237-0738
3.7	N.A.	6.7	Japan (69)	Takeo Nakamura, N.A. (6)	None	1.42	74	46	10,000	800-833-0018
2.7	N.A.	6.8	United Kingdom (18.5)	Hakan Castegren, 56 (5)	None	1.66	90	29	1,000	800-235-3322
4.3	N.A.	5.0	Japan (76.5)	Stephen Silverman, 40 (7)	6.5	1.07	120	31	250	800-637-3863
3.7	N.A.	10.0	Japan (17.3)	Jarrod Wilcox, 47 (6 months)	None	0.44	25	18	10,000	800-662-7447
1.9	N.A.	16.7	United Kingdom (15)	Multiple portfolio counselors	5.75	1.28	122	26	250	800-421-0180
1.3	N.A.	9.5	Japan (18)	Christian Wignall, 35 (4)	4.75	1.93	147	58	500	800-824-1580
2.7	N.A.	12.3	United States (30)	Multiple portfolio counselors	5.75	0.82	100	14	250	800-421-0180
0.8	N.A.	5.4	Japan (84.5)	Robert Theurkauf, 63 (5)	None	1.05	56	60	1,000	800-535-2726
1.7	N.A.	10.1	Japan (19.4)	Martin Wade, 48 (11)	None	1.09	60	47	2,500	800-541-8832
0.3	N.A.	7.7	United States (24.4)	Kenneth Oberman, 61 (9)	5.75	1.68	144	48	1,000	800-525-7048
1.0	N.A.	3.0	Japan (16.4)	Team management	None	1.82	103	52	1,000	800-237-4218
0.0	N.A.	3.1	United Kingdom (24)	John Legat, 28 (6)	4.75	1.93	147	34	500	800-824-1580
3.5	N.A.	9.2	United States (34.3)	John Templeton, 78 (36)	8.5	0.67	123	18	500	800-237-0738
1.6	N.A.	4.0	Japan (23.9)	Nicholas Bratt, 43 (15)	None	1.24	65	70	1,000	800-225-2470
3.6	N.A.	14.0	Japan (17)	Gordon Wilson, 50 (2)	5.75	1.20	133	191	1,000	800-621-1048
1.9	N.A.	9.6	Japan (29.2)	Richard Foulkes, N.A. (10)	None	0.68	38	45	3,000	800-662-7447
2.4									◀ **CATEGORY AVERAGE**	
0.5	34.0	13.4	Consumer goods (53.9)	John Kaweske, 49 (6)	None	1.12	78	242	250	800-525-8085
1.7	22.5	12.4	Consumer goods (56.7)	Edward Owens, 44 (7)	None[2]	0.36	33	28	3,000	800-662-7447
0.5	31.3	1.5	Consumer goods (110.9)[1]	Andrew Offit, 31 (1)	3.0[2]	1.55	129	184	1,000	800-544-8888
0.9	20.4	17.3	Consumer goods (90.9)	David Calabro, 31 (3)	3.0[2]	2.16	168	160	1,000	800-544-8888
3.0	19.4	7.2	Energy (56.3)	Ernst von Metzsch, 51 (7)	None[2]	0.35	32	44	3,000	800-662-7447
0.0	27.1	8.5	Consumer goods (140)[1]	Charles Mangum, 26 (5 months)	3.0[2]	2.0	150	178	1,000	800-544-8888
0.1	60.7	15.2	Consumer goods (110.4)[1]	Michael Gordon, 26 (1)	3.0[2]	1.64	146	280	1,000	800-544-8888
1.8	22.3	8.7	Utilities (70.4)	Jennifer Uhrig, 30 (3)	3.0[2]	1.86	135	210	1,000	800-544-8888
1.2	N.A.	12.8	N.A.	Cheryl Alexander, N.A. (5)	5.75	1.18	124	37	500	800-225-1581
0.0	27.0	6.8	Capital goods (65.8)	Dan Leonard, 56 (7)	None	1.25	69	345	250	800-525-8085
3.1	N.A.	1.2	Energy (61.2)	Edward Shadek, N.A. (6 months)	5.75	1.50	140	48	500	800-225-1581
2.4	16.0	0.4	Energy (47.9)	Diane Lisa Sobin, N.A. (1)	None[2]	1.80	117	22	1,000	800-869-3863
1.5	31.0	9.3	Capital goods (31.7)	Abel Garcia, 42 (7)	8.5	0.90	131	64	500	913-236-1303
1.7	20.9	18.0	Energy (28)	Richard Price, N.A. (6)	None[2]	1.96	106	57	500	800-637-3863
0.1	18.9	5.4	Energy (44.7)	David Neisser, 29 (9 months)	3.0[2]	1.76	139	48	1,000	800-544-8888
3.0	17.8	14.3	Energy (29)	George Roche, 50 (12)	None	0.83	46	9	2,500	800-541-8832
0.1	14.7	7.1	Finance (87.1)	Philip Dubuque, 28 (1)	None	2.50	92	528	250	800-525-8085
2.0	24.7	20.9	Capital goods (34.9)	Rupert Johnson, 50 (23)	4.0	0.79	82	11	100	800-342-5236
1.9	16.5	6.0	Consumer cyclical (17.7)	Larry Marx, 45 (2)	None	0.92	51	60	1,000	800-877-9700
0.0	14.9	10.0	Capital goods (64.8)	Paul Wick, 28 (1)	4.75	1.67	134	123	1,000	800-221-2450
1.5									◀ **CATEGORY AVERAGE**	
0.4	N.A.	18.9	Gold mines, Canada (23.8)	Kenneth Oberman, 61 (3)	5.75	1.37	128	76	1,000	800-525-7048
2.7	N.A.	17.0	Gold mines, South Africa (32.3)	Martin Wiskemann, 64 (19)	4.0	0.75	80	3	100	800-342-5236
3.3	N.A.	3.1	Gold mines, South Africa (42.1)	David Hutchins, 30 (6)	None[2]	0.42	36	17	3,000	800-662-7447
2.2	N.A.	14.6	Gold mines, North America (75)	Dick Warden, N.A. (4 months)	5.0	1.48	127	76	2,000	800-328-8300
1.8	N.A.	2.2	Gold mines, South Africa (50.1)	John Van Eck, 75 (36)	8.5	0.97	134	2	1,000	800-221-2220
3.3	**17.7**									

MONEY's grades compare domestic equity, overseas, and sector funds by five-year, risk-adjusted return. The top 20% in each group receive an A, the next 20% a B and so on.

THE MONEY RANKINGS: TOP TAXABLE BOND FUNDS

Ranked by five-year performance	Type	Money risk-adjusted grade	% gain (or loss) to July 1, 1991				% compound annual return		Five-year analysis		Lipper market-phase rating			Net assets (millions)
			1991	One year	Three years	Five years	Three years	Five years	Best quarter	Worst quarter	Current	Prior up	Prior down	
U.S. GOVERNMENTS			**3.4**	**9.5**	**29.5**	**45.8**	**9.0**	**7.8**						
1. FPA New Income	USG	A	8.2	14.0	33.1	61.8	10.0	10.1	6.9	(0.9)	A	C	A	$38.6
2. Federated GNMA	MBS	A	4.5	11.6	35.9	58.6	10.8	9.7	8.7	(2.8)	A	B	A	1,240.5
3. Vanguard Fixed Income–GNMA	MBS	A	4.7	11.7	35.8	58.5	10.7	9.7	7.8	(3.8)	A	A	B	2,944.0
4. Smith Barney U.S. Gov. Securities	MBS	A	4.4	11.4	35.4	57.9	10.6	9.6	8.5	(3.6)	A	—	A	343.9
5. Franklin U.S. Government Series	MBS	A	5.1	12.3	33.8	57.9	10.2	9.6	6.9	(1.5)	A	B	B	11,576.4
6. Benham GNMA Income	MBS	A	4.7	11.4	34.5	57.3	10.4	9.5	7.7	(3.1)	B	—	B	405.8
7. Princor Gov. Securities Income	MBS	A	4.1	10.8	34.3	56.1	10.3	9.3	8.7	(4.2)	C	—	C	78.2
8. First Trust U.S. Government Securities	USG	A	4.3	11.1	33.5	56.0	10.1	9.3	7.4	(3.3)	A	—	B	191.4
9. Alliance Mortgage Income Securities	MBS	A	4.8	12.9	31.1	55.6	9.4	9.2	5.9	(2.6)	B	C	B	491.7
10. Putnam U.S. Government Income	MBS	A	3.9	10.5	31.3	55.1	9.5	9.2	6.5	(2.0)	D	D	A	1,879.8
HIGH-GRADE CORPORATES			**5.0**	**9.5**	**29.0**	**45.2**	**8.9**	**7.7**						
1. UST Master Managed Income	HGC	A	3.0	10.8	34.2	63.8	10.3	10.4	8.9	(1.8)	A	—	A	52.5
2. MacKenzie Fixed Income	HGC	A	2.2	7.6	28.0	53.2	8.6	8.9	9.6	(4.5)	E	—	A	89.9
3. Vanguard Fixed Income–Invest. Grade	HGC	A	5.7	10.0	34.8	52.0	10.5	8.7	9.6	(5.8)	A	B	B	1,305.6
4. Columbia Fixed Income Securities	HGC	A	4.4	10.2	32.6	51.7	9.9	8.7	8.0	(3.3)	A	D	C	144.1
5. John Hancock Bond	HGC	B	5.6	9.9	31.6	49.2	9.6	8.3	6.6	(3.5)	C	B	B	1,127.6
6. Vanguard Preferred	HGC	B	7.0	11.7	40.7	49.0	12.1	8.3	13.1	(6.6)	C	C	C	57.1
7. Scudder Income	HGC	B	4.5	10.3	32.7	48.9	9.9	8.3	6.8	(3.5)	A	C	C	311.2
8. Putnam Income	HGC	B	7.1	10.8	30.0	48.8	9.2	8.3	6.5	(3.8)	E	C	A	463.5
9. Sentinel Bond	HGC	B	5.4	10.0	31.4	47.8	9.5	8.1	8.6	(4.3)	D	D	D	37.1
10. IDS Selective	HGC	B	4.7	10.5	29.9	47.8	9.1	8.1	9.2	(4.5)	B	C	C	1,276.7
HIGH-YIELD CORPORATES			**21.1**	**9.3**	**13.1**	**28.1**	**4.1**	**4.9**						
1. Merrill Lynch Corporate–High Income A	HYC	A	25.0	13.3	29.2	51.5	8.9	8.7	15.9	(5.4)	A	C	B	483.3
2. Kemper High Yield	HYC	B	31.4	11.7	17.3	48.9	5.5	8.3	23.4	(11.8)	B	A	A	1,481.5
3. Aegon USA–High Yield Portfolio	HYC	B	10.3	10.2	32.8	48.3	9.9	8.2	6.8	(3.4)	A	—	B	38.2
4. Bartlett Fixed Income	HYC	B	4.2	8.5	27.0	46.6	8.3	8.0	6.4	(1.4)	B	—	B	159.2
5. Oppenheimer High Yield	HYC	B	18.3	11.9	23.0	45.2	7.1	7.8	12.9	(4.1)	A	E	A	618.5
6. IDS Bond	HYC	C	7.7	12.1	29.6	44.5	9.0	7.7	10.9	(4.3)	C	B	D	1,798.3
7. Delaware Group–Delchester Bond I	HYC	B	28.2	13.5	18.7	43.5	5.9	7.5	18.4	(8.2)	B	A	B	468.6
8. Cigna Income	HYC	C	4.7	7.8	27.0	42.2	8.3	7.3	10.3	(4.4)	C	C	C	219.7
9. Liberty High Income Bond	HYC	B	38.3	18.5	26.7	41.9	8.2	7.3	25.6	(8.7)	B	C	B	252.0
10. Federated High Yield	HYC	C	33.2	15.1	21.6	41.8	6.7	7.2	21.4	(7.4)	B	—	C	118.3
SHORT/INTERMEDIATE TAXABLES			**4.0**	**9.3**	**28.0**	**43.7**	**8.6**	**7.5**						
1. Smith Barney–Income Return	STT	A	3.6	9.1	28.8	53.7	8.8	9.0	6.5	0.6	B	—	A	28.1
2. Scudder Short-Term Bond	STT	A	6.2	12.6	34.9	52.0	10.5	8.7	7.0	(4.6)	A	A	E	483.8
3. Eaton Vance Government Obligations	STT	A	4.2	10.6	31.5	51.9	9.6	8.7	7.6	(1.3)	A	—	A	281.2
4. IDS Federal Income	STT	A	4.0	10.6	30.9	50.0	9.4	8.4	5.3	(3.0)	A	—	C	344.6
5. Vanguard Fixed Income–Short-Term Bond	STT	A	4.7	10.4	31.1	49.2	9.4	8.3	5.0	(0.2)	A	C	C	922.9
6. Federated Intermediate Government	STT	B	3.8	10.5	29.4	46.4	9.0	7.9	6.6	(0.9)	A	A	D	754.5
7. Merrill Lynch Corporate–Intermed. Bond	STT	B	4.5	10.2	30.5	45.7	9.3	7.8	6.8	(2.9)	A	B	D	93.0
8. Federated Short-Intermed. Government	STT	C	3.9	9.6	28.1	44.9	8.6	7.7	4.6	0.6	C	D	C	1,256.9
9. Oppenheimer Investment Grade Bond	STT	B	5.1	8.3	25.9	44.5	8.0	7.6	5.9	(1.5)	D	D	B	86.7
10. Delaware Treas. Rsvs.–Inves. II	STT	D	4.3	10.1	28.3	44.3	8.7	7.6	3.4	0.7	C	—	B	109.4
WORLD INCOME			**(0.4)**	**8.7**	**23.3**	**36.3**	**7.1**	**5.4**						
1. Mass. Financial Worldwide Governments	WI	A	(3.4)	8.4	30.3	73.3	9.2	11.6	17.7	(3.4)	B	C	B	153.9
2. Huntington Intl. Cash–Global Currency	WI	A	(0.2)	9.0	28.3	57.9	8.7	9.6	14.4	(4.0)	D	—	C	73.9
3. Scudder International Bond	WI	—	0.3	14.9	38.0	—	11.3	—	7.6	(2.6)	A	—	—	182.9
4. Van Eck World Income	WI	—	0.5	9.9	34.7	—	10.4	—	6.2	(2.2)	A	—	—	76.5
5. Putnam Global Governmental Income	WI	—	0.8	14.2	34.1	—	10.3	—	11.8	(1.7)	A	—	—	269.6
Salomon Bros. broad investment-grade bond index			4.5	10.8	37.1	57.1	11.1	9.5	8.0	(2.8)				

Types: HGC-High-grade corporates; HYC-High-yield corporates; MBS-Mortgage-backed securities; STT-Short/intermediate-term taxables; USG-U.S. Governments; WI-World income
[1] Figure reflects borrowing to boost investments.   [2] Manager absorbed a portion of operating expenses.   N.A. Not available

% yield	Portfolio analysis				Senior fund manager, age (years managing fund)	Expense analysis				Minimum initial investment	Telephone
	Average maturity (years)	% cash	% of assets rated at least AA	BBB		% maximum initial sales charge	Annual expenses (% of assets)	Five-year projection	% annual portfolio turnover		
8.1										◀ CATEGORY AVERAGE	
8.1	7.0	7.2	74.2	84.2	Robert Rodriguez, 42 (7)	4.5	0.94	$95	29	$1,500	800-421-4374
8.8	9.7	0.0	99.9	99.9	Gary Madich, 36 (7)	None	0.52	29	27	25,000	800-245-2423
8.6	9.5	5.0	99.9	99.9	Paul Sullivan, 48 (11)	None	0.34	19	9	3,000	800-662-7447
8.9	11.1	4.1	99.9	99.9	Committee management	4.0	0.41	62	6	3,000	800-544-7835
9.5	25.0	2.7	100.0	100.0	Jack Lemein, 46 (6)	4.0	0.52	68	18	100	800-342-5236
8.6	26.8	6.4	100.0	100.0	Randy Merk, 37 (4)	None	0.75	42	433	1,000	800-472-3389
8.0	26.0	3.0	99.9	99.9	Martin Schafer, 37 (6)	5.0	1.07	106	22	1,000	800-247-4123
8.5	7.0	3.0	100.0	100.0	Arthur Steinmetz, 32 (1)	4.5	0.93	75	60	1,000	800-848-8222
9.9	5.0	14.7	100.0	100.0	Michael Jones, N.A. (3 months)	4.75	1.12	106	393	250	800-227-4618
9.6	10.0	0.0	100.0	100.0	Jaclyn Conrad, N.A.	4.75	0.75	104	63	500	800-225-1581
8.6										◀ CATEGORY AVERAGE	
7.4	13.0	2.1	87.4	99.9	Hank Milkewicz, 50 (5)	4.5	1.11	107	350	1,000	800-233-1136
6.3	15.9	0.0	99.9	99.9	Committee management	4.75	1.36	125	0	250	800-456-5111
8.9	24.4	4.0	51.9	96.9	Paul Sullivan, 48 (15)	None	0.37	21	62	3,000	800-662-7447
8.0	7.8	4.1	80.1	99.8	Tom Thomsen, 47 (8)	None	0.73	41	132	1,000	800-547-1707
8.9	17.1	0.7	49.6	82.1	James Ho, 39 (4)	4.5	1.31	114	64	1,000	800-225-5291
9.2	N.A.	2.0	31.0	97.0	Earl McEvoy, 43 (9)	None	0.65	36	15	3,000	800-662-7447
8.2	8.0	2.0	74.0	89.0	William Hutchinson, 43 (5)	None	0.95	51	45	1,000	800-225-2470
10.0	14.8	2.6	36.4	73.7	John Geissinger, 32 (5)	4.75	0.80	103	68	500	800-225-1581
8.2	9.4	7.0	64.7	99.4	Richard Temple, 47 (6)	5.25	0.83	96	108	250	800-233-4332
8.1	13.3	5.7	62.0	83.0	Ray Goodner, N.A. (6)	5.0	0.76	90	54	2,000	800-328-8300
13.0										◀ CATEGORY AVERAGE	
13.9	8.8	8.0	7.0	8.0	Vincent Lathbury, 50 (9)	4.0	0.68	75	48	1,000	800-637-3863
14.7	7.4	8.0	17.0	17.0	Michael McNamara, 46 (1)	4.5	0.73	91	37	1,000	800-621-1048
10.4	13.1	1.2	10.7	54.9	David Halfpap, 39 (1)	4.75	0.69	113	19	1,000	800-288-2346
7.4	4.4	2.4	87.3	92.7	Dale Rabiner, 39 (5)	None	1.00	55	95	5,000	800-800-4612
14.7	N.A.	3.1	2.2	9.2	Ralph Stellmacher, 32 (3)	4.75	0.93	97	68	1,000	800-525-7048
8.4	13.3	3.4	49.0	75.0	Frederick Quirsfeld, N.A. (6)	5.0	0.75	91	81	2,000	800-328-8300
13.5	7.9	3.2	8.2	8.2	J. Michael Pokorny, 51 (10)	6.75	0.85	111	72	250	800-523-4640
8.4	16.5	9.9	73.6	92.2	Gary Brown, 37 (1)	5.0	1.00	103	106	500	800-572-4462
12.9	18.7	0.0	4.6	4.6	Mark Durbiano, 31 (4)						
14.8	N.A.	0.0	3.8	3.8	Mark Durbiano, 31 (4)	None	0.76	42	24	25,000	800-245-2423
7.8										◀ CATEGORY AVERAGE	
8.6	1.8	39.5	96.3	99.8	Committee management	1.5	0.43	43	28	10,000	800-544-7835
9.1	2.7	13.0	65.0	100.0	Thomas Poor, 48 (2)	None	0.41[2]	28	53	1,000	800-225-2470
9.8	5.1	(11.3)[1]	100.0	100.0	Mark Venezia, 41 (7)	4.75	1.22	170	22	1,000	800-225-6265
8.0	6.4	4.4	100.0	100.0	Stuart Sedlacek, 33 (1)	5.0	0.82	93	104	2,000	800-328-8300
8.2	2.3	4.8	61.7	99.7	Ian MacKinnon, 43 (9)	None	0.31	17	107	3,000	800-662-7447
7.5	3.4	0.0	99.9	99.9	Roger Early, 37 (4)	None	0.51	29	166	25,000	800-245-2423
8.6	5.1	7.0	51.7	96.5	Martha Reed, 53 (9)	2.0	0.71	59	103	1,000	800-637-3863
7.4	1.7	0.0	99.8	99.8	Roger Early, 37 (4)	None	0.48	27	172	25,000	800-245-2423
8.3	8.8	50.0	46.9	98.8	Mary Wilson, 37 (9)	4.75	1.24	112	80	1,000	800-525-7048
8.2	4.4	1.7	100.0	100.0	David Rosenberg, 32 (1)	None	0.97	50	175	1,000	800-523-4640
10.5										◀ CATEGORY AVERAGE	
8.0	6.5	13.0	N.A.	N.A.	Leslie Nanberg, 45 (8)	4.75	1.44	128	282	1,000	800-225-2606
7.5	0.1	100.0	N.A.	N.A.	Christopher Wyke, N.A. (3)	2.25	2.09	110	0	2,500	800-354-4111
9.7	9.0	18.0	N.A.	N.A.	Mark Turner, 38 (2)	None	1.25[2]	69	216	1,000	800-225-2470
12.5	4.5	10.7	N.A.	N.A.	Klaus Buescher, 60 (4)	4.75	1.42	128	290	1,000	800-221-2220
8.1	9.3	8.0	N.A.	N.A.	Gary Kreps, 37 (2)	4.75	1.58	133	498	500	800-225-1581
8.3	**9.5**		**88.3**	**100.0**							

MONEY's grades compare long-term and short/intermediate-term taxable bond funds by five-year, risk-adjusted return. The top 20% in each group receive an A, the next 20% a B and so on.

THE ALPHABETICAL GUIDE TO
1,020 MUTUAL FUNDS

BENCHMARKS FOR INVESTORS

	% gain (or loss) to Jan. 1, 1991				
	One year	Three years	Five years	10 years	% yield
S&P 500-stock index	(3.1)	48.7	85.7	268.6	3.8
Dow Jones industrial average	(5.6)	38.3	65.8	216.5	3.9
Russell 2000 small-company stock index	(19.5)	16.9	12.7	125.3	2.3
Average equity fund	(5.3)	35.7	58.9	222.2	3.3
Salomon Bros. investment-grade bond index	9.1	34.8	59.6	240.8	8.5
Shearson Lehman Bros. long-term Treasury index	6.3	38.4	66.7	265.0	8.3
Shearson Lehman Bros. municipal bond index[1]	7.7	32.3	59.3	180.4	6.8

[1] All figures to Dec. 1, 1990

THE MONEY RANKINGS: EQUITY FUNDS

FUND NAME	Type	MONEY risk-adjusted grade	% gain (or loss) to Jan. 1, 1991				Portfolio analysis			Net assets (millions)	Expense analysis	
			One year	Three years	Five years	10 years	% yield	P/E ratio	% cash		% max. initial sales charge	Five-year projection
ABT Growth & Income Trust	G&I	D	(9.3)	24.8	51.6	134.6	3.9	12.0	19.7	$76.2	4.75	$111
ABT Utility Income	Sec	B	(6.2)	45.5	65.2	179.7	5.8	15.3	2.8	139.2	4.75	110
Acorn Fund[1]	SCG	C	(18.0)	28.5	56.8	193.4	1.9	18.5	15.0	719.4	None[3]	41
Advantage Growth	Gro	—	(5.2)	37.4	—	—	0.9	16.4	19.0	24.8	None[3]	123
Advantage Income	Flex	—	0.8	34.5	—	—	6.4	N.A.	12.5	44.5	None[3]	108
Aegon USA Growth Portfolio	Gro	D	(5.5)	20.8	45.0	181.7	4.7	14.4	23.0	31.3	4.75	119
AFA–National Aviation & Technology	Sec	D	(19.3)	40.7	42.2	113.5	1.1	13.2	18.2	61.5	4.75	127
AFA–National Telecom. & Technology	Sec	E	(18.5)	5.1	11.2	—	0.0	13.9	17.8	26.7	4.75	152
AIM Charter	G&I	A	8.2	55.4	100.9	233.0	2.2	20.4	19.0	632.5	5.5	126
AIM Constellation	Max	A	(4.1)	54.0	103.6	161.9	0.0	22.0	14.0	83.3	5.5	143
AIM Summit[2]	Gro	B	0.9	55.5	68.9	—	2.0	19.1	4.35	279.1	8.5	46
AIM Weingarten	Gro	A	5.6	59.8	119.3	311.8	0.7	18.9	12.0	632.5	5.5	120
Alliance Balanced Shares	Bal	D	(2.2)	30.0	54.5	258.6	3.6	17.9	16.0	139.3	5.5	128
Alliance Convertible	Conv	—	(24.0)	(0.4)	—	—	6.8	N.A.	18.0	34.7	5.5	148
Alliance Counterpoint	G&I	A	(4.6)	53.4	82.9	—	1.4	17.4	0.3	48.7	5.5	142
Alliance Fund	Gro	C	(4.4)	38.2	63.1	158.9	3.2	17.2	0.1	559.6	5.5	94
Alliance Global Small Cap A	Glo	E	(24.9)	20.6	31.5	83.2	0.0	N.A.	7.1	63.5	5.5	149
Alliance Growth & Income	G&I	A	(1.7)	44.1	76.7	278.6	3.9	16.8	8.4	314.7	5.5	112
Alliance International A	Intl	D	(21.0)	36.0	85.2	—	0.2	N.A.	4.3	230.3	5.5	141
Alliance Quasar A	SCG	E	(23.4)	27.3	33.9	183.7	0.4	19.6	9.5	234.0	5.5	139

MONEY's grades compare domestic equity, international equity and gold and sector funds by five-year, risk-adjusted return. The top 20% in each group receive an A, the next 20% a B and so on.   [1] Currently closed to new investors   [2] Investment by contractual plan only   [3] Fund may impose back-end load or exit fee.   N.A. Not available

ABBREVIATIONS: AA Asset allocation; **Bal** Balanced; **Conv** Convertibles; **Eql** Equity income; **Flex** Flexible income; **G&I** Growth and income; **Glo** Global; **Gold** Gold/metals; **Gro** Growth; **HGC** High-grade corporates; **HGT** High-grade tax-exempts; **HYC** High-yield corporates; **HYT** High-yield tax-exempts; **Intl** International; **ITT** Short/intermediate-term tax-exempts; **Max** Maximum capital gains; **MBS** Mortgage-backed securities; **OpInc** Option income; **SCG** Small-company growth; **Sec** Sectors; **STT** Short/intermediate-term taxables; **USG** U.S. Government bonds; **WI** World income.

THE MONEY RANKINGS: EQUITY FUNDS

FUND NAME	Type	MONEY risk-adjusted grade	% gain (or loss) to Jan. 1, 1991				Portfolio analysis			Net assets (millions)	Expense analysis	
			One year	Three years	Five years	10 years	% yield	P/E ratio	% cash		% max. initial sales charge	Five-year projection
Alliance Technology	Sec	E	(3.1)	3.4	38.0	—	0.0	15.3	20.5	$109.6	5.5	$128
AMA Global Growth	Glo	—	(10.1)	28.6	—	—	3.0	N.A.	12.0	87.8	None	92
AMCAP Fund	Gro	B	(4.0)	32.9	71.3	241.3	2.4	17.7	8.1	1,652.4	5.75	95
American Balanced	Bal	B	(1.6)	35.0	64.5	264.7	6.0	12.3	13.3	330.3	5.75	98
American Capital Comstock	Gro	C	(3.4)	44.8	63.6	262.9	3.3	14.7	7.6	762.6	8.5	126
American Capital Emerging Growth	Max	E	2.0	36.5	48.3	203.8	0.5	21.8	8.3	181.5	5.75	116
American Capital Enterprise	Gro	C	(2.9)	42.8	58.5	141.3	2.1	17.1	3.6	496.6	5.75	107
American Capital Equity Income	Eql	D	(4.7)	30.7	49.4	259.7	5.8	16.0	8.4	80.5	5.75	108
American Capital Growth & Income	G&I	D	(5.2)	27.4	48.3	221.4	3.3	15.2	11.5	134.7	5.75	108
American Capital Harbor	Conv	D	(1.2)	39.1	52.2	212.1	6.7	N.A.	1.6	324.2	5.75	102
American Capital Pace	Max	D	(5.8)	35.8	52.9	288.2	2.6	15.8	8.0	2,001.6	5.75	108
American Gas Index	Sec	—	(10.5)	—	—	—	5.3	16.3	1.0	112.9	None	42
American Growth	Gro	E	(6.9)	25.9	38.8	143.9	3.7	N.A.	33.0	52.5	8.5	153
American Investors Growth	Gro	E	(17.4)	30.9	25.7	(9.8)	0.5	21.9	0.5	54.0	8.5	162
American Leaders	G&I	D	(1.8)	23.0	47.4	263.0	3.7	13.8	2.0	119.2	4.5	98
American Mutual	G&I	A	(1.6)	39.1	72.0	315.3	5.2	12.6	24.4	3,196.0	5.75	89
American National Growth	Gro	C	(2.9)	27.9	59.7	216.5	2.2	18.5	12.7	90.8	8.5	140
American National Income	Eql	C	0.8	42.1	59.7	275.3	4.2	16.2	12.6	68.6	8.5	144
AMEV Capital	G&I	C	(9.5)	31.6	65.4	261.2	2.0	20.2	39.1	133.2	4.75	117
AMEV Fiduciary	Gro	C	(11.1)	33.5	60.7	—	1.1	20.5	29.9	28.45	4.5	119
AMEV Growth	Max	B	(6.3)	44.1	72.1	258.8	1.3	26.4	26.1	202.7	4.75	113
Analytic Optioned Equity	OpInc	B	1.5	38.2	59.3	178.6	10.7	17.5	5.5	100.6	None	62
Axe-Houghton Fund B	Bal	B	7.2	41.0	67.7	227.8	6.4	12.4	1.6	156.4	5.75	97
Axe-Houghton Growth	Gro	D	6.4	37.8	43.0	136.5	0.7	20.5	12.7	58.7	5.75	108
Babson Enterprise	SCG	E	(15.9)	36.5	35.2	—	1.2	13.4	0.7	70.4	None	68
Babson Growth	Gro	C	(9.4)	28.3	57.7	156.1	2.6	13.8	6.0	207.0	None	48
Bailard Biehl & Kaiser Diversa	AA	—	(9.5)	8.8	—	—	3.0	N.A.	14.4	75.2	None	73
Baird Blue Chip	G&I	—	3.0	40.8	—	—	1.7	17.3	16.9	33.0	5.75	144
Baron Asset	SCG	—	(18.6)	37.1	—	—	1.7	24.8	25.0	38.1	None[2]	96
Bartlett Basic Value	G&I	E	(9.6)	27.5	39.5	—	4.8	9.5	4.5	80.0	None	66
Benham Gold Equities Index	Gold	—	(19.4)	—	—	—	0.6	N.A.	3.2	95.5	None	42
Blanchard Precious Metals	Gold	—	(22.9)	—	—	—	0.0	N.A.	8.0	29.5	None	130[3]
Blanchard Strategic Growth	AA	—	(6.4)	16.3	—	—	2.3	N.A.	25.0	206.9	$125	164
Boston Co. Capital Appreciation	Gro	C	(13.5)	29.3	58.7	211.2	2.4	20.6	10.5	397.6	None	68
Boston Co. Investors–International	Intl	—	(18.5)	—	—	—	1.5	N.A.	6.0	30.2	None	95
Boston Co. Special Growth	Gro	D	(4.9)	37.4	41.7	—	0.2	28.3	6.0	28.5	None	93
Brandywine Fund	Gro	B	0.6	57.3	87.9	—	1.7	N.A.	78.0	282.0	None	62
Bull & Bear Capital Growth	Gro	E	(26.2)	9.4	8.3	50.0	0.0	17.4	12.0	41.2	None	141
Bull & Bear Gold Investors	Gold	D	(22.1)	(19.7)	41.5	(4.8)	0.3	N.A.	10.0	32.5	None	139
Burnham Fund	G&I	A	(2.0)	34.8	76.0	233.9	6.2	15.9	27.8	122.6	5.0	114
Calvert Ariel Growth[1]	SCG	—	(16.1)	46.9	—	—	1.2	13.0	1.0	175.3	4.5	119
Calvert Social Investment Managed Growth	Bal	B	1.8	33.8	65.8	—	4.9	N.A.	6.0	245.0	4.5	113
Capital Income Builder	Eql	—	4.0	40.5	—	—	5.3	12.5	3.0	206.3	5.75	115
Cardinal Fund	G&I	C	(6.3)	33.5	61.5	261.0	4.1	11.4	14.0	167.8	8.5	120
Carnegie Cappiello–Growth	Gro	C	(12.5)	54.8	59.4	—	1.9	14.5	6.5	51.0	4.5	109
Carnegie Cappiello–Total Return	AA	E	(17.9)	33.8	42.6	—	6.8	11.9	3.7	62.7	4.5	127
Century Shares Trust	Sec	D	(7.8)	51.0	52.2	307.2	2.9	N.A.	3.5	107.0	None	52
CGM Capital Development[1]	Gro	B	1.5	19.3	77.6	412.2	0.5	23.2	0.7	150.3	None	51
CGM Mutual	Bal	A	1.1	26.9	80.5	299.9	4.3	18.2	0.7	282.5	None	54
Cigna Growth	Gro	C	(5.0)	34.8	57.6	172.8	1.6	15.9	7.3	139.1	5.0	107
Cigna Utilities	Sec	—	(3.0)	—	—	—	5.6	19.0	17.1	65.4	5.0	114
Cigna Value	G&I	A	1.9	61.6	86.3	—	1.8	19.9	9.3	75.7	5.0	112

MONEY's grades compare domestic equity, international equity and gold and sector funds by five-year, risk-adjusted return. The top 20% in each group receive an A, the next 20% a B and so on. [1] Currently closed to new investors [2] Fund may impose back-end load or exit fee. [3] Three years N.A. Not available

THE Money RANKINGS: EQUITY FUNDS

FUND NAME	Type	Money risk-adjusted grade	% gain (or loss) to Jan. 1, 1991				Portfolio analysis			Net assets (millions)	Expense analysis	
			One year	Three years	Five years	10 years	% yield	P/E ratio	% cash		% max. initial sales charge	Five-year projection
Clipper Fund	G&I	B	(7.6)	35.1	65.3	—	2.9	12.7	1.3	$119.3	None	$64
Colonial Advanced Strategies Gold	Gold	E	(26.4)	(26.4)	40.1	—	1.0	N.A.	5.5	53.2	5.75	157
Colonial Diversified Income	Flex	E	(6.9)	19.4	29.8	123.5	11.6	N.A.	5.7	438.4	5.75	124
Colonial Fund	G&I	B	(7.9)	34.8	62.5	221.5	4.2	12.2	21.4	290.0	5.75	113
Colonial Growth Shares	Gro	B	(10.7)	45.2	76.8	187.8	1.9	11.6	8.5	101.2	5.75	115
Colonial Small Stock Index	SCG	—	(23.7)	8.6	—	—	0.4	15.9	5.8	29.3	5.75	144
Colonial U.S. Equity Index	G&I	—	(4.2)	42.6	—	—	2.3	16.3	1.4	33.5	5.75	140
Colonial VIP–Diversified Return	AA	—	(8.6)	—	—	—	4.3	N.A.	9.6	25.8	None[1]	140
Columbia Growth	Gro	B	(3.3)	38.6	69.5	263.5	2.2	21.1	14.7	244.0	None	53
Columbia Special	Max	A	(12.4)	64.8	96.3	—	0.1	15.1	1.8	91.0	None	74
Common Sense–Growth	Gro	—	(3.4)	38.3	—	—	1.8	17.3	21.0	865.9	8.5	166
Common Sense–Growth & Income	G&I	—	(3.1)	35.7	—	—	2.6	14.4	6.0	366.3	8.5	155
Compass Capital–Equity Income	Eql	—	2.0	—	—	—	4.2	N.A.	0.0	45.6	4.5	77
Compass Capital–Growth	Gro	—	(3.1)	—	—	—	2.1	N.A.	0.0	79.5	4.5	75
Composite Bond & Stock	Bal	D	0.1	28.9	46.4	192.8	5.4	12.5	2.5	61.7	4.0	102
Composite Growth	G&I	D	(6.0)	25.1	49.0	200.9	3.5	12.6	13.0	55.8	4.0	100
Composite Northwest 50 Index	Gro	—	(1.1)	67.8	—	—	0.7	14.0	2.3	42.6	4.5	123
Connecticut Mutual–Growth	Gro	C	(8.0)	41.9	58.7	—	3.0	9.6	10.0	32.6	6.25	123
Connecticut Mutual–Total Return	Bal	C	(0.2)	35.1	57.1	—	5.5	9.6	9.0	63.0	6.25	124
Copley Fund	G&I	D	(1.5)	39.1	49.9	223.2	0.0	11.2	15.0	27.0	None	101
Counsellors Capital Appreciation	Gro	—	(5.5)	45.5	—	—	2.1	N.A.	21.1	76.5	None	61
Counsellors International Equity	Intl	—	(4.6)	—	—	—	3.5	N.A.	20.0	38.9	None	47[2]
Cowen Income & Growth	Eql	—	(8.6)	32.6	—	—	4.3	N.A.	2.2	32.9	4.85	156
Dean Witter American Value	Gro	B	(0.9)	37.7	64.1	152.8	1.9	19.6	17.6	88.1	None[1]	110
Dean Witter Convertible Securities	Conv	E	(11.7)	6.9	10.6	—	5.5	N.A.	6.6	375.2	None[1]	122
Dean Witter Developing Growth Securities	SCG	E	(3.8)	20.5	18.7	—	0.0	18.2	5.3	69.3	None[1]	129
Dean Witter Dividend Growth	G&I	B	(7.2)	45.0	71.8	—	3.8	15.3	0.6	2,701.1	None[1]	97
Dean Witter Managed Assets	AA	—	(1.0)	—	—	—	5.1	15.8	26.4	217.7	None[1]	116
Dean Witter Natural Resources Development	Sec	B	(8.7)	37.5	71.5	—	2.7	18.8	0.5	148.8	None[1]	118
Dean Witter Option Income	OpInc	E	1.5	41.6	40.1	—	8.7	13.8	5.0	146.2	None[1]	130
Dean Witter Strategist	AA	—	2.6	—	—	—	2.3	17.8	18.0	180.6	None[1]	104
Dean Witter Utilities	Sec	—	(0.3)	—	—	—	5.6	14.2	6.8	1,337.6	None[1]	111
Dean Witter Value Added–Equity	G&I	—	(11.7)	28.2	—	—	1.9	15.1	1.9	112.5	None[1]	117
Dean Witter World Wide Investment	Glo	D	(10.2)	19.5	66.4	—	1.6	N.A.	14.8	271.4	None[1]	138
Delaware Fund	Bal	C	(0.5)	51.2	57.5	281.9	5.2	18.8	6.2	349.7	6.75	107
Delaware Group–Decatur I	Eql	C	(12.4)	27.7	60.4	264.8	6.7	12.1	10.8	1,470.5	8.5	119
Delaware Group–Decatur II	Eql	—	(8.3)	45.9	—	—	5.0	15.3	12.0	329.8	4.75	112
Delaware Group–Delcap I	Max	—	(3.5)	52.2	—	—	2.4	16.8	21.4	15.9	4.75	121
Delaware Group–Trend	Max	D	(24.6)	43.1	38.9	211.0	0.7	15.8	17.1	53.3	4.75	114
Dreyfus Capital Value	Max	A	1.4	37.3	113.5	—	7.2	35.2	37.8	729.5	4.5	111
Dreyfus Convertible Securities	Conv	D	(16.7)	17.8	43.4	175.1	6.6	N.A.	17.0	194.3	None	60
Dreyfus Fund	G&I	B	(3.3)	30.0	63.6	205.0	4.6	14.1	22.3	2,160.3	None	42
Dreyfus General Aggressive Growth	Max	B	(1.9)	45.7	74.9	—	2.0	N.A.	21.4	42.4	None	65
Dreyfus Growth Opportunity	Gro	C	(6.6)	26.5	56.0	107.4	3.0	22.9	28.4	387.2	None	55
Dreyfus Leverage	Max	C	(1.5)	20.8	60.1	193.0	5.2	15.1	13.1	392.2	4.5	127
Dreyfus New Leaders	SCG	D	(11.9)	42.7	52.2	—	1.9	19.0	18.8	95.5	None	75
Dreyfus Strategic Aggressive Investing	Max	—	(7.2)	11.5	—	—	0.0	19.5	6.0	58.8	3.0	186
Dreyfus Strategic Investing	Max	—	0.7	26.7	—	—	1.8	26.1	58.0	102.4	4.5	152
Dreyfus Third Century	Gro	C	3.6	49.7	60.7	135.4	1.8	21.4	15.6	159.6	None	58
Eaton Vance Growth	Gro	C	(5.5)	33.7	61.9	215.3	1.1	18.0	21.3	71.6	4.75	99
Eaton Vance Investors	Bal	C	1.0	35.0	55.9	222.4	6.1	16.5	6.0	186.7	4.75	96
Eaton Vance Special Equities	Gro	D	2.5	40.9	41.3	155.7	0.0	17.4	13.7	43.8	4.75	111

Money's grades compare domestic equity, international equity and gold and sector funds by five-year, risk-adjusted return. The top 20% in each group receive an A, the next 20% a B and so on.   [1]Fund may impose back-end load or exit fee.   [2] Three years   N.A. Not available

THE MONEY RANKINGS:EQUITY FUNDS

FUND NAME	Type	MONEY risk-adjusted grade	% gain (or loss) to Jan. 1, 1991				Portfolio analysis			Net assets (millions)	Expense analysis	
			One year	Three years	Five years	10 years	% yield	P/E ratio	% cash		% max. initial sales charge	Five-year projection
Eaton Vance Stock	G&I	A	0.6	49.1	75.6	240.9	4.5	17.0	5.6	$77.5	4.75	$95
Eaton Vance Total Return Trust	G&I	B	0.2	49.6	65.7	—	5.9	15.2	1.7	491.7	4.75	116
Eclipse Equity	SCG	—	(13.6)	13.4	—	—	3.5	N.A.	15.0	123.7	None	60
Enterprise Growth & Income	G&I	—	(8.2)	22.1	—	—	4.7	14.2	4.0	27.6	4.75	125
Enterprise Growth Portfolio	Gro	B	(2.3)	35.1	69.7	294.6	1.2	17.8	2.0	49.0	4.75[4]	130
Equitec Siebel Total Return	G&I	D	(2.3)	23.4	43.5	—	3.0	18.6	1.0	99.0	4.75[4]	109
EuroPacific Growth	Intl	B	(0.1)	50.2	125.7	—	2.3	N.A.	29.7	880.8	5.75	122
European Emerging Companies	Intl	—	(7.7)	—	—	—	0.3	N.A.	16.5	33.5	5.75	171
Evergreen Fund	Gro	E	(11.7)	24.9	36.9	184.0	1.7	15.5	13.0	502.6	None	62
Evergreen Limited Market[1]	SCG	D	(10.4)	36.4	51.8	—	3.5	11.6	56.3	32.5	None	73
Evergreen Total Return	Eql	E	(6.3)	26.7	40.5	276.3	6.5	13.2	12.2	1,024.6	None	65
Evergreen Value Timing	Max	—	(4.5)	49.2	—	—	2.7	17.8	27.0	33.5	None	84
FBL Series–Growth Common Stock	G&I	E	5.2	33.5	31.7	106.7	5.7	14.1	66.7	32.9	None[4]	66
Fenimore International–Equity Series	Intl	—	(11.9)	25.8	—	—	0.0	N.A.	13.8	38.0	5.0[4]	178
Fidelity Asset Manager	AA	—	5.4	—	—	—	6.0	11.2	11.8	343.8	None	44[5]
Fidelity Balanced	Bal	—	(0.5)	38.0	—	—	6.4	13.4	14.4	250.4	None	81
Fidelity Blue Chip Growth	Gro	—	3.5	49.3	—	—	1.0	18.1	17.5	102.0	3.0	97
Fidelity Capital Appreciation	Max	—	(15.7)	47.3	—	—	1.2	16.8	8.2	1,349.2	3.0	93
Fidelity Contrafund	Gro	A	3.9	80.1	100.2	248.4	0.5	13.7	5.0	289.6	3.0	53
Fidelity Convertible Securities	Conv	—	(2.9)	42.1	—	—	5.8	N.A.	11.5	54.1	None	76
Fidelity Destiny I[2]	Gro	A	(3.2)	45.3	82.4	400.3	2.0	12.1	5.1	1,475.3	9.0	30
Fidelity Destiny II[2]	Gro	A	(2.5)	51.3	160.0	—	1.8	12.3	4.0	192.0	9.0	48
Fidelity Disciplined Equity	Gro	—	(0.8)	—	—	—	2.3	12.4	4.6	96.1	None[4]	132
Fidelity Equity-Income	Eql	D	(14.1)	24.9	43.9	278.6	7.2	11.9	12.0	3,689.9	2.0	59
Fidelity Europe	Intl	—	(4.6)	33.6	—	—	2.4	N.A.	18.9	390.0	3.0	120
Fidelity Freedom[3]	Max	B	(10.2)	35.4	68.9	—	0.8	13.9	4.9	1,193.1	None	51
Fidelity Fund	G&I	B	(5.0)	44.1	72.3	255.9	4.5	15.6	13.7	994.4	None	36
Fidelity Growth & Income	G&I	A	(6.8)	48.6	112.0	—	3.8	14.9	11.1	1,592.5	2.0	67
Fidelity Growth Company	Gro	A	3.6	70.3	89.2	—	0.0	17.4	23.2	422.8	3.0	81
Fidelity International Growth & Income	Intl	—	(3.2)	28.6	—	—	3.3	N.A.	9.7	35.5	2.0	113
Fidelity Magellan	Gro	A	(4.5)	57.8	97.2	588.0	1.5	14.0	11.0	11.143.8	3.0	85
Fidelity OTC	SCG	B	(4.8)	52.6	72.7	—	0.3	N.A.	14.6	543.5	3.0	102
Fidelity Overseas	Intl	B	(6.6)	18.2	136.9	—	2.7	N.A.	1.4	1,013.1	3.0	87
Fidelity Pacific Basin	Intl	—	(27.2)	(10.4)	—	—	1.4	N.A.	9.8	89.7	3.0	95
Fidelity Puritan	Eql	C	(6.4)	33.2	57.9	304.6	6.6	13.1	3.4	4,067.6	2.0	55
Fidelity Real Estate	Sec	—	(8.7)	14.7	—	—	6.2	N.A.	13.5	36.3	None	76
Fidelity Select–American Gold	Gold	D	(17.2)	(11.5)	46.7	—	0.0	N.A.	6.6	180.3	3.0	135
Fidelity Select–Biotechnology	Sec	A	44.4	116.3	116.4	—	0.0	45.7	25.5	169.6	3.0	146
Fidelity Select–Energy	Sec	C	(4.5)	58.2	63.8	—	0.9	33.3	6.5	114.4	3.0	139
Fidelity Select–Energy Services	Sec	E	1.8	61.6	20.1	—	0.2	36.6	7.2	95.1	3.0	156
Fidelity Select–Environmental Services	Sec	—	(2.5)	—	—	—	0.0	N.A.	15.1	93.1	3.0	154
Fidelity Select–Food & Agriculture	Sec	A	9.3	92.4	153.4	—	1.1	16.0	16.2	30.0	3.0	168
Fidelity Select–Health Care	Sec	A	24.3	92.7	133.5	—	0.3	22.9	14.6	328.9	3.0	129
Fidelity Select–Leisure	Sec	C	(22.3)	28.8	57.6	—	1.0	15.7	17.2	33.0	3.0	140
Fidelity Select–Medical	Sec	—	16.2	112.7	—	—	1.4	N.A.	13.2	25.3	3.0	150
Fidelity Select–Precious Metals	Gold	D	(21.1)	(20.6)	45.0	—	1.3	N.A.	8.6	174.0	3.0	139
Fidelity Select–Technology	Sec	E	10.5	25.8	2.6	—	0.0	19.5	5.8	61.4	3.0	147
Fidelity Select–Telecommunications	Sec	A	(16.4)	61.2	122.4	—	1.9	15.8	24.7	51.4	3.0	135
Fidelity Select–Utilities	Sec	A	0.6	62.8	83.3	—	1.7	14.6	15.2	160.6	3.0	126
Fidelity Special Situations–Plymouth	Max	—	(7.2)	50.5	—	—	4.3	N.A.	7.1	169.7	4.75	130
Fidelity Trend	Gro	D	(12.7)	43.0	55.6	168.3	0.6	16.1	7.1	602.9	None	32
Fidelity Utilities Income	Sec	—	1.9	47.2	—	—	5.8	14.9	16.3	186.7	None	56

MONEY's grades compare domestic equity, international equity and gold and sector funds by five-year, risk-adjusted return. The top 20% in each group receive an A, the next 20% a B and so on.   [1]Currently closed to new investors   [2]Investment by contractual plan only   [3]Open only to retirement plans   [4]Fund may impose back-end load or exit fee.   [5]Three years   N.A. Not available

THE MONEY RANKINGS: EQUITY FUNDS

FUND NAME	Type	MONEY risk-adjusted grade	% gain (or loss) to Jan. 1, 1991				Portfolio analysis			Net assets (millions)	Expense analysis	
			One year	Three years	Five years	10 years	% yield	P/E ratio	% cash		% max. initial sales charge	Five-year projection
Fidelity Value	Max	D	(12.8)	38.3	45.1	209.1	4.9	24.4	28.0	$92.4	None	$62
Financial Dynamics	Max	D	(6.4)	25.3	38.2	136.9	1.7	25.4	19.0	49.0	None	68
Financial Industrial	G&I	D	(1.2)	37.2	48.4	152.8	2.5	20.5	11.0	315.0	None	46
Financial Industrial Income	Eql	A	1.0	53.5	84.4	303.4	4.2	17.1	8.0	489.0	None	55
Financial Strategic–Energy	Sec	C	(16.5)	37.8	54.8	—	1.0	34.9	1.5	31.0	None	96
Financial Strategic–European	Intl	—	0.7	38.4	—	—	2.4	N.A.	12.0	85.0	None	97
Financial Strategic–Gold	Gold	E	(23.2)	(25.5)	19.8	—	0.1	N.A.	7.0	38.8	None	89
Financial Strategic–Health Sciences	Sec	A	25.8	132.8	224.1	—	0.7	28.2	10.0	88.0	None	78
Financial Strategic–Utilities	Sec	—	(10.0)	35.2	—	—	3.9	22.4	12.0	35.0	None	74
First Eagle Fund of America	Max	—	(17.6)	28.1	—	—	2.8	N.A.	22.0	66.7	None[3]	113
First Investors Blue Chip	G&I	—	(3.5)	—	—	—	3.0	15.4	5.0	42.7	6.9	127
First Investors Global	Glo	A	(12.2)	40.3	162.3	—	0.0	N.A.	9.2	226.3	6.9	172
Flag Investors Emerging Growth	SCG	—	(21.1)	22.3	—	—	0.0	24.4	18.1	32.0	4.5	126
Flag Investors International	Intl	—	(20.2)	13.8	—	—	0.0	N.A.	14.0	44.0	4.5	126
Flag Investors Quality Growth	Gro	—	3.7	—	—	—	2.1	18.4	20.5	37.0	4.5	113
Flag Investors Telephone Income	Eql	A	(7.6)	64.9	109.3	—	4.6	14.0	4.6	174.0	4.5	95
Flexfunds–Muirfield	Gro	—	1.7	—	—	—	14.3	N.A.	100.0	29.8	None	81
Fortress Utility	Sec	—	0.9	44.8	—	—	7.2	13.5	7.0	39.6	1.0[3]	58
Founders Blue Chip	G&I	A	0.4	49.9	79.2	247.3	2.3	18.5	38.3	227.8	None	55
Founders Frontier	SCG	—	(7.5)	72.6	—	—	1.4	30.3	63.4	34.7	None	82
Founders Growth	Gro	B	(10.6)	32.8	75.1	200.9	1.7	23.1	58.1	76.1	None	72
Founders Special	Max	B	(10.4)	41.2	76.6	150.5	1.7	23.4	58.3	46.2	None	59
FPA Capital	Gro	C	(13.8)	27.5	59.3	147.4	1.9	9.2	6.7	53.9	6.5	125
FPA Paramount[1]	G&I	A	1.6	49.2	91.6	381.5	4.4	20.4	51.7	195.7	6.5	114
FPA Perennial	G&I	B	1.0	52.3	66.1	—	5.8	12.3	23.9	52.6	6.5	123
Franklin DynaTech Series	Sec	D	3.2	42.5	52.7	166.3	2.4	19.2	21.6	33.8	4.0	84
Franklin Equity	Gro	C	(9.0)	34.2	58.5	200.3	2.8	10.2	4.7	294.8	4.0	77
Franklin Gold	Gold	B	(19.6)	2.1	102.2	75.3	3.6	N.A.	15.3	261.1	4.0	82
Franklin Growth Series	Gro	A	2.1	37.9	90.1	294.8	2.3	16.5	16.6	173.4	4.0	81
Franklin Income Series	Eql	E	(8.8)	11.3	39.7	206.1	13.1	N.A.	3.6	1,232.8	4.0	71
Franklin Managed Rising Dividend	G&I	—	0.3	42.4	—	—	3.5	10.2	15.1	35.0	4.0	129
Franklin Option	OpInc	E	(8.7)	23.8	35.3	136.2	3.5	15.5	15.5	30.9	4.0	83
Franklin Utilities Series	Sec	B	0.4	41.1	64.9	353.3	7.2	10.3	20.1	820.7	4.0	73
Freedom Global	Glo	—	(19.6)	16.7	—	—	0.0	N.A.	0.6	33.3	None[3]	152
Freedom Gold & Government	Gold	E	0.4	19.8	46.9	—	7.9	N.A.	27.0	65.5	None[3]	121
Freedom Regional Bank	Sec	D	(20.6)	21.2	45.2	—	3.8	N.A.	20.0	39.0	None[3]	117
Fundamental Investors	G&I	B	(6.2)	39.8	77.6	308.7	3.3	16.7	20.6	741.7	5.75	93
FundTrust–Growth & Income	G&I	E	(8.0)	30.1	42.9	—	5.8	N.A.	0.8	29.7	1.5	145
Gabelli Asset	Gro	—	(5.8)	57.1	—	—	4.9	23.4	36.6	318.5	None	69
Gabelli Convertible Securities	Conv	—	6.3	—	—	—	6.6	N.A.	80.4	78.9	4.5	119[4]
Gabelli Growth	Gro	—	(2.0)	91.0	—	—	2.4	15.5	36.9	184.4	None	100
Gabelli Value	Max	—	(5.6)	—	—	—	6.3	25.3	17.7	802.0	5.5	99[4]
Gateway Index Plus	G&I	A	10.3	57.8	67.8	166.0	2.5	17.1	0.0	37.0	None	77
Gintel Capital Appreciation	Max	B	(9.8)	53.3	69.8	—	2.5	N.A.	49.0	26.9	None	99
Gintel ERISA[2]	G&I	C	(5.1)	33.7	62.0	—	4.6	10.9	59.0	74.2	None	73
GIT Equity–Special Growth	SCG	D	(15.9)	31.3	49.1	—	2.1	N.A.	26.7	32.9	None	77
Gradison Established Growth	Gro	B	(8.1)	22.8	68.8	—	3.3	11.5	24.0	116.2	None	76
Growth Fund of America	Gro	A	(4.1)	47.7	85.4	256.0	2.5	17.7	18.5	1,784.9	5.75	99
Growth Fund of Washington	Gro	E	(18.5)	10.4	31.3	—	2.4	N.A.	6.5	35.4	5.0	133
Growth Industry Shares	Gro	C	(2.0)	36.9	62.4	193.5	1.7	21.7	20.0	58.8	None	51
G.T. Global–America Growth	Gro	—	(7.4)	59.3	—	—	0.0	17.8	37.1	59.1	4.75	148
G.T. Global–Europe Growth	Intl	C	(14.7)	33.3	100.4	—	0.0	N.A.	13.6	1,493.7	4.75	144

MONEY's grades compare domestic equity, international equity and gold and sector funds by five-year, risk-adjusted return. The top 20% in each group receive an A, the next 20% a B and so on.   [1]Currently closed to new investors   [2]For retirement plans only   [3]May impose back-end load or exit fee.   [4]Three years   N.A. Not available

THE MONEY RANKINGS: EQUITY FUNDS

| FUND NAME | Type | MONEY risk-adjusted grade | % gain (or loss) to Jan. 1, 1991 | | | | Portfolio analysis | | | Net assets (millions) | Expense analysis | |
			One year	Three years	Five years	10 years	% yield	P/E ratio	% cash		% max. initial sales charge	Five-year projection
G.T. Global–Healthcare	Sec	—	13.1	—	—	—	1.1	N.A.	24.9	$145.6	4.75	$166
G.T. Global–International Growth	Intl	B	(14.3)	41.8	131.3	—	1.4	N.A.	17.3	349.0	4.75	146
G.T. Global–Japan Growth	Intl	A	(28.7)	39.6	242.5	—	0.0	N.A.	28.5	63.1	4.75	155
G.T. Global–Pacific Growth	Intl	A	(11.0)	62.5	191.9	320.1	3.0	N.A.	21.4	251.0	4.75	150
G.T. Global–Worldwide Growth	Glo	—	(12.5)	40.0	—	—	0.8	N.A.	22.2	84.0	4.75	150
Guardian Park Avenue	Gro	C	(12.2)	31.1	59.6	307.9	3.9	12.7	6.4	198.0	4.5	82
Harbor Capital Appreciation	Gro	—	(1.8)	40.7	—	—	1.2	N.A.	6.0	54.5	None	52
Harbor Growth	Gro	—	(6.7)	31.2	—	—	0.7	19.3	2.0	122.6	None	58
Harbor International	Intl	—	(9.8)	70.1	—	—	2.3	N.A.	8.0	63.7	None	83
Heritage Capital Appreciation	Max	D	(12.9)	25.4	42.7	—	3.0	N.A.	39.0	53.7	4.0	147
IAI International	Intl	—	(13.3)	21.1	—	—	0.0	N.A.	9.0	35.4	None	109
IAI Regional	Gro	A	(0.3)	55.2	103.8	319.7	1.8	15.1	35.0	191.1	None	69
IAI Stock	Max	B	(6.7)	31.4	70.9	234.8	2.1	18.0	20.5	70.3	None	69
IDEX Fund	Gro	A	(1.0)	68.1	114.1	—	1.1	19.8	52.0	89.8	8.5	155
IDEX II	Gro	—	(0.6)	73.1	—	—	1.4	18.6	46.0	72.4	8.5	156
IDEX III	Gro	—	(2.0)	63.9	—	—	1.5	19.9	47.0	131.3	8.5	155
IDS Discovery	SCG	D	0.0	48.0	40.8	—	1.4	22.8	14.0	133.0	5.0	85
IDS Equity Plus	G&I	B	(3.2)	35.5	75.0	203.6	3.0	18.8	23.0	338.0	5.0	80
IDS Growth	Gro	B	3.3	51.4	79.2	220.5	1.7	22.0	22.0	590.2	5.0	84
IDS International	Intl	D	(6.2)	25.0	92.5	—	1.8	N.A.	14.0	214.8	5.0	123
IDS Managed Retirement	G&I	A	0.1	41.9	93.2	—	3.1	22.1	30.0	682.4	5.0	98
IDS Mutual	Bal	A	(3.0)	29.6	69.6	251.4	6.4	12.2	21.0	333.0	5.0	86
IDS New Dimensions	Gro	A	5.4	50.1	106.2	330.9	2.2	21.4	19.0	836.0	5.0	77
IDS Precious Metals	Gold	C	(23.7)	(22.8)	71.9	—	2.3	N.A.	10.0	73.1	5.0	123
IDS Progressive	Max	E	(17.7)	9.9	23.0	164.5	4.2	21.7	39.0	115.9	5.0	90
IDS Stock	G&I	A	1.7	45.6	90.0	226.5	4.4	15.1	21.0	1,212.8	5.0	82
IDS Strategy–Aggressive Equity	Max	C	(0.7)	42.8	65.9	—	1.3	17.5	22.0	251.6	None[1]	115
IDS Strategy–Equity Portfolio	G&I	B	(5.9)	42.2	65.6	—	3.7	N.A.	20.0	287.1	None[1]	112
IDS Strategy–Worldwide Growth	Intl	—	(13.5)	8.5	—	—	0.0	N.A.	16.0	38.2	None[1]	152
IDS Utilities Income	Sec	—	(1.7)	—	—	—	6.9	N.A.	25.0	202.3	5.0	96
Income Fund of America	Eql	B	(3.6)	36.2	57.8	313.6	7.1	16.5	16.2	1,989.9	5.75	93
International Investors	Gold	D	(27.0)	(14.0)	55.3	56.3	2.1	N.A.	2.3	630.9	8.5	130
Investment Co. of America	G&I	A	0.7	47.7	88.5	335.3	4.0	15.6	21.2	5,372.6	5.75	85
Investment Portfolio–Equity	Gro	C	(1.7)	41.6	57.4	—	0.0	19.4	22.0	282.0	None[1]	128
Investment Portfolio–Total Return	Bal	—	0.3	34.7	—	—	4.2	16.4	28.0	489.0	None[1]	127
Investment Trust of Boston–Growth Opp.	G&I	D	(4.3)	34.2	51.0	118.9	3.2	15.7	5.7	52.4	5.75	113
Investors Research	Max	C	(1.9)	18.0	66.4	195.4	4.7	23.6	62.0	56.9	8.5	111
Ivy Growth	Gro	C	(3.8)	37.6	59.2	307.9	2.3	16.7	16.4	169.3	None	73
Ivy International	Intl	—	(13.0)	44.8	—	—	3.0	N.A.	8.7	71.1	None	97
Janus Fund	Max	A	(0.7)	69.3	96.3	331.4	2.2	26.1	54.1	1,100.0	None	51
Janus Twenty	Max	B	0.6	80.7	79.5	—	1.3	27.0	46.8	200.0	None	72
Janus Venture	SCG	A	(0.4)	65.3	109.3	—	0.3	25.2	56.0	234.0	None	64
Japan Fund	Intl	B	(16.4)	11.5	148.7	397.1	1.8	N.A.	4.0	366.7	None	56
John Hancock Global Trust	Glo	E	(13.1)	12.8	50.6	—	1.4	N.A.	9.8	81.9	4.5	150
John Hancock Growth	Gro	C	(8.6)	32.9	60.1	137.0	1.2	N.A.	12.0	100.0	4.5	121
Kaufmann Fund	SCG	—	(6.1)	118.6	—	—	0.0	N.A.	10.0	33.5	None	182
Kemper Blue Chip	G&I	—	2.4	21.7	—	—	1.2	17.9	17.0	32.0	4.5	152
Kemper Growth	Gro	A	3.9	50.5	80.5	203.7	1.8	22.0	15.0	310.0	5.75	101
Kemper International	Intl	C	(7.5)	28.6	97.4	—	3.6	N.A.	28.0	201.0	5.75	114
Kemper Summit	SCG	D	(5.2)	28.8	48.2	171.3	1.5	16.0	26.0	179.0	5.75	104
Kemper Technology	Sec	C	0.4	29.2	58.0	135.5	2.0	20.7	12.0	473.0	4.5	94
Kemper Total Return	Bal	C	4.1	35.7	55.8	192.8	6.1	17.7	28.0	489.0	5.0	127

MONEY's grades compare domestic equity, international equity and gold and sector funds by five-year, risk-adjusted return. The top 20% in each group receive an A, the next 20% a B and so on. [1]Fund may impose back-end load or exit fee. N.A. Not available

THE MONEY RANKINGS: EQUITY FUNDS

| FUND NAME | Type | MONEY risk-adjusted grade | % gain (or loss) to Jan. 1, 1991 | | | | Portfolio analysis | | | Net assets (millions) | Expense analysis | |
			One year	Three years	Five years	10 years	% yield	P/E ratio	% cash		% max. initial sales charge	Five-year projection
Keystone America Omega	Max	B	(3.2)	47.1	78.4	140.5	1.2	20.9	17.0	$37.2	2.0[1]	$118
Keystone International	Intl	E	(24.0)	(7.5)	50.8	142.3	0.5	N.A.	9.0	79.7	None[1]	141
Keystone K-1	Eql	C	(1.8)	31.3	58.8	230.7	6.3	N.A.	5.0	773.0	None[1]	107
Keystone K-2	Gro	D	(7.0)	27.8	51.7	170.1	2.3	16.3	14.0	239.7	None[1]	87
Keystone Precious Metals	Gold	D	(26.3)	(22.3)	54.8	4.8	2.2	N.A.	8.9	151.5	None[1]	118
Keystone S-1	G&I	C	(5.2)	32.9	61.8	154.3	2.5	16.5	13.0	147.2	None[1]	110
Keystone S-3	Gro	D	(8.8)	29.9	51.5	157.3	1.0	18.3	15.0	188.9	None[1]	82
Keystone S-4	SCG	E	(6.0)	29.9	29.7	50.5	0.0	22.5	10.0	418.6	None[1]	70
Kidder Peabody Equity Income	Eql	B	2.0	32.9	60.7	—	2.8	N.A.	10.0	60.5	4.0	132
Kleinwort Benson–International Equity	Intl	C	(14.8)	26.9	111.6	166.6	1.1	N.A.	8.0	78.7	None	116
Legg Mason Special Investment	SCG	D	0.5	58.9	52.8	—	2.0	9.6	21.9	65.8	None	120
Legg Mason Value Trust	Gro	E	(17.0)	25.5	27.3	—	3.0	10.9	19.4	608.6	None	101
Lexington Global	Glo	—	(16.8)	21.2	—	—	1.2	N.A.	17.5	51.0	None	89
Lexington Goldfund	Gold	C	(20.7)	(16.7)	61.8	21.5	0.8	N.A.	4.0	110.0	None	78
Lexington Research	G&I	D	(10.3)	25.3	50.9	180.3	2.1	14.5	16.0	102.0	None	56
Liberty Utility	Sec	—	2.0	45.1	—	—	7.2	13.6	8.0	83.2	4.5	99
Lindner Dividend	Eql	D	(6.5)	30.0	50.5	384.1	9.4	N.A.	9.0	145.3	None[1]	48
Lindner Fund	Gro	B	(11.3)	29.4	60.6	362.9	5.4	13.5	20.7	637.4	None[1]	41
Lord Abbett Affiliated	G&I	B	(5.4)	32.1	67.9	256.3	4.5	12.8	5.3	3,034.4	6.75	94
Lord Abbett Developing Growth	SCG	E	(6.4)	10.5	11.9	73.7	0.0	15.1	14.5	92.3	6.75	135
Lord Abbett Global Equity	Glo	—	(12.1)	—	—	—	1.9	N.A.	13.0	32.1	6.75	137
Lord Abbett Value Appreciation	Gro	D	(4.7)	32.4	48.1	—	3.1	17.8	8.3	140.6	6.75	121
MacKenzie American	Gro	E	(14.9)	14.5	35.9	—	1.3	22.5	9.0	37.9	5.75	161
MacKenzie North American Total Return	Bal	E	(8.2)	8.2	20.0	—	5.6	13.2	3.0	62.7	5.75	151
MainStay Capital Appreciation	Max	—	4.1	34.6	—	—	0.0	24.7	23.9	34.8	None[1]	170
MainStay Total Return	Bal	—	5.1	30.1	—	—	2.6	22.9	19.6	50.0	None[1]	170
MainStay Value	G&I	—	(6.1)	32.4	—	—	1.4	14.7	17.4	29.5	None[1]	170
Mass. Capital Development	Gro	D	(4.4)	34.0	47.2	189.0	3.2	15.4	23.0	679.8	5.75	112
Mass. Fin. Lifetime–Capital Growth	Max	—	(2.0)	46.3	—	—	1.5	14.0	25.0	232.8	None[1]	131
Mass. Fin. Lifetime–Emerging Growth	SCG	—	(2.5)	33.6	—	—	0.0	N.A.	8.0	74.4	None[1]	148
Mass. Fin. Lifetime–Global Equity	Glo	—	(4.7)	22.5	—	—	0.3	N.A.	31.0	82.4	None[1]	160
Mass. Fin. Lifetime–Managed Sectors	Sec	—	(13.7)	27.2	—	—	0.0	N.A.	20.0	152.3	None[1]	134
Mass. Fin. Lifetime–Total Return	Bal	—	2.2	31.7	—	—	4.8	N.A.	15.0	220.8	None[1]	122
Mass. Financial Development	G&I	C	(6.0)	30.8	57.4	176.2	3.5	16.8	21.0	204.6	5.75	118
Mass. Financial Emerging Growth	SCG	E	(11.5)	27.8	29.3	—	0.0	25.1	15.0	161.9	5.75	140
Mass. Financial Managed Sectors Trust	Sec	—	(13.4)	28.6	—	—	0.4	21.9	22.0	98.5	5.75	125
Mass. Financial Special	Max	C	(11.8)	36.5	65.0	—	2.5	14.0	22.0	101.8	5.75	121
Mass. Financial Total Return Trust	Bal	A	(2.3)	38.3	71.7	280.1	6.3	14.4	15.0	745.3	5.75	99
Mass. Investors Growth Stock	Gro	C	(4.7)	34.6	60.3	168.8	0.6	20.9	10.0	767.4	5.75	100
Mass. Investors Trust	G&I	A	(0.1)	50.1	89.1	231.4	3.2	16.6	25.0	1,286.4	5.75	98
Mathers Fund	Gro	A	10.4	38.7	100.8	206.9	5.5	25.0	93.0	274.0	None	56
Merrill Lynch Basic Value A	G&I	D	(13.1)	25.4	54.2	269.5	5.9	13.3	13.0	1,231.4	6.5	95
Merrill Lynch Capital A	G&I	A	1.1	45.5	82.5	320.3	5.5	14.1	20.0	904.4	6.5	96
Merrill Lynch Developing Capital Markets	Intl	—	(5.3)	—	—	—	7.1	N.A.	22.0	95.0	4.0[1]	129
Merrill Lynch Eurofund B	Intl	—	(3.3)	24.9	—	—	1.2	N.A.	6.0	499.8	None[1]	127
Merrill Lynch Fund for Tomorrow B	Gro	C	(8.0)	44.8	57.9	—	1.5	18.5	11.0	413.9	None[1]	104
Merrill Lynch Global Allocation B	Glo	—	0.8	—	—	—	7.3	N.A.	2.0	168.0	None[1]	128
Merrill Lynch International A	Glo	D	(9.2)	23.4	71.3	—	2.5	N.A.	35.0	181.5	6.5	141
Merrill Lynch Natural Resources B	Sec	B	(1.7)	14.2	83.3	—	1.7	21.8	20.0	384.6	None[1]	106
Merrill Lynch Pacific A	Intl	A	(9.2)	36.5	176.4	577.5	4.2	N.A.	5.0	267.3	6.5	120
Merrill Lynch Phoenix A	G&I	E	(20.7)	20.3	42.0	—	7.2	21.9	9.0	107.5	6.5	133
Merrill Lynch Retirement Benefit B	Bal	E	(3.3)	22.4	41.3	—	5.0	N.A.	2.0	1,145.4	None[1]	100

MONEY's grades compare domestic equity, international equity and gold and sector funds by five-year, risk-adjusted return. The top 20% in each group receive an A, the next 20% a B and so on.   [1]Fund may impose back-end load or exit fee.   N.A. Not available

THE MONEY RANKINGS: EQUITY FUNDS

FUND NAME	Type	MONEY risk-adjusted grade	% gain (or loss) to Jan. 1, 1991				Portfolio analysis			Net assets (millions)	Expense analysis	
			One year	Three years	Five years	10 years	% yield	P/E ratio	% cash		% max. initial sales charge	Five-year projection
Merrill Lynch Retirement Equity B	G&I	—	(1.0)	51.2	—	—	0.0	16.4	2.0	$438.3	None[3]	$106
Merrill Lynch Science-Tech. Holdings A	Sec	D	(6.2)	11.2	44.5	—	6.0	24.1	40.0	111.8	6.5	144
Merrill Lynch Special Value A	Gro	E	(27.5)	(14.8)	(29.3)	12.7	1.8	16.8	6.0	35.5	6.5	139
MetLife–State Street Capital Appreciation	Max	—	(13.7)	38.0	—	—	0.4	20.8	5.9	42.2	4.5	123
MetLife–State Street Equity Income	Eql	—	(10.8)	30.2	—	—	5.8	20.1	18.2	42.6	4.5	123
MetLife–State Street Equity Investments	G&I	—	(9.5)	26.4	—	—	1.9	18.0	17.9	29.9	4.5	123
MetLife–State Street Managed Assets	AA	—	(3.2)	—	—	—	6.6	20.6	14.0	60.0	4.5	111
Mutual Benefit	G&I	A	(4.8)	58.9	85.7	327.0	3.4	14.7	17.4	34.1	4.75	123
Mutual of Omaha Growth	Gro	C	(8.4)	50.6	68.5	169.1	1.0	19.1	10.2	46.6	4.75	118
Mutual of Omaha Income	Flex	B	3.5	34.7	57.2	202.8	7.8	N.A.	4.6	158.8	4.75	102
Mutual Qualified[1]	G&I	B	(10.1)	34.1	68.9	363.9	6.6	19.3	31.3	1,000.0	None	44
Mutual Shares[1]	G&I	B	(9.8)	35.7	68.6	313.0	5.8	19.1	34.0	2,400.0	None	42
N&B Guardian	G&I	C	(4.7)	48.3	64.3	239.9	2.9	12.6	6.2	453.0	None	49
N&B Manhattan	Max	C	(8.1)	40.4	65.1	267.5	1.7	17.2	12.3	320.0	None	63
N&B Partners	Gro	B	(5.1)	34.5	64.2	269.0	4.6	14.0	28.9	679.0	None	50
N&B Selected Sectors Plus Energy	Sec	C	(5.9)	42.2	57.5	123.7	2.0	18.8	3.4	351.0	None	51
National Aggressive Growth	SCG	E	(22.7)	(6.3)	(6.2)	44.5	5.2	N.A.	17.1	53.1	7.25	155
National Industries	G&I	C	3.1	44.6	62.9	81.8	1.7	25.2	85.0	27.6	None	92
National Stock	G&I	C	(6.6)	43.2	59.3	181.6	2.5	N.A.	19.1	181.6	5.75	129
National Strategic Allocation	AA	—	(6.2)	16.4	—	—	3.8	N.A.	5.3	69.1	5.75	174
National Total Income	Flex	A	(1.5)	41.1	75.5	312.1	5.6	N.A.	16.0	206.1	5.75	136
National Total Return	Eql	C	(6.1)	36.0	58.4	230.5	4.3	13.6	5.1	215.9	5.75	133
Nationwide Fund	G&I	A	0.3	56.7	88.0	292.9	2.7	16.3	8.0	441.2	7.5	108
Nationwide Growth	Gro	C	(7.6)	30.2	57.8	288.5	3.1	17.1	11.8	198.7	7.5	110
New Beginning Growth	SCG	B	(2.0)	45.3	69.2	—	1.0	N.A.	10.0	58.1	None	65
New Economy	Gro	C	(10.1)	37.1	63.3	—	2.6	17.2	21.0	718.0	5.75	101
New England Balanced	Bal	E	(10.6)	8.6	33.7	170.6	4.5	12.2	2.0	47.2	6.5	142
New England Growth	Gro	B	5.3	30.4	83.2	373.8	1.0	26.4	0.3	556.7	6.5	128
New England Retirement Equity	G&I	D	(13.6)	3.6	43.5	214.0	3.4	11.0	0.3	123.9	6.5	131
New Perspective	Glo	C	(2.2)	36.0	96.2	308.9	2.8	N.A.	25.9	1,495.4	5.75	97
Newton Growth	Gro	E	(4.5)	28.1	35.7	164.3	2.7	13.9	13.0	29.9	None	69
New York Venture	Gro	A	(2.9)	58.7	90.7	328.5	2.0	18.3	2.5	305.3	4.75	99
Nicholas Fund	Gro	D	(4.8)	39.9	55.0	303.8	2.3	12.3	9.0	1,201.9	None	46
Nicholas Income	Flex	E	(1.0)	14.8	31.1	182.8	13.2	N.A.	8.2	62.3	None	45
Nicholas Limited Edition	SCG	—	(1.7)	46.8	—	—	1.0	12.8	7.7	56.5	None	62
Nicholas II	SCG	D	(6.2)	29.5	53.9	—	1.8	13.9	6.6	314.7	None	41
Nomura Pacific Basin	Intl	A	(15.4)	20.8	181.2	—	3.0	N.A.	9.2	51.1	None	74
North American Securities–Moderate	AA	—	(8.8)	—	—	—	3.9	12.7	3.7	34.7	4.75	127[4]
Northeast Investors Trust	Flex	E	(9.7)	3.7	25.0	185.9	17.2	N.A.	13.0	255.0	None	40
Oppenheimer Asset Allocation	AA	—	0.9	38.3	—	—	5.0	20.1	25.6	80.9	4.75	124
Oppenheimer Directors	Max	E	(5.4)	37.2	37.8	112.9	3.1	14.9	4.6	107.4	8.5	149
Oppenheimer Discovery	SCG	—	(15.1)	36.3	—	—	1.0	25.2	34.0	50.1	4.75	123
Oppenheimer Equity Income	Eql	A	(1.4)	33.3	68.4	317.6	5.6	21.1	31.8	1,200.0	8.5	125
Oppenheimer Fund	Gro	E	(4.5)	28.0	26.9	70.7	2.5	17.0	18.8	162.9	8.5	138
Oppenheimer Global	Glo	B	(0.7)	65.0	133.3	248.2	0.3	N.A.	9.4	785.8	8.5	179
Oppenheimer Gold & Special Minerals	Gold	A	(26.8)	6.8	150.8	—	0.4	N.A.	36.9	150.5	8.5	154
Oppenheimer Premium Income	OpInc	D	(7.7)	3.4	49.2	183.4	4.5	21.7	4.3	187.9	8.5	139
Oppenheimer Regency[2]	Max	E	(6.4)	26.5	39.2	—	1.8	17.3	19.2	97.9	8.5	152
Oppenheimer Special	Gro	D	(2.5)	39.6	46.0	124.9	3.0	16.3	26.6	424.2	8.5	134
Oppenheimer Target	Max	E	(2.1)	53.3	36.2	388.4	2.3	12.6	16.8	43.0	4.75	114
Oppenheimer Time	Max	B	(7.1)	35.2	75.8	238.5	3.4	20.2	29.4	270.0	8.5	136
Oppenheimer Total Return	G&I	A	(3.9)	30.0	74.9	176.9	3.9	23.7	17.3	367.3	4.75	99

MONEY's grades compare domestic equity, international equity and gold and sector funds by five-year, risk-adjusted return. The top 20% in each group receive an A, the next 20% a B and so on.   [1]Currently closed to new investors   [2]For retirement plans only   [3]May impose back-end load or exit fee   [4]Three years   N.A. Not available

THE MONEY RANKINGS: EQUITY FUNDS

FUND NAME	Type	MONEY risk-adjusted grade	% gain (or loss) to Jan. 1, 1991				Portfolio analysis			Net assets (millions)	Expense analysis	
			One year	Three years	Five years	10 years	% yield	P/E ratio	% cash		% max. initial sales charge	Five-year projection
Over-the-Counter Securities	SCG	E	(20.5)	20.5	10.5	141.9	0.7	16.1	7.7	$203.0	5.75	$132
Pacific Horizon Aggressive Growth	Max	A	5.1	44.8	94.5	—	0.0	38.0	7.0	68.8	4.5	121
Paine Webber Asset Allocation	AA	—	1.9	25.8	—	—	6.5	13.7	32.7	433.6	None[1]	110
Paine Webber Classic Atlas	Glo	C	(7.3)	33.6	94.0	—	2.8	N.A.	32.0	199.1	4.5	127
Paine Webber Classic Growth	Gro	C	(7.3)	51.6	67.2	—	1.2	21.4	11.2	66.9	4.5	140
Paine Webber Classic Growth & Income	G&I	C	(1.0)	45.3	58.7	—	1.9	16.5	11.4	55.9	4.5	134
Paine Webber Classic World	AA	—	1.1	—	—	—	5.9	N.A.	49.4	96.5	4.5	111
Paine Webber Master Energy	Sec	—	(4.3)	45.1	—	—	0.9	N.A.	1.6	59.1	None[1]	194
Paine Webber Master Growth	Gro	—	(11.6)	36.0	—	—	0.3	17.6	6.0	90.1	None[1]	121
Pasadena Growth	Gro	—	(4.6)	78.7	—	—	0.0	17.8	2.0	66.4	5.5	171
Pax World	Bal	A	10.5	54.0	71.1	243.0	4.1	20.3	17.8	111.5	None	59
Penn Square Mutual	G&I	C	(5.3)	36.2	61.3	226.6	4.1	16.1	20.0	178.5	4.75	96
Pennsylvania Mutual	SCG	D	(11.5)	28.6	45.0	257.8	2.7	15.3	7.0	496.7	None[1]	54
Permanent Portfolio	AA	E	(3.9)	3.6	33.1	—	3.2	N.A.	35.0	80.7	None	105
Philadelphia Fund	G&I	D	(11.5)	35.4	51.2	123.8	3.3	20.6	55.0	82.3	None	60
Phoenix Balanced Series	Bal	A	7.3	37.9	81.5	361.3	4.7	17.5	7.0	472.9	6.9	117
Phoenix Convertible Series	Conv	A	4.1	30.7	69.3	304.6	5.8	N.A.	15.0	143.3	6.9	122
Phoenix Growth	Gro	A	6.1	44.6	91.7	420.4	3.4	18.8	21.0	678.3	6.9	123
Phoenix Stock Series	Max	D	(5.6)	20.0	55.4	311.5	0.8	23.0	21.0	99.4	6.9	125
Phoenix Total Return	G&I	B	4.5	27.8	63.5	140.8	5.1	20.4	7.0	28.7	4.75	123
Pilgrim MagnaCap	Gro	C	(3.1)	36.8	61.3	307.8	1.6	19.1	0.0	179.7	4.75	127
Pine Street	G&I	D	(3.5)	40.0	50.4	177.0	4.3	18.8	6.5	43.6	None	65
Pioneer Fund	G&I	D	(10.5)	30.7	53.6	164.0	3.3	16.2	1.2	1,326.0	8.5	123
Pioneer II	G&I	D	(12.0)	30.9	46.7	224.5	3.8	14.4	7.7	3,523.0	8.5	126
Pioneer Three	G&I	E	(13.0)	36.3	39.6	—	3.3	12.7	2.1	538.0	8.5	123
Piper Jaffray Value	Gro	—	1.2	58.0	—	—	1.6	N.A.	3.4	48.0	4.0	108
Plymouth–Growth Opportunities	Gro	—	(1.7)	62.7	—	—	1.1	12.8	4.0	50.9	4.75	169
Plymouth–Income & Growth	G&I	—	(2.9)	46.2	—	—	5.3	12.1	7.9	60.8	4.75	146
Primary Trend	G&I	—	(1.7)	26.7	—	—	5.3	N.A.	30.0	30.2	None	61
Princor Capital Accumulation	Max	D	(10.6)	16.7	41.3	252.9	3.5	13.2	5.5	109.5	5.0	108
Princor Growth	Gro	D	(1.4)	29.2	53.3	156.2	2.0	14.8	13.3	28.9	5.0	114
ProvidentMutual Growth	Gro	E	(8.7)	13.2	23.7	208.9	0.9	18.8	7.2	96.9	6.0	140
ProvidentMutual Investment Shares	G&I	D	(15.9)	20.9	55.3	219.2	2.5	15.1	0.9	158.4	6.0	119
ProvidentMutual Total Return	Bal	E	(10.2)	23.9	43.8	194.2	5.4	N.A.	3.2	55.7	6.0	124
Pru-Bache Equity B	Gro	B	(4.3)	44.6	67.2	—	2.4	16.2	13.0	513.4	None[1]	109
Pru-Bache Equity Income B	Eql	—	(5.7)	37.1	—	—	3.1	15.7	1.3	121.1	None[1]	122
Pru-Bache Flexifund–Conservative B	AA	—	2.9	27.2	—	—	3.8	N.A.	11.1	139.2	None[1]	121
Pru-Bache Flexifund–Strategy B	AA	—	1.1	33.6	—	—	3.1	N.A.	4.0	162.4	None[1]	140
Pru-Bache Global B	Glo	E	(16.5)	0.8	58.5	—	1.2	N.A.	8.0	261.0	None[1]	132
Pru-Bache Global Genesis B	Glo	—	(17.3)	—	—	—	0.0	N.A.	2.2	34.5	None[1]	212
Pru-Bache Global Natural Resources B	Sec	—	(15.0)	15.3	—	—	0.9	N.A.	8.5	40.1	None[1]	161
Pru-Bache Growth Opportunity B	SCG	E	(12.5)	31.1	31.6	—	1.2	15.6	8.7	80.6	None[1]	126
Pru-Bache IncomeVertible B	Sec	C	(6.1)	27.6	51.9	—	7.2	N.A.	9.0	421.9	None[1]	119
Pru-Bache Option Growth B	Max	C	(3.1)	34.1	58.6	—	1.9	17.6	16.0	53.3	None[1]	148
Pru-Bache Research B	Gro	C	(10.0)	22.1	60.4	—	1.1	17.9	8.5	360.7	None[1]	122
Pru-Bache Utility B	Sec	A	(6.5)	57.5	90.5	—	4.3	16.6	8.0	2,334.5	None[1]	105
Putnam Convertible Income & Growth	Conv	E	(10.0)	17.6	28.7	177.4	7.9	N.A.	8.1	528.9	5.75	119
Putnam Energy Resources	Sec	B	(4.9)	54.2	63.8	36.0	3.2	N.A.	0.3	123.8	5.75	142
Putnam Fund for Growth & Income	G&I	A	2.4	49.2	87.7	268.6	5.3	13.5	18.5	1,920.9	5.75	109
Putnam (George) Fund of Boston	Bal	A	(0.9)	37.3	69.2	257.2	5.4	13.5	1.4	394.1	5.75	113
Putnam Global Growth	Glo	D	(9.2)	23.3	84.1	327.8	2.1	N.A.	4.1	560.0	5.75	136
Putnam Health Sciences Trust	Sec	A	15.5	81.3	121.5	—	1.4	N.A.	13.3	335.1	5.75	129

MONEY's grades compare domestic equity, international equity and gold and sector funds by five-year, risk-adjusted return. The top 20% in each group receive an A, the next 20% a B and so on.   [1]Fund may impose back-end load or exit fee.   N.A. Not available

THE MONEY RANKINGS: EQUITY FUNDS

FUND NAME	Type	MONEY risk-adjusted grade	% gain (or loss) to Jan. 1, 1991				Portfolio analysis			Net assets (millions)	Expense analysis	
			One year	Three years	Five years	10 years	% yield	P/E ratio	% cash		% max. initial sales charge	Five-year projection
Putnam Information Sciences	Sec	C	(6.2)	37.1	70.2	—	0.6	N.A.	12.4	$73.2	5.75	$146
Putnam Investors	Gro	B	(2.8)	40.0	68.5	194.5	2.4	15.2	6.4	576.8	5.75	112
Putnam Option Income	OpInc	E	(7.3)	31.3	35.8	143.5	3.6	16.1	0.8	725.8	6.75	124
Putnam Option Income II	OpInc	E	(3.0)	36.5	40.5	—	4.0	19.2	10.0	78.8	6.75	123
Putnam OTC Emerging Growth	SCG	C	(9.8)	35.1	67.8	—	0.0	N.A.	5.5	145.0	5.75	141
Putnam Vista	Max	B	(7.0)	34.1	68.3	271.6	2.4	12.1	11.3	217.1	5.75	116
Putnam Voyager	Max	A	(2.8)	46.3	94.6	266.9	0.9	N.A.	5.1	609.0	5.75	122
Quest for Value	Max	D	(6.9)	31.5	46.9	399.3	1.9	11.4	18.3	49.8	5.5	148
Rea-Graham Balanced	Bal	E	(5.7)	12.9	24.3	—	6.7	N.A.	58.0	35.1	4.75	148
Reich & Tang Equity	Gro	B	(5.8)	36.7	65.1	—	2.8	14.5	21.0	87.7	None	61
Rightime Blue Chip	G&I	—	1.3	24.3	—	—	2.1	16.3	83.0	128.7	4.75	177
Rightime Fund	G&I	D	0.7	11.1	47.1	—	1.9	N.A.	66.0	134.2	None	137
Rightime Growth	Gro	—	(13.8)	—	—	—	2.4	N.A.	97.0	37.3	4.75	178
Rodney Square Growth	Gro	—	(7.2)	42.8	—	—	1.0	N.A.	17.6	33.7	5.75	147
Rodney Square International Equity	Intl	—	(14.3)	12.4	—	—	1.2	N.A.	12.8	58.5	5.75	147
Royce Value	SCG	E	(13.6)	23.8	32.5	—	2.1	15.1	1.0	139.7	2.5[3]	113
Safeco Equity	G&I	B	(8.6)	55.6	66.9	192.9	1.8	18.7	2.5	51.0	None	53
Safeco Growth	Gro	E	(15.0)	23.8	34.9	132.7	0.3	13.0	1.9	55.0	None	52
Safeco Income	Eql	D	(10.8)	26.6	42.9	247.0	6.4	11.8	1.7	165.0	None	51
Salomon Bros. Capital	Max	D	(9.1)	21.3	39.8	244.9	1.9	21.9	18.0	76.1	5.0	127
Salomon Bros. Investors	G&I	D	(6.5)	33.2	53.2	212.6	3.7	16.5	11.0	327.5	5.0	83
Salomon Bros. Opportunity	Max	E	(16.0)	25.3	39.2	269.6	3.1	12.9	16.0	85.8	None	65
SBSF Growth	Gro	C	(2.5)	53.0	59.5	—	3.9	N.A.	35.0	92.5	None	64
Schroder Capital–International Equity	Intl	C	(11.4)	29.0	100.2	—	4.5	N.A.	2.0	62.5	None	71
Scudder Capital Growth	Gro	C	(17.0)	44.1	66.8	239.7	2.3	18.1	7.0	690.9	None	49
Scudder Development	SCG	D	1.5	38.9	47.6	136.0	0.0	26.5	6.0	236.4	None	73
Scudder Global	Glo	—	(6.4)	53.5	—	—	3.6	N.A.	0.0	234.6	None	98
Scudder Gold	Gold	—	(16.7)	—	—	—	0.0	N.A.	38.0	23.1	None	138
Scudder Growth & Income	G&I	B	(2.3)	38.2	69.3	183.8	5.2	19.0	14.0	454.4	None	48
Scudder International	Intl	C	(8.9)	37.5	109.0	292.3	2.2	N.A.	7.0	833.8	None	65
Security Action[1]	Gro	E	(10.1)	23.0	32.2	—	0.8	16.3	5.0	190.7	8.5	46
Security Equity	Gro	B	(4.6)	48.6	76.3	179.0	2.9	15.9	14.7	223.9	5.75	114
Security Investment	G&I	D	(2.9)	29.4	45.6	114.4	7.2	12.6	13.4	70.9	5.75	120
Security Ultra	Max	E	(27.5)	(0.2)	(14.0)	24.6	0.0	16.7	15.4	29.8	5.75	235
Selected American Shares	G&I	B	(3.9)	40.8	65.4	279.2	3.4	14.6	0.3	327.5	None	60
Selected Special Shares	Gro	D	(6.9)	43.6	54.9	153.0	2.1	15.6	12.2	45.9	None	67
Seligman Capital	Max	C	1.4	37.7	59.3	217.0	0.0	21.8	4.8	99.3	4.75	94
Seligman Common Stock	G&I	B	(4.0)	34.0	65.3	245.4	3.6	14.9	0.7	392.4	4.75	82
Seligman Communications & Information	Sec	B	(11.0)	24.6	71.0	—	0.0	14.9	7.5	30.0	4.75	124
Seligman Growth	Gro	C	(5.2)	35.9	66.4	153.3	2.1	19.0	7.4	430.6	4.75	82
Seligman Income	Flex	E	(8.3)	16.6	31.1	185.1	10.2	N.A.	5.5	122.8	4.75	87
Sentinel Balanced	Bal	B	1.9	33.6	60.1	280.3	6.3	14.0	8.7	72.1	8.5	134
Sentinel Common Stock	G&I	B	(2.7)	40.7	74.0	320.4	4.2	13.8	4.4	515.8	8.5	126
Sentinel Growth	Gro	C	0.5	32.1	58.0	229.5	1.3	17.9	2.9	46.4	5.25	120
Sentry Fund	Gro	B	5.2	52.7	65.6	168.2	2.6	16.3	0.1	43.9	8.0	114
Sequoia Fund[2]	Gro	B	(3.8)	36.6	66.4	411.9	3.2	12.4	44.0	789.0	None	56
Shearson Aggressive Growth	Max	A	(6.0)	45.7	97.6	—	0.0	15.5	12.5	80.2	5.0	109
Shearson Appreciation	Gro	A	(0.3)	46.7	88.0	297.9	3.3	16.7	23.2	1,008.6	5.0	95
Shearson Equity–Growth & Opportunity	Gro	—	(15.3)	18.6	—	—	2.9	12.9	8.1	123.1	None[3]	125
Shearson Equity-International	Intl	—	(10.6)	16.1	—	—	0.1	N.A.	5.9	47.5	None[3]	167
Shearson Equity–Sector Analysis	Max	—	(7.3)	(1.4)	—	—	3.8	17.0	0.6	148.4	None[3]	126
Shearson Equity–Strategic Investors	AA	—	(2.2)	38.7	—	—	3.3	17.3	7.5	179.8	None[3]	130

MONEY's grades compare domestic equity, international equity and gold and sector funds by five-year, risk-adjusted return. The top 20% in each group receive an A, the next 20% a B and so on.   [1]Investment by contractual plan only   [2]Currently closed to new investors   [3]Fund may impose back-end load or exit fee.   N.A. Not available

THE MONEY RANKINGS: EQUITY FUNDS

FUND NAME	Type	MONEY risk-adjusted grade	% gain (or loss) to Jan. 1, 1991				Portfolio analysis			Net assets (millions)	Expense analysis	
			One year	Three years	Five years	10 years	% yield	P/E ratio	% cash		% max. initial sales charge	Five-year projection
Shearson Fundamental Value	Gro	E	(8.4)	31.8	40.9	—	4.2	16.4	17.7	$59.6	5.0	$113
Shearson Global Opportunities	Glo	E	(11.3)	14.1	36.1	—	1.6	N.A.	15.5	64.2	5.0	134
Shearson Income–Convertible	Conv	—	(8.7)	15.2	—	—	7.3	N.A.	21.3	74.9	None[1]	110
Shearson Income–Option Income	OpInc	C	2.0	50.6	58.1	—	7.3	11.9	15.4	405.7	None[1]	106
Shearson Investment–Directions Value	Gro	D	(6.8)	28.6	43.8	—	1.6	11.0	12.1	231.8	None[1]	111
Shearson Investment–European	Intl	—	0.9	38.9	—	—	1.2	N.A.	6.9	27.7	None[1]	127
Shearson Investment–Growth	Gro	D	(4.5)	28.8	52.5	—	4.2	18.0	31.1	720.5	None[1]	111
Shearson Investment–Precious Metals	Gold	C	(23.7)	(23.5)	58.9	—	0.3	N.A.	36.2	58.8	None[1]	142
Shearson Investment–Special Equities	SCG	E	(24.4)	1.0	(3.7)	—	3.1	17.4	40.0	73.2	None[1]	135
Shearson Precious Metals & Minerals	Gold	—	(19.7)	(27.1)	—	—	0.0	N.A.	11.2	22.6	5.0	169
Shearson Principal Return–Zero & Apprec.	Bal	—	3.2	—	—	—	6.7	N.A.	0.2	119.4	5.0	86[2]
Shearson Special Income–Utilities	Sec	—	3.3	—	—	—	6.7	N.A.	12.3	624.3	None[1]	102
Smith Barney Equity	Gro	B	(3.2)	28.0	66.1	185.3	3.0	19.3	10.4	68.4	5.75	99
Smith Barney Income & Growth	G&I	C	(9.6)	33.1	57.2	270.0	6.5	16.1	7.1	491.0	5.75	81
SoGen International	Gro	A	(1.3)	32.2	88.2	354.3	4.2	21.6	25.0	197.0	3.75	110
Sound Shore	Gro	D	(10.6)	32.6	53.7	—	4.4	N.A.	28.0	27.9	None	68
Southeastern Growth	Gro	E	(11.3)	21.7	26.6	—	0.6	16.3	11.0	78.0	None[1]	128
Sovereign Investors	G&I	A	4.4	43.7	75.2	300.9	4.7	13.2	18.7	76.0	5.0	113
SteinRoe Capital Opportunities	Max	E	(29.1)	(6.7)	19.2	45.9	1.0	14.4	6.7	79.5	None	63
SteinRoe Prime Equities	G&I	—	(1.7)	40.4	—	—	2.6	N.A.	18.2	43.6	None	55
SteinRoe Special	Gro	A	(5.8)	56.1	86.8	288.7	2.0	16.2	21.1	356.4	None	56
SteinRoe Stock	Gro	B	0.9	37.7	69.9	136.7	2.3	17.6	23.1	207.0	None	41
SteinRoe Total Return	Eql	D	(1.7)	27.6	50.6	142.6	4.7	15.3	8.1	123.3	None	50
Strategic Investments	Gold	E	(42.4)	(47.1)	(15.9)	(52.9)	3.7	N.A.	4.0	35.0	8.5	165
Stratton Monthly Dividend Shares	Sec	E	(3.8)	25.4	33.8	221.5	9.7	9.7	10.8	29.6	None	68
Strong Discovery	Max	—	(2.7)	50.1	—	—	2.5	14.3	68.6	53.8	2.0	121
Strong Income	Flex	E	(6.2)	5.9	44.4	—	11.9	N.A.	8.3	100.1	None	66
Strong Investment	Bal	D	2.8	24.8	46.4	—	7.9	N.A.	66.1	215.0	1.0	80
Strong Opportunity	Max	A	(11.3)	22.4	119.0	—	4.6	17.4	67.6	130.0	2.0	105
Strong Total Return	G&I	E	(7.1)	10.2	40.2	—	7.4	17.2	41.6	658.7	1.0	76
SunAmerica Capital Appreciation	Gro	E	(25.2)	9.0	17.9	—	0.5	N.A.	22.6	109.7	None[1]	139
SunAmerica Equity–Growth	Gro	—	(15.0)	35.1	—	—	2.5	N.A.	39.6	24.8	5.75	143
SunAmerica Multi-Asset–Total Return	AA	—	(12.3)	21.6	—	—	2.2	N.A.	31.3	25.6	5.75	150
Templeton Foreign	Intl	A	(3.0)	54.5	148.1	—	3.6	N.A.	17.5	899.5	8.5	126
Templeton Growth	Glo	D	(9.1)	37.8	72.2	230.2	3.9	N.A.	8.5	2,206.4	8.5	119
Templeton Smaller Companies Growth	Glo	E	(15.7)	28.0	34.5	—	2.6	N.A.	11.2	655.5	8.5	133
Templeton World	Glo	E	(15.9)	23.4	51.1	250.8	4.0	N.A.	3.5	3,516.8	8.5	120
Thomson Convertible B	Conv	—	(15.5)	—	—	—	5.7	N.A.	34.0	23.5	None[1]	123
Thomson Global B	Glo	—	(15.5)	20.1	—	—	0.0	N.A.	2.9	38.3	None[1]	143
Thomson Growth B	Gro	A	0.3	50.8	100.2	—	1.2	18.1	13.6	312.4	None[1]	112
Thomson Opportunity B	Max	D	(7.3)	38.0	53.2	—	0.0	25.3	35.1	35.1	None[1]	123
Transamerica Growth & Income	G&I	C	(0.5)	29.8	54.7	201.7	1.8	19.3	1.0	59.9	4.75	118
Transamerica Technology	Sec	B	(6.4)	36.1	111.8	—	1.2	19.4	7.0	48.7	4.75	146
T. Rowe Price Capital Appreciation	Max	—	(1.3)	45.3	—	—	3.8	19.8	16.5	139.9	None	69
T. Rowe Price Equity Income	Eql	A	(6.8)	35.3	77.6	—	5.2	15.4	14.4	788.5	None	61
T. Rowe Price Growth & Income	G&I	E	(11.1)	32.6	37.2	—	5.0	15.3	10.0	427.2	None	53
T. Rowe Price Growth Stock	Gro	C	(4.3)	27.3	60.8	145.3	2.8	15.0	11.5	1,270.2	None	42
T. Rowe Price International Discovery	Intl	—	(12.9)	—	—	—	1.3	N.A.	18.5	168.2	None	82
T. Rowe Price International Stock	Intl	B	(8.9)	32.9	131.6	325.2	1.7	N.A.	14.4	1,072.5	None	61
T. Rowe Price New America Growth	Gro	D	(12.2)	43.9	49.1	—	1.2	15.8	9.0	85.5	None	69
T. Rowe Price New Era	Sec	B	(8.8)	25.1	71.0	136.0	3.2	19.6	17.1	672.7	None	46
T. Rowe Price New Horizons	SCG	E	(9.6)	30.0	20.5	83.1	0.8	15.0	8.2	726.7	None	44

MONEY's grades compare domestic equity, international equity and gold and sector funds by five-year, risk-adjusted return. The top 20% in each group receive an A, the next 20% a B and so on.   [1]Fund may impose back-end load or exit fee.   [2]Three years   N.A. Not available

THE MONEY RANKINGS: EQUITY FUNDS

FUND NAME	Type	MONEY risk-adjusted grade	% gain (or loss) to Jan. 1, 1991				Portfolio analysis			Net assets (millions)	Expense analysis	
			One year	Three years	Five years	10 years	% yield	P/E ratio	% cash		% max. initial sales charge	Five-year projection
T. Rowe Price Science & Technology	Sec	—	(1.3)	57.2	—	—	0.9	N.A.	26.0	$47.6	None	$69
T. Rowe Price Small-Cap Value	SCG	—	(11.3)	—	—	—	2.9	14.2	20.7	24.3	None	69
Twentieth Century Balanced	Bal	—	1.8	—	—	—	3.6	25.9	1.4	66.3	None	55
Twentieth Century Growth	Max	A	(3.9)	41.4	90.1	190.1	0.7	24.2	7.2	1,695.0	None	55
Twentieth Century Heritage	Gro	—	(9.2)	42.9	—	—	1.6	21.6	7.3	198.0	None	55
Twentieth Century Select	Gro	A	(0.4)	46.7	87.1	332.9	1.8	18.5	2.4	2,900.0	None	55
Twentieth Century Ultra	Max	A	9.4	69.7	99.6	—	0.0	38.9	1.9	329.0	None	55
Twentieth Century Vista	Max	C	(15.7)	31.4	76.0	—	0.0	22.3	18.9	340.0	None	55
United Accumulative	Gro	B	(10.2)	34.1	65.8	261.7	4.7	14.4	38.9	723.8	8.5	117
United Continental Income	Bal	E	(6.1)	29.9	42.3	257.3	5.5	12.6	22.4	275.3	8.5	127
United Gold & Government	Gold	C	(21.6)	(10.8)	64.6	—	1.8	N.A.	7.6	55.7	8.5	159
United Income	Eql	A	(5.5)	44.5	89.3	379.1	3.7	14.0	12.5	1,420.0	8.5	118
United International Growth	Intl	E	(13.7)	7.7	64.3	288.9	2.6	N.A.	11.4	255.0	8.5	144
United New Concepts	SCG	E	2.0	15.0	27.4	—	1.7	19.2	26.4	50.7	8.5	151
United Retirement Shares	G&I	C	1.7	47.8	61.0	230.9	4.4	20.3	26.2	154.9	8.5	132
United Science & Energy	Sec	B	(3.5)	34.1	78.4	186.1	2.2	21.1	21.4	219.0	8.5	130
United Services Global Resources	Sec	D	(16.0)	(9.9)	45.8	—	0.6	32.9	6.1	29.7	None	119
United Services Gold Shares	Gold	E	(34.2)	(30.4)	26.3	(18.3)	4.5	N.A.	13.0	270.4	None	83
United Services World Gold	Gold	E	(27.9)	(31.7)	24.0	—	0.0	N.A.	2.7	61.4	None	110
United Vanguard	Gro	B	(3.6)	29.6	65.9	270.6	3.1	15.6	21.5	665.8	8.5	135
USAA Investment Trust–Balanced	Bal	—	1.4	—	—	—	5.0	17.5	0.0	37.7	None	32[1]
USAA Investment Trust–Cornerstone	AA	A	(9.2)	20.0	84.1	—	3.8	N.A.	0.0	527.4	None	66

MONEY's grades compare domestic equity, international equity and gold and sector funds by five-year, risk-adjusted return. The top 20% in each group receive an A, the next 20% a B and so on. [1]Three years   N.A. Not available

THE MONEY RANKINGS: EQUITY FUNDS

FUND NAME	Type	MONEY risk-adjusted grade	% gain (or loss) to Jan. 1, 1991				Portfolio analysis			Net assets (millions)	Expense analysis	
			One year	Three years	Five years	10 years	% yield	P/E ratio	% cash		% max. initial sales charge	Five-year projection
USAA Investment Trust–Gold	Gold	E	(26.6)	(28.1)	29.6	—	0.9	N.A.	8.9	$134.7	None	$82
USAA Mutual–Aggressive Growth	SCG	E	(11.9)	17.3	22.8	—	0.7	16.3	6.7	112.6	None	50
USAA Mutual–Growth	Gro	C	(0.1)	35.6	57.1	124.1	3.3	17.0	2.7	224.2	None	65
USAA Mutual–Income	Flex	A	7.7	37.7	60.6	240.3	9.0	N.A.	1.8	452.0	None	28
USAA Mutual–Income Stock	Eql	—	(1.4)	49.7	—	—	5.9	18.0	4.8	83.2	None	55
U.S. Trend	Gro	B	(3.3)	42.1	69.5	180.4	3.0	16.0	2.1	76.7	4.75	98
Value Line Convertible	Conv	E	(3.7)	23.7	35.0	—	6.6	N.A.	28.0	33.1	None	58
Value Line Fund	G&I	B	(0.8)	43.1	75.5	161.3	1.9	18.7	12.9	171.1	None	39
Value Line Income	Eql	B	2.0	40.2	59.9	227.4	6.1	13.5	24.2	135.6	None	42
Value Line Leveraged Growth	Max	B	(1.6)	38.5	75.3	226.8	1.6	17.2	4.1	202.3	None	56
Value Line Special Situations	Gro	E	(4.5)	20.2	14.9	48.7	1.3	22.8	11.6	89.8	None	60
Vance Sanders Special	Gro	E	(23.5)	2.3	(10.6)	27.6	0.4	N.A.	6.9	33.8	4.75	105
Van Eck Gold Resources	Gold	—	(26.4)	(31.1)	—	—	0.6	N.A.	6.7	172.2	6.75	143
Van Eck World Trends	Glo	D	(7.9)	10.8	68.3	—	3.0	N.A.	6.8	48.1	5.75	135
Vanguard Asset Allocation	AA	—	0.9	—	—	—	5.4	16.3	2.2	161.8	None	27
Vanguard Convertible	Conv	—	(8.2)	23.1	—	—	7.0	N.A.	14.0	41.2	None	47
Vanguard Equity Income	Eql	—	(11.9)	—	—	—	6.9	12.7	5.5	337.0	None	25
Vanguard Explorer	SCG	E	(10.8)	22.8	4.7	78.9	1.3	14.8	7.7	207.5	None	32
Vanguard High Yield Stock[1]	Eql	E	(29.5)	(8.5)	6.2	281.2	12.4	12.4	2.0	65.3	None	28
Vanguard Index Trust–Extended Market	SCG	—	(14.1)	27.7	—	—	2.8	17.6	2.8	155.0	1.0	73
Vanguard Index Trust–500 Portfolio	G&I	A	(3.3)	47.6	82.5	253.7	3.7	16.3	4.2	1,900.0	None	62
Vanguard PRIMECAP	Gro	C	(2.8)	35.5	63.6	—	1.1	14.1	6.2	257.0	None	41

MONEY's grades compare domestic equity, international equity and gold and sector funds by five-year, risk-adjusted return. The top 20% in each group receive an A, the next 20% a B and so on.   [1]Currently closed to new investors   N.A. Not available

THE MONEY RANKINGS: EQUITY FUNDS

FUND NAME	Type	MONEY risk-adjusted grade	% gain (or loss) to Jan. 1, 1991				Portfolio analysis			Net assets (millions)	Expense analysis	
			One year	Three years	Five years	10 years	% yield	P/E ratio	% cash		% max. initial sales charge	Five-year projection
Vanguard Quantitative Portfolio	G&I	—	(2.4)	50.4	—	—	3.5	13.1	2.7	$195.0	None	$30
Vanguard Small Capitalization Stock	SCG	E	(18.1)	12.8	5.1	62.8	2.0	16.1	2.9	39.0	None	70
Vanguard Specialized Portfolio–Energy	Sec	A	(1.4)	71.7	105.4	—	3.1	22.9	5.2	131.8	None[2]	34
Vanguard Special. Portfolio–Gold & PM	Gold	B	(19.9)	(10.3)	86.5	—	3.5	N.A.	4.7	158.0	None[2]	38
Vanguard Special. Portfolio–Health Care	Sec	A	16.8	99.4	140.9	—	2.1	17.2	9.4	129.5	None[2]	34
Vanguard STAR	Bal	C	(3.7)	36.2	57.7	—	6.7	N.A.	12.8	951.8	None	24
Vanguard Trustees' Commingled–Intl.	Intl	A	(12.2)	31.4	145.3	—	3.5	N.A.	10.7	788.1	None	26
Vanguard Trustees' Commingled–U.S.	G&I	D	(8.3)	33.9	57.0	226.8	4.7	14.2	12.0	98.3	None	29
Vanguard Wellesley Income	Flex	A	3.8	42.6	65.5	290.8	8.1	10.4	4.3	930.0	None	25
Vanguard Wellington	Bal	B	(2.8)	37.2	66.2	274.5	6.2	12.8	2.2	2,100.0	None	24
Vanguard Windsor[1]	G&I	D	(15.5)	25.1	52.3	330.6	7.0	8.7	8.8	5,800.0	None	23
Vanguard Windsor II	G&I	B	(10.0)	43.5	70.5	—	5.7	14.9	5.3	2,100.0	None	30
Vanguard W.L. Morgan Growth	Gro	B	(1.5)	47.8	67.4	219.6	3.0	15.4	9.0	624.0	None	29
Vanguard World–International Growth	Intl	B	(12.1)	22.5	115.9	—	1.9	N.A.	1.4	792.5	None	38
Vanguard World–U.S. Growth	Gro	C	4.6	56.7	58.7	223.6	1.8	17.1	9.4	318.0	None	41
Van Kampen Merritt Growth & Income	G&I	—	(7.9)	27.8	—	—	3.7	N.A.	7.6	21.0	4.9	127
Washington Mutual Investors	G&I	A	(3.8)	46.0	81.3	375.0	4.5	14.8	5.3	4,946.3	5.75	93
Westwood Fund	Max	—	(6.2)	35.7	—	—	4.8	N.A.	20.0	53.0	4.0	107
Winthrop Focus Growth	Gro	—	(7.3)	33.0	—	—	2.8	21.2	15.0	42.9	None[2]	75
WPG Fund	Max	D	(10.4)	25.2	48.9	179.1	2.0	15.8	11.3	27.6	None	77
WPG Tudor	Max	D	(5.2)	36.6	55.1	283.6	1.1	20.1	11.4	163.2	None	61
Yamaichi Global	Glo	—	(19.4)	—	—	—	0.0	N.A.	1.0	70.0	4.75	137
Zweig Series–Priority	Max	—	(3.1)	47.1	—	—	2.0	18.3	28.6	39.2	5.5[2]	142

THE MONEY RANKINGS: TAXABLE BOND FUNDS

FUND NAME	Type	MONEY risk-adjusted grade	% gain (or loss) to Jan. 1, 1991				Portfolio analysis			Net assets (millions)	Expense analysis	
			One year	Three years	Five years	10 years	% yield	Average maturity (years)	% cash		% max. initial sales charge	Five-year projection
Advantage Government Securities	USG	—	8.6	24.9	—	—	8.1	10.0	4.0	$106.6	None[2]	$78
Aegon USA Managed High Yield Portfolio	HYC	C	2.9	28.2	47.6	—	11.3	13.8	0.6	32.7	4.75	122
AIM High-Yield Securities	HYC	E	(17.4)	(14.8)	(4.7)	98.4	17.8	8.4	12.5	36.4	4.75	122
AIM Limited Maturity Treasury Shares	STT	—	9.0	26.5	—	—	7.6	N.A.	0.0	101.6	1.75	137
Alliance Bond–High Yield Portfolio	HYC	E	(15.1)	(18.5)	(12.0)	—	15.3	8.3	7.1	94.6	5.5	125
Alliance Bond–Monthly Income Portfolio	HGC	B	5.5	29.1	51.1	233.1	10.8	14.4	0.6	68.3	5.5	133
Alliance Bond–U.S. Gov. Portfolio	USG	C	7.9	29.3	47.3	—	10.2	N.A.	0.3	493.8	5.5	112
Alliance Mortgage Income	MBS	A	11.0	33.8	53.9	—	9.9	N.A.	14.7	527.5	5.5	114
Alliance Short-Term Multi-Market A	WI	—	12.2	—	—	—	11.0	1.1	60.0	1,343.1	3.0	65
AMA Income–U.S. Gov. Plus Portfolio	USG	D	8.4	25.7	41.0	170.8	8.3	21.6	9.0	40.0	None	100
American Capital Corporate Bond	HGC	C	7.0	25.6	48.5	211.8	10.1	17.2	1.1	186.0	4.75	96
American Capital Federal Mortgage	MBS	—	9.5	30.9	—	—	9.2	6.2	0.0	31.9	4.75	116
American Capital Government Securities	USG	C	8.7	33.6	45.4	—	9.1	9.5	0.0	3,883.3	4.75	95
American Capital High Yield	HYC	E	(15.8)	(16.1)	(7.8)	101.2	18.7	10.6	8.4	270.6	4.75	97
American High-Income Trust	HYC	—	0.1	—	—	—	13.5	11.0	6.2	137.7	4.75	100
AMEV U.S. Government Securities	USG	A	10.4	33.3	55.3	219.7	9.3	16.7	2.7	188.1	4.5	89
Axe-Houghton Income	HGC	C	4.2	24.8	47.4	221.8	8.0	N.A.	12.2	62.2	4.75	91
Babson Bond Trust–Long-Term Portfolio	HGC	B	7.8	30.7	51.7	207.5	8.7	N.A.	6.0	87.0	None	54
Baker U.S. Government	STT	—	5.7	22.3	—	—	6.7	N.A.	100.0	46.5	None	55
Bartlett Fixed Income	HYC	—	6.0	28.7	—	—	7.8	N.A.	2.9	154.0	None	55
Benham GNMA Income	MBS	A	10.2	36.1	55.6	—	8.8	27.0	5.0	329.1	None	42
Benham Government Treasury Note	STT	C	9.2	28.6	47.8	174.1	7.4	3.8	2.0	117.1	None	42
Benham Target–1995	STT	A	9.2	35.9	65.0	—	0.0	5.2	0.4	62.2	None	39

MONEY's grades compare taxable bond funds by five-year, risk-adjusted return. The top 20% receive an A, the next 20% a B and so on.
[1]Currently closed to new investors   [2]Fund may impose back-end load or exit fee.   N.A. Not available

THE MONEY RANKINGS: TAXABLE BOND FUNDS

FUND NAME	Type	MONEY risk-adjusted grade	% gain (or loss) to Jan. 1, 1991				Portfolio analysis			Net assets (millions)	Expense analysis	
			One year	Three years	Five years	10 years	% yield	Average maturity (years)	% cash		% max. initial sales charge	Five-year projection
Benham Target–2000	USG	A	6.3	42.0	76.8	—	0.0	9.9	0.2	$56.4	None	$39
Benham Target–2005	USG	A	3.6	46.9	87.3	—	0.0	14.4	0.2	51.3	None	39
Benham Target–2010	USG	A	0.3	48.5	94.4	—	0.0	19.5	0.0	40.7	None	39
Benham Target–2015	USG	—	(3.4)	43.3	—	—	0.0	24.4	0.0	306.0	None	39
Benham Target–2020	USG	—	(4.5)	—	—	—	0.0	28.7	0.0	57.9	None	39
Bond Fund of America	HGC	C	3.3	25.9	47.8	225.9	10.0	16.1	6.2	1,766.4	4.75	85
Boston Co. Managed Income	STT	C	4.5	21.4	47.6	178.2	9.7	N.A.	1.0	75.1	None	63
Bull & Bear High Yield	HYC	E	(3.0)	(1.3)	(2.1)	—	12.5	9.7	6.0	43.6	None	93
Bull & Bear U.S. Government Securities	MBS	—	7.8	24.4	—	—	7.3	23.9	0.0	32.1	None	107
Calvert Income	HGC	B	4.2	32.2	50.5	—	8.5	17.8	3.0	32.4	4.5	101
Capital World Bond	WI	—	11.5	19.8	—	—	8.0	8.1	15.0	45.2	4.75	115
Cardinal Government Guaranteed	MBS	—	10.4	33.1	—	—	9.4	N.A.	1.0	114.3	4.75	86
Carnegie Government Securities	USG	C	8.3	28.3	46.5	—	7.7	12.5	18.0	41.5	4.5	109
Cigna Government Securities	USG	—	9.4	29.6	—	—	8.4	N.A.	7.4	59.0	5.0	102
Cigna High Yield	HYC	D	(9.0)	7.1	28.1	186.7	15.8	8.8	7.8	204.5	5.0	107
Cigna Income	HGC	B	3.8	28.5	52.5	220.3	8.7	15.5	9.1	209.5	5.0	100
Colonial Government Securities Plus	USG	B	6.7	31.6	52.2	—	8.4	16.8	5.7	2,200.0	6.75	126
Colonial High Yield Securities	HYC	E	(14.9)	(3.8)	15.2	147.6	17.9	8.5	5.9	250.0	4.75	111
Colonial Income Trust	HGC	D	2.3	24.3	40.5	193.2	10.3	19.0	2.6	140.0	4.75	108
Colonial U.S. Government Trust	MBS	—	9.7	29.9	—	—	10.2	N.A.	3.2	106.0	4.75	113
Colonial VIP–Federal Securities	USG	—	8.2	—	—	—	8.5	N.A.	2.1	35.5	None[2]	140
Colonial VIP–High Income	HYC	—	(8.3)	—	—	—	13.7	8.3	1.8	50.0	None[2]	139
Columbia Fixed Income Securities	HGC	B	8.3	33.4	51.8	—	8.1	N.A.	2.5	126.0	None	41
Common Sense Government	USG	—	8.1	31.7	—	—	8.5	7.1	3.0	139.9	6.75	127
Compass Capital–Fixed Income	HGC	—	7.1	—	—	—	7.5	14.8	1.0	42.8	4.5	75[3]
Compass Capital–Short-Intermediate	STT	—	8.1	—	—	—	7.4	4.2	0.0	84.5	4.5	75[3]
Composite Income	HGC	D	8.4	23.8	44.6	207.1	8.8	N.A.	4.3	67.0	4.0	94
Composite U.S. Government Securities	USG	B	9.5	33.5	50.0	—	8.4	16.6	3.3	84.5	4.0	95
Connecticut Mutual–Government	MBS	A	9.4	34.9	55.2	—	7.9	25.3	7.0	45.5	4.5	107
Counsellors Fixed Income	STT	—	2.9	22.2	—	—	9.5	8.3	3.6	60.8	None	42
Counsellors Government–Intermediate Mat.	STT	—	8.8	—	—	—	7.4	4.2	2.5	63.7	None	28
Dean Witter Government Sec. Plus	USG	—	7.1	30.2	—	—	7.8	21.3	0.4	1,404.6	None[2]	100
Dean Witter High Yield Securities	HYC	E	(40.1)	(43.0)	(34.0)	42.6	31.4	10.1	4.9	397.2	5.5	87
Dean Witter Intermediate Income	STT	—	2.2	—	—	—	9.2	6.9	3.4	109.1	None[2]	115
Dean Witter U.S. Government Securities	MBS	D	8.5	28.7	44.7	—	9.6	13.0	2.1	9,782.1	None[2]	85
Dean Witter Worldwide Income	WI	—	16.6	—	—	—	12.2	6.1	23.2	465.1	None[2]	90[3]
Delaware Group–Delchester I	HYC	E	(11.9)	1.5	24.8	161.9	16.9	8.7	4.2	419.0	6.75	111
Delaware Group–Delchester II	HYC	—	(12.2)	0.5	—	—	16.5	8.7	4.2	78.9	4.75	108
Delaware Group–Government Income	MBS	C	8.8	29.3	48.2	—	8.5	N.A.	6.2	150.7	4.75	107
Delaware Treasury Rsvs.–Investors Series	STT	D	9.3	27.4	44.8	—	8.3	N.A.	6.7	119.6	None	54
Dreyfus A Bond Plus	HGC	C	4.8	30.5	48.3	205.8	8.6	20.7	5.0	315.8	None	48
Dreyfus GNMA	MBS	C	9.8	30.3	46.5	—	8.8	24.9	4.4	1,517.5	None	54
Dreyfus Short-Intermediate Government	STT	—	10.0	29.3	—	—	8.8	1.8	3.1	58.4	None	0[4]
Dreyfus Strategic Income	HYC	—	5.5	33.5	—	—	9.2	17.1	4.7	41.9	4.5	89
Dreyfus U.S. Government Bond	USG	—	7.0	34.5	—	—	8.8	15.4	5.8	30.9	None	0[4]
Dreyfus U.S. Government Intermediate	STT	—	8.6	29.6	—	—	9.0	4.1	3.5	64.2	None	44
Eaton Vance Government Obligations	STT	A	9.0	32.6	56.5	—	9.8	N.A.	(12.0)[1]	277.5	4.75	166
Eaton Vance High Income Trust	HYC	—	(18.4)	(4.1)	—	—	19.4	N.A.	6.3	177.5	None[2]	138
Eaton Vance Income of Boston	HYC	E	(15.5)	1.5	20.6	156.0	18.6	N.A.	8.1	62.0	4.75	120
Enterprise U.S. Government Securities	USG	—	9.3	25.7	—	—	8.5	28.5	7.0	30.5	4.75	115
Equitec Siebel U.S. Government	USG	—	9.0	27.1	—	—	9.6	N.A.	2.0	435.6	None[2]	112
Fidelity Flexible Bond	HGC	C	6.1	29.4	47.1	187.0	9.0	10.2	4.6	379.9	None	39

MONEY's grades compare taxable bond funds by five-year, risk-adjusted return. The top 20% receive an A, the next 20% a B and so on.
[1] Figure reflects borrowing to boost investments. [2] Fund may impose back-end load or exit fee. [3] Three years [4] Manager absorbing expenses   N.A. Not available

THE MONEY RANKINGS: TAXABLE BOND FUNDS

FUND NAME	Type	MONEY risk-adjusted grade	% gain (or loss) to Jan. 1, 1991				Portfolio analysis			Net assets (millions)	Expense analysis	
			One year	Three years	Five years	10 years	% yield	Average maturity (years)	% cash		% max. initial sales charge	Five-year projection
Fidelity Global Bond	WI	—	12.3	25.6	—	—	9.2	2.7	36.8	$125.4	None	$87
Fidelity Government Securities	USG	B	9.5	31.2	52.0	194.4	8.6	8.1	1.3	453.1	None	41
Fidelity High Income	HYC	E	(3.9)	4.8	25.2	198.5	12.2	6.1	33.0	870.2	None	45
Fidelity Income–GNMA Portfolio	MBS	A	10.5	34.8	54.0	—	8.1	21.9	7.9	672.8	None	46
Fidelity Income–Mortgage Securities	MBS	A	10.4	33.8	52.9	—	8.0	21.3	2.0	380.2	None	46
Fidelity Intermediate Bond	STT	B	7.5	28.9	49.0	211.1	8.2	7.5	15.0	748.7	None	40
Fidelity Short-Term Bond Portfolio	STT	—	5.8	23.6	—	—	8.9	2.6	4.2	216.8	None	46
Fidelity Spartan Government	USG	—	9.2	—	—	—	8.4	19.5	8.0	361.0	None	5[2,3]
Fidelity Spartan Limited Maturity Gov.	STT	—	9.1	—	—	—	8.2	3.8	16.1	138.0	None	41
Financial Bond Shares–High Yield	HYC	D	(4.6)	12.3	33.3	—	14.1	7.9	9.0	40.0	None	60
Financial Bond Shares–Select Income	HGC	C	4.9	25.3	46.7	173.2	9.8	14.5	11.0	36.0	None	68
First Investors Fund for Income	HYC	E	(17.2)	(13.1)	(4.8)	68.6	17.3	7.2	10.2	731.1	6.9	130
First Investors Government	MBS	C	9.3	33.1	47.5	—	8.1	N.A.	5.0	235.9	6.9	128
First Investors High Yield	HYC	—	(17.3)	(14.3)	—	—	15.7	7.8	9.8	484.8	6.9	140
First Trust U.S. Government Securities	USG	—	10.4	34.6	—	—	8.5	N.A.	1.1	211.9	4.5	75
Flag Investors–Total Return Treasury	USG	—	6.1	—	—	—	8.3	N.A.	9.0	199.0	4.5	97
FPA New Income	MBS	A	8.4	32.0	58.4	207.3	7.9	N.A.	1.9	35.5	4.5	103
Franklin AGE High Income	HYC	E	(14.4)	(5.9)	7.6	125.3	19.7	N.A.	7.1	253.1	4.0	70
Franklin I.S. Trust–Adj. U.S. Gov. Sec.	MBS	—	9.6	28.7	—	—	10.3	29.0	0.0	770.8	4.0	86
Franklin I.S. Trust–Global Income	WI	—	7.6	—	—	—	11.9	5.0	0.1	24.3	4.0	91
Franklin I.S. Trust–Short-Intermed. U.S.	STT	—	9.7	27.2	—	—	8.4	N.A.	11.6	41.4	1.5	57
Franklin Partners–Tax-Adv. High Yield	HYC	—	(16.4)	(1.6)	—	—	18.6	9.8	4.8	27.3	4.0	82
Franklin Partners–Tax-Adv. U.S. Gov.	MBS	—	10.2	34.8	—	—	9.0	27.3	4.4	85.7	4.0	81
Franklin U.S. Government Series	MBS	A	10.8	34.6	55.5	228.8	9.8	26.5	3.2	11,189.3	4.0	68
Freedom Global Income	WI	—	11.7	36.0	—	—	8.6	N.A.	0.0	186.4	None[1]	111
Freedom Government Income	USG	—	8.1	33.6	—	—	8.7	N.A.	0.5	133.8	None[1]	97
Fund for U.S. Government Securities	MBS	A	9.7	33.7	52.9	211.6	9.3	N.A.	3.2	1,060.0	4.5	96
FundTrust–Income	HYC	E	3.9	22.0	31.9	—	7.8	N.A.	5.8	39.5	1.5	144
GNA Investors–U.S. Government	USG	—	9.0	32.0	—	—	8.1	24.8	1.6	72.3	None	116
Government Income Securities	USG	—	9.5	33.5	—	—	9.5	N.A.	3.1	1,002.0	1.0[1]	61
Gradison Government Income	USG	—	8.8	31.4	—	—	8.0	N.A.	12.0	68.5	2.0	86
G.T. Global–Bond Income	WI	—	8.4	—	—	—	7.6	N.A.	29.5	44.5	4.75	143
G.T. Global–Government Income	WI	—	8.8	—	—	—	11.1	N.A.	64.8	259.1	4.75	137
IAI Bond	HGC	B	7.1	32.0	50.7	209.7	7.6	N.A.	6.0	96.9	None	61
IAI Reserve	STT	—	8.4	25.8	—	—	7.9	0.7	6.0	89.2	None	69
IDS Bond	HYC	B	4.8	27.6	52.4	233.9	8.5	13.8	1.0	1,709.0	5.0	90
IDS Extra Income	HYC	E	(10.5)	(2.7)	14.1	—	13.8	11.4	3.0	817.6	5.0	93
IDS Federal Income	STT	B	10.1	32.6	51.7	—	8.3	6.0	4.0	266.3	5.0	92
IDS Selective	HGC	A	6.7	31.1	56.7	243.9	8.1	14.7	4.0	1,169.0	5.0	91
IDS Strategy–Income Portfolio	HYC	B	5.7	26.5	50.3	—	7.3	17.7	1.0	234.6	None[1]	117
IDS Strategy–Short-Term Income	STT	E	7.2	25.0	38.0	—	6.9	3.1	32.0	141.0	None[1]	119
Intermediate Bond Fund of America	STT	—	7.9	—	—	—	9.1	8.4	5.9	199.3	4.75	100
International Cash–Global Portfolio	WI	—	14.4	22.2	—	—	6.9	0.1	100.0	78.4	2.25	110
Investment Portfolio–Diversified Income	HYC	E	(15.8)	3.7	(4.6)	—	17.2	11.8	2.0	202.0	None[1]	123
Investment Portfolio–Government	USG	D	7.1	24.7	41.7	—	8.9	N.A.	0.0	4,936.0	None[1]	117
Investment Portfolio–High Yield	HYC	E	(15.7)	(8.5)	15.0	—	17.7	12.1	3.0	525.0	None[1]	120
Investment Portfolio–Short-Inter. Gov.	STT	—	7.1	—	—	—	8.6	N.A.	2.0	61.0	None[1]	123
Investment Trust of Boston–Premium Inc.	STT	—	10.5	—	—	—	7.4	N.A.	10.7	38.7	2.5[1]	92
John Hancock Bond	HGC	B	6.7	31.4	51.7	218.7	9.5	15.9	3.5	1,092.6	4.5	113
John Hancock Government Spectrum	MBS	B	9.0	32.2	49.8	—	8.3	N.A.	1.6	296.6	4.5	117
John Hancock High Income–Federal Sec.	USG	—	7.5	24.9	—	—	8.7	N.A.	1.5	66.9	4.5	124
John Hancock High Income–Fixed Income	HYC	—	(9.8)	2.0	—	—	14.9	8.9	5.4	66.8	4.5	125

MONEY's grades compare taxable bond funds by five-year, risk-adjusted return. The top 20% receive an A, the next 20% a B and so on.
[1]Fund may impose back-end load or exit fee. [2]Three years [3]Manager absorbing expenses N.A. Not available

THE MONEY RANKINGS: TAXABLE BOND FUNDS

FUND NAME	Type	MONEY risk-adjusted grade	One year	Three years	Five years	10 years	% yield	Average maturity (years)	% cash	Net assets (millions)	% max. initial sales charge	Five-year projection
John Hancock U.S. Gov. Securities	STT	C	7.8	27.1	45.0	145.4	8.7	N.A.	2.2	$178.9	4.5	$124
Kemper Diversified Income	HYC	D	(12.6)	11.0	4.9	76.8	17.5	11.4	6.0	180.0	4.5	134
Kemper Enhanced Government Income	USG	—	7.2	25.4	—	—	9.7	N.A.	0.0	73.0	4.5	99
Kemper High Yield	HYC	D	(13.0)	(1.6)	26.9	207.0	18.4	11.6	3.0	1,116.0	4.5	81
Kemper Income & Capital Preservation	HGC	B	6.5	27.7	50.8	216.5	10.1	10.0	3.0	394.0	4.5	81
Kemper U.S. Government Securities	MBS	A	9.7	33.0	58.7	206.7	9.3	N.A.	4.0	4,564.0	4.5	71
Keystone America Government	USG	—	8.4	26.1	—	—	7.5	N.A.	2.6	58.1	2.0[1]	121
Keystone America High Yield	HYC	—	(25.4)	(17.3)	—	—	20.6	N.A.	8.0	57.8	2.0[1]	126
Keystone B-1	HGC	D	6.7	27.0	40.9	197.6	7.8	N.A.	5.5	412.0	None[1]	99
Keystone B-2	HYC	E	(2.1)	14.2	29.0	173.5	12.3	N.A.	4.9	794.9	None[1]	100
Keystone B-4	HYC	E	(21.8)	(17.2)	(12.8)	85.3	23.0	N.A.	5.1	595.9	None[1]	112
Kidder Peabody Government Income	USG	D	5.8	27.8	40.4	—	8.6	27.5	1.1	98.5	4.0	115
Legg Mason Income–Gov. Intermediate	STT	—	9.1	30.9	—	—	7.6	N.A.	9.9	59.9	None	45
Lexington GNMA Income	MBS	A	9.2	35.0	53.6	178.9	8.4	N.A.	0.0	96.0	None	57
Liberty Advantage–U.S. Government	MBS	—	10.3	29.5	—	—	9.2	22.0	5.1	321.9	4.5	98
Liberty High Income Bond	HYC	E	(12.8)	0.1	12.6	139.4	17.5	10.2	4.5	218.1	4.5	99
Lord Abbett Bond Debenture	HYC	E	(7.6)	10.5	24.4	148.3	14.1	12.5	2.4	476.6	4.75	103
Lord Abbett Global Income	WI	—	11.9	—	—	—	12.6	17.2	15.6	58.6	4.75	95
Lord Abbett U.S. Government Securities	USG	A	9.3	33.6	55.7	246.0	10.5	N.A.	2.6	1,491.4	4.75	94
MacKenzie Fixed Income	HGC	B	4.3	33.8	53.4	—	7.0	19.0	13.0	76.0	4.75	125
MainStay Government Plus	USG	—	6.9	27.6	—	—	9.5	11.5	24.4	479.6	None[1]	129
MainStay High Yield Bond	HYC	—	(7.9)	2.3	—	—	17.3	11.0	13.1	184.2	None[1]	134

MONEY's grades compare taxable bond funds by five-year, risk-adjusted return. The top 20% receive an A, the next 20% a B and so on.
[1]Fund may impose back-end load or exit fee.   N.A. Not available

THE MONEY RANKINGS: TAXABLE BOND FUNDS

FUND NAME	Type	MONEY risk-adjusted grade	One year	Three years	Five years	10 years	% yield	Average maturity (years)	% cash	Net assets (millions)	% max. initial sales charge	Five-year projection
Mass. Financial Bond	HGC	B	8.0	32.8	52.6	230.7	9.0	8.3	9.0	$308.5	4.75	$111
Mass. Fin. Government Income Plus	USG	—	3.5	26.1	—	—	6.6	14.6	2.0	1,068.0	4.75	119
Mass. Fin. Government Premium	STT	—	4.8	—	—	—	5.6	4.9	51.0	423.4	3.75	113
Mass. Fin. Government Securities Trust	USG	D	7.8	28.5	42.9	—	7.7	7.2	0.0	327.1	4.75	115
Mass. Financial High Income Trust I[1]	HYC	E	(16.7)	(8.3)	2.0	146.9	19.6	8.9	9.0	390.5	4.75	117
Mass. Fin. High Income Trust–Series II	HYC	—	(14.9)	(5.8)	—	—	18.0	8.6	14.0	28.3	4.75	125
Mass. Fin. Lifetime–Gov. Income Plus	USG	—	4.4	23.9	—	—	6.0	17.8	0.0	3,182.9	None[2]	105
Mass. Fin. Lifetime–High Income	HYC	—	(14.2)	(8.7)	—	—	17.5	8.6	11.0	107.3	None[2]	127
Mass. Fin. Lifetime–Intermed. Income	STT	—	7.2	—	—	—	5.9	2.5	12.0	127.6	None[2]	132
Mass. Fin. Worldwide Governments Trust	WI	A	17.9	32.1	114.2	—	7.6	3.3	12.0	149.6	4.75	132
Merrill Lynch Corporate–High Income A	HYC	D	(4.6)	12.2	32.9	172.8	17.1	9.0	9.0	442.5	4.0	75
Merrill Lynch Corporate–High Quality A	HGC	B	7.0	31.6	51.1	230.8	8.4	10.3	11.0	307.5	4.0	75
Merrill Lynch Corporate–Intermed. Bond	STT	B	8.4	30.9	50.7	218.4	8.8	4.9	10.0	88.2	2.0	59
Merrill Lynch Federal Securities	MBS	A	10.4	35.4	56.2	—	8.8	7.6	2.0	2,318.6	4.0	80
Merrill Lynch Retirement Global Bond B	WI	—	14.7	26.9	—	—	12.0	10.4	15.0	268.3	None[2]	94
Merrill Lynch Retirement Income	MBS	—	9.6	32.7	—	—	8.2	N.A.	3.0	1,578.0	None[2]	78
MetLife–State Street Gov. Income	USG	—	8.9	30.6	—	—	8.2	18.9	0.9	894.6	None	58
MetLife–State Street Gov. Securities	USG	—	8.4	29.4	—	—	7.9	13.5	3.9	34.3	4.5	111
MetLife–State Street High Income	HYC	—	(16.6)	(1.4)	—	—	17.7	6.3	23.9	162.1	4.5	110
Midwest Income–Intermediate-Term Gov.	STT	D	7.0	24.1	41.2	—	7.5	7.5	9.6	38.1	1.0	66
Midwest Strategic–Treasury Allocation	USG	—	3.6	—	—	—	6.9	23.9	14.7	68.3	4.0	102
Midwest Strategic–U.S. Gov. Securities	MBS	C	8.1	28.6	44.1	—	8.2	19.2	8.4	42.3	4.0	109

MONEY's grades compare taxable bond funds by five-year, risk-adjusted return. The top 20% receive an A, the next 20% a B and so on.
[1]Currently closed to new investors   [2]Fund may impose back-end load or exit fee.   N.A. Not available

THE MONEY RANKINGS: TAXABLE BOND FUNDS

FUND NAME	Type	MONEY risk-adjusted grade	% gain (or loss) to Jan. 1, 1991				Portfolio analysis			Net assets (millions)	Expense analysis	
			One year	Three years	Five years	10 years	% yield	Average maturity (years)	% cash		% max. initial sales charge	Five-year projection
Mutual of Omaha America	USG	B	7.8	33.5	49.5	170.1	7.7	13.5	12.2	$51.9	4.75	$113
N&B Limited Maturity	STT	—	8.7	29.0	—	—	7.9	N.A.	4.0	100.0	None	36
N&B Money Market Plus	STT	—	8.4	26.7	—	—	7.8	N.A.	3.4	85.0	None	36
National Bond	HYC	E	(14.0)	(18.0)	(17.5)	70.2	19.9	8.9	10.1	297.7	4.75	103
National Federal Securities Trust	USG	E	4.5	23.6	27.9	—	8.9	29.1	2.4	381.6	4.75	115
Nationwide Bond	HGC	C	8.2	29.6	46.7	182.9	9.7	21.0	7.3	36.4	7.5	110
New England Bond Income	HGC	B	7.5	29.1	51.4	198.0	8.1	N.A.	7.0	81.9	4.5	107
New England Global Government	WI	—	10.5	—	—	—	7.9	N.A.	1.0	26.3	4.5	162
New England Government Securities	USG	D	5.6	26.6	41.5	—	7.8	N.A.	10.0	173.4	4.5	108
North American Sec.–U.S. Government	MBS	—	8.2	—	—	—	8.4	17.5	8.6	43.3	4.75	124[2]
Olympus U.S. Government Plus	USG	—	10.8	30.1	—	—	8.4	N.A.	1.0	80.0	4.25	124
Oppenheimer GNMA	MBS	—	10.1	31.6	—	—	9.0	N.A.	8.5	68.6	4.75	119
Oppenheimer High Yield	HYC	E	(3.2)	12.6	32.4	155.6	16.1	7.6	13.0	564.0	6.75	113
Oppenheimer Strategic Income	HYC	—	7.8	—	—	—	13.7	N.A.	20.9	192.8	4.75	87
Oppenheimer U.S. Government Trust	USG	C	7.6	28.7	48.0	—	9.4	N.A.	1.0	275.1	4.75	110
Paine Webber Fixed Income–High Yield	HYC	E	(8.8)	(2.3)	9.5	—	16.8	N.A.	10.0	209.9	4.25	80
Paine Webber Fixed Inc.–Investment Grade	HGC	C	6.4	29.8	46.3	—	8.6	13.9	10.0	227.2	4.25	77
Paine Webber Fixed Inc.–U.S. Government	USG	B	9.7	33.1	48.9	—	8.2	11.0	10.3	807.2	4.25	81
Paine Webber Master Global	WI	—	17.7	39.3	—	—	9.0	N.A.	0.0	1,272.0	None[1]	125
Paine Webber Master Income	HGC	—	2.0	21.2	—	—	9.2	15.1	3.6	152.6	None[1]	123
Phoenix High Yield Series	HYC	D	(1.1)	11.3	31.2	169.5	11.3	8.6	8.0	80.5	4.75	92
Pilgrim GNMA	MBS	D	8.0	30.9	40.7	—	9.4	25.9	0.4	118.0	4.75	77
Pioneer Bond	HGC	C	7.3	28.9	47.0	198.5	9.0	13.7	6.7	74.0	4.5	104
Piper Jaffray Government Income	USG	—	8.7	27.9	—	—	8.7	N.A.	15.9	72.0	4.0	102
Premier GNMA	MBS	—	10.6	40.5	—	—	9.2	22.5	4.5	49.0	4.5	95
Principal Preservation Government Port.	USG	B	8.7	29.1	52.3	—	8.3	N.A.	2.0	28.7	4.5	108
Princor Government Securities Income	MBS	A	9.5	36.9	54.4	—	7.9	26.3	2.4	71.8	5.0	106
ProvidentMutual U.S. Government Income	USG	—	6.8	22.5	—	—	7.5	21.5	15.3	55.3	4.5	126
Pru-Bache GNMA B	MBS	D	7.9	27.7	42.9	—	7.9	N.A.	13.0	220.9	None[1]	104
Pru-Bache Government–Intermed. Term	STT	C	8.0	27.3	47.8	—	8.8	4.1	17.6	328.7	None	38
Pru-Bache Government Plus B	USG	C	7.1	27.6	43.9	—	6.8	N.A.	1.5	3,280.1	None[1]	97
Pru-Bache High Yield B	HYC	E	(9.6)	(0.2)	16.5	138.6	15.5	N.A.	5.0	1,600.0	None[1]	90
Pru-Bache Structured Maturity	STT	—	9.4	—	—	—	8.6	3.0	12.0	111.1	3.25	57
Pru-Bache U.S. Government B	USG	—	3.5	26.6	—	—	6.8	N.A.	24.2	172.7	None[1]	97
Putnam Capital Preservation/Income	STT	—	8.6	—	—	—	9.2	4.3	5.9	57.8	4.75	114
Putnam Diversified Income	HYC	—	5.0	—	—	—	10.5	14.0	7.9	127.6	4.75	114
Putnam Global Government Income	WI	—	16.3	43.9	—	—	12.0	5.0	0.0	238.8	4.75	131
Putnam GNMA Plus	MBS	—	8.2	30.9	—	—	8.2	21.0	4.9	808.1	4.75	105
Putnam High Income Government	USG	C	7.4	28.3	45.0	—	7.9	11.6	5.6	5,919.1	6.75	115
Putnam High Yield	HYC	E	(5.9)	4.0	23.5	169.7	17.1	7.2	5.0	1,462.5	6.75	106
Putnam High Yield Trust II	HYC	—	(8.1)	1.2	—	—	16.8	6.8	11.1	252.5	6.75	131
Putnam Income	HGC	C	4.4	29.2	48.3	235.3	10.4	15.7	5.0	429.0	6.75	90
Putnam U.S. Gov. Guaranteed Securities	MBS	A	9.9	33.3	54.8	—	9.6	N.A.	4.2	1,634.6	4.75	82
Quest for Value–U.S. Gov. High Income	USG	—	9.4	—	—	—	7.5	24.8	2.0	52.8	4.75	108
Rightime Government Securities	USG	—	(3.6)	21.4	—	—	6.5	N.A.	0.0	49.5	4.75	130
Rodney Square Benchmark–U.S. Treasury	STT	—	7.3	7.0	—	—	6.8	N.A.	29.0	32.1	4.5	103
Safeco U.S. Government	MBS	—	8.7	32.3	—	—	8.2	24.1	3.2	29.0	None	56
Scudder GNMA	MBS	B	10.1	32.7	49.8	—	8.4	N.A.	1.0	243.2	None	58
Scudder Income	HGC	A	8.3	32.9	53.7	216.1	8.5	N.A.	8.0	287.4	None	51
Scudder International Bond	WI	—	21.1	—	—	—	8.8	5.0	7.0	145.0	None	69
Scudder Short-Term Bond	STT	A	9.9	32.1	53.6	—	9.3	2.9	11.0	265.7	None	28
Scudder Trust–Zero Coupon 2000	USG	—	4.6	40.7	—	—	6.8	N.A.	0.0	27.0	None	55

MONEY's grades compare taxable bond funds by five-year, risk-adjusted return. The top 20% receive an A, the next 20% a B and so on.
[1] Fund may impose back-end load or exit fee.   [2] Three years   N.A. Not available

THE MONEY RANKINGS: TAXABLE BOND FUNDS

FUND NAME	Type	MONEY risk-adjusted grade	% gain (or loss) to Jan. 1, 1991				Portfolio analysis			Net assets (millions)	Expense analysis	
			One year	Three years	Five years	10 years	% yield	Average maturity (years)	% cash		% max. initial sales charge	Five-year projection
Security Income–Corporate Bond	HGC	D	6.6	24.7	44.0	194.9	9.5	22.0	4.5	$57.1	4.75	$104
Seligman High Yield–Bond	HYC	E	(6.9)	7.5	28.3	—	14.9	N.A.	1.0	30.3	4.75	107
Seligman High Yield–Secured Mortgage	MBS	D	7.4	27.3	40.4	—	8.0	N.A.	1.9	27.8	4.75	107
Seligman High Yield–U.S. Government	USG	D	6.6	25.4	41.4	—	8.4	N.A.	1.4	70.3	4.75	105
Sentinel Bond	HGC	B	7.2	31.0	53.0	199.7	8.5	9.9	11.0	35.2	5.25	131
Sentinel Government Securities	USG	—	9.2	31.9	—	—	8.0	10.5	16.6	39.7	5.25	93
SFT U.S. Government Series	USG	B	4.4	29.0	49.2	—	10.9	N.A.	7.0	32.5	5.0	141
Shearson High Yield	HYC	E	(11.9)	(6.6)	10.2	131.2	18.0	N.A.	15.7	211.6	5.0	96
Shearson Income–Global Bond	WI	—	9.1	17.8	—	—	15.7	N.A.	11.6	58.1	None[3]	120
Shearson Income–High Income Bond	HYC	—	(13.2)	(6.9)	—	—	16.7	N.A.	16.1	235.2	None[3]	101
Shearson Inc.–Intermed.-Term Government	STT	D	9.4	25.8	41.9	—	6.7	8.5	10.1	35.9	None[3]	108
Shearson Income–Mortgage Securities	MBS	—	9.2	28.0	—	—	8.3	25.0	2.9	597.9	None[3]	100
Shearson Investment–Gov. Securities	USG	D	7.0	31.7	42.0	—	8.0	N.A.	1.9	1,529.0	None[3]	87
Shearson Investment–Investment Grade	HGC	C	3.0	27.0	46.5	—	8.3	28.0	2.7	399.5	None[3]	99
Shearson Managed Governments	MBS	C	10.1	29.2	46.0	—	9.0	N.A.	4.2	491.5	5.0	93
Smith Barney U.S. Gov. Securities	MBS	A	10.0	37.6	56.8	—	9.0	11.4	1.5	330.0	4.0	62
SteinRoe Government Income	USG	—	8.2	31.0	—	—	7.5	N.A.	7.5	47.7	None	55
SteinRoe Income	HGC	—	6.1	26.7	—	—	9.5	N.A.	15.1	87.1	None	51
SteinRoe Intermediate Bond	STT	B	7.1	29.2	50.7	196.4	8.5	N.A.	12.6	162.0	None	41
Strong Advantage	STT	—	6.6	—	—	—	8.6	N.A.	80.0	129.8	None	63
Strong Government Securities	USG	—	8.7	32.0	—	—	7.7	N.A.	2.4	29.7	None	69
Strong Short-Term Bond	STT	—	5.3	25.3	—	—	8.5	N.A.	16.2	81.2	None	62
SunAmerica Home Investors Gov. Guar.	MBS	C	9.5	31.8	46.3	—	7.5	N.A.	1.1	129.8	None[3]	105
SunAmerica Income–Government Plus	USG	—	5.4	23.2	—	—	9.8	24.9	1.5	37.1	4.75	128
Templeton Income	WI	—	9.9	27.7	—	—	9.3	6.4	13.9	114.2	4.5	103
Thomson Government B	USG	D	6.5	26.8	42.5	—	8.8	N.A.	28.0	441.2	None[3]	112
Thomson Income B	HGC	E	2.1	18.6	37.0	—	10.9	N.A.	9.6	345.4	None[3]	107
Transamerica Bond–Government Securities	USG	D	9.1	27.7	41.3	—	10.8	13.8	4.0	782.7	4.75	105
Transamerica Investment Quality Bond	HGC	B	7.8	28.0	49.2	214.3	9.7	N.A.	0.0	81.3	4.75	109
Transamerica Special–Gov. Income Trust	USG	—	7.8	—	—	—	10.2	13.8	5.0	64.7	None[3]	131
Transamerica Special–High Yield	HYC	—	(6.6)	(5.2)	—	—	15.3	N.A.	6.0	37.1	None[3]	141
T. Rowe Price GNMA	MBS	C	10.0	32.9	48.7	—	8.8	N.A.	0.0	420.9	None	50
T. Rowe Price High Yield Bond	HYC	E	(11.0)	3.5	22.6	—	16.2	8.1	19.5	504.6	None	56
T. Rowe Price International Bond	WI	—	16.0	10.9	—	—	8.6	6.2	19.2	379.1	None	68
T. Rowe Price New Income	HGC	A	8.8	31.3	52.6	192.2	8.2	7.6	4.4	1,018.7	None	48
T. Rowe Price Short-Term Bond	STT	D	8.6	26.0	44.4	—	7.9	2.2	24.2	211.8	None	53
T. Rowe Price Treasury–Intermediate	STT	—	9.0	—	—	—	8.1	3.9	2.3	34.9	None	44
Twentieth Century Long-Term Bond	HGC	—	6.0	30.9	—	—	8.7	N.A.	2.6	76.0	None	55
Twentieth Century U.S. Governments	STT	D	7.5	24.9	42.5	—	8.5	2.4	1.5	452.0	None	55
United Bond	HGC	B	4.2	25.7	51.3	236.8	8.6	N.A.	4.4	421.1	8.5	118
United Government Securities	USG	C	7.1	28.0	44.8	—	8.4	28.3	(7.2)[2]	108.7	4.25	86
United High Income[1]	HYC	E	(14.8)	(12.4)	1.0	117.5	17.7	8.6	13.7	705.0	8.5	123
United High Income II	HYC	—	(5.3)	3.7	—	—	13.5	12.8	18.5	242.2	8.5	128
U.S. Government Securities	USG	C	9.8	31.1	48.8	—	9.4	16.6	11.2	674.8	4.75	93
UST Master Managed Income	HGC	—	8.6	37.1	—	—	7.5	12.0	8.0	42.6	4.5	107
Value Line U.S. Government Securities	USG	A	10.3	33.3	52.8	—	8.4	25.6	8.0	266.0	None	37
Van Eck World Income	WI	—	16.8	44.8	—	—	9.4	3.2	29.6	55.0	4.75	128
Vanguard Bond Market	STT	—	8.7	32.6	—	—	8.5	9.9	2.3	225.4	None	64
Vanguard Fixed Income–GNMA	MBS	A	10.3	37.8	57.2	226.9	8.7	10.3	2.9	2,400.0	None	17
Vanguard Fixed Income–High Yield	HYC	D	(6.0)	8.8	30.5	175.6	14.7	10.1	6.0	680.5	None	21
Vanguard Fixed Income–Invest. Grade	HGC	B	6.2	34.2	53.8	220.5	9.0	25.2	4.8	1,100.0	None	19
Vanguard Fixed Income–Short-Term Bond	STT	A	9.2	30.2	51.5	—	8.4	2.3	4.0	738.5	None	16

MONEY's grades compare taxable bond funds by five-year, risk-adjusted return. The top 20% receive an A, the next 20% a B and so on.
[1] Currently closed to new investors   [2] Figure reflects borrowing to boost investments.   [3] Fund may impose back-end load or exit fee.   N.A. Not available

THE MONEY RANKINGS: TAXABLE BOND FUNDS

FUND NAME	Type	MONEY risk-adjusted grade	% gain (or loss) to Jan. 1, 1991				Portfolio analysis			Net assets (millions)	Expense analysis	
			One year	Three years	Five years	10 years	% yield	Average maturity (years)	% cash		% max. initial sales charge	Five-year projection
Vanguard Fixed Income–Short-Term Gov.	STT	—	9.3	28.7	—	—	8.0	2.2	9.2	$368.9	None	$16
Vanguard Fixed Income–U.S. Treasury	USG	—	5.8	36.2	—	—	8.0	19.8	3.7	568.9	None	16
Vanguard Preferred	HGC	A	6.4	36.4	57.0	244.2	9.4	N.A.	3.3	53.5	None	37
Van Kampen Merritt High Yield	HYC	—	(11.6)	(8.2)	—	—	17.0	8.7	8.6	181.9	4.9	116
Van Kampen Merritt U.S. Government	MBS	A	9.6	34.3	55.5	—	9.2	13.8	2.7	3,291.4	4.9	83
Venture Income Plus	HYC	E	(16.1)	(14.8)	(12.6)	102.3	23.9	5.7	18.0	23.3	4.75	126
Venture Ret. Plan of America–Bond	USG	D	6.1	22.4	37.4	144.1	9.1	N.A.	0.8	54.6	None[2]	132
WPG Government Securities	USG	—	9.0	34.0	—	—	8.0	N.A.	3.0	117.1	None	42
Zweig Series–Government Securities	USG	D	6.1	24.8	34.8	—	7.3	N.A.	27.4	102.9	4.75	119

THE MONEY RANKINGS: TAX-EXEMPT BOND FUNDS

FUND NAME	Type	MONEY risk-adjusted grade	% gain (or loss) to Dec. 1, 1990				Portfolio analysis			Net assets (millions)	Expense analysis	
			One year	Three years	Five years	10 years	% yield	Average maturity (years)	% cash		% max. initial sales charge	Five-year projection
Advance America Tax-Free Income	HGT	—	6.0	—	—	—	6.1	17.6	0.0	$30.5	4.75	$75[3]
Alliance Muni Income–Insured National	HGT	—	6.9	36.9	—	—	6.5	21.0	2.4	118.2	4.5	88
Alliance Muni Income–National Portfolio	HGT	—	7.8	36.9	—	—	7.0	26.0	(0.5)[1]	185.8	4.5	75
American Capital Muni Bond	HGT	D	5.9	34.4	48.5	173.8	6.9	24.0	0.3	241.1	4.75	93
American Capital Tax-Exempt High Yield	HYT	—	6.4	27.0	—	—	8.0	21.2	0.7	220.9	4.75	103
American Capital Tax-Exempt Insured	HGT	—	6.2	26.4	—	—	6.8	23.5	1.3	40.8	4.75	110
AMEV Tax-Free National	HGT	—	5.8	27.6	—	—	6.8	24.5	2.1	40.3	4.5	95

MONEY's grades compare tax-exempt bond funds by five-year, risk-adjusted return through Nov. 30, 1990. The top 20% receive an A, the next 20% a B and so on.
[1] Figure reflects borrowing to boost investments.   [2] Fund may impose back-end load or exit fee.   [3] Three years   N.A. Not available

Important Mutual-Fund Terms That You Should Know

Clone fund. A portfolio spun off by a popular fund when its manager decides the original has become too large to accept new investors. A clone follows its parent's investment philosophy.

Growth fund. One whose main objective is capital appreciation rather than income.

Income fund. A portfolio managed to generate steady income, rather than capital gains, by investing in bonds, high-dividend stocks, and other income-producing investments.

Load. A sales charge, usually 8½%, that you pay when buying fund shares through a broker or financial planner. Some funds that sell their shares directly to the public also charge loads, usually 2% to 3%. A charge imposed when you sell your shares is called a back-end load or exit fee.

Net asset value (NAV). The value of a share of a mutual fund. A fund computes its NAV daily by taking the closing prices of all securities in its portfolio, adding the value of all other assets such as cash, subtracting the fund's liabilities, and dividing the result by the number of fund shares outstanding.

Prospectus. The official document that a mutual fund supplies to all prospective shareholders, identifying the fund's management company, outlining its investment objective, and assessing the risks involved. A corollary document, called Part B or the statement of additional information, generally describes in detail the fees that are charged and often the fund's holdings.

Sector fund. One that restricts its holdings to the securities of companies in a particular industry, region, or country. Sector funds are often grouped into families, and investors switch among funds as economic conditions warrant.

Total return. The dividends, interest, and capital gains that a fund achieves in a given period. A total-return fund is one that pursues both growth and income by investing in a mix of growth stocks, high-dividend stocks, and bonds.

THE MONEY RANKINGS: TAX-EXEMPT BOND FUNDS

FUND NAME	Type	MONEY risk-adjusted grade	% gain (or loss) to Dec. 1, 1990				Portfolio analysis			Net assets (millions)	Expense analysis	
			One year	Three years	Five years	10 years	% yield	Average maturity (years)	% cash		% max. initial sales charge	Five-year projection
Babson Tax-Free Income–Long Term	HGT	D	6.2	31.1	52.9	147.2	6.3	23.5	1.0	$27.7	None	$55
Benham National Tax-Free–Intermediate	ITT	E	7.7	24.8	45.2	—	6.0	7.6	5.4	26.2	None	28
Benham National Tax-Free–Long-Term	HGT	D	6.7	31.3	46.8	—	6.5	19.9	15.0	39.9	None	28
Calvert Tax-Free Reserves–Limited-Term	ITT	E	6.3	22.2	36.7	—	6.3	N.A.	5.0	141.0	2.0	62
Calvert Tax-Free Reserves–Long-Term	HGT	D	4.9	29.0	46.9	—	6.4	23.0	9.0	45.1	4.5	90
Carnegie Tax-Exempt–National High Yield	HYT	—	7.0	31.1	—	—	7.1	19.2	2.2	35.2	4.5	99
Cigna Municipal Bond	HGT	B	5.8	32.3	58.8	166.4	7.0	26.1	11.1	254.3	5.0	97
Colonial Tax-Exempt	HGT	D	7.0	27.5	50.1	192.1	7.7	12.6	5.5	1,800.0	4.75	102
Colonial Tax-Exempt Insured	HGT	D	6.7	29.2	52.0	—	6.7	9.4	2.5	139.0	4.75	106
Colonial VIP–High-Yield Muni	HYT	—	5.3	—	—	—	7.1	18.6	7.6	49.4	None[2]	140
Common Sense Municipal Bond	HGT	—	6.0	—	—	—	6.1	21.8	2.0	37.0	4.75	113
Composite Tax-Exempt Bond	HGT	C	7.2	28.8	54.2	159.2	6.6	8.4	4.9	107.5	4.0	83
Dean Witter Tax-Exempt Securities	HGT	B	6.3	34.9	59.3	198.0	7.2	22.0	0.1	1,021.0	4.0	67
Delaware Group Tax-Free–USA	HGT	A	4.0	33.2	60.3	—	7.2	25.0	0.7	617.0	4.75	87
Delaware Group Tax-Free–USA Insured	HGT	B	6.5	30.3	55.4	—	6.7	22.0	2.0	63.3	4.75	91
Dreyfus General Municipal	HGT	D	8.2	37.0	53.4	—	7.8	24.0	11.0	244.4	None	16
Dreyfus Insured Municipal	HGT	D	7.2	29.9	50.5	—	6.5	25.0	5.0	198.5	None	55
Dreyfus Intermediate Municipal	ITT	D	7.2	26.6	48.7	—	6.9	9.4	2.1	1,119.0	None	40
Dreyfus Short-Intermediate Tax-Exempt	ITT	—	6.7	20.7	—	—	6.2	2.6	11.7	73.8	None	27
Dreyfus Tax Exempt Bond	HGT	D	6.7	31.7	52.7	162.2	7.2	23.0	7.0	3,750.0	None	38
Eaton Vance High Yield Muni Trust	HYT	—	3.8	24.7	—	—	7.7	23.4	2.0	1,071.7	None[2]	123
Eaton Vance Muni Bond	HGT	A	7.1	35.5	61.1	190.4	7.2	23.9	0.4	78.3	4.75	96
Fidelity Aggressive Tax-Free	HYT	A	7.5	34.8	61.8	—	7.7	20.5	12.9	636.1	None[2]	38
Fidelity High Yield Tax-Free	HYT	B	8.9	37.2	58.9	186.6	6.8	20.8	5.3	1,705.1	None	32
Fidelity Insured Tax-Free	HGT	C	7.3	32.4	55.0	—	6.4	21.1	13.5	188.2	None	39
Fidelity Limited Term Muni	ITT	E	7.2	25.9	46.5	146.4	6.6	9.4	15.1	440.6	None	37
Fidelity Municipal Bond	HGT	B	6.8	33.4	57.3	164.6	6.6	19.6	21.1	1,051.0	None	39
Fidelity Spartan Short-Intermed. Muni	ITT	—	6.6	18.8	—	—	5.9	1.9	22.6	59.5	None	36
Financial Tax-Free Income Shares	HGT	A	6.7	40.3	65.3	—	6.6	25.3	5.0	180.0	None	41
First Investors Insured Tax Exempt	HGT	C	6.2	29.7	54.0	173.1	7.0	N.A.	1.0	1,119.9	6.9	130
Flagship All-American Tax Exempt	HGT	—	6.2	—	—	—	7.4	25.0	0.3	56.0	4.2	90
Fortress Municipal Income	HGT	—	6.5	33.3	—	—	7.1	15.4	5.7	96.3	1.0[2]	59
Franklin Federal Tax-Free Income	HGT	C	6.4	34.0	55.3	—	7.6	25.0	3.0	3,998.5	4.0	67
Franklin High Yield Tax-Free Income	HYT	—	6.1	33.9	—	—	8.1	24.0	7.7	1,673.9	4.0	69
Franklin Insured Tax-Free Income	HGT	C	7.1	34.0	56.1	—	7.0	24.0	3.4	788.4	4.0	69
Freedom Managed Tax-Exempt	HGT	—	6.4	35.0	—	—	6.7	25.0	0.0	140.8	None[2]	72
GIT Tax-Free–High Yield	HYT	D	5.6	24.8	50.3	—	6.5	18.6	11.4	40.2	None	65
IDS High-Yield Tax-Exempt	HYT	B	5.7	31.4	58.3	190.5	7.5	21.8	4.0	4,645.0	5.0	82
IDS Insured Tax-Exempt	HGT	—	6.2	30.4	—	—	6.4	23.8	8.0	144.7	5.0	88
IDS Tax-Exempt Bond	HGT	B	6.3	30.6	57.3	178.6	6.5	24.2	12.0	1,074.8	5.0	82
John Hancock Tax-Exempt Income	HGT	B	6.5	30.8	60.2	163.4	6.4	24.5	6.1	375.5	4.5	109
Kemper Municipal Bond	HGT	A	6.9	33.4	62.1	195.4	7.0	20.0	3.0	2,114.0	4.5	71
Keystone America Tax-Free Income	HGT	—	6.9	29.2	—	—	6.8	25.8	4.0	146.4	2.0[2]	106
Keystone Tax-Exempt Trust	HGT	D	5.5	30.9	51.2	—	6.6	22.6	7.0	582.4	None[2]	97
Keystone Tax-Free	HGT	C	5.6	29.3	53.7	174.5	6.9	22.7	6.0	856.9	None[2]	68
Liberty Advantage–Tax-Free Bond	HGT	—	6.9	31.5	—	—	6.4	22.3	6.9	31.3	4.5	85
Liberty Tax-Free Income	HGT	B	5.9	32.4	59.2	169.7	6.8	27.2	6.5	504.8	4.5	93
Limited Term Muni–National Portfolio	ITT	E	6.6	24.5	43.5	—	6.8	4.7	0.1	234.0	2.75	87
Lord Abbett Tax-Free Income–National	HGT	A	7.5	34.3	61.8	—	6.8	23.6	1.4	323.5	4.75	83
MainStay Tax-Free Bond	HGT	—	4.9	24.3	—	—	6.3	23.2	5.0	135.7	None[2]	108
Mass. Fin. Lifetime–Managed Muni	HGT	—	4.2	29.2	—	—	6.0	24.4	3.0	378.6	None[2]	111
Mass. Fin. Managed High Yield Muni[1]	HYT	E	4.2	25.3	44.5	—	8.6	21.2	3.0	645.8	4.75	82

MONEY's grades compare tax-exempt bond funds by five-year, risk-adjusted return through Nov. 30, 1990. The top 20% receive an A, the next 20% a B and so on.
[1] Currently closed to new investors   [2] Fund may impose back-end load or exit fee.   N.A. Not available

THE MONEY RANKINGS: TAX-EXEMPT BOND FUNDS

FUND NAME	Type	MONEY risk-adjusted grade	% gain (or loss) to Dec. 1, 1990				Portfolio analysis			Net assets (millions)	Expense analysis	
			One year	Three years	Five years	10 years	% yield	Average maturity (years)	% cash		% max. initial sales charge	Five-year projection
Mass. Fin. Managed Muni Bond	HGT	B	6.5	32.2	58.1	226.2	6.6	21.1	4.0	$1,463.4	4.75	$81
Merrill Lynch Muni–High Yield A	HGT	C	6.4	30.8	54.9	191.4	7.3	21.0	8.0	1,300.6	4.0	70
Merrill Lynch Muni Income B	ITT	—	5.9	22.4	—	—	6.1	10.0	8.0	112.0	None[1]	64
Merrill Lynch Muni–Insured A	HGT	C	7.3	31.9	55.5	164.9	7.0	21.0	4.0	1,949.5	4.0	65
Merrill Lynch Muni–Limited Maturity	ITT	E	6.2	20.7	32.8	90.5	6.2	1.2	12.0	338.2	0.75	30
MetLife–State Street Tax-Exempt	HGT	—	5.1	32.1	—	—	6.3	25.3	6.0	81.3	4.5	111
Mutual of Omaha Tax-Free Income	HGT	A	7.4	34.6	67.5	175.3	6.6	23.6	1.6	355.1	4.75	94
National Securities Tax-Exempt	HGT	B	7.1	32.6	59.8	172.9	6.7	24.9	5.7	92.1	4.75	88
Nationwide Tax-Free Income	HGT	—	6.3	30.8	—	—	6.5	22.9	1.4	89.3	None[1]	58
New Beginning–Tax-Free	HGT	—	7.2	—	—	—	8.3	18.9	6.0	41.2	None	44
New England Tax-Exempt Income	HGT	C	5.7	30.8	55.6	198.6	6.4	19.8	10.0	143.4	4.5	96
Nuveen Insured Tax-Free–National Port.	HGT	—	6.6	37.1	—	—	6.4	25.1	3.4	148.8	4.75	91
Nuveen Municipal Bond	HGT	A	6.5	32.8	61.2	174.2	6.8	21.3	1.0	1,341.6	4.75	80
Oppenheimer Tax-Free Bond	HGT	C	5.8	29.2	55.8	201.3	6.7	9.7	3.3	247.3	4.75	91
Paine Webber Classic High Yield Muni	HYT	—	6.2	34.4	—	—	7.9	21.3	7.0	63.0	4.0	118
Paine Webber Managed Tax-Exempt Income	HGT	B	7.5	31.0	57.0	—	7.3	18.0	4.0	337.3	4.25	76
Pioneer Municipal	HGT	—	6.8	34.2	—	—	6.5	18.8	6.9	33.0	4.5	90
Piper Jaffray National Tax-Exempt	HGT	—	7.2	—	—	—	6.7	25.0	0.9	36.0	4.0	88
Premier Muni Bond	HGT	—	7.8	37.5	—	—	7.7	25.0	6.7	161.3	4.5	77
Principal Preservation–Tax-Exempt	HGT	E	6.6	23.6	24.8	—	6.5	16.9	1.0	64.7	4.5	98
Princor Tax-Exempt Bond	HGT	—	5.3	34.6	—	—	6.1	23.9	3.6	46.8	5.0	115
ProvidentMutual Tax-Free Bond	HGT	C	6.2	31.4	54.3	147.8	6.1	24.6	8.7	27.3	4.5	105
Pru-Bache Muni–High Yield Series B	HYT	—	4.7	34.4	—	—	7.5	24.7	2.9	668.5	None[1]	74
Pru-Bache Muni–Insured Series B	HGT	—	6.3	32.5	—	—	6.0	24.7	10.0	524.3	None[1]	75
Pru-Bache Muni–Modified-Term Series B	ITT	—	6.8	27.3	—	—	5.7	N.A.	0.1	46.3	None[1]	97
Pru-Bache National Municipal B	HGT	D	6.2	27.5	47.0	168.3	6.0	21.5	7.3	878.1	None[1]	64
Putnam Tax-Exempt Income	HGT	B	5.0	34.0	60.8	227.1	6.7	22.8	5.1	1,329.1	4.75	61
Putnam Tax-Free–High Income	HYT	—	7.6	—	—	—	8.1	24.7	3.4	220.7	4.75	101
Putnam Tax-Free–High Yield	HYT	C	4.2	27.5	52.3	—	7.5	24.4	5.3	651.5	None[1]	113
Putnam Tax-Free–Insured	HGT	D	5.3	29.8	52.8	—	5.8	24.9	7.6	308.4	None[1]	108
Safeco Municipal Bond	HGT	A	6.9	35.5	62.7	—	6.7	20.0	3.2	300.0	None	32
Scudder Managed Muni Bond	HGT	C	6.8	35.3	54.0	178.9	6.5	16.0	11.0	697.5	None	26
Scudder Medium-Term Tax-Free	ITT	E	6.2	19.0	33.9	—	5.3	1.5	77.0	32.5	None	37
Scudder Muni High Yield	HYT	—	6.3	36.1	—	—	6.8	20.3	6.0	124.8	None	55
Scudder Tax-Free Target–1993	ITT	E	6.5	21.5	38.3	—	6.3	2.7	8.0	74.5	None	43
Scudder Tax-Free Target–1996	ITT	E	7.1	25.1	43.1	—	5.9	4.9	6.0	37.5	None	56
Seligman Tax-Exempt–National	HGT	A	6.2	34.1	61.8	—	6.5	23.5	2.4	136.3	4.75	89
Shearson Income–Tax-Exempt	HGT	C	5.4	30.6	53.2	—	6.5	22.3	1.5	569.7	None[1]	90
Shearson Managed Muni	HGT	B	5.6	30.5	57.0	—	7.3	23.8	9.6	1,399.9	5.0	81
Smith Barney Muni–Limited Term Portfolio	ITT	—	8.0	—	—	—	6.9	6.1	5.4	39.0	2.0	38
Smith Barney Muni–National Portfolio	HGT	—	7.8	36.5	—	—	7.4	26.8	3.0	179.0	4.0	60
SteinRoe High-Yield Municipals	HYT	A	7.8	37.7	65.2	—	7.1	17.1	11.6	321.7	None	40
SteinRoe Intermediate Municipals	ITT	E	8.0	24.4	41.8	—	5.9	7.3	16.8	101.2	None	44
SteinRoe Managed Municipals	HGT	A	7.1	32.7	63.8	216.5	6.5	14.5	11.6	598.3	None	37
SunAmerica Tax-Free–STRIPES	HGT	—	6.0	27.9	—	—	6.8	23.6	7.9	89.8	4.75	118
Tax-Exempt Bond of America	HGT	C	6.2	29.3	53.9	177.3	6.6	20.9	14.2	568.9	4.75	82
Thomson Tax Exempt B	HGT	C	5.1	29.2	54.6	—	5.6	20.9	3.4	49.5	None[1]	112
Transamerica Special–High Yield Tax-Free	HYT	—	4.5	29.6	—	—	6.2	21.4	7.0	35.8	None[1]	147
T. Rowe Price Tax-Free–High Yield	HYT	A	7.5	32.4	62.6	—	7.3	19.6	6.2	487.6	None	49
T. Rowe Price Tax-Free Income	HGT	D	6.3	25.9	46.1	144.5	6.6	19.9	8.5	1,101.7	None	36
T. Rowe Price Tax-Free Short-Intermediate	ITT	E	6.3	19.5	33.0	—	5.7	1.9	35.1	221.6	None	42
Twentieth Century Tax Exempt–Long Term	HGT	—	6.1	30.3	—	—	6.1	19.9	7.8	27.6	None	55

MONEY's grades compare tax-exempt bond funds by five-year, risk-adjusted return through Nov. 30, 1990. The top 20% receive an A, the next 20% a B and so on.
[1] Fund may impose back-end load or exit fee.   N.A. Not available ·

THE MONEY RANKINGS: TAX-EXEMPT BOND FUNDS

FUND NAME	Type	MONEY risk-adjusted grade	% gain (or loss) to Dec. 1, 1990				Portfolio analysis			Net assets (millions)	Expense analysis	
			One year	Three years	Five years	10 years	% yield	Average maturity (years)	% cash		% max. initial sales charge	Five-year projection
United Municipal Bond	HGT	A	6.1	37.4	66.7	182.3	7.0	23.5	4.6	$660.8	4.25	$74
United Municipal High Income	HYT	—	7.0	29.9	—	—	8.0	23.2	4.4	195.5	4.25	83
USAA Tax Exempt–High-Yield	HGT	B	6.8	35.9	57.7	—	7.2	22.3	3.0	1,274.0	None	23
USAA Tax Exempt–Intermediate-Term	ITT	D	7.3	29.8	48.6	—	6.9	8.8	3.7	514.6	None	25
USAA Tax Exempt–Short-Term	ITT	E	5.8	22.3	35.8	—	6.5	1.9	0.0	335.1	None	28
UST Master Intermediate-Term Tax-Exempt	ITT	—	6.5	24.7	—	—	6.4	6.7	4.0	96.0	4.5	83
UST Master Tax-Exempt–Long Term	HGT	—	7.0	36.1	—	—	5.9	19.0	12.0	34.2	4.5	95
Value Line Tax Exempt–High Yield	HGT	D	6.9	29.4	48.5	—	7.6	23.3	5.0	272.9	None	35
Vanguard Muni–High-Yield	HYT	B	6.3	36.0	60.9	180.9	7.2	21.5	0.1	986.2	None	14
Vanguard Muni–Insured Long-Term	HGT	A	7.1	34.7	61.5	—	6.8	21.0	0.0	1,800.0	None	14
Vanguard Muni–Intermediate-Term	ITT	C	7.8	31.3	54.4	145.2	6.7	9.3	3.0	1,300.0	None	14
Vanguard Muni–Limited-Term Portfolio	ITT	—	7.4	23.5	—	—	6.2	3.5	2.0	251.0	None	14
Vanguard Muni–Long-Term Portfolio	HGT	B	7.0	35.2	60.8	170.3	6.9	20.8	2.0	689.9	None	14
Vanguard Muni–Short-Term Portfolio	ITT	E	6.6	20.8	34.2	92.5	5.9	1.3	1.7	735.2	None	14
Van Kampen Merritt Insured Tax Free Inc.	HGT	A	7.2	32.8	61.3	—	6.9	21.2	3.5	663.8	4.9	95
Van Kampen Merritt Tax Free High Income	HYT	A	3.6	27.1	60.6	—	8.5	23.4	3.8	631.1	4.9	93
Venture Muni Plus	HYT	E	3.8	27.8	43.4	—	8.5	19.8	1.8	81.7	None[1]	128
Zweig Tax-Free–Limited-Term Portfolio	ITT	E	6.2	21.1	40.2	—	6.3	N.A.	1.9	25.4	1.5	63

MONEY's grades compare tax-exempt bond funds by five-year, risk-adjusted return through Nov. 30, 1990. The top 20% receive an A, the next 20% a B and so on.
[1] Fund may impose back-end load or exit fee.   N.A. Not available

Notes: To be ranked, a fund must be at least one year old, accept a minimum investment of $25,000 or less and have had assets of at least $25 million as of Sept. 30, 1990. Gain or loss figures include reinvestment of all dividends and capital-gains distributions. The MONEY risk-adjusted grade appears for funds with records of at least five years and covers the 60-month period through Dec. 31, 1990. The prospectuses of bond funds in the high-grade categories require them to invest primarily in issues rated BBB or better by Moody's or Standard & Poor's. Short/intermediate-term taxable and tax-exempt bond funds have average weighted maturities of up to 10 years. Stock and bond fund yields are the latest 12 months' dividends divided by the most recent share prices adjusted for capital-gains distributions. **Source: Lipper Analytical Services**

Index